Also by Arthur Hertzberg

The Jews in America
The Zionist Idea
The Outbursts That Await Us (coauthor)
The French Enlightenment and the Jews
Being Jewish in America

JUDAISM

The Key Spiritual Writings
of the
Jewish Tradition

The Revised Edition

edited and interpreted by
Arthur Hertzberg

Simon & Schuster Paperbacks
New York   London   Toronto   Sydney

Simon & Schuster Paperbacks
A Division of Simon & Schuster, Inc.
1230 Avenue of the Americas
New York, NY 10020

This Simon & Schuster trade paperback edition July 2008

SIMON & SCHUSTER PAPERBACKS and colophon are registered trademarks of Simon & Schuster, Inc.

For information about special discounts for bulk purchases, please contact Simon & Schuster Special Sales at 1-800-456-6798 or business@simonandschuster.com.

Manufactured in the United States of America

10 9 8 7 6 5 4 3 2 1

Library of Congress Cataloging-in-Publication Data is available.

ISBN-13: 978-1-4165-6137-8
ISBN-10:   1-4165-6137-4

לזכר נשמות הורי
א"מ הרב צבי אלימלך זצ"ל
בן הרב אברהם זצ"ל
א"מ נחמה שפרה נ"ע
בת הקדוש משולם שו"ב מלמברג הי"ד
צדיקים במיתתם קרואים חיים

IN MEMORY OF MY PARENTS

Rabbi Zvi Elimelech

and Rebbetzin Nechama Shifra

WHOSE LIVES REMAIN A LESSON

IN THE WAY OF JEWISH FAITH

Contents

8 Contents

Acknowledgments

In the early months of 1960 my friend, the late George Brantl, who was then editor of Braziller Books, proposed an idea—to publish together six books of text and commentary that would summarize and explain "the great religions of modern man." He defined the format of these volumes very rigorously: they were to consist of original texts through which the reader, with the help of commentary, would come into direct contact with the spirit and values of each of the great religious traditions. Brantl invited me to do the volume on Judaism. I accepted on the understanding that I would need the help of a young scholar in finding appropriate texts from a vast literature. Jules Harlow, who had very recently been ordained a rabbi, worked hard with me then on the first edition of this book, choosing and translating the texts.

Thirty years later, another editor who has become a friend, Carole Hall of Touchstone Books, encouraged a revised edition of this book to take account of the new questions which have been debated within Judaism in recent decades. Fortunately, I could again turn to Rabbi Harlow, who unhesitatingly agreed to resume the collaboration. We defined the new issues, read in the literature of all the elements within Jewry, and added roughly a third to the earlier book—and we made many corrections in the text of 1961. Rabbi Harlow's energy has not lessened with the passing of time, and his wisdom and insight have increased. Working together with him for the second time has been an even greater joy than the remembered pleasure of thirty years ago.

On the technical side of typing and assembling the manuscript, I am very grateful to two diligent and devoted students of mine at Dartmouth College, Meredith Katz, who gave up a term at school to work with me full-time on this revised edition, and Joshua Wesoky, who helped between and after classes. Near the end of the task, a former student of mine at Dartmouth, Edward Nelson, volunteered to help tie up all the loose ends. Sandra Curtis, the administrative assistant who runs the Department of Religion at Dartmouth, and her staff were unfailingly kind as this manuscript, in all of its revisions, kept turning up on the machines in their domain. My colleagues in Thornton Hall were, without exception, supportive of one of their own who was coping this spring with teaching and finishing this work.

Looking at this book, both in its original version and in this expanded and radically revised second edition, I am even more grateful than I was thirty years ago for the unstinting labors of Jules Harlow. My gratitude to the memory of George Brantl has increased, and my sorrow at his untimely death is greater. When this book was first done, it was my second published work, and I did not yet really know how much the labor on a book takes away from the family of the author. Since then, Phyllis, my wife of more than forty years, has seen me through a number of books and hundreds of essays. None of these tasks could have been completed without her support and patience. As first reader, she continues to make each page better.

To the degree to which it is possible, this work, both text and commentary, takes no sides. Original sources, from ancient to contemporary, are presented and explained in their own terms. The basic texts, with some necessary explanations, are here for the reader to contemplate. They will add to knowledge, or perhaps even serve as markers on the path of a journey of the spirit.

—Arthur Hertzberg
June 9, 1991

PREFACE TO THE REVISED EDITION

This book was finished once in quiet times; it has now been redone, three turbulent decades later. Many of the answers to questions of values and of life and death are different now than they were thirty years ago. The easy conclusion would be the cliché that religion changes with changing times, as indeed it does—and that the believers themselves change, as I know I have in the years between my fortieth birthday, when I signed the preface to the first edition, and my seventieth birthday, when I signed the present text. What seems more remarkable is that even in very stressful times, in the recent years of often angry sectarianism, Judaism has remained very much a unity. The hundred pages or so of new material in this revised edition are culled from clashing, but basically not discordant, discussions of all the major new issues of the last three decades.

The foundations of the world seemed secure in the late 1950s. America was at the zenith of its influence as the preeminent power in the world. The five million Jews within its borders were less persecuted and excluded than Jews had ever been in the many centuries of their wanderings among the gentiles. Judaism could be described as a confident religion, the faith of a community which no longer had much to fear from the hand of man. American Jews could, so I hoped, begin to find their way back to the inherited religious tradition. To be sure, the faithful, those in each of the several denominations who lived by the rules, were a minority. Most Jews were impressionistic in their beliefs and practices, but what Judaism taught seemed clear. The maleness of God, or at least of His authorized representatives, was hardly in question, even though more and more women, in Judaism as in all the major biblical faiths, had begun to demand equality.

In the late 1950s fundamentalism had not yet risen to major power in America. The religious scene was still dominated by theological and social moderates who wanted to dampen conflicts and accommodate differences. The major religious groups did differ, as they always had, on such issues as abortion or state aid to parochial education, but they were perceived to be moving away from their quarrels and towards pragmatic entente. To be sure, there was deep division within American society on the question of race. Large groups among the Christians of the South fought actively to retain segregation, and some of the synagogue congregations in the region did not speak above a whisper—but the overwhelming bulk of the organized religious community, both Jewish and Christian, joined in active commitment to the cause of civil rights. It was widely believed that this unity would lead to an era of peace and cooperation among the faiths; they were perceived to be working together towards a more just and peaceful society in the near future.

Looking inward, most Jews believed that the future would be more peaceful. They thought that harmony would be growing within their community. The Orthodox were led then by moderates who cooperated easily with the more liberal wings, the Conservative and the Reform. To be sure, the atmosphere was beginning to change in the late 1950s. Some forces among the Orthodox were becoming assertive. More fundamentalist elements were insisting on erecting barriers to keep the true believers inside their own fold. The Reform and the Conservative were moving towards gender equality, and thus the more liberal denominations were fashioning themselves to be ever less like the Orthodox. Within the Jewish community, as among both the Protestants and the Catholics, the religious moderates had begun to be challenged by confrontationists, but few thought that the future would bring a sometimes embittered polarization.

Perhaps most important of all, Judaism in America, and even in Israel, thought of itself as a Western religion, primarily in dialogue with Christianity. The Jews in America were still fighting for complete social equality in an overwhelmingly Christian society. In Israel the bid of the Jews from Islamic lands for equal respect for their cultural heritage was in its early stages. Culture and society were dominated, seemingly permanently, by earlier immigrants who had come from Europe.

The relationship between religion and the West has changed, fundamentally, in the last three decades. Christianity itself, in both its Catholic and Protestant versions, has been working to break the connection between the Christian faith and Western culture. The new thinking asserts that the civilizations of Asia and Africa must have an equal stake in the Christian message, lest Christianity be regarded as merely an agent of colonial oppression. In the West itself, religion is no longer only either Christian or Jewish. The wars and political turmoil of the last three decades have propelled millions of Muslims, Buddhists, and Hindus to all the major European countries and to the United States. In every major city west of the Elbe river, the boundary of West Germany before the reunification, there is a marked and growing presence of mosques, Buddhist temples, and ashrams. In the ten largest cities of the United States, taken together, white Europeans are now the minority. To be sure, Blacks and Hispanics are generally Christians, but even among them, third-world religions are growing.

In this ever more complicated society, Jews are well on the way to defining themselves, and their religion, independent of supposed Western norms. The re-creation of a Jewish State in Asia is a strong force moving the Jewish community, and Judaism, away from its Western presumptions of three decades ago. One of the deepest themes in Zionism is the quest for a redefinition of the Jewish soul through reencounter with the ambiance in which Judaism was first defined. Judaism was distorted, so this argument goes, by its life in the Exile, under unremitting pressure of various majority cultures. The authentic Jewish spirit belongs not to the West, to which Jews were once sent in slavery, but to the Middle East, where this people was born. The religious dialogue with the West has become less important in recent years for immediate political reasons as well. Arabs have challenged the Zionists with the argument that Jews returning to the Land of Israel are Western interlopers who had long since become alien to the region. Jewish thinkers have replied by insisting on the Middle Eastern character which had been stamped on Judaism when it began, and which it had retained even during the long centuries of the exile of the Jews to alien lands. Quite apart from Zionist ideology, a fundamental demographic and cultural change has taken place in Israel in the last thirty years. Jews of European origin are now a minority, and some of its most distinguished religious authorities are people for whom Islam and not Christianity is the point of reference.

The religious experience of Jews is indissolubly linked to what happens to the Jewish people in history. Both the Holocaust, the unprecedented murder of six million Jews by the Nazis for the "crime" of being born Jews, and the creation of the State of Israel, a Jewish commonwealth reestablished nearly nineteen centuries after the destruction of the Second Temple, had occurred in the 1940s. Obviously, Jewish thought and feeling in the 1950s were deeply affected by these seminal events, but it is clear now, thirty years later, that the transforming impact of the Holocaust and of the State of Israel on Jewish spirituality had just begun to be felt. In the last three decades the murder of European Jewry has become more than a memory of the ultimate pogrom. The Holocaust cannot be discussed without raising the question of God's justice. The religious significance of the State of Israel was transformed even more dramatically. Since 1967, the State of Israel has controlled all the territory west of the Jordan river, including, for the first time, a very large Arab minority within the borders of the "undivided Land of Israel." Very soon after the victory an explosive issue developed: on national and religious grounds, is it permissible to give back even one inch of the land that "God gave to the Jews"? More generally, what moral responsibilities come with power?

On rereading the new material, after this revised edition was finished, I was astonished to find that on most issues—old and new—the combatting views belonged together.

One source of coherence is the method of argument. It has remained the same for many centuries. Biblical and rabbinic precedents are invariably cited today as in the past. In most cases, it is argued that Talmudic norms can be stretched to apply to situations that the ancient rabbis could not possibly have imagined. As the reader will see, all of the opinions on medical questions, regardless of whether their authors are Orthodox or Liberal rabbis, are argued on the basis of Talmudic law, and the conclusions are indistinguishable. Indeed, on the question of abortion, Rabbi Solomon Freehof, an American Reform rabbi, was no more permissive than the Orthodox leaders, Rabbi Eliezer Waldenberg and Rabbi Ben Zion Hai Ouziel: all three permit abortions when the mother's physical health or her psychological well-being are in danger, but they reject the opinion that the decision to abort is entirely and always a matter of her personal choice.

On the equally difficult issue of the "undivided Land of Israel," the tempers of the opposing opinions are hotter, but the clashing arguments cite the same texts. The debate revolves around two rabbinic rulings: the undoubted principle that saving life takes precedence over almost every other commandment of the Jewish religion, and the insistence by one of the greatest rabbinic authorities, Nachmanides, writing in thirteenth-century Spain, that the restoration of Jewish rule to the Holy Land is a Biblical commandment which Jews must always strive to fulfill. Must one, so the arguments go, fulfill this commandment even at danger to life, or is human life, even that of a single individual, too precious to be destroyed even to bring the Messiah? Rabbi Zvi Yehudah Kook, the spiritual leader of the annexationists, ruled that the commandment to restore the Holy Land to Jewish sovereignty takes precedence even over the danger to the lives of those who fight for this cause. Rabbi Ovadiah Yosef, the former Sephardi Chief Rabbi of Israel, has argued that the ruling by Nachmanides was meant to be carried out only at a time of peace, when it will cost no lives.

Some contemporary issues cannot be debated by arguing about the meaning, and the limitations, of ancient texts. Even one of the most conservative of all the rabbinic authorities, Rabbi Moshe Feinstein, revised the definition of death in the light of new medical knowledge. He accepted the contemporary view that proof of death is the cessation of all activity in the brain. To be sure, he satisfied the Talmudic ruling that death is established by the end of heartbeat and breathing. Rabbi Feinstein suggested that the oxygen tank in a heart-lung machine not be replaced when it becomes empty, thus "testing" whether the patient can breathe and maintain heart activity independently.

But the greatest difficulties for those who would remain within the confines of Tamudic precedent have been presented by the questions of gender. The Talmud presumed a patriarchal society as the dominant social form. To be sure, a number of rulings were made by the ancient rabbis to protect the rights of women. In Biblical law, where there are male heirs, only they inherit. The Talmud altered the rule to include unmarried daughters, arguing that if they had no means, they might be forced into wicked ways of making a living. The ancient rabbis added conditions to the Biblical laws of marriage. They ruled that no wedding could take place unless the groom first agreed by pre-marital contract (the *Ketubah*) that in case of divorce or of his death the wife was automatically entitled to a substantial settlement. Nevertheless, these progressive injunctions belonged to a world of male domination, tempered by some concern for women. In recent decades, Rabbi Yechiel Weinberg ruled in favor of bat-mitzvah ceremonies for girls (though not in synagogue, where men and women must in Orthodox practice be kept separate) on the grounds that in modern times girls are as well educated as boys.

Rabbi Menachem Mendel Schneerson, the Rebbe of Lubavitch, has recently gone even farther. He interpreted the Talmudic dictum that women are not to be taught the Torah as applying only to past centuries, when women were usually not given much education; women are now free to become scientists and scholars, and so their education in religious texts must be broad and deep. A liberal Orthodox thinker, Rabbi Eliezer Berkovits, has gone farther still, declaring with passion and eloquence that the inherited patriarchal attitudes, which the law of the Talmud reflects, must be discarded. In Rabbi Berkovits's view, these attitudes are repugnant to contemporary moral sense. Nevertheless, despite his discomfort, he suggested no radical change in Orthodox behavior. Total gender equality in all aspects of Jewish practice, including the ordination of women as rabbis, was proclaimed very recently by the liberal elements of the Jewish religious community. The Reform movement began to ordain women in 1972, and the Conservative movement followed in 1984. There was little pretense in either group that these decisions were made on the basis of Talmudic precedent. On the contrary, as Rabbi Simon Greenberg, the senior vice-chancellor of the Conservative Jewish Theological Seminary of America, asserted: separate and unequal status for women had been the undoubted law of the past—but Rabbi Greenberg's sense of himself as a moral Jew could not survive if he obeyed such precedent.

The tension between inherited teaching and contemporary sensibility has become all the sharper, and more painful, in recent years in face of the rising demands of homosexuals for equality not only in the marketplace and in society but also in the religious community. Here the precedents are unmistakable and univocal: homosexuality is a sin, both in the Bible and in the literature of the Talmud. It goes without saying that a homosexual is inconceivable as a role-model. The ordination of a gay man or lesbian woman to be a rabbi is totally beyond the parameters of the halakhah, the religious law that was first defined in the Talmud. Yet the dominant view today among many Jews is that homosexuality is most often innate and that, even if it is not, homosexuality is not a crime. Jewish religious liberals continue to debate whether homosexuals should be encouraged and supported in founding their own synagogues or whether they should be welcomed in existing congregations, but exclusion of homosexuals from the institutions of Judaism of all the denominations is no longer possible. The Reform and Reconstructionist rabbinical seminaries now ordain men and women who are avowed homosexuals. This policy is justified by those who have accepted it as their way of responding to a profound, and recent, change in moral outlook.

Many pointed, even heated disagreements appear in the new pages of this revised edition, and yet all of the disputants of the last thirty years belong together. These contemporaries are part of an ancient and continuing dialectic. Throughout the centuries the Jewish religion has imagined human life to exist in tension between the demand of justice for all of God's creatures and the fear of sin. The moral command, at its most inclusive, was first pronounced by Abraham when he pleaded with God to save the people of Sodom and Gomorrah: "Shall not the Judge of all the world do justice?" [Genesis 18:5]. The people of Sodom and Gomorrah were idolaters; yet Abraham pleaded for their lives, for the sake of the righteous who might be among them. Nonetheless, the prohibitions against idolatry, the injunction to uproot pagan cults from the Land of Israel, and to maintain distance from idol worshippers are repeated in the Bible over and over again. But, who is an idol worshipper? The definition is debated in the Talmud, especially in the tractate *Avodah Zarah*. How much distance from idolaters is required? What relations with them are permitted by the need to maintain peace in society? Were not even the worst enemies of the Jewish people, the idolatrous Egyptians who pursued the Jews to the Red Sea, also children of God whose deaths God Himself mourned? They, too, were His handiwork.

This ancient struggle between inclusive justice and the need to exclude sin remains the basic quandary today. What is justice towards the dying? Is reverence for life absolute, under all conditions, or must it be balanced with compassion for suffering patients and for the families which suffer with them? On what principles does one resolve the claims of Jews and Arabs to the same land? Does love for all of humanity require us to be equally accepting of all values and of all forms of conduct? These ancient questions were discussed in the first edition of this book, in excerpts from many authorities throughout the centuries. The readers of this second edition will find that the demands of justice and the fear of sin have been debated again, in the last three decades, by men and women who care passionately about the issues of our time.

INTRODUCTION

God made covenant with a particular people that it should be His priesthood. To this people, the seed of Abraham, the slaves He had just redeemed from Egypt, He revealed the Torah, the Law which they were to obey, as the particular burden of the Jews and as the sign of their unique destiny in the world. He chose the land of Canaan as His inheritance and that of His people, the Holy Land which would forever remain the place in which He would most clearly be manifest.

God exists in the world and cares for all humanity, for are not the children of Israel, as Amos said, no more to Him than the Ethiopians? It was out of His love for mankind as a whole that He taught to all His way of redemption, the Torah, in His revelation in the desert of Sinai, to show that, like the desert, the Law belongs to anyone who dares to claim it. God does not speak to mortals only in the Holy Land, for He addressed Noah in the land between the rivers, Abraham in Ur, Moses in Midian, and He spoke even to Balaam, who came to curse the Israelites in the desert of Sinai. The Talmud contains a vision of the end of days, in which the holiness that is particular to the land of Israel will "spread out" to encompass all the lands.

Either of the two sets of assertions just above is true as description of Judaism, but neither is true without the other. It would be easy to say that these two versions of Judaism, the so-called "universal" and "particular" aspects, are in uneasy tension; this has indeed been said by non-Jewish commentators and polemicists for many centuries. From the perspective of one who stands inside the Jewish tradition, in the faith and experience of the Jewish believer, such a distinction does not exist. Jewish faith addresses itself not only to the Jews; it prescribes the Law and the way of salvation for all mankind.

The Jewish ideas of God, Torah, and the people Israel, as well as the lesser but quite important doctrine of the Holy Land, do not represent a catechism or a theology, for there is none such in Judaism. They are the lasting values, areas of concern, foci, or problems (call them what you will) around which the mass of Jewish spiritual devotion and thought through the ages has organized itself. Men of simple faith, scholars, mystics, and philosophers have differed from one another in their understanding and interpretation of these values. Nonetheless Judaism has remained recognizably one faith through all these permutations because, at least until the last century or so, the contemporary age of doubt, the normative tradition has been believed, and obeyed, by all Jews who intended to remain within the fold. Jews have regarded it as self-evident that the God of all the world had made them His priest-people, His "suffering servant," to live by the Law and to bear the burden of the woes that might come to them. Their task is to achieve redemption for themselves and to lead mankind to the day when, in the words of Zechariah, quoted in the liturgy, "the Lord will be One and His name One."

The truest key to understanding Judaism in its own terms is to be found in its concept of the "chosen people." This doctrine of "chosenness" is a mystery—and a scandal. It was already a mystery to the Bible itself, which ascribed the Divine choice not to any inborn merits of the Jews, but to the unknowable will of God. It soon became, and has remained, a scandal to the Gentiles—and even to some Jews. There have been many attempts through the ages to defend and explain this doctrine. Several such explanations, culled from the writings of medieval and modern Jewish thinkers, appear in this book, as well as a modern attack on this doctrine by a radical American Jewish theologian, whose version of Judaism is naturalist and religio-cultural. Certainly the secularist versions of Jewish experience, like some forms of Zionism, have tended to abandon this doctrine. It is nonetheless my view that Judaism is inconceivable without it. This does not mean that anyone, certainly not in our own troubled times, can dare assert that he or she knows the meaning of this mystery. Perhaps it is enough for this moment to know that the mystery exists; perhaps that is all that any other generation really knew. Nevertheless, a few words about what the idea of the "chosen people" implies need to be added.

Obviously there can be no "chosen people" unless there is a God who does the choosing. History, especially modern history, knows too many examples of self-chosen peoples. No matter how high and humanitarian a "civilizing mission" such a people may assign to itself, self-chosenness has invariably degenerated into some form of the notion of a master race. Nor can we attempt to rationalize the classical Jewish concept of the chosen people, as some nineteenth-century Jewish theologians did, by arguing that various peoples have particular talents innate within them, e.g. the Greeks for art and philosophy, the Germans for order, the English and Americans for liberty, and the Jews for religion. Quite apart from the massive evidence from sociology and allied disciplines that such thinking is untrue, it has about it an air of arrogance which is morally repugnant. A "chosen people" has a right to exist and so think of itself only if there is a God in the world who is more than a First Cause or the order of the cosmos. He has to be conceived as the Creator who has not washed His hands of creation, who cares for and speaks to human beings, to whom what they do is not a matter of indifference. Such a God can be imagined as choosing a particular people for the task of strictest obedience to His will, as an instrument in His hand for the redemption of mankind and as a teacher whom God Himself keeps from pride by applying to His chosen people the severest of judgments.

Classical Judaism is, therefore, a *revealed* religion. The very notion of revelation is in itself of the utmost difficulty, not only to the unbeliever but especially to the believer. What need does God have of mortals at all? Why should He have wished to speak to them? Even if one's faith in His revelation is of the most orthodox kind, there still remains the question: What does the Divine command require of me, of my individual life in the context of my immediate situation?

Stripped bare of all arguments, there are only two possible

approaches to religion: either we invented God for our own purposes, or God created us to achieve His purposes. The first alternative is the favorite one of the last several centuries. Some have approved of human inventiveness and others have denounced it as an unnecessary and even harmful illusion. Especially since Voltaire, the idea of God has been explained as the antidote that mortals have devised to the menace of the world and to death. It is a crutch that humanity can, indeed ought to, discard—so this argument goes. There is no real comfort for the traditionalist in the classical philosophical and theological attempts to prove that God exists. Each of the well-known "proofs"—that creation implies a Creator, that the design of the world implies a Designer, etc.—has been refuted in the realm of philosophical argument, and a verdict of "not proved" has been returned by the jury of reason.

I say not *proved*, and not *disproved*. Philosophical argument can indeed produce no undeniable proof of God's existence, but neither can it make it certain beyond argument that there is no God. The choice can only be made by faith. As human beings survey the world, it can appear to be an uncaring universe, indifferent and perhaps chaotic, to which we give some passing meaning, or we can view it as purposeful, though like Job, we may not comprehend its purposes. Here we are confronted by an ultimate choice, and we cannot argue ourselves into one or the other position.

Judaism, the religion of the Bible, is the classical paradigm of a God-made religion. It is the assertion—not the philosophical proof—that God exists and that He has spoken and speaks to His creatures, giving them clues to the road that they must follow. A God who cares about humanity is likely to have revealed Himself to His favorite creation, though this is not an absolute necessity, for He could have so created the world that human destiny would work itself out without immediate contact with the Divine; but a God who has chosen a people for a role of transcendent importance in the scheme of redemption must have informed it of His choice, though here, too, it is just possible that the choice can exist without its knowledge. Classical Judaism believes that this people is conscious of its appointment, for God has spoken to it. The Jewish faith therefore, from the earliest time, even in the Bible itself, has confronted the question of what is true and what is false revelation.

To be sure, every individual can experience the Divine revelation, but one can also imagine that it is being experienced while actually one is engaged in self-delusion. Revelation must therefore be personal and not personalist. For the Jew, the form into which the revelation is cast is the Law, and Judaism throughout all the ages is therefore a tension between true and false prophets, between religious enthusiasts who come to recharge the experience of the obedient believer with refreshed devotion to the Law and those enthusiasts who come to break it in the name of some "higher" experience.

> If a prophet or a dreamer of dreams should arise among you, one who gives you a sign or a miracle, and these signs and miracles of which he speaks to you come to pass, as he says, Let us follow other gods which you have not known and let us serve them, do not listen to the words of that prophet or that dreamer of dreams. For the Lord your God is testing you to know whether you love the Lord your God with all your heart and with all your soul. You shall follow after the Lord your God and fear Him, keeping His commandments and obeying His voice; you shall serve Him and cleave unto Him [Deut. 13:2–5].

In every age Jewish religious expression is rich in mystical fervor. Such fervor is regarded as valid so long as it remains the handmaiden of obedience to the original revelation, so long as it is judged by it and does not presume to become its judge.

What the Divine revelation contains has of course been at issue between Judaism and both Christianity and Islam for many centuries. In the realm of history, in the actual living experience of an all too often persecuted minority, this debate has had large and tragic consequences, but it has had relatively little effect on the Jewish faith. Occasionally a philosophical theologian within Jewry, such as Franz Rosenzweig in our century, has posited a missionary role among the Gentiles for the daughter religions which have sprung from the Bible, but throughout the ages all Israel has stood fast in the faith that the Torah is the inheritance of the congregation of Jacob. It is only in the modern age that the meaning of revelation, which means, most crucially, the binding character of the Torah, has become the most serious and severe problem for Jewish religious thought.

Biblical criticism of the modern kind has tended to undermine the Talmudic notions that every word in the Torah was dictated by the Lawgiver to Moses on Sinai and that the further tradition of interpretation in the Talmud and the later writings has been guided by Divine inspiration. Religious anthropology has called into question the idea that the ritual prescriptions of the Bible are unique and God-given, for many parallels to them have been found, especially in ancient near-Eastern religions. Above all, the political and intellectual emancipation of modern Jewry, the entry of large segments of this community into the general life of Western man, has been regarded by most Jews as a primary practical objective. The life of obedience to the inherited Law requires of the Jew a considerable conscious apartness. Inevitably, it has therefore been regarded as a bar on the road to complete social integration.

The first two attacks, from Biblical criticism and the anthropology of religion, were not directed against Judaism alone. They were part of a major current which has dominated Western thought in the last several centuries, the criticism of revealed religion in the name of reason and science. The story of the defense of Judaism against such attack is not essentially different from the history of Western religious thought as a whole. It is by now commonly agreed that scholarly investigation into the composition of the text of the Bible, no matter what the results of such study may be, cannot by its very nature pass final judgment on the faith in revelation. As for the argument from anthropology, a person is obviously more than the chemical elements that make up his body. By the same token, a religious system is more than the sum of its individual practices.

For Judaism, however, the theological problem in modern times has been made more acute by the historic implications of the changing political and social history of the Jews. From the beginning of the Exile in the year 70 until the eighteenth century all Jews lived as a separate enclave both in Christian Europe and in Moslem North Africa and the Near East. With the beginning of the social and political emancipation of Jewry, the overarching theme of Jewish experience in the nineteenth century became the finding of ways to cease being outside society. Jewish thought devoted itself to definitions of Jewish faith and identity which would make it possible for the Jews to think about themselves as very much like everybody else, as a religion among religions, a group among groups, or as a nation among nations. Hence Jewish religious thought was more radically "Westernized" than it had ever been before, even by the most philosophical of medieval Jewish theologians. It was defined, especially by liberal theologians, as a religious denomination among the several which dominated West European culture. The Law therefore became a problem not only because it was socially inconvenient. It was even more fundamentally in question because, of all the key values of Judaism, it was the most foreign, the hardest to explain, within an outlook that proceeded in the form and mode of Western philosophical theology.

Authentic Judaism is inconceivable without the Law. To be sure, there is a difference between moral principle and ceremonial observance. The Talmudic tradition rules that on the Day of Atonement people can find forgiveness from God for their sins in the realm of ritual, but no ceremony can absolve them of their sins against others. Such absolution can be gained only by reconciliation with the wronged. Many other proofs of this distinction could be added. It is nonetheless an essential of the faith that the regimen which has been ordained for the religious practice of the Jew is God-given. This people was chosen to be a corporate priesthood, to live within the world and yet apart from it. Its way of life is the appointed sign of its difference. At the end of time, in a completely redeemed world, this unique way will perhaps disappear, but the world is not yet redeemed and the Messiah has not yet come.

It remains to be added, in terms of a famous distinction, that Judaism is a religion not of nature but of history. There are many passages in the Bible which sing the praises of God in nature, but the characteristic Jewish experience of God is the awareness of His presence in human events. Every aspect of the Jewish tradition is pervaded by the memory of His redemptive act in the exodus from Egypt. Almost the whole of the religious calendar is an act of recalling the past experience of the Jewish people as the record of God's relationship to it. The emphasis of Jewish faith is therefore neither on metaphysical speculation nor on dogma but on human action. Life is the arena of moral choice, and each individual can choose the good. One can become worse than the beast or can ascend to a level little lower than the angels. Every individual plays a role, for good or ill, in the redemptive history of mankind, for human beings are God's partners in the work of creation.

Judaism constructs its present out of a memory reaching back to Abraham and looking forward to the Messianic age for humanity as a whole. It is the way which began with the breaking of the idols and with risking all for the sake of God. To lead is often to suffer, and throughout the centuries Judaism has found in the tragedy which is so much of Jewish history, in its role as the "suffering servant" of God, the surest sign of its ordained task.

The Jews have often been restless under the burden. Even before the modern age, some have longed for peace and ease, for the quest for a "normal" identity and destiny is human, all too human. It is, at the very least, untrue to history. Jewish experience has not been like that of all the nations, and the generation which has witnessed both Hitler and the third return to Zion engages in great self-delusion if it imagines that the place of the Jew in the world is as yet "normalized." Like Jonah, some Jews may attempt to cease prophesying against Nineveh, but Nineveh is always there. Jonah's knowledge that God wants something special from him is the inescapable and continuing groove of Jewish experience.

1

PEOPLE

THE FACT OF THE COVENANT

God's initial covenant, with Abraham, was with the head of a family, and the Jewish people was conceived as the ever-increasing number of his descendants. Hence to this day the convert to Judaism is not only accepted into the faith; the ritual prescribes that he or she be adopted into the family as a child of Abraham. The covenant with Moses is a new and wider one, with a people as a whole. This is symbolized by the "new name" by which God makes Himself known to Moses.

And when Abram was ninety-nine years old, the Lord appeared to Abram and said to him, "I am God Almighty; walk before Me, and be perfect. And I will make My covenant between Me and you and I will multiply you exceedingly." Abram fell on his face and God spoke with him, saying "As for Me, behold, My covenant is with you, and you shall be the father of a multitude of nations. Neither shall your name be called any more Abram, but your name shall be Abraham, because I have made you the father of a multitude of nations. And I will make you exceedingly fruitful, and I will make nations of you, and kings shall come out of you. And I will establish My covenant between Me and you and your seed after you throughout their generations for an everlasting covenant, to be God to you and to your seed after you. And I will give to you, and to your seed after you, the land of your sojournings, all the land of Canaan, for an everlasting possession, and I will be their God."[1]

And God spoke to Moses saying, "I am the Lord. I appeared to Abraham, to Isaac and to Jacob as God Almighty but by My name of Lord I did not make Myself known to them. And I established My covenant with them, to give them the land of Canaan, the land of their sojournings, wherein they dwelled. Moreover I have heard the groaning of the children of Israel whom the Egyptians keep in bondage and I have remembered My covenant. Therefore say to the children of Israel, 'I am the Lord, who will bring you out from under the burdens of the Egyptians, and will deliver you from their bondage, and will deliver you with an outstretched arm and with great judgments. And I will take you to Myself for a people and I will be your God; and you shall know that I am the Lord your God who brought you out from under the burdens of the Egyptians. And I will bring you into the land concerning which I lifted My hand to give it to Abraham, Isaac and Jacob. I will give it to you for a heritage; I am the Lord.' "[2]

THE NATURE OF THE COVENANT

The covenant with God binds the Jewish people to the task of being a corporate priesthood. God redeemed them from slavery in Egypt, let them hear His voice, led them to the promised land and vowed to keep faith with all future generations of this people. They in turn must keep His statutes as ordained in the Bible. The covenant is, however, unbreakable. They will be punished for their sins and judged by stricter standards than those God applies to other men, but He will never put them utterly aside and find a new love.

Now, therefore, if you will obey My voice and keep My covenant, you shall be My own possession among all the peoples, for all the earth is Mine, and you shall be to Me a kingdom of priests and a holy nation.[3]

You shall therefore keep all My statutes and all My ordinances, and do them, lest the land, into which I bring you to dwell, vomit you out. And you shall not walk in the customs of the nations which I am casting out before you; they have done all these things and therefore I abhorred them. But to you I say: Possess their land which I will give you for an inheritance, a land flowing with milk and honey. I am the Lord your God, who have set you apart from other people. You shall therefore separate the clean beast from the unclean, and the clean fowl from the unclean; you shall not defile yourselves by beast or by fowl or by anything with which the ground teems, which I have set apart for you to hold unclean. You shall be holy to Me, because I the Lord am holy, and I have separated you from other people, that you should be Mine.[4]

You shall not defile the land in which you live, in the midst of which I dwell, for I the Lord dwell in the midst of the people Israel.[5]

Ask of the days of old, that have been before your time from the day that God created man upon the earth, from one end of heaven to the other, whether a great thing like this has ever happened or was ever heard of. Did ever a people hear the voice of God speaking out of the midst of fire, as you have heard, and live? Has God attempted to go and take to Himself a nation from the midst of another nation, by trials, signs and wonders, by war, a mighty hand and an outstretched arm, and by great terrors, according to all that the Lord your God did for you in Egypt before your eyes? To you it was shown, that you might know that the Lord, He is God, and there is no other besides Him. From heaven He made you hear His voice, that He might teach you. And on earth He showed you His great fire, and you heard His words out of the midst of the fire. And because He loved your fathers, and chose their seed after them, He brought you out of Egypt with His Presence, with His great power, to drive out nations greater and mightier than you from before you, to bring you in, to give you their land for an inheritance, as it is this day. Know therefore this day and lay it to your heart, that the Lord, He is God in heaven above and in the earth beneath, and there is no other.[6]

Moses summoned all Israel and said to them: Hear, O Israel, the statutes and the ordinances which I speak in your hearing this day, and you shall learn them and be careful to do them. The Lord our God made a covenant with us in Horeb. Not with our fathers did the Lord make this covenant, but with us, who are all of us here alive this day.[7]

You all stand this day before the Lord your God, your princes, your tribes, your elders and your officers, all the people of Israel, your children and your wives, and the stranger that is in the midst of your camp, from those that hew wood to those that draw water; that you enter into the covenant of the Lord your God, and into His oath, which this day the Lord your God makes with you, that He may establish you this day as a people to Himself, and that He may be your God, as He has spoken to you, and as He swore to your fathers, Abraham, Isaac and Jacob. Not with you only do I make this covenant and this oath, but with him that stands here with us this day before the Lord our God and also with him that is not here with us this day.[8]

I will betroth you to Me forever. I will betroth you to Me in righteousness and in justice, in love and in mercy. I will betroth you to Me in faithfulness, and you shall love the Lord.[9]

The Holy One, praised be He, said to Hosea "Your children have sinned." Hosea should have said "They are Your children, children of Your dear ones, children of Abraham, Isaac and Jacob; show them Your mercy." However, not only did he not say this, but he said "Lord of the universe! The entire world belongs to You. Displace them with another people." The Holy One, praised be He, thought: What shall I do with this old man? I shall tell him to marry a harlot and to beget children of harlotry and then I shall tell him to send her away. If he will be able to send her away, I will send Israel away. And it is written "The Lord said to Hosea: Go, take to yourself a wife of harlotry and have children of harlotry. . . . So he went and took Gomer the daughter of Dibla'im . . ." [Hosea 1:2–3]. When two sons and a daughter had been born to him, the Holy One, praised be He, said to Hosea "Could you not have learned from Moses, your teacher? Whenever I spoke with him he separated from his wife. You must do likewise." Hosea answered "Lord of the universe! I have children from her. I cannot put her away or divorce her." The Holy One said to him "Your wife is a harlot and your children are children of harlotry; you do not even know if they are really yours. Yet you refuse to divorce her. How, then, should I act toward Israel? They are the children of those whom I have tested, the children of Abraham, Isaac and Jacob, and one of the four possessions which I have acquired in My world: The Torah, heaven and earth, the Temple and Israel. And yet you tell Me to supersede them with another people!"

When he realized that he had sinned, Hosea rose to ask mercy for himself. The Holy One, praised be He, said to him "Before you ask mercy for yourself, ask mercy for Israel."[10]

In the Rabbinic commentary on the Song of Songs the Biblical image is changed. This great paean to love is interpreted as referring to the love between God and His people, Israel. The beloved is beautiful because she decks herself as a bride in her proper jewelry, i.e. deeds which represent the obedient and sacrificial love borne by Israel to God. Israel is adorned by daily prayer (the Shema, i.e. "Hear, O Israel, the Lord our God, the Lord is One"); the receptacle on the right front doorpost of every Jewish home which contains the Shema (the *mezuzah*); the phylacteries (*tephillin*, or *tefillin*), the black receptacles to be worn on head and arm, near the heart, by every adult male in weekday morning prayer; and the citron (*ethrog*, or *etrog*) and palm tree (*lulab*, or *lulav*) used in the ritual of the Sukkot holiday (see chapter 4).

> "You are beautiful, my love" (Song of Songs 1:15). You are beautiful through the commandments, both positive and negative, beautiful through loving deeds, beautiful in your house with the heave-offering and the tithes . . . beautiful in the law of circumcision, beautiful in prayer, in reciting the *Shema*, in observing the laws of *Mezuzah* and *Tefillin*, *etrog* and *lulav*, beautiful too in repentance and in good works, beautiful in this world and beautiful in the world to come.[11]

The author of the following epistle is Maimonides (1135–1206), Moses ben Maimon, the towering figure of medieval Jewish learning in both philosophy and rabbinic law. He is here (in 1172) strengthening the resolve of Yemenite Jewry to withstand persecution.

> . . . And now let me deal with the rest of the contents of your epistle. I reply to it in the Arabic language, in order that all may easily understand, for all are concerned in what I shall communicate. The news that the government under which you live ordered all Jews in South Arabia to apostacize, in the same manner as the ruling powers in Western countries have acted towards us, made us turn pale with terror. The whole community shares your grief. . . . Our minds are bewildered; we feel unable to think calmly, so terrible is the alternative in which Israel has been placed on all sides, from the East and from the West. . . .
>
> Know for certain that what we believe in is the Law of God given through the father of the prophets. That by its teaching the

heavenly legislator intended to constitute us an entirely distinct people. The selection was not due to our inherent worth. Indeed we have been distinctly told so in the Scriptures. But because our progenitors acted righteously through their knowledge of the Supreme Being, therefore we, their descendants, reap the benefit of their meritorious deeds. . . .

My brethren, it behooves us to keep ever present before our minds the great day of Sinai, for the Lord has forbidden us ever to forget it. Rear your offspring in a thorough understanding of that all-important event. Explain before large assemblies the principles it involves, show that it is a lucid mirror reflecting the truth: aye, the very pivot upon which our religion turns. . . . Know, moreover, you who are born in this covenant and raised in this belief, that the stupendous occurrence, the truth of which is testified by the most trusty of witnesses, stands in very deed alone in the annals of mankind. For a whole people heard the word of God and saw the glory of the Divinity. From this lasting memory we must draw our power to strengthen our faith even in a period of persecution and affliction such as the present one.

My brethren! Hold fast to the covenant, be immovable in your convictions, fulfill the statutes of your religion. . . . Rejoice that you suffer trials, confiscation, contumely, all for the love of God, to magnify His glorious name. It is the sweetest offering you can make. . . . Should ever the necessity of fleeing for your lives to a wilderness and inhospitable regions arise, painful as it may be to sever oneself from dear associations or to relinquish one's property, you should still endure all, and be supported by the consoling thought that the Omnipresent Lord, who reigns supreme, can recompense you commensurately to your deserts, in this world and in the world to come. . . . It often happens that a man will part from his kindred and friends and travel abroad, because he finds his earnings inadequate to his wants. How much more readily ought we to follow the same course, when we stand in danger of being denied the means to supply our *spiritual* necessities.[12]

THE NATURE OF
THE COVENANT PEOPLE

By obeying the divine commandments the people that God has chosen will experience His nearness to a degree greater than that of all other peoples. Obedience to the Law is therefore not slavery to a divine despot; it is the way of regular encounter with God. Law in Judaism is not the enemy of mystical experience; it *is* that experience, generalized and regularized for all kinds and conditions of Jews.

But why did God choose this people? There are several partial answers: the merits of their ancestors, chiefly Abraham, who accepted the One God and broke with idolatry; their comparative virtue; their humility and their faithfulness. The first reason, the argument based on the merit of Abraham, recurs everywhere in Jewish literature, and especially in the liturgy. The others (and more could be added) indicate that the question remained a question—and a source and guarantor of humility.

> I have taught you statutes and ordinances, as the Lord my God has commanded me; so shall you do in the land which you shall possess. And you shall observe and fulfill them, for this is your wisdom and your understanding in the sight of the peoples that, hearing all these statutes, they may say: Behold a wise and un- derstanding people, a great nation. For what great nation is there that has God so near to them, as the Lord our God whenever we call upon Him? And what great nation is there that has statutes and ordinances so righteous as all this law which I set before you this day?[13]

> For you are a holy people to the Lord your God; the Lord your God has chosen you to be His own treasure, out of all the peoples that are upon the earth. Not because you surpass all nations in number did the Lord set His love upon you and choose you, for you are the fewest of any people, but because the Lord has loved you, and because He would keep His oath which He swore to your fathers has He brought you out with a mighty hand and redeemed you from the house of bondage, out of the hand of Pharaoh, king of Egypt. Know therefore that the Lord your God is God, the faithful God, keeping His covenant and mercy with those who love Him and keep His commandments to a thousand

generations, and repaying those who hate Him, to destroy them, immediately rendering to them what they deserve. Keep therefore the commandments and the statutes and the ordinances which I command you this day to do.[14]

Not because of your righteousness or the uprightness of your heart are you going in to possess their land, but because of the wickedness of these nations the Lord your God is driving them out from before you, and that He may confirm the word which the Lord swore to your fathers, to Abraham to Isaac and to Jacob.[15]

The people Israel are beloved for they are called God's children. They are especially beloved in that they were made aware of this, as it is written, "You are children of the Lord your God . . ." [Deut. 14:1]. The people Israel are beloved, for to them was given a precious instrument [the Torah]. They are especially beloved in that they were made aware that to them was given the precious instrument by which the world was created, as it is written, "For I have given you good doctrine; do not forsake My Torah" [Prov. 4:2].[16]

"You have declared this day concerning the Lord that He is your God and that you will walk in His ways . . . and the Lord has declared this day that you are a people for His own possession . . ." [Deut. 26:17–18]. The Holy One, praised be He, said to Israel: You have made Me unique in the world and I shall make you unique in the world. You have made Me unique, by proclaiming "Hear, O Israel, the Lord is our God, the Lord is One" [Deut. 6:4], and I will make you unique, by agreeing "Who is like Your people Israel, a nation that is one in the earth . . ." [I Chron. 17:21].[17]

"It was not because you were more in number than any other people that the Lord set His love upon you and chose you, for you were the fewest of all peoples" [Deut. 7:7]. The Holy One praised be He said to Israel: I set My love upon you because even when I grant you greatness you make yourselves small [i.e. humble] before Me. I gave greatness to Abraham, and he said "Behold, I am dust and ashes" [Gen. 18:27]; to Moses and Aaron, and they said "But what are we?" [Ex. 16:7]; to David, and he said "I am a worm, not a man" [Ps. 22:7]. But the other nations of the world are not like you. I gave greatness to Nimrod, and he said "Let us build for ourselves a city, and a tower with its top in the heavens . . ." [Gen. 11:4]; to Pharaoh and he said "Who is the Lord?"

[Ex. 5:2] . . . to Nebuchadnezzar and he said "I will ascend above the heights of the clouds; I will make myself like the Most High" [Isa. 14:14].[18]

This people has been compared to the dust [". . . your descendants shall be like the dust of the earth . . ." Gen. 28:14] and it has been compared to the stars [". . . I will multiply your descendants as the stars of the heavens . . ." Gen. 22:17]. When they go down, they go down to the dust of the earth; but when they rise, they rise to the stars.[19]

Rabbi Abba bar Acha said: One cannot determine the nature of this people. When asked to contribute for making the golden calf, they give; and when asked to contribute for constructing the Tabernacle, they give.[20]

"And you shall take on the first day [of Sukkot] the fruit of goodly trees, branches of palm trees and boughs of leafy trees, and willows of the brook; and you shall rejoice before the Lord your God seven days" [Lev. 23:40]. ". . . the fruit of goodly trees . . ." refers to Israel. Just as the *etrog* [citron] has both taste and fragrance, so Israel has men who have both learning and good deeds. ". . . branches of palm trees . . ." refer to Israel. Just as the fig has a taste but has no fragrance, so Israel has men who have learning but have no good deeds. ". . . boughs of leafy trees . . ." refer to Israel. Just as the myrtle has fragrance but has no taste, so Israel has men who have good deeds but have no learning. ". . . willows of the brook . . ." refer to Israel. Just as the willow has neither taste nor fragrance, so Israel has men who have neither learning nor good deeds. What does the Holy One, praised be He, do with them? . . . He stated, "Let them be interrelated, united in one group, and they will be able to atone for one another. When Israel does so, I will be exalted. . . ."[21]

Judah Halevi, the author of the following passage, was born in Spain toward the end of the eleventh century, and died either on the way to or in the Holy Land in 1140. He was a great poet in Hebrew and a profound theologian. Tradition and revelation, rather than reason, are the sources of faith—so he argues in his book called the *Kuzari*. The form of this volume, from which the statement here about Israel is excerpted, is based on a historic fact. The Khazars, a people of large though temporary power in southern Russia (740–1250), were converted to Judaism, in preference to Christianity or Islam. The *Kuzari* was written as a series of imaginary religious disputations before the king of the Khazars by representations of all three faiths, culminating in his accepting Judaism.

> Israel amidst the nations is like the heart amidst the organs of the body; it is at one and the same time the most sick and the most healthy of them. . . .
>
> Our relation to the Divine Influence is the same as that of the soul to the heart. For this reason it is said: "You only have I known of all the families of the earth, therefore I will punish you for all your iniquities" [Amos 3:2]. He does not allow our sins to become overwhelming, or they would destroy us completely by their multitude. . . . Just as the heart is pure in substance and matter, and of even temperament, in order to be accessible to the intellectual soul, so Israel is pure in all its parts. But just as the heart may be affected by disease of the other organs . . . caused through contact with malignant elements, so Israel is exposed to ills which originate in its inclinings towards the pagans, as it is said: "They were mingled among the heathens and learned their works" [Ps. 106:35]. . . . The trials which come upon us are meant to prove our faith, to cleanse us completely, and to remove all taint from us.[22]

THE BURDEN OF THE COVENANT

To be God's chosen people is a merit and a distinction. In the Bible and the Talmud, it is also the explanation for Jewry's tragedies. The Babylonian captivity after the destruction of the First Temple in 586 B.C.E. and the Exile of the Jews from the Holy Land after the razing of the Second Temple by the Romans in the year 70 were both great crises of faith. Had God put the Jews aside? No. They had sinned, perhaps no more than other peoples, but it was their duty to be more obedient.

> Hear this word that the Lord has spoken against you, O children of Israel, against the whole family which I brought up out of the land of Egypt, saying: You only have I known of all the families of the earth; therefore will I punish you for all your iniquities.[23]

Are you not as the children of the Ethiopians to Me, O children of Israel? says the Lord. Did I not bring up Israel out of the land of Egypt, and the Philistines out of Caphtor, and the Syrians out of Kir? Behold, the eyes of the Lord God are upon the sinful kingdom, and I will destroy it from the face of the earth, but I will not utterly destroy the house of Jacob, says the Lord. For behold, I will command, and I will sift the house of Israel among all nations, as corn is sifted in a sieve, yet not the least grain shall fall to the ground. All the sinners of My people shall fall by the sword, who say, "The evil shall not approach, and shall not come upon us."[24]

The image here is essentially that of the comment above on the Song of Songs. Israel is God's faithful mate. It is ornamented by obedience to every one of His laws, not to just a few; it is faithful to the home, the Temple, which was its meeting place with its beloved divine mate; it is faithful to God even unto death.

"Your eyes are doves" [Song of Songs 1:15]. The dove is faithful; Israel was likewise faithful to the Holy One, praised be He, at Sinai. For they did not say that ten commandments, or twenty or thirty, were enough for them, but they said, "All that the Lord has spoken we will do and we will obey" [Ex. 24:7]. The dove is distinguishable among all other birds; Israel is likewise distinguished, by deeds. The dove is modest; Israel is likewise modest. . . . The dove does not leave its nest even if someone has taken its brood; Israel likewise continues to visit the Temple site even though the Temple has been destroyed. The dove journeys, and returns to its nest; Israel likewise "shall come eagerly like birds from Egypt and like doves from Assyria" [Hos. 11:11]. Others are attracted to the dove; likewise, converts are attracted to Israel. The dove, unlike other birds, offers its neck for slaughter without struggling; children of Israel likewise give their lives for the Holy One praised be He. The dove does not leave its mate; Israel likewise does not leave the Holy One, praised be He. The dove atones for sins; Israel likewise atones for the nations of the world.[25]

THE COVENANT WITH ALL

Noah is the ancestor of all mankind, and to him God made the promise that no matter what its sins, humanity would never be utterly destroyed, as it had been at the Flood. But covenant here too involves commandment. Noah's descendants must obey the moral law and forsake idolatry. Salvation is not only for the "chosen people," or those who join it by conversion. It is open to all, if they but obey the law of righteousness.

God spoke to Noah and to his sons, saying: Behold, I will establish My covenant with you and with your seed after you, and with every living creature that is with you, the fowl, the cattle, and every beast of the earth with you, that come forth out of the ark, all the beasts of the earth. I will establish My covenant with you; all flesh shall no more be destroyed with the waters of a flood, neither shall there be a flood to waste the earth. And God said: This is the sign of the covenant which I make between Me and you and every living creature with you, for perpetual generations. I will set My bow in the clouds, and it shall be the sign of a covenant between Me and the earth. And whenever I cover the sky with clouds, My bow shall appear in the clouds, and I will remember My covenant with you and with every living creature of all flesh, and there shall no more be waters of a flood to destroy all flesh. [26]

The sons of Noah were given seven commandments, forbidding idolatry, incest, bloodshed, profaning God's name, injustice, robbery, and cutting the flesh or a limb from a living animal. [27]

I call heaven and earth as witnesses: The spirit of holiness rests upon each person according to the deed that each does, whether that person be non-Jew or Jew, man or woman, manservant or maidservant. [28]

The Holy One, praised be He, does not disqualify any creature; He accepts everyone. The gates are always open, and whoever wants to enter may enter. [29]

Rabbi Jeremiah used to say: How do we know that even a non-Jew who fulfills the Torah is to be regarded as equal to the High Priest? Scripture states, "You shall therefore keep My statutes and My ordinances which, if *a man* do, he shall live by them" [Lev. 18:5]. . . . And he said: Scripture does not state "This is the Law of the Priests, Levites and Israelites" but "This is the Law of man, O Lord God" [II Sam. 7:19]. And he said: Scripture does not state "Open the gates, that the Priests, Levites and Israelites may enter" but "Open the gates that the righteous nation that keeps faithfulness may enter" [Isa. 26:2]. And he said: Scripture does not state "This is the gate of the Lord; the Priests, Levites and Israelites shall enter therein" but "This is the gate of the Lord; the righteous shall enter therein" [Ps. 118:20].[30]

. . . As to your question about the nations, know that the Lord desires the heart, and that the intention of the heart is the measure of all things. That is why our sages say, "The pious men among the Gentiles have a share in the world to come," namely, if they have acquired what can be acquired of the knowledge of God, and if they ennoble their souls with worthy qualities. There is no doubt that every man who ennobles his soul with excellent morals and wisdom based on the faith in God certainly belongs to the men of the world to come. That is why our sages say, "Even a non-Jew who studies the Torah of our master Moses may be compared to a High Priest."[31]

Judaism does accept converts. They are indeed especially precious to God. Their virtue is not so much that they have accepted the Jewish faith, for good men can attain salvation in their own religions. It is that they have taken upon themselves the special burden of Jewish destiny and obligation of becoming part of a priest-people, by choice and adoption "children of Abraham."

"You shall have one ordinance both for the stranger and for the native" [Num. 9:14]. [For the rabbis, "stranger" means proselyte.] Thus, this verse teaches that Scripture makes the proselyte equal to the native-born Jew as regards all the commandments of the Torah.[32]

A proselyte who has come of his own accord is dearer to God than all the Israelites who stood before Him at Mount Sinai. Had the Israelites not witnessed the thunders, lightnings, quaking mountains and sound of trumpets, they would not have accepted the Torah. The proselyte, who saw not one of these things, came and surrendered himself to the Holy One, praised be He, and took the yoke of Heaven upon himself. Can anyone be dearer to God than such a person?[33]

If anyone desires to be a convert during these times [*probably a period of persecution*], they should say to him, "Why do you want to convert? Do you not know that Israelites today are harried, and oppressed, persecuted and harassed, and that they suffer?" If he says, "I know and I am not worthy," he is accepted at once, and they explain some of the easier and some of the more stringent commandments to him. . . . And as they tell him of the punishments for transgressing commandments, so they tell him of the rewards for observing them. . . . However, they do not speak with him at great length nor do they go into great detail. If he agrees to accept everything, he is circumcised at once. . . . After he is healed, he must undergo ritual immersion and two scholars stand by, telling him some of the easier and some of the more stringent commandments. After the ritual immersion he is an Israelite in every respect.[34]

Why was Abraham circumcised at the age of ninety-nine? To teach that if a man wants to convert he should not say, "I am too old; how can I convert?" This is the reason why Abraham was not circumcised until the age of ninety-nine.[35]

What follows here is a legal decision by Maimonides in answer to a question posed by a convert.

. . . You ask me if you, too, are allowed to say in the blessings and prayers you offer alone or in the congregation: "*Our* God and God of *our* fathers," "You who have sanctified *us* through Your commandments," "You who have separated *us*," "You who have chosen *us*," . . . "You who have brought *us* out of the land of Egypt," . . . and more of this kind.

Yes, you may say all this in the prescribed order and not change it in the least. In the same way as every Jew by birth says his blessings and prayers, you, too, shall bless and pray alike, whether you are alone or pray in the congregation. The reason for this is that Abraham, our father, taught the people, opened their minds, and revealed to them the true faith and the unity of God; he rejected the idols and abolished their adoration; he brought many children under the wings of the Divine Presence; he gave them counsel and advice, and ordered his sons and the members of his household after him to keep the ways of the Lord forever, as it is written, "For I have known him to the end that he may command his children and his household after him, that they may keep the way of the Lord, to do righteousness and justice" [Gen. 18:19]. Ever since then whoever adopts Judaism and confesses the unity of the Divine Name, as it is prescribed in the Torah, is counted among the disciples of Abraham, our father, peace be with him. These men are Abraham's household, and he it is who converted them to righteousness.

In the same way as he converted his contemporaries through his words and teaching, he converts future generations through the testament he left to his children and household after him. Thus Abraham, our father, peace be with him, is the father of his pious posterity who keep his ways, and the father of his disciples and of all proselytes who adopt Judaism.[36]

JEWISH IDENTITY
IN THE MODERN AGE

In Biblical days, strangers who came to live in the land of Israel, such as Ruth from Moab, became Jews simply by choosing to live in the community. Marriages with such permanent settlers were, with few exceptions, expressly permitted. On the other hand, in the fifth century B.C.E. Ezra, who came to Jerusalem to lead the Jews in the rebuilding of the Temple, insisted that they put aside the foreign women whom they had married. The probable explanation is that in earliest times a secure Jewish majority in the land could assimilate some strangers into its midst; after the destruction of the First Temple in 586 B.C.E, however, the handful of Jews who had returned from the Babylonian exile could easily have been swamped by the pagan majority.

The first sectarian split was with the Samaritans, an ancient tribe who refused to accept the central authority of the Temple in Jerusalem and insisted on their own shrine on Mount Gerizim. In the course of the centuries, their religious practices, and especially their laws of marriage and divorce, were sufficiently different so that, in Talmudic law, they were outside the Jewish people. The next division occurred less than a hundred years after the appearance of Christianity. As the Christian sect became more gentile than Jewish in its membership, the rabbis declared the Christians to be a new community outside the Jewish fold. The Christians did not obey the 613 commandments as defined in the Talmud, and they were no longer ethnically Jewish.

In late antiquity tension began between the large majority who followed the Talmud and the Karaites who pronounced themselves to be bound only by the Bible. Early in the tenth century, Rabbi Saadia Gaon, the greatest authority among the rabbis of that age, excommunicated the Karaites and forbade all connection with them because of their religious ideology. Nonetheless, the connection between these two groups was not broken for many centuries. Maimonides ruled in the twelfth century that Karaites "should be treated with respect" and that one could "circumcise their children, bury their dead, and comfort their mourners." Marriages between the two groups did not cease entirely until the sixteenth century, but they did come to an end. The Karaite practices were so different that their descendants were suspect of being bastards, in the law of the Talmud. In the modern era the destiny of the Karaites diverged almost completely from the main body of the Jews. As early as 1795, the Karaites were exempted from the severe discrimination against Jews in czarist Russia which remained in force until the revolution of 1917. It even became a matter of advantage for Karaites to cultivate the myth that they were not of Jewish origin at all. In 1941, when the Nazis were murdering European Jewry, three scholars from the mainstream of the Jewish community joined in attesting to Nazi authorities that the Karaites were indeed not Jews, and so they were saved from mass deportation. On the other hand, in the struggle for the creation of the state of Israel, some Karaites chose to fight as part of the Jewish community.

An equally complicated question of Jewish identity arose on the Iberian peninsula in the late Middle Ages. In the fourteenth and fifteenth centuries the pressures on Jews to convert to Christianity were intense. In 1492, when the Jews were finally expelled from Spain and five years later when they were expelled from Portugal, some 100,000 converted in order to save themselves from the hardships and the dangers that awaited those who were being expelled. Many became Marranos, that is they practiced Judaism in secret. Some families kept their Jewishness alive for generations. Substantial numbers eventually succeeded in escaping from Spain and Portugal and wanted to be accepted again as Jews. There was debate among rabbinic authorities about the effect of their apostasy, and, soon, about the validity of their marriages which had been contracted under the law of the Church and not under the discipline of the halakhah. Nonetheless, all of the Marranos who fled to places in which they could declare themselves to be Jews were accepted by the Jewish community. Their children were circumcised and they were remarried according to rabbinic law. Some chafed under the burden of obeying the 613 commandments, but the basic rabbinic criterion of belonging to the Jewish community, obedience to the halakhah, remained the guideline for acceptance.

The question of Jewish identity became sharp again in the last two centuries, in the era of the Emancipation, when Jews entered the general society. In law, the separate Jewish community was abolished, except as a voluntary association, and thus Jewish authorities had lost the power to impose rabbinic rules. In Europe and America, more and more Jews entered the culture of the majority. Some chose to assimilate and leave the Jewish community. Others tried to redefine their Jewishness.

The problems for Jewish identity in the new age of the Emancipation were first raised in 1806 by Napoleon, when he convoked as assembly of notables, from his domain in France and Italy. He posed a number of questions to the Jewish leaders. Here are the first six:

1. Are Jews allowed to marry several wives?

2. Does the Jewish faith permit divorce? And is an ecclesiastical divorce valid without the sanction of civil court or valid in the face of the French code?

3. May a Jewess marry a Christian, or a Christian woman a Jew? Or does the Jewish law demand alliances between Jews only?

4. Are the French in the eyes of the Jews their brethren or their enemies?

5. In either case, what duties does the law prescribe for the Jews toward the French who are not of their faith?

6. Do those Jews who are born in France and who are treated as French citizens regard France as their native country, and do they feel themselves obligated to defend it, to obey its laws, and to submit to all regulations of the civil code?[37]

A "Grand Sanhedrin" was convoked in 1808. It consisted of 120 rabbis and laymen whose authority extended to the organized Jewish communities in countries ruled by Napoleon. After suitably fervid patriotic declarations, the Sanhedrin ruled in 1808, as follows:

> We declare that the divine law, the precious heritage of our ancestors, contains religious as well as civil demands;
>
> That by their nature religious demands are absolute and independent of circumstance and time;
>
> That this is not the same with civil commands, that is to say, with those which touch upon government and which were designed to govern the people of Israel in Palestine when it had its kings, its priests, and its magistrates;
>
> That these civil commands ceased to be applicable when Israel ceased to be a nation;
>
> The Grand Sanhedrin, taking cognizance of the fact that in the French Empire and the Kingdom of Italy no marriage is valid unless it has been preceded by a civil contract before a public official, declares in virtue of the authority granted unto it:
>
> That it is a religious obligation for every Israelite in France, as well as in the Kingdom of Italy, to regard from now on civil marriage as a civil obligation, and
>
> Therefore forbids every rabbi or any other person in the two lands to assist in a religious marriage without it having been established beforehand that marriage has been concluded according to the law before a civil officer.
>
> The Grand Sanhedrin declares further that marriages between Jews and Christians which have been contracted in accordance with the laws of the civil code are civilly legal, and that, although they may not be capable of receiving religious sanction, they should not be subject to religious prosecution.[38]

Napoleon's Sanhedrin remained within the bounds of traditional halakhah. Its members had no choice but to accept the civil validity of mixed marriages, but they remained committed to the rabbinic law that such marriages had no religious sanction and that the children of intermarriages were Jews by birth if that was the identity of their mother. This question arose again when the outlook and practices of Reform Judaism, as a new religious movement, were being defined in the 1840s in Germany. At a conference in Brunswick in 1844 the question of intermarriage was debated. Here is an excerpt from that discussion:

Schott: The integrity of the Sanhedrin is proven in the way it formulated its answer. It said: "Marriage between Jews and Christians is not forbidden"; it did not say: "It is permitted." There is a difference. Such a marriage may be permitted, yet there would be practical difficulties, as for instance, in the marriage service or the ritual of engagement or divorce proceedings. Since these questions touch so widely on practical issues, I am for postponing this whole matter for the time being.

The President asks: Shall the proposal of the commission be accepted in the following formulation: Marriages between Jews and Christians, in fact, marriages with monotheists in general are not forbidden.
The vote is taken. The majority votes "No."
Philippson rephrases the motion in the following manner: Members of monotheistic religions in general are not forbidden to marry if the parents are permitted by the laws of the state to bring up children from such wedlock in the Jewish religion.
The majority agrees to the motion.
Jolowicz objects to the formulation and wishes his objection to be recorded, because the resolution goes against the expression of the Paris Sanhedrin as well as against the rules of the Talmud at this point. The latter has not been abrogated.[39]

The problem of Jewish identity was complicated further by the decision of a conference of Reform rabbis in the United States, in Philadelphia in 1869. They formally dispensed with the *get*, the religious rite that the halakhah requires in a case of divorce:

A judgment of divorce pronounced by a civil court has full validity also in the eyes of Judaism, if the court documents reveal that both parties to the marriage agreed to the divorce. If, however, the civil court decreed a forcible divorce against one or the other party in the marriage, then Judaism recognizes the validity of this divorce only after the divorce grounds have been studied and have been found sufficient according to the spirit of the Jewish religion. It is recommended that the rabbi should seek the advice of experts for such a decision.[40]

Formally, therefore, Reform Judaism had instituted marriage practices which distanced it from rabbinic halakhah as much as the Karaites had twelve centuries earlier. This tendency to break with halakhic requirements was equally pronounced in the matter of conversion. The ritual requirements of the halakhah are that a female convert must be totally immersed in a *mikvah*, a pool of "living water," and that a male convert be both circumcised and immersed in a *mikvah*. Various authorities differ on the degree of observance of all the commandments to which a convert is obligated, at least in advance, but there was no dispute about the rituals. In 1892, the Central Conference of American Rabbis, meeting in New York, adopted the following resolution:

> Resolved, that the Central Conference of American Rabbis, assembled this day in this city of New York, considers it lawful and proper for any officiating rabbi, assisted by no less than two associates, and in the name and with the consent of his congregation, to accept into the sacred covenant of Israel, and declare fully affiliated with the congregation *for every religious purpose*, any honorable and intelligent person who desires such affiliation, without any initiatory rite, ceremony, or observance whatever; provided such person be sufficiently acquainted with the faith, doctrine, and religious usages of Israel; that nothing derogatory to such person's moral and mental character is suspected; that it is his or her free will and choice to embrace the cause of Judaism, and that he or she declare verbally, and in a document signed and sealed before such officiating rabbi and his associates, his or her intention and firm resolve—
>
> 1. To worship the One Sole and Eternal God and none besides Him.
> 2. To be conscientiously governed in his or her doings and omissions in life by God's laws, ordained for the child and image of the Father and Maker of all, the sanctified son or daughter of the divine covenant.
> 3. To adhere in life and death, actively and faithfully, to the sacred cause and mission of Israel, as marked out in Holy Writ.[41]

These departures by the Reform inevitably aroused the ire of the Orthodox. In Germany, the Orthodox and the Reform continued to belong, in most places, to the same religious corporation as constituted by local law. Some of the Orthodox found this intolerable and they left the established community to found their own congregations. Most German Jews remained together. This unity was made possible through commitments by the Reform group not to deviate from Orthodox practice in the laws of marriage and conversion. This nonetheless did not satisfy the strictest of the Orthodox authorities. Rabbi Moses Schick of Brezova wrote in this spirit to Rabbi Isaac Beer Bamberger of Wurzberg in 1877:

> . . . I have heard that you rendered a decision that if the Reform Congregation of Frankfurt am Main swears (guarantees) before the Orthodox community that they do not want to separate themselves in regard to every matter of the Torah, it is permitted to be with them within one community.
>
> Truly, I do not know why you said this. In my opinion it is clear that this is prohibited to us by the Torah, by the Hagiographa, by our sages, and by consensus. And this is also supported by experience. Moses said on the occasion of Korah's rebellion: "Depart, I pray you, from the tents of these wicked men, and touch nothing of theirs, lest ye be swept away in all their sins" (Num. 16:26). . . . Our sages learned from this incident that we have to remove and excommunicate the wicked. . . . Thus we are commanded to be separated from them. . . . And Korah did not worship idols. He only rejected some parts of the Torah, just like the reformers of our day. I have no doubts that if excommunication would be permissible today, you would excommunicate them. . . . I am profoundly surprised why you permitted to join them.[42]

Another kind of question about Jewish identity was presented in the nineteenth and twentieth centuries by Jewish communities which had been separated from the mainstream of the Jewish people in very early centuries and which lived in far-off places. One such group were the B'nei Israel who had lived in India since ancient times. Their origins were uncertain, and they practiced a form of Biblical Judaism. In 1944 Rabbi Ben Zion Meir Hai Ouziel (1881–1953), the Sephardi Chief Rabbi of the Holy Land, responded to a letter from a Rabbi in Bombay insisting that the B'nei Israel should not be rejected:

> Delivered into my hands by my colleague, the Gaon, Chief Rabbi Herzog, may he be granted a long and happy life, is his eminence's question about the sect known by the name of *B'nei Israel* found in your land, who follow the laws of Moses and the people Israel but who have no knowledge of religious divorce [*get*], ritual immersion [*mikvah*], or the rules concerning levirate

marriage [*chalitzah*, *yibbum* (Deut. 25:9)], and who maintain no categories of *kohen* or *levi*, and in which he states his desire for an answer to his question whether it is permitted [for Jews] to marry members of their families and whether it is permitted to include them in a *minyan* and to call them to the Torah.

And here is my response to him. . . . The Jews who bear the name of *B'nei Israel* are from the holy seed of Judaism, based on the responsum of Rabbi Hai Gaon (*Shaarei Teshuvah* 46:5), and on the letter of Maimonides to the sages of Lunel, which speaks of the Jews in India, stating that they do not know the Written Law and that they know nothing of the Jewish faith although they are circumcised and they rest on the Sabbath. And they surely were discussing the ancestors of those who are found in your midst and who are known as Jews.

As for the matter of allowing them to come into the community . . . I have written at length about this in my volume *Mishp'tei Ouziel* (*Even Ha-ezer*), and I cited the responsum of Rabbi Isaac ben Sheshet [1326–1408, Spain and North Africa] and the responsum of Rabbi Shimon bar Tzemach [1361–1444, Spain and North Africa] and the notes of Rabbi Moses Isserles [1520–1572, Poland] on *Even Ha-ezer* 4 concerning the matter of the Marranos, and I reached the conclusion that the sect of *B'nei Israel* constitute a branch on the trunk of the people Israel, and are not to be judged as the Karaites [were judged] who cast off the yoke of Torah and commandments as received from Moses at Sinai in the Oral Law. For these [whom we now are considering] did not willingly cast off the Torah and commandments, but the Torah was forgotten from their midst because of their existence in distant, cut off and isolated lands, subjugated to a severe and bitter exile. But since communities of Israel have come into contact with them and have seen their good and upright deeds, for they do cleave to the Torah and commandments, they [the communities] should restore to them and to their children the Torah which has been forgotten by them. Still, since they persisted in their forgetfulness, they are called transgressors, as Rabbi Isaac ben Sheshet wrote about the Marranos. And since until recent years they continued as distant from the organized Jewish community, and their weddings did not take place in the presence of proper Jewish witnesses, their marriages are annulled, though their children are not bastards [*mamzerim*]. . . .

And as for including them in a *minyan* and calling them to the Torah [in a synagogue service], it is also my opinion that those who do not seek the closeness of the faithful of Israel, accepting the yoke of the Torah and commandments, should neither be included in a *minyan* nor called to the Torah, because of the concern expressed by Rav Amram Gaon that in this way they would come to marry into the Jewish community and thus increase [the number of] bastards in the Jewish community. But as for those who seek our company and publicly accept the yoke of the commandments, like other proper Jews, it is a mitzvah [for us] to seek their company, and to involve them in every sacred activity and to call them to the Torah.

And may the Lord God of Israel soon gather our banished from the four corners of the earth, and confirm in our sight His assurance as stated by His Holy prophet: "And He will raise a banner to the nations and assemble the banished of the people Israel, and gather its dispersed from the four corners of the earth." This is as it appears to be in my humble opinion.[43]

Soon after the establishment of the State of Israel in 1948, most of the B'nei Israel emigrated from India to the Jewish Commonwealth where relatively little difficulty was made about their Jewish identity. The problem was more acute in the case of the Falashas, the black Jews of Ethiopia. In the view of most scholars, they were not ethnically of Jewish stock but rather descendants of an indigenous population, some of whom were converted to Judaism in late antiquity by Jewish missionaries from Egypt or, more probably, from Yemen. Their customs are widely different from those enjoined by Rabbinic Judaism. In their own view, the Falashas say that they descend from the Jewish escorts whom King Solomon provided for his son, Menelik, the supposed issue of his union with the Queen of Sheba. In the sixteenth century Rabbi David ben Zimra believed that the Falashas belonged to the tribe of Dan, and he ruled that they were to be accepted as Jews. There was sporadic effort in the nineteenth and twentieth centuries by several Jewish groups to help the Falashas and to bring them into the orbit of world Jewry. In the 1970s they began to arrive in some numbers in Israel and thus the question of their Jewish identity became a matter for serious and sharp debate. The dominant view in the Israeli Chief Rabbinate was that the Falashas were not Jews, according to halakhic norms. Early in 1973 the Sephardi Chief Rabbi, Ovadiah Yosef, declared, following Rabbi David ben Zimra's view of four hundred years earlier, that the Falashas "must be saved from absorption and assimilation" and that bringing them back to the Holy Land would help carry out the prophecy of Isaiah that "the scattered ones of Israel and the dispersed ones of Judah may be gathered together from the four corners of the earth." By 1975 this view was accepted also by the Ashkenazi Chief Rabbi Shlomo Goren. The Falashas could now enter Israel under the Law of Return, as Jews entitled to automatic citizenship in the ancestral land. Some authorities continued to insist that the Ethiopians required a symbolic conversion by immersion in a *mikvah*, but the Falashas resolutely refused, and they have essentially won this battle.

After the 1970s, the largest stream of immigration to Israel was from the Soviet Union. In the two generations since the Bolshevik Revolution in October 1917 the policy of the government was anti-religious. Very few couples were married or, much more important for the halakhah, were divorced in accordance with Jewish religious law. Most of the males were not circumcised and there was much intermarriage. The Jewish identity of many of these immigrants was called into question by various Orthodox authorities, but these objections made no essential difference. Russians who claimed Jewish identity were helped to emigrate. Their status was soon "regularized," especially if they went to Israel, through circumcision, religious marriages, and conversions. When necessary, technical procedures were used to avoid having to declare anyone a *mamzer* (bastard). As in the case of the Marranos after 1492, the Jewish people had made a decision to reintegrate anyone who wanted to claim Jewish identity. The halakhic rules were a necessary second step, to set the seal on this decision, but they were not the determining norm.

This indeed had been the policy of the State of Israel from its very beginning in 1948. In the first several years of its existence it had absorbed more than a million newcomers, and not all were Jews by halakhic standards. The question of who is a Jew was sufficiently troubling, and controversial, so that David Ben-Gurion wrote a circular letter, in 1958, to nearly 100 rabbis, scholars, and thinkers of all persuasions to ask their advice on how to deal with these complexities. One of the most interesting replies was written by a learned American Reform Rabbi, Solomon Freehof (1892–1990):

May I suggest that a solution is possible? The State can make clear that it is not deciding for the Jewish *religion* who is a Jew. It is making only a civic or political decision as to which of the three communities, Christian, Mohammedan, or Jewish, the citizen belongs. The religious tests remain. When this child grows up and is about to marry, it will be the duty of the religious authority to inquire whether this child is born of a Jewish or a Gentile mother. It should have such a questionnaire for *all* who come to be married. If the religious authorities find that the person was born of a Christian mother, then they may demand that certain ceremonials be observed before the marriage is permitted. All that the State now says is that this child is politically or civically Jewish. Whether or not the requirements for being religiously Jewish are also fulfilled is left to the religious authorities to decide whenever the matter comes before them, in such individual cases as marriage or divorce.

Of course, this involves, in effect, the creation of a group of what may be called half-proselytes to Judaism. They will be people who have full Jewish rights civically, but only tentative Jewish rights religiously. Is this possible? Is there a precedent for it? There is, indeed! Besides the full proselytes [*ger zedek*] which Orthodoxy now demands, there was also during the time of the Jewish State, a status of half-proselytes [*ger toshav*]. This is based upon the Talmud (*Avodah Zarah* 64b) and codified by Maimonides (*Hilkhot Issurei Biah* 15:7–8). But, such half-proselytes could only be accepted while the Jewish State existed, the technical phrase for that being, "while the Jubilees were being observed." But after the Jewish State ceased to exist, it was not safe, or permitted, to welcome such half-proselytes (cf. Maimonides, *op. cit.*, 8). However, now there is a Jewish State. Without going into the complex question of the State's status in Jewish religion, it appears to be clear, as you indicate in your letter, that whatever assimilation there is, it will be *toward* Judaism and not away from it. Therefore, it is again possible to have *ger toshav*, half-proselytes.

Actually, this is all that the government of the State of Israel wants. The present difficulty with the religious groups has arisen chiefly because of a confusion between *ger zedek*, the full proselyte, and *ger toshav*, the half- or tentative proselyte. If the State will now declare that it does not proclaim these children *ger zedek* (this [*gerut*] will be a matter for religion to decide, when the problem of the status of the child comes before the religious authorities at marriage and other occasions), the State is only making a *ger toshav* decision affirming the civic right to choose to belong to the Jewish community rather than to the Christian or Mohammedan community. It is with this clear distinction that I believe a solution can be reached.[44]

The sharpest battle of all over the question of Jewish identity remains unresolved. The officially established Rabbinate of Israel, which controls all matters of personal status, is entirely Orthodox. It has consistently refused to recognize the validity of conversions to Judaism performed by rabbis of the Conservative and Reform movements, anywhere. The law of the State is less specific. It recognizes a convert as a Jew, and entitled to the privilege of the Law of Return, without denominational distinction. In Israeli politics a fight has been waged intermittently in the 1980s to amend this policy and to specify that acceptable conversions must be performed "according to the halakhah," that is, by Orthodox rabbis who adhere to Orthodox standards. The force of such legislation would declare anyone converted to Judaism under other than Orthodox auspices not to be a Jew. To date, in 1991, the law has not been changed. Strong forces both in Israel and the Diaspora prefer this untidy status quo. There are, and will continue to be, a growing number of individuals who feel and act as Jews, and who are integrated into the Jewish community, but whom others will not accept as Jews. There can no longer be a set, puristic definition of Jewish identity. I wrote in this spirit in 1971 in the entry "Jewish Identity" in the *Encyclopedia Judaica*:

In the last third of the 20th century there are many Jews, especially that worldwide, intensely Jewish, religiously traditionalist minority for whom the question of Jewish identity is decided by the *halakhah*. The overarching institutions of world Jewry, while paying respect to this view, determine their policy by broader and more amorphous considerations of history and situation. So, when the last remaining, completely dejudaized, almost entirely intermarried communists of Jewish parentage in Poland were purged in 1968, the Israel government provided them with the necessary exit passports, even though few were going to Israel, and the world Jewish social service budget took care of the overwhelming majority who opted to go to other countries. Those who suffer as Jews, regardless of their own perception of that suffering, and those whose Jewish consciousness might one day be rekindled, remain part of world Jewish concern. In the broadest sense, significant elements of world Jewry in the modern era have defined, and are defining, Jewish identity as a community of history and destiny of those who still feel their involvement in this community or about whom others feel strongly that these people belong to Jewry.[45]

MODERN THINKING
ABOUT THE COVENANT

The concepts of revelation, the Law, and the "chosen people" all became problematic for modern Jewish theologians, as stressed above in the essay which introduces this volume. The thinkers represented here are each interpreting it anew, several in the conscious desire to formulate it so that it is consonant with the general thought of their own generations.

Kaufmann Kohler (1843–1926), a leading figure of American Reform Judaism, identified religion with moral progress and chosenness with a corporate mission to effect it. Judaism in Biblical days had been the most progressive faith of its time; it would continue to be so, he asserted, by constantly reforming and purifying itself, by abandoning outworn ideas and practices in the name of ever higher ideals. To Kohler, revelation is thus progressive and not bound even by the event on Sinai.

. . . The election of Israel cannot be regarded as a single divine act, concluded at one moment of revelation, or even during the Biblical period. It must instead be considered a divine call persisting through all ages and encompassing all lands, a continuous activity of the spirit which has ever summoned for itself new heralds and heroes to testify to truth, justice, and sublime faith, with an unparalleled scorn for death, and to work for their dissemination by words and deeds and by their whole life. Judaism differs from all other religions in that it is neither the creation of one great moral teacher and preacher of truth, nor seeks to typify the moral and spiritual sublimity which it aims to develop in a single person, who is then lifted up into the realm of the super-human. Judaism counts its prophets, its sages, and its martyrs by generations; it is still demonstrating its power to reshape and re-generate religion as a vital force. Moreover, Judaism does not separate religion from life, so as to regard only a segment of the common life and the national existence as holy. The entire peo-ple, the entire life, must bear the stamp of holiness and be filled with priestly consecration. Whether this lofty aim can ever be completely attained is a question not to be decided by short sighted humanity, but only by God, the Ruler of history. It is sufficient that the life of the individual as well as that of the people should aspire toward this ideal.

Of course, the election of Israel presupposes an inner calling, a special capacity of soul and tendency of intellect which fit it for the divine task. The people which has given mankind its greatest prophets and psalmists, its boldest thinkers and its noblest martyrs, which has brought to fruition the three great world religions, the Church, the Mosque and—mother of them both—the Syn-agogue, must be the religious people *par excellence*. It must have within itself enough of the heavenly spark of truth and of the impetus of the religious genius as to be able and eager, whenever and wherever the opportunity is favorable, to direct the spiritual flight of humanity toward the highest and holiest.[46]

Mordecai Kaplan (1881–1984) was the leader of American Jewish religious naturalism, i.e. of a version of religion without revelation. According to Kaplan, "God" is the term we use for the sum of our highest ideals. Obviously there can be no "chosen people," in such a system. Even here, in the boldest anticlassicist among modern Jewish theologians, one can perceive a re-echo of one part—but only one part—of the teaching of Amos, that the Jews are no better than the Ethiopians. But Amos also believed that they were in covenant with the living God who had chosen them to do and to suffer more than others.

The apologists for the doctrine of Israel's election do not take the trouble to think through to a conclusion the role of religion in human civilization. Formerly the adherents of all the tradi-tional religions of the Western world maintained that religion was supernaturally revealed truth. That such truth was transmitted only by one's own people was sufficient evidence that only one's own people had been chosen. Since it was assumed that salvation could be achieved only through revealed truth, the possession of that truth imposed the obligation to convey it to others and to induct them into one's own "chosen" community by way of conversion.

But when one abandons the idea of supernatural revelation, what becomes of religion? If religious truth is independent of any historic self-revelation of God to a particular people, then it is no different from scientific truth in being accessible to and attainable by all mankind. Indeed, one of the main criteria of truth is its universal applicability to and conformity with universal reason. . . .

A religion is the organized quest of a people for salvation, for helping those who live by the civilization of that people to achieve their destiny as human beings. In the course of that quest, the people discovers religious truth and abiding values. These truths and values, like all others, are universal. They are not the monopoly of the group that discovers them. They may be discovered by other groups as well. Religions are distinct from one another not so much ideationally as existentially. Each religion represents a particular area of collective life marked out by the *sancta* of the group. These are a definite product of the group's unique historic experience. Such *sancta* are its saints and heroes, its sacred literature, its holy places, its common symbols, its customs and folkways, and all objects and associations which have been hallowed, because of their relation to that people's quest for salvation. There is no more reason for having all the world adopt the *sancta* of one people or church than for all people to wear an identical type of garment. What is important is that the *sancta* of each people or church help to humanize all who belong to it, by implementing those universal values which it should share with all other peoples and churches. *A religion is universal, if its conception of God is one that imposes on its adherents loyalty to a universally valid code of ethics. It is only in that sense that the Jewish religion is universal.*[47]

Martin Buber (1878–1965), the leading Jewish existentialist theologian, believed profoundly in the fact of the encounter between God and the Jewish people. For him it was an event which recurs in the personal experience of each Jew, so long as one chooses to be a Jew and to hear the voice of God's direct declarations. Buber thus affirmed the classical notions of both God and Israel, but the traditional idea of the Law is absent. In the encounter with God, as the individual hears Him speaking to the deepest recesses of his or her being, everyone hears what he or she can hear—and obeys that which has been personally heard.

What does it mean to become a "people of God"? A common belief in God and service to His name do not constitute a people of God. Becoming a people of God means rather that the attributes of God revealed to it, justice and love, are to be made effective in its own life, in the lives of its members with one another; justice materialized in the indirect mutual relationships of these individuals; love in their direct mutual relationships, rooted in their personal existence. Of the two, however, love is the higher, the transcending principle. This becomes unequivocally clear from the fact that man cannot be just to God; he can, however, and should, love God. And it is the love of God which transfers itself to man; "God loves the stranger," we are told, "so you too shall love him." The man who loves God loves also him whom God loves.[48]

Edmond Fleg (1874–1963), the Franco-Jewish man of letters, was a historical mystic. The ancient tradition could find only one reason for God's choice on which all agreed, the merit of Abraham and the virtue of those of his progeny who followed in his courageous and faithful ways. This affirmation is here used as the central value, blended with intellectual liberalism and passionate love for the Jewish past.

People ask me why I am a Jew. It is to you that I want to answer, little unborn grandson. . . .

I am a Jew because, born of Israel and having lost her, I have felt her live again in me, more living then myself.

I am a Jew because, born of Israel and having regained her, I wish her to live after me, more living than in myself.

I am a Jew because the faith of Israel demands of me no abdication of the mind.

I am a Jew because the faith of Israel requires of me all the devotion of my heart.

I am a Jew because in every place where suffering weeps, the Jew weeps.

I am a Jew because at every time when despair cries out, the Jew hopes.

I am a Jew because the word of Israel is the oldest and the newest.

I am a Jew because the promise of Israel is the universal promise.

I am a Jew because, for Israel, the world is not yet completed; men are completing it.

I am a Jew because, above the nations and Israel, Israel places Man and his Unity.

I am a Jew because, above Man, image of the divine Unity, Israel places the divine Unity, and its divinity. . . .

And I say to myself: From this remote father [Abraham] right up to my own father, all these fathers have handed on to me a truth which flowed in their blood, which flows in mine; and shall I not hand it on, with my blood, to those of my blood?

Will you take it from me, my child? Will you hand it on? Perhaps you will wish to abandon it. If so, let it be for a greater truth, if there is one. I shall not blame you. It will be my fault; I shall have failed to hand it on as I received it.[49]

Samson Raphael Hirsch (1808–1888) was a rabbi in Germany and the founder of neo-orthodox Judaism. These words of his are not different, except in rhetoric, from what we have found in earlier centuries.

Because men had eliminated God from life, nay, even from nature, and found the basis of life in possessions and its aim in enjoyment, deeming life the product of the multitude of human desires, just as they looked upon nature as the product of a multitude of gods, therefore, it became necessary that a people be introduced into the ranks of the nations which, through its history and life, should declare God the only creative cause of existence, fulfillment of His will the only aim of life; and which should bear the revelation of His will, rejuvenated and renewed for its sake, unto all parts of the world as the motive and incentive of its coherence. This mission required for its carrying out a nation poor in everything upon which the rest of mankind reared the edifice of its greatness and its power; externally subordinate to the nations armed with proud reliance on self, but fortified by direct reliance on God; so that by suppression of every opposing force God might reveal Himself directly as the only Creator, Judge and Master of nature and history. . . .

"One God, Creator, Lawgiver, Judge, Guide, Preserver, and Father of all beings; all beings His servants, His children, man also His child and servant, from His hand all, and this all to be used only for the fulfillment of His will, since this alone is sufficient for a proper attainment of the purposes of life, while all other human occupations and pursuits are but paths which lead to the goal of the fulfillment of the mission of humanity."

The proclaiming of these great truths was to be the chief, if not the sole, life-task of this people.[50]

Has Israel any other task than to teach all the races of man to recognize and worship the Only-One as their God? Is it not Israel's unceasing duty to proclaim, through the example of its life and history, Him as the universal Lord and Sovereign? The Bible terms Israel *segulah*, "a peculiar treasure," but this designation does not imply, as some have falsely interpreted, that Israel has a monopoly of the Divine love and favor, but, on the contrary, that God has the sole and exclusive claim to Israel's devotions and service; that Israel may not render Divine homage to any other being. [*Segulah* means a property belonging exclusively to one owner, to which no other has any right or claim.] Israel's most cherished ideal is that of the universal brotherhood of mankind.[51]

The greatest spiritual representative of classical Judaism in the twentieth century was Abraham Isaac Kook (1865–1935), who became in 1921 the chief rabbi of Palestine. Kook's mysticism was a reaffirmation of the holiness of the Jewish faith, practices, land, and people and of the divine meaning of their interaction and unity. The selection from his writings should be read, though he did not write it as such, as a homily on the passage from the prescribed daily morning prayers, which concludes this chapter.

The world and all that it contains is waiting for the Light of Israel, for the Exalted Light radiating from Him Whose Name is to be praised. This people was fashioned by God to speak of His glory; it was granted the heritage of the blessing of Abraham so that it might disseminate the knowledge of God and it was commanded to live its life apart from the nations of the world. God chose it to cleanse the whole world of all impurity and darkness; this people is endowed with a hidden treasure, with the Torah, the means by which the Heaven and the Earth were created.

The Light of Israel is not a utopian dream, or some abstract morality, or merely a pious wish and a noble vision. It does not wash its hands of the material world and all its values, abandoning the flesh, and society and government to wallow in their impurity, and forsaking the forces of nature, which fell in the Fall of Man, to remain in their low estate. It is, rather, a raising of all of life. . . .

Redemption is continuous. The Redemption from Egypt and the Final Redemption are part of the same process, "of the mighty hand and outstretched arm," which began in Egypt and is evident in all of history. Moses and Elijah belong to the same redemptive act; one represents its beginning and the other its culmination, so that together they fulfill its purpose. The spirit of Israel is attuned to the hum of the redemptive process, to the sound of the waves of its labors which will end only with the coming of the days of the Messiah.

It is a grave error to be insensitive to the distinctive unity of the Jewish spirit, to imagine that the Divine stuff which uniquely characterizes Israel is comparable to the spiritual content of all the other national civilizations. This error is the source of the attempt to sever the national from the religious element of Judaism. Such a division would falsify both our nationalism and our religion, for every element of thought, emotion, and idealism that is present in the Jewish people belongs to an indivisible entity, and all together make up its specific character.[52]

Deep is Your love for us, O Lord our God;
Bounteous is Your compassion and tenderness.
You taught our fathers the laws of life,
And they trusted in You, Father and King.

For their sake be gracious to us, and teach us,
That we may learn Your laws, and trust in You.
Father, merciful Father, have compassion upon us;
Endow us with discernment and understanding.

Grant us the will to study Your Torah,
To heed its words and to teach its precepts.
May we observe and practice its instruction,
Lovingly fulfilling all its teachings.

Enlighten our eyes in Your Torah,
Open our hearts to Your commandments.
Unify our hearts with singleness of purpose
To hold You in reverence and in love.

Unify our hearts to revere and to love You;
Then shall we never be brought to shame.
We will delight and exult in Your help;
In Your holiness do we trust.

Bring us safely from the corners of the earth,
And lead us in dignity to our holy land.
You, O God, are the Source of salvation;
You have chosen us from all peoples and tongues.

You have drawn us close to You;
We praise You and thank You in truth.
With love do we thankfully proclaim Your unity,
And praise You who chose Your people Israel in love.[53]

2

GOD

GOD IS

The Bible is the account of God's work. His existence is the given: it does not need to be proved. None of the Biblical writers, with the possible exception of the author of Ecclesiastes, ever entertained the thought that the universe is self-created or that it is eternal. And if the universe had a beginning in time, who but God could have created it? Surely God has not abandoned creation. He cares for all humanity, indeed for everything that is.

In the beginning God created the heavens and the earth.[1]

Who has measured the waters in the hollow of His hand, and weighed the heavens with His palm? Who has measured the dust of the earth in a measure and weighed the mountains in scales, and the hills in a balance? Who has meted out the spirit of the Lord? Who has been His counsellor; who has taught Him? With whom has He consulted and who has instructed Him, and taught Him the path of justice, and taught Him knowledge and showed Him the way of understanding? Behold, the nations are a drop in a bucket, and are counted as the smallest grain on a balance; behold the islands are as a little dust. And Lebanon is not enough to burn, nor the beasts thereof sufficient for a burnt offering. All nations are before Him as if they had no being at all, and are counted to Him as nothing, and vanity. To whom then will you liken God? What likeness will you compare to Him? The image which the craftsman has melted and the goldsmith spread over with gold, the silversmith casting silver chains? He has chosen strong wood, that will not rot; he seeks a skillful workman to set up an idol that will not be moved.

Do you not know? Have you not heard? Has it not been told you from the beginning? Have you not understood the foundations of the earth? It is He that sits above the globe of the earth, and the inhabitants thereof are as grasshoppers, He that stretches out the heavens as a curtain, and spreads them out as a tent to dwell in; that brings princes to nothing; He makes the judges of the earth as a thing of nought. Scarce are they planted, scarce are they sown, scarce has their stock taken root in the earth when He blows upon them, and they are withered, and a whirlwind takes them away as stubble. To whom, then, would you liken Me, that I should be equal? says the Holy One.[2]

Praised are You, Lord our God, King of the universe, creating light and fashioning darkness, ordaining the order of all creation. You illumine the world and its creatures with mercy; in Your goodness, day after day, You renew Creation. How manifold Your works, O Lord; with wisdom You fashioned them all. The earth abounds with Your creations.[3]

The Lord is my shepherd, I shall not want.
He gives me repose in green meadows.
He leads me beside the still waters to revive my spirit.
He guides me on the right path, for that is His nature.
Though I walk in the valley of the shadow of death,
I fear no harm, for You are with me.
Your staff and Your rod comfort me.
You prepare a banquet for me in the presence of my foes.
You anoint my head with oil; my cup overflows.
Surely goodness and kindness shall be my portion
all the days of my life.
And I shall dwell in the House of the Lord forever.[4]

The proper response to such a God is gratitude and reverence. The psalm and prayer of thanksgiving that follow here are prescribed in the prayer book for the festivals of Passover, Shabuot, and Sukkot; for the first day of the lunar month, which is a half holiday; and for Hanukkah, the holiday which commemorates the victory of the Jews over their Syrian Greek persecutors of the second century B.C.E.

> Sing praises, O you servants of the Lord;
> Praise the glory of the Lord. Halleluyah!
>
> Praised is the glory of the Lord, now and always;
> From sunrise to sunset, praised is the Lord.
>
> Supreme over all nations is the Lord;
> His glory is high over all the heavens.
>
> Who is like the Lord our God, enthroned on high,
> Yet bending low to survey all heaven and earth?
>
> He raises the poor from the dust;
> He lifts the needy from the ash heap.
>
> He places them in the seats of the noble;
> He seats them with the princes of His people.
>
> He transforms the childless mistress of a home
> Into a joyous mother of children. Halleluyah![5]
>
> All creation praises You, O Lord our God.
> The pious and the just who do Your will,
> And all Your people of the house of Israel
> Join in thanking You with joyous song.
>
> They praise, exalt, sanctify and revere
> Your sovereign glory, O our King.
>
> To You it is good to give thanks;
> To Your glory it is fitting to sing.
>
> You are God from beginning of time to its end.
> Praised are You, O Lord, acclaimed with praises.[6]

The world is not God, that is, Judaism is not a pantheistic religion, but God is in the world. Man's sins may make Him more remote, but that is man's fault, for God is always present for "those who call upon Him in truth."

> Am I not a God near at hand, says the Lord, and not a God far off? Can any hide himself in secret places that I shall not see him? Do I not fill heaven and earth?[7]

> There is nothing on earth which is apart from the *Shekhinah* [God's Presence in the world].[8]

> God fills the universe just as the soul fills the body of man.[9]

> An emperor said to Rabbi Joshua ben Chananya: "I want to see your God." He replied, "You cannot see Him." "Nevertheless," the emperor said, "I want to see Him!" Rabbi Joshua stood him in the summer sun, and said "Look at the sun." "I cannot," answered the emperor. Rabbi Joshua said, "The sun is but one of the servants who stand in the presence of the Holy One, praised be He, and you cannot look at the sun. Is it not truer still that you cannot see God's Presence?"[10]

> Originally, the *Shekhinah* [Presence of God] was on earth. When Adam sinned, it rose to the nearest firmament. When Cain sinned, it rose to the second. When the generation of Enosh sinned [in idolatry], it rose to the third. When the generation of the Flood sinned, it rose to the fourth. When the generation of the dispersal of nations [who tried to erect the Tower of Babel] sinned, it rose to the fifth firmament. When the men of Sodom sinned, it rose to the sixth. The wickedness of the Egyptians in the time of Abraham caused the *Shekhinah* to retreat to the seventh and most remote firmament.
>
> The righteous counteracted the above effect. Abraham brought the *Shekhinah* down to the sixth firmament, Isaac brought it to the fifth, Jacob brought it to the fourth, Levi to the third, Kehat to the second and Amram to the first firmament. Moses brought it back from the heavens to earth.[11]

The passage immediately below is from the *Zohar* (Book of Splendor), the basic text of the *kabbalah* (cabala), the Jewish mystical tradition. In its present form this book dates from the thirteenth century, when it was "edited" by the Spanish mystic

Moses de León, who announced it as an ancient text of the second century. This is almost certainly not true, but the book does reflect a well-developed older tradition of mystical speculation. The dominant Jewish tradition has always regarded *kabbalah* gingerly and with some suspicion. Mystic speculation can enrich the faith, but it must be curbed lest it substitute mystical transports, and even magic, for the life of obedience to divine commandment.

The Holy One, praised be He, is transcendent in His glory, He is hidden and removed far beyond all ken; there is no one in the world, nor has there ever been one whom His wisdom and essence do not elude, since He is recondite and hidden and beyond all ken, so that neither the supernal nor the lower beings are able to commune with Him until they utter the words: "Blessed is the glory of the Lord from His place" [Ezek. 3:12].

The creatures of the earth think of Him as being on high, declaring "His glory is above the heavens" [Ps. 113:4], while the heavenly beings think of Him as being below, declaring "His glory is over all the earth" [Ps. 57:12], until they both, in heaven and on earth, concur in declaring "Blessed be the glory of the Lord from His place" [Ezek. 3:12], because He is unknowable and no one can truly understand Him. . . .

For there is door within door, grade behind grade, through which the glory of the Holy One is made known. Hence here the "tent door" is the door of righteousness, referred to in the words, "Open to me the gates of righteousness" [Ps. 118:19], and this is the first entrance door; through this door a view is opened to all the other higher doors. He who succeeds in entering this door is privileged to know both it and all the other doors, since they all rest on this one.

At the present time this door remains unknown because Israel is in exile; and therefore all the other doors are removed from them, so that they cannot know or commune with God; but when Israel will return from exile, all the higher grades are destined to rest harmoniously upon this one. Then men will obtain a knowledge of the precious higher wisdom of which hitherto they knew not, as it is written, "And the spirit of the Lord shall rest upon him, the spirit of wisdom and understanding, the spirit of counsel and might, the spirit of knowledge and of the fear of the Lord" [Isa. 11:2].[12]

Under the challenge of Aristotelian philosophy, as understood by the Arabs after the ninth century, Jewish thinkers felt constrained to develop their own philosophical apologetics. Here are two famous examples of such explanations of the doctrine of God. The first is by Saadia (882–942), who is second only to Maimonides among medieval Jewish authorities. Saadia was a native of Egypt and head (*gaon*) of the academy in Sura, Babylonia. His *Book of Beliefs and Opinions*, from which this passage is taken, is the first major work of medieval Jewish philosophical theology.

> With respect to the category of *relation*, I say that it would be improper to connect anything with the Creator in an anthropomorphic manner or to relate it to Him, because He has existed since eternity, that is a time when none of the things created were connected with Him or related to Him. . . . When, therefore, we note that the Scriptures call God *king* and present human beings as His slaves and the angels as ministering to Him . . . all that is merely a means of expressing reverence and esteem. For the human beings most highly esteemed by us are the kings. God is also called "king" in the sense that He can do whatever He wishes and that His command is always carried out. . . .
>
> Apropos of the category of *place*, I say that it is inconceivable for several reasons that the Creator should have any need for occupying any place whatsoever. First of all He is Himself the Creator of all space. Also He originally existed alone, when there was as yet no such thing as place. It is unthinkable, therefore, that as a result of His act of creation He should have been transported into space. Furthermore, space is required only by a material object. . . .
>
> As for the assertion of the prophets that God dwells in heaven, that was merely a way of indicating God's greatness and His elevation, since heaven is for us the highest thing we know of. . . . The same applies to statements to the effect that God dwells in the Temple, such as "And I will dwell among the children of Israel" [Ex. 29:45] and "The Lord dwells in Zion" [Joel 4:21]. The purpose of all this was to confer honor upon the place and the people in question. . . .
>
> As regards the category of *time*, it is inconceivable that the concept of time could be applied to the Creator because He Himself is the Creator of all time. Furthermore, He existed orig-

inally alone when there was as yet no such thing as time. It is, therefore, unthinkable that time should have effected any loco-motion or change in Him. Moreover, time is nothing else than the measurement of the duration of corporeal beings. He, how-ever, who has no body, is far removed from such concepts as time and duration. If, nevertheless, we do describe God as being en-during and permanent, that is done only as a metaphor. . . .

As regards the matter of *possession*, inasmuch as all creatures are God's creation and handiwork, it is not seemly for us to say that He possesses one thing to the exclusion of another, nor that He possesses the one to a greater and the other to a lesser degree. If we, nevertheless, see Scriptures assert that a certain people is His peculiar property and His possession and His portion, as they do in the statement, "For the portion of the Lord is His people, Jacob the lot of His inheritance" [Deut. 32:9], that is done merely as a means of conferring honor and distinction. For, as it appears to us, every man's portion and lot are precious to him. Nay the Scriptures even go so far as to declare God, too, figuratively to be the lot of the pious and their portion, as they do in their statement, "O Lord, the portion of mine inheritance and of my cup" [Ps. 16:5]. This is, therefore, also an expression of special devotion and esteem. . . .

As for the category of *position*, inasmuch as the Creator is not a physical being, it is unseemly to speak of Him as having any such position as sitting or standing or the like. Nay, it is impossible because He is not a physical being, and because originally there existed nothing outside of Himself.[13]

Maimonides here expounds the doctrine of God's "negative attributes," which means that anything which may be ascribed to God is a limitation of His absolute being. This passage is a crucial point in the argument of the greatest Jewish philosophical work, *The Guide of the Perplexed*.

It would be extremely difficult for us to find, in any language whatsoever, words adequate to this subject, and we can only employ inadequate language. In our endeavour to show that God does not include a plurality, we can only say "He is one," although "one" and "many" are both terms which serve to distinguish quantity. We therefore make the subject clearer, and show to the understanding the way of truth by saying that He is one but does not possess the attribute of unity.

The same is the case when we say God is the First (*kadmon*), to express that He has not been created; the term *kadmon*, "First," is decidedly inaccurate, for it can in its true sense only be applied to a being that is subject to the relation of time; the latter, however, is an accident to motion which again is connected with a body. Besides, the attribute *kadmon* ("first" or "eternal") is a relative term, being in regard to time the same as the terms "long" and "short" are in regard to a line. Both expressions, "created" and "eternal" (or "first"), are equally inadmissible in reference to any being to which the attribute of time is not applicable, just as we do not say "crooked" or "straight" in reference to taste, "salted" or "insipid" in reference to the voice. These subjects are not unknown to those who have accustomed themselves to seek a true understanding of the things, and to establish their properties in accordance with the abstract notions which the mind has formed of them, and who are not misled by the inaccuracy of the words employed. All attributes, such as "the First," "the Last," occurring in the Scriptures in reference to God, are as metaphorical as the expressions "ear" and "eye." They simply signify that God is not subject to any change or innovation whatever; they do not imply that God can be described by time, or that there is any comparison between Him and any other being as regards time, and that He is called on that account "the first" and "the last." In short, all similar expressions are borrowed from the language commonly used among the people. In the same way we see "One" (*echad*) in reference to God, to express that there is nothing similar to Him, but we do not mean to say that an attribute of unity is added to His essence.

Know that the negative attributes of God are the true attributes. . . . God's existence is absolute. . . . We comprehend only the fact that He exists, not His essence (i.e. we comprehend only that He is, but not what He is). Consequently it is a false assumption to hold that He has any positive attribute; for He does not possess existence in addition to His essence; it therefore cannot be said that the one (either existence or essence) may be described as an attribute of the other; much less has He in addition to His existence a compound essence, consisting of two constituent elements to which the attribute could refer; still less has He accidents, which could be described by an attribute. Hence it is clear that He has no positive attribute whatever. The negative attributes, however, are those which are necessary to direct the mind to the truths which we must believe concerning God; for, on the one hand, they do not imply any plurality, and, on the other, they convey to man the highest possible knowledge of God; e.g. it has been established by proof that some being must exist besides those things which can be perceived by the senses, or apprehended by the mind; when we say of this being, that it exists, we mean that its non-existence is impossible. We thus perceive that such a being is not, for instance, like the four elements, which are animate, and we therefore say it is living, expressing thereby that it is not dead. We call such a being incorporeal, because we notice that it is unlike the heavens, which are living, but material.

Seeing that it is also different from the intellect, which, though incorporeal and living, owes its existence to some cause, we say it is the first (*kadmon*), expressing thereby that its existence is not due to any cause. We further notice that the existence, that is the essence, of this being is not limited to its own existence; many existences emanate from it, and its influence is not like that of the fire in producing heat or that of the sun in sending forth light, but consists in constantly giving them stability and order by well-established rule, as we shall show (heat comes from fire, light from the sun, as natural consequences of the properties of fire and of the sun. There is no intention or will in either of them; but that which comes from God emanates from His will). We say, on that account, it has power, wisdom and will, i.e. it is not feeble or ignorant, or hasty, and does not abandon its creatures; when we say that it is not feeble, we mean that its existence is capable of producing the existence of many other things; by saying it is not ignorant, we mean "it perceives" or "it lives,"—for everything that perceives is alive—by saying "it is not hasty, and does not abandon its creatures," we mean that all these creatures preserve a certain order and arrangement; they are not left to themselves, or produced aimlessly, but whatever condition they receive from that being is given them with design and intention. We thus learn that there is no other being like unto God, and we say that He is One, i.e. there are not more Gods than one.[14]

The Rabbinic tradition was largely antispeculative.

Why was the world created with the letter *Beth*? [*Beth* is the first letter of the first word in the Torah, *Bereshith*, "In the beginning."] Just as the shape of the letter *Beth* is closed on three sides and open toward the front, so you do not have permission to be concerned with that which is below or above the earth, nor with what happened before this world came to be. Rather, you should be concerned with what happened since the Creation of the world, with what lies before you on earth.[15]

There were four who entered the Pardes [*Rashi:* they ascended to the highest firmament, that of *God*]: Ben Azai, Ben Zoma, Elisha ben Abuyah, and Rabbi Akiva. Ben Azai looked in the direction of the *Shekhinah* and died. . . . Ben Zoma looked and went mad. . . . Elisha ben Abuyah abandoned the faith. Rabbi Akiva came out unharmed.[16]

Maimonides as guide to Jewish law was accepted as the paramount authority. As philosophical theologian his work occasioned embittered controversy. Pietists were less impressed by his brilliant answers to doubters than they were upset by the clarity with which he, and his intellectual successors, posed the arguments of the unbelievers. They preferred not to enter this field at all. Here Hayyim ibn Musa (1390–1460), a Spanish rabbi and writer, expresses this view.

In my youth I heard a preacher preach about God's being one and one only, in a speculating manner—in the manner of philosophers. And he said many times over that if He were not one only God, then this and that would necessarily follow. Thereupon a man rose, one of those who "tremble at the word of the Lord" [Isa. 66:5], and said: "Misfortune came upon me and mine at the great disaster in Sevilla (Pogrom of 1391). I was beaten and wounded, until my persecutors desisted because they thought I was dead. All this have I suffered for my faith in 'Hear, O Israel, the Lord our God, the Lord is One.' And here you are, dealing with the traditions of our fathers in the manner of a speculating philosopher, and saying: 'If He were not one only God, then this and that would necessarily follow.' I have greater faith in the tradition of our fathers, and I do not want to go on listening to this sermon." And he left the house of prayer and most of the congregation went with him.[17]

Here are three nonphilosophical views of God, which are quite characteristic of Rabbinic piety and its sense of at-homeness with Him.

How do we know that the Holy One, praised be He, prays? It is written, "I will bring them to My holy mountain and make them rejoice in My house of prayer" [Isa. 56:7]. This verse states not *"their* house of prayer" but *"My* house of prayer," from which we infer that the Holy One, praised be He, prays. What is His prayer? Rav Tuviah bar Zutra, quoting Rav, said, "May it be My will that My compassion overcomes My wrath, and that it prevail over My attribute of strict justice. May I deal with My children according to the attribute of compassion; may I not deal with them according to the strict line of justice."[18]

Rabbi Judah said, quoting Rav: The day consists of twelve hours. During the first three hours, the Holy One, praised be He, is engaged in the study of Torah. During the second three He sits in judgment over His entire world. When He realizes that the world is deserving of destruction, He rises from the Throne of Justice, to sit in the Throne of Mercy. During the third group of three hours, He provides sustenance for the entire world, from huge beasts to lice. During the fourth, He sports with the Leviathan, as it is written, "Leviathan, which You did form to sport with" [Ps. 104:26]. . . . During the fourth group of three hours (according to others) He teaches schoolchildren.[19]

Rabbi Nehemiah said: When the Israelites did that wicked deed [i.e. when they constructed and worshiped the golden calf] Moses sought to appease God, who was angry with them. He said, "Lord of the universe! They have made an assistant for You. Why should You be angry with them? This calf will assist You: You will cause the sun to shine, and the calf will cause the moon to shine; You will take care of the stars, and the calf will take care of the planets; You will cause the dew to fall, and the calf will make the winds to blow; You will cause the rain to fall, and the calf will cause vegetation to sprout." The Holy One, praised be He, said to Moses, "You are making the same mistake that the people are making! This calf is not real!" Moses then replied, "If that is so, why should You be angry with Your children?"[20]

Rabbi Israel Baal Shem Tov (1698–1760), the founder of Hasidism, summed up the mainstream of Jewish thought about God's existence. The faith of Jewish belief that God exists comes from three sources: reason, faith, and tradition. All these sources of knowledge are indispensable. Incidentally, exactly this view had already been stated by Saadia more than eight centuries before in his *Book of Beliefs and Opinions* (See chapter 3).

Why do we say "Our God and the God of our fathers"? [Introductory phrase in many prayers.] There are two sorts of persons who believe in God. The one believes because his faith has been handed down to him by his fathers; and his faith is strong. The other has arrived at faith by dint of searching thought. And this is the difference between the two: the first has the advantage that his faith cannot be shaken, no matter how many objections are raised to it, for his faith is firm because he has taken it over from his fathers. But there is a flaw in it: it is a commandment given by man, and it has been learned without thought or reasoning. The advantage of the second man is that he has reached faith through his own power, through much searching and thinking. But his faith too has a flaw: it is easy to shake it by offering contrary evidence. But he who combines both kinds of faith is invulnerable. That is why we say "Our God," because of our searching, and "the God of our fathers," because of our tradition.

And a like interpretation holds when we say "The God of Abraham, the God of Isaac, and the God of Jacob" [Introductory phrase of the *Amidah* prayer], for this means: Isaac and Jacob did not merely take over the tradition of Abraham, but sought out the divine for themselves.[21]

GOD IS ONE

On this subject all Jewish teachings throughout the ages speak with one voice. For this faith countless martyrs have died in all the centuries.

Hear O Israel, the Lord our God, the Lord is one.[22]

You shall have no gods before Me. You shall not make to yourself a graven image, or the likeness of anything that is in heaven above or on the earth beneath or in the waters under the earth. You shall not bow down to them or serve them, for I, the Lord your God, am a jealous God, visiting the iniquity of the fathers upon the children to the third and fourth generations of those who hate Me, and showing mercy to the thousandth generation of those that love Me and keep My commandments.[23]

Not for us, Lord, not for us but for Yourself
win praise through Your love and faithfulness.

Why should the nations say: "Where is their God?"
Our God is in heaven; He does whatever He wills.

Their idols are silver and gold, made by human hands. ·
They have a mouth and cannot speak, eyes and cannot see.
They have ears and cannot hear, a nose and cannot smell.
They have hands and cannot feel, feet and cannot walk.
They cannot make a sound in their throat.
Their makers shall become like them; all who trust in them.

Let the House of Israel trust in the Lord;
He is their help and their shield.
Let the House of Aaron trust in the Lord;
He is their help and their shield.
Let those who revere the Lord trust in the Lord;
He is their help and their shield.

The Lord remembers us with blessing.
He will bless the House of Israel.
He will bless the House of Aaron.
He will bless those who revere Him, young and old alike.

May the Lord increase your blessings, yours and your children's.
May you be blessed by the Lord, Maker of heaven and earth.

Heaven belongs to the Lord,
and the earth He has entrusted to mortals.

The dead cannot praise the Lord,
nor can those who go down into silence.
But we shall praise the Lord now and forever.
Halleluyah![24]

The law against idolatry is basic to all the commandments in the Torah. . . . Whoever transgresses all of the commandments breaks from himself the yoke of the Torah, annulling the covenant between God and Israel and misrepresenting the Torah. The same is true of whoever transgresses the one commandment against idolatry. [25]

Rabbi Chanina said: The seal of the Holy One, praised be He, is truth. [In Hebrew, the word for *truth* is spelled with three letters, אמת , the first, middle, and last letters of the alphabet.] Resh Lakish said: Truth (*emet*) is spelled with the first, middle and last letters of the alphabet to teach that "I am first, I am last, and beside Me there is no God" [Isa. 44:6]. "I am first" for I received nothing from another; "and beside Me there is no God," for I have no partner; "and with the last, I am He" [Isa. 41:4]— I shall never transmit My sovereignty to another. [26]

We rise to our duty to praise the Lord of all, to acclaim the Creator. He made our lot unlike that of other people, assigning to us a unique destiny. We bend the knee and bow, acknowledging the King of kings, the Holy One praised be He, who spread out the heavens and laid the foundations of the earth, whose glorious abode is in the highest heaven, whose mighty dominion is in the loftiest heights. He is our God, there is no other. In truth, He is our King, as it is written in His Torah: "Know this day and take it to heart that the Lord is God in heaven above and on earth below; there is no other."

And so we hope in You, Lord our God, soon to see Your splendor, sweeping idolatry away so that false gods will be utterly destroyed, perfecting earth by Your kingship so that all mankind will invoke Your name, bringing all the earth's wicked back to You, repentant. Then all who live will know that to You every knee must bend, every tongue pledge loyalty. To You, Lord, may all bow in worship, may they give honor to Your glory. May everyone accept the rule of Your kingship. Reign over all, soon and for all time. Sovereignty is Yours in glory, now and forever. Thus is it written in Your Torah: The Lord reigns for ever and ever. Such is the assurance of Your prophet Zechariah: The Lord shall be acknowledged King of all the earth. On that day the Lord shall be One and His name One. [27]

GOD IS MORAL

He is the Lord of all the world, creating evil as well as good, but He desires the good. The classic ages of Judaism, in Bible and

Talmud, did not really imagine or regard as real the question whether the good is whatever God wills, or whether God is bound to will only the good. It was certain that He is especially identified with the good and responsive to finding it in man's conduct. As we have already seen, Judaism does not insist that the faithful can or even should know all the attributes of God, or even very much about God's action in the world. One thing, however, is undoubted, that He demands proper conduct from people and will punish them for their transgressions.

> The Lord, the Lord, a God merciful and gracious, slow to anger, abounding in steadfast love and faithfulness, keeping steadfast love for thousands of generations, forgiving iniquity and transgression and sin, but who will by no means clear the guilty, visiting the iniquity of the fathers upon the children and the children's children, to the third and the fourth generations.[28]

> Know in your heart that as a man disciplines his son the Lord your God disciplines you.[29]

> When you come to appear before Me, who required this from you, that you should trample My courts? Offer vain sacrifices no more, incense is an abomination to Me. New Moon and Sabbath, the holding of convocations—I cannot endure iniquity along with solemn assembly. My soul hates your new moons and your appointed seasons; they have become burdensome to Me. I am weary of bearing them. When you stretch forth your hands, I will turn My eyes away from you; when you increase prayer, I will not hear, for your hands are full of blood. Wash yourselves, be clean, put away the evil of your devices from before My eyes; cease to do perversely. Learn to do good; seek justice, relieve the oppressed, uphold the orphan's rights, defend the widow's cause.

> Come now and let us reason together, says the Lord. Though your sins be as scarlet, they shall become white as snow; though they be red as crimson, they shall become white as wool. If you are willing, and hearken to Me, you shall eat the good things of the earth; but if you refuse, and rebel, the sword shall devour you. The mouth of the Lord Himself has spoken.[30]

> "The Rock, His work is perfect, for all His ways are just. A God of faithfulness without iniquity, just and right is He" [Deut. 32:4]. His work is perfect as regards all who come into the world, and one should not criticize His ways. One should not ponder,

saying "If I had three hands or three feet, if I could walk on my head, if I had eyes in the back of my head, how nice it would be." He is a God of justice. He judges each person justly and gives him what he deserves. He is a God of faithfulness. He had faith in the world and so He created it. He did not create human beings that they should be wicked, but that they should be righteous, as it is written "God made man upright, but they have sought out many devices" [Eccles. 7:29].[31]

Rabbi Joshua said "Wherever you find a description of the greatness of the Holy One, praised be He, you find a description of His consideration for the lowly. This is written in the Torah, repeated in the Prophets, and stated for the third time in the Writings. In the Torah it is written: "For the Lord your God is God of gods and Lord of lords . . ." [Deut. 10:17], and in the verse following it is written, "He executes justice for the fatherless and the widow" [Deut. 10:18]. It is repeated in the Prophets: "For thus says the high and lofty One who inhabits eternity, whose name is holy; 'I dwell in the high and holy place' " [Isa. 57:15]. And the verse continues "and also with the contrite and the humble spirit" (ibid.). It is stated for the third time in the Writings: "Extol Him who rides upon the skies, whose name is the Lord" [Ps. 68:5], and in the verse following it is written "Father of the fatherless and protector of widows" [Ps. 68:6].[32]

"Then Moses said to God 'If I come to the people Israel and say to them "The God of your fathers has sent me to you" and they ask "What is His name?" what shall I say to them?' " [Ex. 3:13]. Moses asked the Holy One, praised be He, to tell him His great name. "And God said to Moses 'I am what I am' " [Ex. 3:14]. Rabbi Abba bar Mamal said: The Holy One, praised be He, said to Moses "You want to know My name. I am called according to My deeds. At various times I am called Almighty, Lord of hosts, God, and Lord. When I judge My creatures, I am called God. When I wage war against the wicked, I am called Lord of hosts. When I suspend the punishment of man's sins, I am called Almighty. And when I have compassion upon My world, I am called Lord. Thus Scripture states 'I am what I am'; I am called according to My deeds."[33]

"You, O Lord, are ever on high" [Ps. 92:8]. You are always right. When a mortal king sits in judgment, all the people praise him when he grants a pardon. But no one praises him when he orders punishment, for they know that passion has played a part in his judgment. However, this is not so of the Holy One, praised be He. Whether He pardons or punishes, "You, O Lord, are ever on high." . . . Rav Huna, in the name of Rav Acha, said: It is written, "I will sing of mercy and justice; to You, O Lord, will I sing" [Ps. 101:1]. In this Psalm, David was saying: Be it one way or the other [whether God pardons me or punishes me] to You, O Lord, will I sing. . . . Rabbi Judah bar Ilai said: It is written, "The Lord gave, the Lord has taken away; praised be the name of the Lord" [Job 1:21]. When He gives, He gives in mercy; when He takes away, He takes away in mercy.[34]

"Then the Lord said to Cain [after the latter killed Abel] 'Where is Abel, your brother?' He answered, 'I do not know. Am I my brother's keeper?' " [Gen. 4:9]. Cain said: "You, O Lord, are the Keeper, the one who should watch over all creatures, and yet You ask me concerning Abel." This situation may be compared to that of a thief who stole at night and was not caught. The following morning, the watchman caught him and asked, "Why did you steal?" The thief answered, "I am a thief and I did not abandon my profession. But your profession demands that you watch at the gate. Why did you abandon your profession? And now you ask me why I stole!" Thus, too, did Cain speak to God: "I killed Abel; but You have created in me the impulse to evil. You are the Keeper of all and yet You permitted me to kill him. You have killed him! If You had accepted my offering as You accepted his, I would not have been jealous of him."[35]

Thus spoke the Holy One, praised be He: If I create the world solely on the basis of My attribute of Mercy, its sins will become too many. If I create it solely by My attribute of strict Justice, how will the world be able to exist? Therefore, I will create it with both attributes, both Justice and Mercy, and I hope that it will endure![36]

The central paradox of the Bible is that God is identified with power and, as in the Book of Job, with power that need not account to man, and yet He is the God of justice who can be challenged. When the angels came to Abraham to announce the divine intention to destroy Sodom and Gomorrah because of their sins, Abraham asked that they be spared for the sake of the righteous who might be among them: "Shall not the Judge of all the earth act justly?!" (Genesis 18:25) Franz Rosenzweig (1887–

1929), the great theologian of German Jewry, here speaks for the whole of Jewish thought about God and His moral nature:

To His people, God the Lord is simultaneously the God of retribution and the God of love. In the same breath, they call on Him as "our God" and as "King of the universe," or—to indicate the same contrast in a more intimate sphere—as "our Father" and "our King." He wants to be served with trembling and yet rejoices when His children overcome their fear at His wondrous signs. Whenever the Scriptures mention His majesty, the next verses are sure to speak of His meekness. He demands the visible signs of offering and prayer brought to His name, and of the "affliction of our soul" in His sight. And almost in the same breath He scorns both and wants to be honored only with the secret fervor of the heart, in the love of one's neighbor, and in anonymous works of justice which no one may recognize as having been done for the sake of His name. He has elected His people, but elected it to visit upon them all their iniquities. He wants every knee to bend to Him and yet He is enthroned above Israel's songs of praise. [Ps. 22:4] Israel intercedes with Him in behalf of the sinning peoples of the world and He afflicts Israel with disease so that those other people may be healed [Isa. 53]. Both stand before God: Israel His servant, and the kings of the peoples; and the strands of suffering and guilt, of love and judgment, of sin and atonement, are so inextricably twined that human hands cannot untangle them.[37]

MORTALS MUST LOVE AND SERVE GOD

How do mortals serve God? By imitating His ways—"as He is just and merciful so must you be just and merciful"—and by absolute devotion, even to death.

You shall love the Lord your God with all your heart, with all your might, and with all your soul.[38]

And now, Israel, what does the Lord your God require of you? Only that you fear the Lord your God, and walk in His ways, and love Him, and serve the Lord your God with all your heart and with all your soul, keeping the commandments of the Lord, and His statutes, which I command you this day for your good. Behold, heaven and the heaven of heavens, the earth and all things therein, belong to the Lord your God. Yet the Lord had delight in your fathers, and He loved them, and chose their seed after them, that is to say, you, out of all peoples, as it is this day. Circumcise therefore the foreskin of your hearts, and stiffen your necks no more, because the Lord your God is the God of gods, the Lord of lords, the great God, the mighty and the awesome, who favors no person, and takes no bribe. He executes justice for the orphan and the widow, loves the stranger, and gives him food and raiment. Do you therefore love the stranger, for you were strangers in the land of Egypt. You shall fear the Lord your God, and serve Him only; to Him shall you cleave and by His name shall you swear. He is your glory and your God, who has done for you these great and awesome things which your eyes have seen. Seventy persons in all your ancestors went down into Egypt; and behold now the Lord your God has made you numerous as the stars of heaven.[39]

Praise the Lord, all nations. Laud Him, all peoples. Great is His love for us; everlasting His faithfulness. Halleluyah![40]

"You shall love the Lord your God with all your heart, with all your soul, and with all your might" [Deut. 6:5] . . . Rabbi Eliezer said, "Since this verse states 'with all your soul' [i.e. life], why does it state 'with all your might' [i.e. substance]? And since it states 'with all your might,' why does it state 'with all your soul'? For one who holds his life as more precious than his wealth, it is written 'with all your soul.' And for one who holds his wealth as more precious than his life it is written 'with all your might.' " Rabbi Akiva said, " 'With all your soul' means that you should love Him even if He takes your soul."[41]

Rabbi Shabtai Hurwitz (1590–1660), an East European scholar, is the author of a will in which this passage occurs.

My master, my father, of blessed memory, wrote in his book that when the time of death draws near, Satan stands near the dying man and tempts him saying, "Deny the God of Israel." The mind of a man in that state is weakened—may the Merciful one save us. Therefore I proclaim from this time forth before God praised be He and His *Shekhinah*, before the heavenly court and the earthly court, that if, God forbid, I should make any unseemly statement near the time of my death, the words shall be null and void, without any binding power. But what I say now does have validity: I accept and bear witness that the Holy One, praised be He, is the First Cause, Creator of all things, eternal, existing before the first and enduring after the last. "Hear, O Israel, the Lord our God, the Lord is One." "Praised be His glorious sovereignty for ever and ever." These are the principles which I accept now and to eternity.[42]

Moses Luzatto (1707–1747) was an Italian poet and mystic. He wrote a famous ethical tract, *Mesillat Yesharim* ("Way of the Upright"), which is the source of the next three passages.

There are many ways of profaning the Name, and one must be constantly mindful of the glory of his Creator. In whatever one does, he must be alert and careful that it does not produce anything which could be a profanation of the glory of Heaven. We have learned, "Whoever profanes the name of Heaven in secret will be punished openly. It makes no difference whether the Name was profaned unwittingly or intentionally" [Mishnah *Avot* 4:4]. When the sages asked for an example of profaning the Name, Rav said, "If a man of my reputation should buy meat without paying for it immediately" [*Yoma* 86a]. Rabbi Johanan said, "If a man of my reputation should walk a distance of four *amot* without meditating on the Torah or without *tefillin*." Every man, according to his status and how he is looked upon by his contemporaries, must be careful not to do anything which is improper for a man of his standing. The more one is honored and learned, the more must he be careful in his religious observance. If he does not act in this way, the Name of Heaven is profaned through him. For it honors the Torah when one who devotes a great amount of time to studying it also devotes a great amount of time to virtue and to self-improvement. But whoever lacks such virtue, though he studies a great deal, disgraces the study of Torah. This is a profanation of the name of God, praised be He, who gave us His holy Torah and commanded us to be occupied in studying it as a means to attaining our perfection.[43]

A major principle in the service of God is joy. David declares, "Serve the Lord with gladness; come into His Presence with singing" [Ps. 100:2]. "Let the righteous be joyful; let them exult before God; let them be jubilant with joy" [Ps. 68:4]. Our sages said, "The *Shekhinah* rests only upon one who performs a commandment in a joyous spirit" (*Shabbat* 30b).[44]

There are three elements in the love of God: joy, devotion and zeal. To love God is to passionately desire His nearness, praised be He, and to pursue His holiness, as one pursues something he strongly desires, until mentioning His name, praised be He, or speaking His praise, or studying His Torah or His divine nature, becomes a source of pleasure and delight as real as that of one who strongly loves the wife of his youth, or his only son. In the latter case, even speaking of them is a delight. And Scripture states, "As often as I speak of Him, I remember Him still; therefore my heart yearns for Him . . ." [Jer. 31:19]. Surely whoever truly loves his Creator will not neglect serving Him for any reason in the world, unless he is physically prevented from doing so. He will not need to be coaxed or enticed into serving Him. On the contrary, unless prevented by some great obstacle, his heart itself will lift him. This is the desirous quality which the early saints, the holy ones of the Highest, were privileged to attain. . . .

Surely there must be no ulterior motives in such love. One should love the Creator, praised be He, not because He is good to him, or grants him wealth or success, but one should love Him as naturally and as obligingly as a son loves his father. Indeed, Scripture states, "Is He not your father, who created you?" [Deut. 32:6]. The test of this love is during a time of hardship and trouble. . . . "Whatever Heaven does is for the best" (*Berakhot* 60b). This means that even hardship and trouble are apparent evils which in reality are good. . . . Thus one should realize that whatever the Holy One praised be He does to him, whether it affect his body or his property, is for his own good, even though he does not understand how it could be for his own good. Thus neither hardship nor suffering would lessen his love for God.[45]

Here, too, Rabbi Israel Baal Shem Tov's words, from his "testament," can stand as a summary of the view of Judaism.

. . . A man who makes efforts to cleave to God has no time to think of unimportant matters; when he constantly serves the Creator, he has no time to be vain. . . . If a man should suddenly be faced by a beautiful woman, or by any other of the fair and lovely objects of this world, he should immediately think to himself: "Where does this beauty come from, if not from the divine power which permeates the world? It follows that the source of this beauty is on high. Why, then, should I be drawn after a part? It would be better for me to be drawn after the All, the Source and Root of all partial beauty." When a man tastes something good and sweet, he should realize that the sweetness on high is the power which sustains it. Perception of any good quality is an experience of the Eternal, praised be He. . . . Thus when a man hears something amusing which brings him some joy, he should realize that it is but a portion from the world of love. Every man must serve God, praised be He, with all his might, for all of this is a divine need. God desires that man serve Him in all ways. At times a man walks and speaks with other men, and then he is unable to study the Torah. Even then he must cleave to God and be conscious of His uniqueness. When a man travels and can neither pray nor study in his usual manner, he must serve Him in other ways. Let him not be troubled over this, for God, praised be He, desires that man serve Him in all ways, sometimes one way, sometimes another. . . . A major principle in serving the Creator is to be rid of sadness as much as possible. Weeping is very bad, for man must serve God in joy. However, if the weeping is caused by joy, then it is very good. One should not thoroughly investigate each one of his acts, for through such a state of mind the impulse to evil intends to make one fearful that he is not fulfilling his duties, and thus bring him to sadness. And sadness is a great obstacle to the service of the Creator, praised be He. Even if a man has committed a sin he should not be overly sad, lest he neglect the service of God. He should, of course, be sad because of the sin, but he should then return to rejoice in the Creator, praised be He.[46]

3

TORAH: TEACHING AND COMMANDMENT

RATIONALE FOR COMMANDMENT

"The Torah was given only as a means of purifying mortals"—so runs a famous rabbinic dictum. It is not an impossible set of demands, meant for angels or a very few people of superior piety. Its wisdom and ordinances are the way of holiness for all mortals, even the most ordinary among them. Through obedience we resist the temptations that come to mislead us each and every day—so Rashi, Rabbi Solomon ben Isaac (1040–1105), the classic commentator on the Bible and Talmud, explains the third of the passages immediately below.

> And when your son asks you in time to come, saying, "What mean the testimonies, the statutes and the ordinances which the Lord our God has commanded us?" then you shall say to your son, "We were slaves to Pharaoh in Egypt, and the Lord brought us out of Egypt with a mighty hand. And the Lord wrought signs and wonders, great and grievous, in Egypt against Pharaoh and all his house, before our eyes. And He brought us out from there, that He might bring us in and give us the land which He swore to our fathers. And the Lord commanded that we should observe all these statutes, and that we should fear the Lord our God, that it might be well with us all the days of our life, as it is at this day. And it will be to our merit if we keep all this commandment before the Lord our God, as He has commanded us."[1]

This commandment which I command you this day is not too hard for you, nor is it far away from you. It is not in heaven, that you should say, "Who shall go up to heaven, to bring it to us, and make us hear it, that we may fulfill it?" Nor is it beyond the sea, that you should say, "Who shall go over the sea for us, to bring it to us, and make us hear it, that we may fulfill it?" But the word is very near to you, in your mouth and in your heart, that you may fulfill it.[2]

Rabbi Simlai expounded: Six hundred and thirteen commandments were transmitted to Moses on Mount Sinai. Three hundred sixty five of them are negative commandments [i.e. prohibitions], corresponding to the number of days in the solar year. The remaining two hundred forty eight are positive commandments [i.e. injunctions], corresponding to the number of limbs in the human body.[3]

After Moses, David the Psalmist came and reduced the six hundred thirteen commandments to eleven, as it is written: "Lord, who shall sojourn in Your tabernacle? Who shall dwell on Your holy mountain? He who walks blamelessly, and does what is right, and speaks truth in his heart, who does not slander with his tongue, and does no evil to his friend, nor takes up a reproach against his neighbor, in whose eyes a reprobate is despised, but honors those who fear the Lord, who swears to his own hurt and does not change, who does not put out his money at interest, and does not take a bribe against the innocent" [Ps. 15:1–5]. . . .

Then Isaiah came and reduced the commandments to six, as it is written "He who walks in righteousness and speaks uprightly, he who spurns the gain of oppressions, who shakes his hands lest they hold a bribe, who stops his ears from hearing of bloodshed, and shuts his eyes from looking upon evil" [Isa. 33:15]. . . . Then Micah came and reduced them to three, as it is written, "It has been told you, O man, what is good, and what the Lord requires of you: To do justice, to love mercy, and to walk humbly with your God" [Mic. 6:8]. . . . Then Isaiah came again and reduced them to two. "Thus says the Lord: Keep justice and do righteousness" [Isa. 56:1]. Amos came and reduced them to one, as it is written, "Thus says the Lord to the house of Israel: Seek Me and live" [Amos 5:4]. . . . Habakkuk came and also reduced them to one, as it is written, "The righteous shall live by his faith" [Hab. 2:4].[4]

Rabbi Huna and Rabbi Jeremiah said in the name of Rabbi Hiyya bar Abba: It is written, "They have forsaken Me and have not kept My law" [Jer. 16:11]. This is to say: "If only they *had* forsaken Me but kept My law! Since they then would have been occupied with it, the light which is in it would have restored them to the right path."[5]

". . . remember all the commandments of the Lord, to obey them, not to follow your heart and your eyes, which you are inclined to go after wantonly" [Num. 15:39]. The heart and the eyes are the panders of the body; they excite the senses. "So you shall remember and obey all My commandments, and be holy to your God" [Num. 15:41]. The human situation may be compared to that of a man who fell into the sea. The helmsman threw him a rope and said "Hold on to the rope. Do not let go, for should you let go of it, you will lose your life." Thus spoke the Holy One, praised be He, to Israel: "So long as you hold fast to the commandments, 'you who hold fast to the Lord your God are all alive this day' " [Num. 4:4]. And it is written, "Hold on to instruction, do not let go; guard it, for it is your life" [Prov. 4:13].[6]

The accepted Jewish view of Torah as the way of "normal holiness" was expounded by a contemporary theologian, Rabbi Louis Finkelstein (1895–).

Judaism is a way of life that endeavors to transform virtually every human action into a means of communion with God. Through this communion with God, the Jew is enabled to make his contribution to the establishment of the Kingdom of God and the brotherhood of man on earth. So far as its adherents are concerned, Judaism seeks to extend the concept of right and wrong to every aspect of their behavior. Jewish rules of conduct apply not merely to worship, ceremonial and justice between man and man, but also to such matters as philanthropy, personal friendships and kindnesses, intellectual pursuits, artistic creation, courtesy, the preservation of health and the care of diet.

So rigorous is this discipline, as ideally conceived in Jewish writing, that it may be compared to those specified for members of religious orders in other faiths. A casual conversation or a thoughtless remark may, for instance, be considered a grave violation of Jewish Law. It is forbidden, as a matter not merely of good form but of religious law, to use obscene language, to rouse a person to anger or to display unusual ability in the presence of the handicapped. The ceremonial observances are equally detailed. The ceremonial law expects each Jew to pray thrice every day, if possible at the synagogue; to recite a blessing before and after each meal; to thank God for any special pleasure, such as a curious sight, the perfume of a flower, or the receipt of good news; to wear a fringed garment about his body; to recite certain passages from Scriptures each day and to don *tephillin* [cubical receptacles containing certain Biblical passages] during the morning prayers. . . .

Like every other authentic experience, piety cannot stop short of the home. If religion were to be merely ecclesiastical, it would soon cease to be that too. The Psalmist who was told "Let us go up to the house of the Lord" rejoiced because in his own house the reality of God was never forgotten. Throughout Jewish history the attempt to reproduce in the home the order and mood of the place of worship has never been relaxed.

The interrelationship of sanctity and home has been responsible for at least two significant results. On the one hand, the Jew did not remain a stranger to the ceremonial and purpose of his sacred institutions. On the other hand, his home and home life were transfigured. His residence became a habitation of God.

This sanctification of the home was achieved by a religious discipline whose purpose was constantly to prompt a remembrance of God. The Jew who visited the ancient Temple, for example, readily understood that the elaborate rites, precautions, exactitudes and purifications were the appropriate expression of the beauty of holiness. "If you were to serve a king of flesh and blood," the saintly Hillel once reminded a guest, "would you not have to learn how to make your entrances and exits and obeisances? How much more so in the service of the King of kings!"

That such fastidiousness was therefore required in God's House the Jew accepted unquestionably. The forms reminded him of God. And because they did, and because Israel's teachers tried to prevent the Jew from forgetting God even when he was away from the Sanctuary, corresponding rituals were introduced into the Jewish home. Thus the Jewish home became a sanctuary in miniature, its table an altar, its furnishings instruments for sanctity.[7]

THE TORAH AS WISDOM

The Torah is commandment, but it is much more than that. At its widest, the concept means more than even the teaching contained in the Bible. It is the whole of the sacred tradition, especially as expressed in all the writings of the faith, from the Bible to the present. Study of Torah is a commandment several times enjoined in the Bible itself. To know that such study is as important an act of Jewish piety as prayer, in some senses indeed more important, is crucial to understanding the genius of Judaism and of Jewry. Hence, in all the past ages, when few people could read, illiteracy was least known among Jews and learning was always the most highly prized of all attainments.

The words of the Torah are compared to a life-giving medicine. A king who inflicted a severe wound upon his son put a plaster upon the wound. He said, "My son, so long as this plaster is on your wound, eat and drink what you like, wash with either hot or cold water, and you will suffer no harm. But if you should remove this plaster, you will suffer." Thus the Holy One, praised be He, said to the Israelites, "I created within you the impulse to evil, but I created the Torah as a medicine. So long as you occupy yourselves with the Torah, the impulse to evil will not dominate you. But if you do not occupy yourselves with the Torah, you will be delivered into the power of the impulse to evil."[8]

Rabbi Joshua ben Levi said: What is the meaning of the verse, "This is the Torah which Moses *set* before the children of Israel"? [Deut. 4:44]. [Note: The Hebrew word for "set" (*sahm*) is a homonym of the Hebrew word for "medicine" or "drug."] It teaches that for one who is deserving the Torah becomes a life-giving medicine; otherwise it becomes a death-dealing drug. . . . ". . . the word of the Lord is purified . . ." [Ps. 18:31] Resh Lakish said: For one who is deserving, the word purifies him to life; otherwise the word melts him down to death.[9]

Rabbi Meir said: Whoever occupies himself with the study of Torah with no ulterior motive merits many things. Furthermore, the entire world is indebted to him. He is called beloved friend [of God]. He loves God and mankind, and he causes God and mankind to rejoice. The Torah clothes him with humility and fear of the Lord, and it prepares him to be just, pious, upright and faithful. It keeps him far from sin and it brings him near to virtue. Through him people enjoy counsel and sound wisdom, insight and strength, as it is written, "I have counsel and sound wisdom, I have insight, I have strength" [Prov. 8:14]. [In that chapter of Proverbs, wisdom, or Torah, is personified as the speaker.] It gives him sovereignty and dominion and discerning judgment. The secrets of the Torah are revealed to him; he becomes like a never-failing spring and like a river which never halts. He becomes modest, patient and forgiving of insult; it magnifies him and exalts him above all the works of creation.

Rabbi Joshua ben Levi said: Every day a heavenly voice echoes forth from Mount Horeb [Sinai, where the Torah was given], proclaiming "Woe to mankind for contempt of Torah." . . .

This is the way to acquire knowledge of Torah: Eat bread with salt, drink water by measure [Ezek. 4:11], sleep on the ground, live a life of constraint, and toil in the Torah. If you do this, "You shall be blessed and it shall be well with you" [Ps. 128:2]. You shall be blessed in this world, and it shall be well with you in the world to come. Seek not greatness for yourself, and do not covet honor. Let your deeds surpass your learning. Crave not after the table of kings, for your table is greater than theirs and your crown is greater than theirs, and your master is faithful; He will reward you for your labors. . . .

Rabbi Jose ben Kisma said: I once was walking on a road when a man met me and greeted me, "Shalom." I returned his greeting. "Shalom." He said, "Rabbi, where are you from?" I said, "From a great city of sages and scribes." He said, "Rabbi, should you wish to live with us in our place, I would give you thousands of gold dinars, and precious stones and pearls." I said, "Were you to give me all the silver, gold, precious stones and pearls in the world, I would live only in a place of Torah. . . . Thus is it written in the book of Psalms by David, the king of Israel, 'The Torah [teaching] that You proclaimed is better to me than thousands of gold and silver pieces' " [Ps. 119:72]. Furthermore, when a man dies, neither silver, gold, precious stones nor pearls accompany him; only Torah and good deeds alone, as it is written, "When you walk it shall lead you, when you lie down it shall watch over you, and when you awake it shall be with you" [Prov. 6:22]. "When you walk it shall lead you" in this world. "When you lie down it shall watch over you" in the grave. "And when you awake it shall be with you" in the world to come. . . .

Rabbi Hananiah ben Akashya said: The Holy One, praised be He, desired to favor the people Israel. Therefore He increased for them the Torah and commandments, as it is written, "The Lord was pleased, for His righteousness' sake, to magnify Torah and to make it glorious" [Isa. 42:21].[10]

"On the third new moon after the Israelites had gone forth out of the land of Egypt, on this day they came into the wilderness of Sinai" [Exodus 19:1]. Ben Zoma said: This verse does not state "on that day" but "on this day," as if to say that on *this* day they have come to the wilderness of Sinai [the site of Revelation]. Whenever you are engaged in the study of Torah, you can say, "It is as though I have received the Torah at Sinai on *this* day." Furthermore, it is written, "*This* day the Lord your God commands you to observe these statutes and ordinances. . . ." [Deut. 26:16].[11]

Rabbi Judah would send Rabbi Assi and Rabbi Ammi to organize religious education in the towns of the Land of Israel. When they came to a town they would say to the people, "Bring to us the guardians of the town." The people would bring to them the captain of the guard and the magistrate. The rabbis would say, "These are not the guardians of the town. These are its destroyers!" When the people asked, "Who are the guardians of the town?" the rabbis would answer, "The scribes and the teachers, who meditate upon, teach and preserve the Torah day and night." This is in accordance with what is written, "You shall meditate therein day and night" [Joshua 1:8]. And it is written, "Unless the Lord builds the house, those who build it labor in vain" [Ps. 127:1]. . . . Rabbi Huna said: Study Torah, even if not for its own sake. Though it be studied at first not for its own sake, this will lead one to study it for its own sake.[12]

Lest you say "I will study Torah that I might be called wise, or sit in the Academy, or be rewarded with length of days in the world to come," it is written "You shall love the Lord your God" [Deut. 6:5]. [The action must be motivated only by love of God.][13]

Rabbi Eliezer said: When the evil power comes to seduce man, let him drag it to the Torah, and thus he will depart from the evil power. Come and see that thus have we learned: When the evil power stands before the Holy One, praised be He, to accuse the world for evil deeds, the Holy One, praised be He, shows compassion for the world and gives mankind counsel by which it can escape the evil power, so that it will dominate neither them nor their deeds. What is this counsel?—To be occupied with the Torah. How do we know this? It is written, "The commandment is a lamp and the Torah is a light, and the reproofs of discipline are the ways of life" [Prov. 6:23]. What words follow that verse? "To preserve you from the evil woman, from the smooth tongue of the adventuress" [Prov. 6:24]. The latter verse refers to the impurity in the world, the "other force" continually standing before the Holy One, praised be He, to accuse mankind for its sins.[14]

The Torah declares, "I was the instrument of the Holy One, praised be He." It is the way of the world that when a mortal king builds a palace he builds it not from his own plans but with the advice of an architect. And the architect, in turn, has blueprints and charts to guide him how to construct the rooms and chambers. So, too, the Holy One, praised be He, was guided by the Torah in creating the world.[15]

The Torah was given publicly and openly, in a place to which no one had any claim. Had it been given in the land of Israel, the nations of the world could have said "We have no portion in it." Therefore it was given in the wilderness, publicly and openly, in a place to which no one had any claim. Everyone who desires to accept, let him come and accept it.[16]

The next passage is from the daily evening service. That He gave Israel the Torah is the surest sign of God's love.

With constancy You have loved Your people Israel, teaching us Torah and mitzvot [commandments], statutes and laws. Therefore, Lord our God, when we lie down to sleep and when we rise, we shall think of Your laws and speak of them, rejoicing in Your Torah and mitzvot always. For they are our life and length of days; we will meditate on them day and night. Never take away Your love from us. Praised are You, Lord who loves His people Israel.[17]

CHALLENGES TO FAITH IN TORAH

Persecution makes living the life ordained by the Torah difficult and dangerous. In the face of Roman tyranny after the destruction of the Second Temple in the year 70 the Rabbis had to distinguish between those laws for which man should accept martyrdom and those which he could disobey rather than risk his life.

"You shall therefore keep My statutes and My ordinances, by doing which a man shall live" [Lev. 18:5]. Rabbi Ishmael said: If in a time of persecution an Israelite should be told in private "Worship this idol and you shall not be killed," he should worship the idol. How do we know this to be so? Because it is written, "by doing which a man shall live," not "by doing which a man shall die." However, if he is told to do this in public, is he to obey? No. For it is written, "you shall not profane My holy name, but I will be hallowed among the children of Israel" [Lev. 22:32].[18]

It was resolved in the upper chambers of the house of the Natzah family in Lydda [in southern Palestine] by a majority vote that should a man be offered the alternative of transgressing one of the Torah's commandments or be killed, he may transgress, except for the commandments against idolatry, prohibited sexual relations, and murder.[19]

Doubt is the other danger to the life of Torah. Saadia attempts to deal with this problem in the three paragraphs quoted next.

There may be some men who would give up their adherence to the Bible because many of the commandments are not clearly explained in it. My answer to them is that the Bible is not the sole basis of our religion, for in addition to it we have two other bases. One of these is anterior to it; namely, the fountain of reason. The second is posterior to it; namely, the source of tradition. Whatever, therefore, we may not find in the Bible, we can find in the two other sources. Thus are the commandments rounded out quantitatively as well as qualitatively.[20]

"Could not God have bestowed upon His creatures complete bliss and permanent happiness without giving them commandments and prohibitions? Indeed, it would seem that such kindness would have contributed even more to human well-being, because they would be relieved of all exertion for the attainment of their bliss."

Let me, then, say in explanation of this matter that, on the contrary, God's making His creatures' diligent compliance with His commandments the means of attaining permanent bliss is the better course. For according to the judgment of reason the person who achieves some good by means of the effort that he has ex-

pended for its attainment obtains double the advantage gained by
him who achieves this good without any effort but merely as a
result of the kindness shown him by God. In fact, reason recognizes no equality between these two. This being the case, then,
the Creator preferred to assign to us the ampler portion in order
that our reward might yield us a double benefit, not merely a
compensation exactly equivalent to the effort, as Scripture also
says: "Behold, the Lord God will come as a Mighty One, and
His arm will rule for Him; behold, His reward is with Him, and
His recompense before Him" [Isa. 40:10].[21]

The paragraphs of apologetics for the Law that follow are by
Samson Raphael Hirsch.

And as for the Law, is it really a preventative of all the joys of
life, a hindrance and an obstacle to the gratification of the natural
human craving for pleasure? Examine once the precepts and ordinances of the Law from beginning to end and tell me what
legitimate desire it forbids to gratify, what natural impulse it would
destroy or extirpate.

On the contrary, it purifies and sanctifies even our lower im-
pulses and desires by applying them with wise limitation to the
purposes designated by the Creator.

Righteousness is the Law's typical end and aim, the gratification of physical lust and passion is never its object. Therefore
are the lower cravings subordinated to higher law and limited by
the Creator's wisdom for His infinitely wise purposes; but as means
of attaining proper and necessary ends, the Law recognizes these
desires as perfectly moral, pure and human, and their carrying
out as just and as legitimate as the fulfillment of any other human
task or mission.

What the Law, however, firmly and unyieldingly opposes is
the deification of wealth and lust as the sole aim and controlling
impulse of our lives; but it not only permits their pursuit within
the limits set by Divine wisdom, but declares the effort to gain
them a duty as sacred and binding as any other human obligation,
and condemns the purposeless and unreasonable abstinence from
permitted indulgences as sin . . .

Does not this law erect a wall of separation between its adherents and the rest of mankind? It does, I admit, but had it not
done so Israel would long since have lost all consciousness of its
mission, would long since have ceased to be itself.[22]

Solomon Schechter (1847–1915), the greatest figure of Conservative Judaism, was perhaps the most eloquent "defender of the faith" ever to write in English.

It is an illusion to speak of the burden which a scrupulous care to observe six hundred and thirteen commandments must have laid upon the Jew. Even a superficial analysis will discover that in the time of Christ many of these commandments were already obsolete (as for instance those relating to the tabernacle and to the conquest of Palestine), while others concerned only certain classes, as the priests, the judges, the soldiers, the Nazirites, or the representatives of the community, or even only one or two individuals among the whole population, as the King and the High Priest. Others, again, provided for contingencies which could occur only to a few, as for instance the laws concerning divorce or levirate marriages, whilst many—such as those concerning idolatry, and incest, and the sacrifice of children to Moloch—could scarcely have been considered as a practical prohibition by the pre-Christian Jew, just as little as we can speak of Englishmen as lying under the burden of a law preventing them from burning widows or marrying their grandmothers, though such acts would certainly be considered as crimes. Thus it will be found by a careful enumeration that barely a hundred laws remain which really concerned the life of the bulk of the people. If we remember that even these include such laws as belief in the unity of God, the necessity of loving and fearing Him, and of sanctifying His name, of loving one's neighbour and the stranger, of providing for the poor, exhorting the sinner, honoring one's parents and many more of a similar character, it will hardly be said that the ceremonial side of the people's religion was not well balanced by a fair amount of spiritual and social elements. Besides, it would seem that the line between the ceremonial and the spiritual is too often only arbitrarily drawn. With many commandments it is rather a matter of opinion whether they should be relegated to the one category or the other.

Thus the wearing of the Tephillin or phylacteries has, on the one hand, been continually condemned as a meaningless superstition, and a pretext for formalism and hypocrisy. But, on the other hand, Maimonides, who can in no way be suspected of superstition or mysticism, described their importance in the following words: "Great is the holiness of the Tephillin; for as long as they are on the arm and head of man, he is humble and God-fearing and feels no attraction for frivolity or idle things, nor has he any evil thoughts, but will turn his heart to the words of truth and righteousness." The view which Rabbi Johanan, a Palestinian preacher of the third century, took of the fulfillment of the Law will probably be found more rational than that of many a rationalist of today. Upon the basis of the last verse in Hosea, "The ways of the Lord are right, and the just shall walk in them, but the transgressors shall fall therein," he explains that while one man, for instance, eats his paschal lamb with the purpose of doing the will of God who commanded it, and thereby does an act of righteousness, another thinks only of satisfying his appetite by the lamb, so that his eating it (by the very fact that he professes at the same time to perform a religious rite) becomes a stumbling block for him. Thus all the laws by virtue of their divine authority—and in this there was in the first century no difference of opinion between Jews and Christians—have their spiritual side, and to neglect them implies, at least from the individual's own point of view, a moral offense.

The legalistic attitude may be summarily described as an attempt to live in accordance with the will of God, caring less for what God is than for what He wants us to be. But, nevertheless, on the whole this life never degenerated into religious formalism. Apart from the fact that during the Second Temple there grew up laws, and even beliefs, which show a decided tendency towards progress and development, there were also ceremonies which were popular with the masses, and others which were neglected. Men were not, therefore, the mere soulless slaves of the Law; personal sympathies and dislikes also played a part in their religion. Nor were all the laws actually put upon the same level. With a happy inconsistency men always spoke of heavier and slighter sins, and by the latter—excepting, perhaps, the profanation of the Sabbath—they mostly understood ceremonial transgressions.[23]

Kaufmann Kohler here states the Reform doctrine of the Law—or rather its rationale for abandoning it. He is obviously impaled on the dilemmas of wanting Israel separate as a "priest-people" and yet wanting it to be part of society as a whole; of desiring the life of obedience and wanting to loose the ancient bonds.

Undoubtedly the Law, as it embraced the whole of life in its power, sharpened the Jewish sense of duty, and served the Jew as an iron wall of defense against temptations, aberrations, and enticements of the centuries. As soon as the modern Jew, however, undertook to free himself from the tutelage of blind acceptance of authority and inquired after the purpose of all the restrictions of the Law laid upon him, his ancient loyalty to the same collapsed and the pillars of Judaism seemed to be shaken. Then the leaders of Reform, imbued with the prophetic spirit, felt it to be their imperative duty to search out the fundamental ideas of the priestly law of holiness and, accordingly, they learned how to separate the kernel from the shell. In opposition to the orthodox tendency to worship the letter, they insisted on the fact that Israel's separation from the world—which it is ultimately to win for the divine truth—cannot itself be its end and aim, and that blind obedience to the law does not constitute true piety. Only the fundamental idea, that Israel as the "first-born" among the nations has been elected as a priest-people, must remain our imperishable truth, a truth to which the centuries of history bear witness by showing that it has given its lifeblood as a ransom for humanity, and is ever bringing new sacrifices for its cause. Only because it has kept itself distinct as a priest-people among the nations could it carry out its great task in history; and only if it remains conscious of its priestly calling, and therefore maintains itself as the people of God, can it fulfill its mission. Not until the end of time, when all of God's children will have entered the kingdom of God, may Israel, the high-priest among the nations, renounce his priesthood.[24]

The greatest of modern Hebrew poets, Hayyim Nahman Bialik (1873–1934), speaks here in exalted summary of the meaning of Torah within the Jewish heritage.

The concept of "Torah" attained in the esteem of the [Jewish] people an infinite exaltation. For them the Torah was almost another existence, a more spiritual and loftier state, added to or even taking the place of secular existence. The Torah became the center of the nation's secret and avowed aspirations and desires in its exile. The dictum "Israel and the Torah are one" was no mere phrase; the non-Jew cannot appreciate it, because the concept of "Torah," in its full national significance, cannot be rendered adequately in any other tongue. Its content and connotations embrace more than "religion" or "creed" alone, or "ethics" or "commandments" or "learning" alone, and it is not even just a combination of all these, but something far transcending all of them. It is a mystic, almost cosmic, conception. The Torah is the tool of the Creator; with it and for it He created the universe. The Torah is older than creation. It is the highest idea and the living soul of the world. Without it the world could not exist and would have no right to exist. "The study of the Torah is more important than the building of the Temple." "Knowledge of the Torah ranks higher than priesthood or kingship." "Only he is free who engages in the study of the Torah." "It is the Torah that magnifies and exalts man over all creatures." "Even a heathen who engages in the study of the Torah is as good as a High Priest." "A bastard learned in the Torah takes precedence over an ignorant High Priest." [These quotations are well known, oft-repeated dicta from Rabbinic literature.]

Such is the world outlook to which almost seventy generations of Jews have been educated. In accordance therewith their spiritual life was provisionally organized for the interim of the exile. For it they suffered martyrdom and by virtue of it they lived. The Jewish elementary school was established shortly before the destruction of Jerusalem and has survived to this day. As a result of such prolonged training, the nation has acquired a sort of sixth sense for everything connected with the needs of the spirit, a most delicate sense and always the first to be affected, and one possessed by almost every individual. There is not a Jew but would be filled with horror by a cruel decree "that Jews shall not engage in the Torah." Even the poorest and meanest man in Israel sacrificed for the teaching of his children, on which he spent sometimes as much as half of his income or more. Before asking for the satisfaction of his material needs, the Jew first prays daily: "And graciously bestow upon us knowledge, understanding, and comprehension." And what was the first request of our pious mothers over the Sabbath candles? "May it be Your will that the eyes of my children may shine with Torah." Nor do I doubt that if God had appeared to one of these mothers in a dream, as He did once to Solomon, and said, "Ask, what shall I give unto you?" she would have replied even as Solomon did, "I ask not for myself either riches or honor, but O Lord of the universe, may it please You to give unto my sons a heart to understand Torah and wisdom to distinguish good from evil" [Based on I Kings 3:9–11].[25]

CIRCUMCISION

The rest of this section is devoted to the characteristic precision with which Judaism defines ritual and moral obligations. Circumcision is the most ancient of Jewish rituals.

And God said to Abraham: You therefore shall keep My covenant, and your seed after you, throughout their generations. This is My covenant, which you shall keep, between Me and you and your seed after you, every male among you shall be circumcised. You shall be circumcised in the flesh of your foreskin, that it may be a sign of the covenant between Me and you. An infant of eight days old shall be circumcised among you, every male throughout your generations, he that is born in your house, as well as he that is bought with money of any foreigner, that is not of your seed. He that is born in your house and he that is bought with your money must be circumcised, and My covenant shall be in your flesh for an everlasting covenant. If any male who is uncircumcised fails to circumcise the flesh of his foreskin, that person shall be destroyed out of his people, because he has broken My covenant. [26]

If a child is sick he is not circumcised until he becomes well. [27]

Rabbi Ishmael says: Great is circumcision, whereby the covenant was made thirteen times [the word "covenant" is repeated thirteen times in the seventeenth chapter of Genesis, where the commandment is given]. Rabbi Jose says: Great is circumcision, for it overrides even the stringency of the Sabbath [circumcision must be performed on the Sabbath when it is the eighth day after birth]. Rabbi Joshua ben Korha says: Great is circumcision, for it was not suspended so much as an hour even for the sake of Moses [See Ex. 4:24f]. . . . Rabbi says: Great is circumcision, for despite all the religious duties which Abraham fulfilled, he was not called "perfect" until he was circumcised, as it is written, "Walk before Me and be perfect, and I will make My covenant [i.e. circumcision] between Me and you" [Genesis 17:1–2]. Great is circumcision, for the Holy One, praised be He, had not created the world but for it, as it is written "Thus says the Lord: But for My covenant [i.e. circumcision] day and night, I had not set forth the ordinances of heaven and earth" [Jer. 33:25]. [28]

A man who brings his son to be circumcised is to be compared to a High Priest bringing meal offering and libation to the Temple altar. From this they say that a man is obliged to prepare a joyous feast on the day on which he is privileged to circumcise his son.[29]

The Israelites who came out of Egypt faithfully observed one commandment: they circumcised their infant sons. The Egyptians told them: Why must you circumcise your sons? Let them grow up like the Egyptians and you will eventually take the heavy load of slavery off your shoulders. The Israelites answered: Did Abraham, Isaac and Jacob forget their Father in heaven? Should their children forget Him?[30]

BAR MITZVAH, CONFIRMATION, AND BAT MITZVAH

Bar mitzvah as a category in rabbinic law is very ancient, but its rituals are not. The Talmud (*Kiddushin* 16b) fixed thirteen as the age when boys become responsible for themselves and twelve as the age for girls. Thus, both genders were obligated henceforth to perform all the rituals incumbent on each according to halakhah. This new maturity entitled the boys to being called to the Torah, among those who were full members of the worshipping community. In recent centuries this occasion has become increasingly festive. The celebration as such has no religious significance, for the rite of passage is in the birth date on which the status of the boy or the girl changes to that of an adult.

In the nineteenth century this halakhic norm was challenged from two perspectives. The first dissent came over its automatic nature. The founders of Reform Judaism introduced the ceremony of confirmation, at first to add resonance to bar mitzvah and soon to supplant it. Girls were treated equally with boys in confirmation classes. All young Jews were expected to learn the principles of the faith, as presented by the Reformers, and to indicate their acceptance of Judaism. The first confirmation ceremony, for boys alone, took place in 1810 in the synagogue of Israel Jacobson in Seesen, Germany. By the middle of the nine-

teenth century, girls were added to this new rite. Solomon Herx-
heimer (1801–1884), writing in Germany, explained and justified
confirmation as a contemporary necessity:

> It is obvious, therefore, that according to Bible and tradition,
> a vow of loyalty concerning individual laws as well as the total
> content of our religion, is not inadmissible and is neither super-
> fluous nor blameworthy, but rather, may be considered required
> in the interest of religion, in the same manner as all covenants
> in the Bible were re-formed and confirmed in order to prevent
> apostasy.
>
> In order that confirmation may, indeed, produce the intended
> strengthening and elevation of Judaism, it must of needs receive
> a form and arrangement which is adequate to its purpose. First
> of all, it would be necessary that an examination in religion be
> connected with it. Such examination should immediately precede
> the confirmation and perhaps would best take place during the
> worship service right after the reading of the Torah. There seems
> to be a direct connection between examination and confirmation,
> and the purpose of the Torah reading, "So that they might hear
> and learn and fear God" [Deut. 31:22–23]. These acts, in their
> total sacred and worshipful character, belong into a sacred place
> in the midst of public worship service and the religious assembly
> which renders them more solemn for all participants. They do
> not belong, therefore, into some school hall or even into the
> family circle where they might become a sort of "breakfast con-
> firmation."[31]

A generation later Kaufmann Kohler, writing in America,
insisted on replacing bar mitzvah entirely:

> I wish to touch upon a subject involving the very principle of
> Reform, being well aware of the fact that we can only discuss
> Congregational customs as to their correctness, but not dictate
> Reform and Progress. We should enlighten our people, working
> for a gradual advancement, following *evolutionary*, not *revolu-
> tionary*, methods, as we want to build up, not to destroy. We
> want peace and harmony while aiming at true progress. The fact
> is beyond dispute that the introduction of the Union Prayer Book
> meant to bring about Union and Unity in our progressive Amer-
> ican Jewry. Now I ask, is the calling of the thirteen-year-old lad
> to become a Bar Mitzvah by reading or by listening to the reading

of the Torah, which is still the practice in many Reform Congregations, in harmony with the whole spirit of our Reform Service? . . .

Since . . . the calling up of the members of the congregation to read from the scroll of the Law has been abolished in the Reform Synagogue, the whole Bar Mitzvah rite lost all meaning, and the calling up of the same is nothing less than a sham. The only place where it might yet have some significance or value would be in a *Children's Service*, in connection with the religious school in which Hebrew is taught. In our regular Congregational service it is an *anachronism*.

Disregarding altogether the false claim of mental maturity of the thirteen-year-old boy for a true realization of life's sacred obligations, I maintain that the Bar Mitzvah rite ought not to be encouraged by any Reform rabbi, as it is a survival of orientalism like the covering of the head during the service, whereas the confirmation—when made as it should, by the rabbi, an impressive appeal to the holiest emotions of the soul and a personal vow of fealty to the ancestral faith—is a source of regeneration of Judaism each year, the value of which none who has the spiritual welfare of Israel at heart can afford to underrate or to ignore.[32]

The earliest Reform rabbis were unequivocal in insisting that the distinctions in the halakhah between men and women had to be abolished. At a conference in Breslau, Germany, in 1846, it was ruled that the female sex is religiously equal with the male in rights and obligations. Women could henceforth be counted among the ten who made up a quorum for public worship. In France, the officially Orthodox synagogues did not go that far, but they did move before 1850 towards a greater role for women. They did follow the lead of the Reformers by instituting a ritual of confirmation for boys and girls together. Here is an account of such a rite in 1852:

The ceremony of confirmation which is called *initiation religieuse* takes place in the synagogue every year after the Shavuot Festival. Even though confirmation has been in existence for only a few years, it has already made a place for itself in the life of the French Jews and has brought them many blessings. Between sixty and eighty children appear at the ceremony. Whether they are poor or rich, they are nicely dressed, and in the holy place confirm their entrance into the synagogue at the end of a meticulous examination.

In this manner children of both sexes from families of the most diverse backgrounds obtain a thorough knowledge and love of their faith. By rearranging and reordering an old form, a need has been satisfied which our times demanded. Such reform is beneficial and after some time it will be firmly rooted in the congregation and amongst our people.[33]

These stirrings towards gender equality moved some in Orthodox circles in Europe to find ways to mark the coming of age of girls. A few congregations began to give the father of girls who reached twelve years of age special recognition at the synagogue service, and their rabbis spoke in honor of the occasion. Rabbi Jacob Etlinger, the major Orthodox authority in mid-nineteenth-century Germany, at first did not oppose these changes, but he soon reversed himself. As Reform Judaism grew stronger, Etlinger counseled resistance even to the most minor, and permissible, modifications of Orthodox practice. In our own time this latter, more stringent view was strongly maintained by Rabbi Moshe Feinstein (1892–1986), the leading authority on Jewish law in America. Bat mitzvah was instituted by Conservative and Reform Jews, and Feinstein ruled it must be totally avoided in any form. He even went so far as to deplore the contemporary form of bar mitzvah, which he saw as emphasizing the celebration at the expense of piety (*Iggerot Moshe, Orah Hayyim* 104). On the other hand, Rabbi Ovadiah Yosef, the leading contemporary Sephardic rabbinic authority, has approved of bat mitzvah celebrations and even suggested that the father recite the same blessings that are prescribed for him at the bar mitzvah of a son (*Yabia Omer* 29).

Those Orthodox authorities who encouraged bat mitzvah did not suggest a role for girls in the actual synagogue service. The separation of sexes at prayer, and for many other public purposes, remains fundamental to Orthodox practice. Nonetheless, the arrival of girls to religious maturity is increasingly marked in even Orthodox circles either in special ceremonies, separate from regular services at synagogue, or in celebrations in the home. The source that is most often quoted to permit such activity is a decision made by Rabbi Yehiel Weinberg (1885–1966), in the 1950s:

. . . And now for the matter under consideration, whether it is permissible to celebrate a bat mitzvah. There are those who want to forbid it since it falls under the category of aping the ways of non-Jews. . . . And in my humble opinion if we state that the confirmation practiced by non-Jews is a matter of alien worship, which must therefore be forbidden, following that reasoning we should have forbidden the celebration of bar mitzvah as well, for they have confirmation for boys as well as for girls . . . And the Reform among our people do not celebrate confirmation in order to be like non-Jews but do so for the sake of a family celebration, rejoicing over the coming of age of their children. And those of our brethren who introduced the celebration of bat mitzvah say that they did so in order to instill in the heart of the young girl who has reached the age of responsibility for fulfilling the commandments a feeling of love for Judaism and its commandments, and to stir up feelings about her Judaism and about being the daughter of a great and holy people. And it is of no concern to us that the gentiles celebrate confirmation of their sons and their daughters. They follow their practices and we follow ours. . . .

There are those who oppose the celebration of a bat mitzvah on the basis of the practices of past generations, who did not have this custom. But this truly is no claim at all, because in our past generations they had no need to be involved in the education of young girls since every single Jew was filled with Torah and the fear of God.

. . . Now it is our duty to concentrate our strength upon the education of young girls. It is a painful matter that in general education, including the study of languages, and secular literature, the physical sciences and the humanities, educators are as concerned about girls as they are about boys, while when it comes to Jewish education, Biblical studies and the ethical literature of the ancient Rabbis, and studying the practical commandments which women are obligated to fulfill, the girls are thoroughly neglected. It is our good fortune that great leaders of our people in the past generation did something about this disgrace and established institutions of Torah and religious strengthening for Jewish girls. They established a great network of *Beis Yaakov* schools [for girls], the most wonderful public demonstration of concern in our time. Simple logic and the duty of fulfilling basic pedagogical principles obliges, almost, that we also celebrate a young girl's reaching the age of responsibility for fulfilling the commandments. And this division made between boys and girls when it comes to celebrating their attaining puberty is a serious blow to the human feelings of the adolescent girl who in other areas already has been accorded the rights of emancipation, so to speak. . . .

. . . [Some maintain that the adoption of bat mitzvah] would strengthen the hands of "the destroyers" among us, who were the first to institute this new practice of bat mitzvah celebration . . . and this is truly a reason for not celebrating the bat mitzvah in the synagogue . . . since celebrating it outside of the synagogue premises makes it apparent that the intention is not one of imitating the practices of heretics. And everyone will see that you do not celebrate the bat mitzvah in the synagogue, as others do, but that you celebrate for the sake of family joy and for educational support of the girl who has reached the age of being responsible for the commandments. . . .

In practice, the matter hinges upon the intent of those who want to institute this practice, whether they intend it for the sake of fulfilling a mitzvah or for the sake of aping the ways of the heretics. Of course it has not escaped my attention that there are those among the pious who [always] forbid and who insist upon stringencies, who in matters of religious practice pay no attention to logical considerations or even to halakhic clarifications; they reach their conclusions solely on the basis of feelings, and the Jewish heart, which clings to the tradition of parents and teachers, and is taken aback at every change in religious practice. . . . However, they should not forget that those who side with the permission for this new practice of celebrating bat mitzvah also have hearts beating with concern for the support of the religious education of Jewish girls. Events of life in our time have created a special need for spiritual strengthening and moral encouragement of girls when they reach the age of obligation to fulfill the commandments. . . .[34]

As a separate ceremony for an individual girl, parallel to the ceremony of bar mitzvah for the individual boy, the first bat mitzvah took place in 1922. The father of the girl was Mordecai M. Kaplan, the founder of the Reconstructionist movement, who decided to institute such a ceremony for his daughter Judith. Many years later she wrote down some of her memories of that occasion:

It was a sunny day early in May of 1922. My two grandmothers, rocking gently in chairs provided for their especial comfort in our house, communed in Yiddish. Their conversation was not intended for my ears, but since Grandma Rubin was slightly hard of hearing, and since both were moved by intense emotion, I could eavesdrop without any difficulty.

"In-law," said my mother's mother, "Talk to your son. Tell him not to do this thing!" "*Mahateineste* [In-law]," said Grandma Kaplan, "you know a son doesn't listen to his mother. You talk to your daughter. Tell her to tell him not to do this thing!"

And what was this terrible deed which my father was about to perform, and which they both sought uselessly to prevent? He was planning to present me in public ceremony in the synagogue as a Bat Mitzvah. . . .

[The following morning] the service proceeded as usual, through *shaharit* [morning prayers], and through the Torah reading. Father was called up for the honor of reading the *Maftir* [concluding portion]. When he finished the *Haftarah* [reading from the Prophets], I was signaled to step forward to a place below the *bimah* at a very respectable distance from the scroll of the Torah, which had already been rolled up and garbed in its mantle. I pronounced the first blessing, and from my own *Humash* [Five Books of Moses] read the selection which Father had chosen for me, continued with the reading of the English translation, and concluded with the closing *brachah* [blessing]. That was it. The scroll was returned to the ark with song and procession, and the service was resumed. No thunder sounded, no lightning struck. The institution of Bat Mitzvah had been born without incident, and the rest of the day was all rejoicing. It was many years before the full privilege of being called to the Torah was granted to a girl, even in the Society for the Advancement of Judaism. By the time my own daughters reached the age of Bat Mitzvah, however, it was taken for granted. They learned to chant both the cantillation of the Torah and of the Haftarah, and each, in turn, read on *Shabbat Kedoshim*, not only the highly ethical code of behavior in the Torah, but the poetic words of the final chapter of the book of Amos.[35]

MARRIAGE

The family is the basic unit of society. Its integrity and purity must be guarded as a sacred obligation. In the Bible and the Talmud, husbands and wives have set obligations to one another.

It is not good that man should be alone. I will make a helper fit for him. [36]

Therefore a man leaves his father and his mother and cleaves to his wife, and they become one flesh. [37]

When a man is newly married, he shall not go out with the army or be charged with any business. He shall be free at home one year, to be happy with his wife, whom he has taken. [38]

A good wife, who can find?
Her worth is far beyond rubies.
The heart of her husband trusts in her,
And no good thing shall he lack.
She provides him with good and not evil
All the days of her life.
She seeks wool and flax
And works them with willing hands.
She is like the merchant ships,
Bringing her food from afar.
She rises when it is still night
To provide food for her household,
A daily portion for her maids.
She considers a field and buys it,
With the fruit of her hands she plants a vineyard.
She girds her loins with power,
And strengthens her arms for her tasks.
She perceives that her business goes well,
Her lamp never goes out at night.
She holds the distaff in her hands,
Her fingers grasp the spindle.
She opens her hand to the needy,
And extends her hands to the poor.
She fears not for her household when it snows,
For her whole household is clothed in crimson.

She makes her own coverings,
Her clothing is fine linen and purple.
Her husband is well known in the city gates
When he takes his place with the land's elders.
She makes cloth and sells it,
Sashes she provides for the merchant.
Strength and splendor are her clothing,
And she cheerfully faces the future.
She opens her mouth with wisdom,
The teaching of kindness guides her tongue.
She attends to the affairs of her household
And eats not the bread of idleness.
Her children step forward and call her blessed,
Her husband sings her praise:
"Many women have done superbly,
But you surpass them all."
Charm is deceptive and beauty is vain,
But a God-fearing woman is to be praised.
Extol her for the fruit of her hands;
Let her deeds praise her in the city gates.[39]

A wife must do the following for her husband: grind flour, bake bread, wash clothes, cook food, give suck to her child, make ready his bed and work in wool. If she brought him one maid-servant [from her father's house], she need not grind or bake or wash. If she brought two maidservants, she need not cook or give her child suck. If she brought three maidservants, she need not make ready his bed or work in wool. If four, she may sit all day and do nothing. Rabbi Eliezer says: Even if she brought one hundred maidservants he should force her to work in wool, for idleness leads to unchastity.[40]

If a man has vowed to have no intercourse with his wife, the School of Shamai say that she may consent for two weeks; the School of Hillel say, for one week. Disciples of the sages, for purposes of study of the Torah, may stay away from their wives for thirty days without their consent. Laborers [whose work takes them to another city] may stay away for one week without their wives' consent. The marital duty enjoined upon husbands by the Torah [. . . he shall not diminish her marital rights . . . Ex. 21:10] is as follows: every day for those that are unemployed, twice a week for laborers, once a week for donkey-drivers [who lead caravans for short distances], once every thirty days for camel drivers, [who lead caravans for longer distances], and once every six months for sailors. This is the ruling of Rabbi Eliezer.[41]

No man may abstain from fulfilling the commandment "Be fruitful and multiply" [Gen. 1:28], unless he already has children. According to the School of Shamai, "children" here means two sons, while the School of Hillel states that it means a son and a daughter, for it is written, "Male and female created He them" [Gen. 5:2]. If he married a woman and lived with her for ten years and she bore no child, he is not permitted to abstain from fulfilling the commandment. If he divorced her, she may marry another, and the second husband may live with her for ten years. If she had a miscarriage, the period of ten years is reckoned from the time of the miscarriage. The duty to be fruitful and multiply is incumbent upon the man but not upon the woman. [This is the view of the Rabbis, in their majority.] Rabbi Johanan ben Baroka dissented, saying: Concerning them both it is written, "God blessed them and God said to them: Be fruitful and multiply" [Gen. 1:28].[42]

Rabbi Eliezer said: Whoever does not fulfill the duty of procreation is compared to a murderer, as it is said: "Whoever sheds the blood of man, by a man shall his blood be shed" [Gen. 9:6], and immediately following it is written "Be fruitful and multiply" [Gen. 9:7]. Rabbi Akiva said: Such a man is compared to one who diminishes the divine image, as it is said "for God made man in His image" [Gen. 9:6] and immediately following it is written "Be fruitful and multiply" [Gen. 9:7]. Ben Azzai said: It is as though he did both.[43]

"I will establish My covenant between Me and you and your descendants after you . . . to be God to you and to your descendants after you" [Gen. 17:7]. If you have no descendants, upon whom will the *Shekhinah* rest? Upon trees and stones?![44]

Rabbi Hanilai said: A man who has no wife lives without joy, without blessing, without good. Without joy, for it is written "you and your household shall rejoice" [Deut. 14:26]. Without blessing, for it is written "that a blessing may rest on your house" [Ezekiel 44:30]. Without good, as it is written "It is not good for man to be alone" [Gen. 2:18]. . . . Rabbi bar Ulla said: He lives without peace. . . . Rabbi Joshua ben Levi said: A man who knows that his wife fears heaven and does not fulfill his marital duty of cohabitation is to be called a sinner. . . . Rabbi Eleazar said: A man who has no wife is not even a man, as it is stated: "Male and female He created them and He named *them* 'man' " [Gen. 5:2]. . . . "I will make man a helper to set over against him" [Gen. 2:18]. If he proves deserving, she will be a helper; if not, she will be against him.[45]

In Palestine, when a man marries, they ask him: "Finds or Found?" "Finds," as it is said "He who finds a wife finds something good" [Prov. 18:22]. "Found," as it is said "I have found a woman whose heart is snares and nets and whose hands are fetters more bitter than death" [Eccles. 7:26].[46]

If a man and wife prove deserving, the *Shekhinah* dwells among them; if not, a fire consumes them.[47]

There is no greater adultery than when a woman thinks of another man while her husband is alone with her.[48]

It is already clear that Judaism does not regard sexual union as a concession to the flesh but as a proper and sacred act. The flesh need not be the enemy of the spiritual life; true spirituality raises the flesh to make it, too, a servant of God. Rabbi Nahman of Bratslav (1772–1811), the great-grandson of the Baal Shem Tov and himself a great figure of the Hasidic movement, is the author of the passage that follows.

The whole world depends on the holiness of the union between man and woman, for the world was created for the sake of God's glory and the essential revelation of His glory comes through the increase of mankind. Man must therefore sanctify himself in order to bring to the world holy people through whom God's glory will be increased. . . .

In truth all experiences of the Divine Unity and Holiness depend on the union between man and woman, for the ultimate meaning of this act is very lofty. Alas, darkness and falsehood tend to grow stronger and to spread so much blackness that we no longer see the truth at all. Union between man and woman becomes so tainted with imperfection that one can almost begin to believe the lie that there is no true holiness in this act.

Union represents the state in which breathing is suspended. It is therefore the opposite of the state of longevity, for, as is well known, many die of this passion. It is also the opposite of wisdom, for many people are driven mad by it. But through the act of union in holiness and purity life is increased and years are added. Through it "man sees life with his wife" and attains wisdom and elevation of the spirit.[49]

A characteristic form of rabbinic legal writing, from its origins two millennia ago, is the responsum, i.e. a question of Jewish law asked of an authority and answered by him in writing, giving his reasons for his decision. The two tragic questions that follow were asked in Kovno, Lithuania, in the Nazi era, of a young rabbi, Ephraim Oshry. That they were asked speaks eloquently of the persistence of Jewish piety under the most extreme of circumstances; that they had to be asked at all shouts out deafeningly the tale of man's inhumanity and of Jewry's suffering.

QUESTION: On the twentieth day of Iyar, 5712 (1942), the wicked ones [i.e. the Germans] published a decree that should they discover a Jewish woman pregnant they would put her to death. I was asked whether it was permissible for Jewish women imprisoned in the ghetto to use contraceptives to prevent pregnancy and thus to avoid endangering their lives.

RESPONSE: In *Yebamot* 12b we read that three categories of women may use contraceptives—a minor [under twelve years of age], a pregnant woman, and a nursing mother. A minor may, lest she become pregnant and, as a result, die. A pregnant woman may, lest she be aborted. And a nursing mother may, lest her child be prematurely weaned and die. . . . In the *Tosafot* it is written that women who are not in any of these categories are forbidden to use contraceptives and willfully destroy seed, even though the obligation "to be fruitful and multiply" is incumbent upon men, not women. . . .

In the case before us, there certainly would be danger to life, for if it would become known to the impure murderers, may they be cursed, that a woman is pregnant, they would put her to death. [As earlier authorities have stated] why should we forbid them the use of contraceptives since in this instance there is not what could be called willful destruction of seed? The latter term applies only when it is fitting to sow this seed. Since this is not a place in which it is fitting to do so, this is not to be termed "destruction of seed." Under these circumstances, a woman is obligated to use contraceptives when a pregnancy would endanger life. There is then no ban of destruction of seed in this case. . . . Furthermore [the discovery by the Germans of pregnant Jewish women, implying disobedience to their decree] can have bad consequences for the entire community. Thus everyone must agree that in this case it is permissible to use contraceptives during intercourse.[50]

QUESTION: Immediately after we were liberated from the ghetto I was asked an important and dreadful question which concerned not only the person who came to me but also many other Jewish women who survived the atrocities committed against them when they were seized by the oppressors and their bodies ravished by German officers, may their name be cursed.

This is the question: A young woman of good family, one of the respected families of Kovno, came to me weeping. She was very unhappy and without comfort, for she, like many of our poor sisters, had been seized and humiliated by the accursed Germans. In addition to abusing her body they had tattooed on her arm the legend: "Whore for Hitler's Troops."

After liberation she had succeeded in finding her husband and the two of them intended to renew their marriage and on the pillars of purity and sanctity to build a proper Jewish home. They wanted to build a family again, since they had lost all their children at the hands of the Germans. However, when her husband saw the dreadful words tattooed on her arm he was taken aback, declaring that they had to clarify whether she was permitted to him or not, since, when the enemy had seized her and had done with her as they pleased, perhaps there had been an element of consent in her submission. Thus she came to me to ask what to do, her eyes asking mercy.

RESPONSE: Maimonides [*Hilkhot Na-arah B'tulah, halakhah* 2], in differentiating between one who seduces and one who rapes, states that the former does so with the woman's consent while the latter acts against her will. If it occurred in the field we assume that she was forced unless witnesses testify that she consented. If it occurred in the city we assume that she was seduced since she did not call out, unless witnesses testify that she had been forced [e.g. he threatened her with a sword, saying he would kill her if she called out]. . . .

The case before us occurred in the city and since she did not cry out you might assume that she consented. However everyone knows that the sword of the oppressors was constantly held over each and every one of these women. Calling out would have been of no avail, for who would have interrupted them? Since there was no escape for these unfortunate women, this case is surely stronger than that cited by Maimonides [when he states that even in the city the girl is considered to have been forced if witnesses testify that she was threatened with the sword], for in the case before us we are all witnesses that the sword was constantly over their heads and that whoever refused was put to death. Thus surely this poor woman is permitted to her husband and there is absolutely no suspicion that she was at all co-operative, for she also saw what they did to Jewish men, women and children, that they slaughtered them without mercy. Surely these oppressors were abominable in her eyes and she could not have willingly consented in any way to lie with them. . . .

This leads to the conclusion that in our case she definitely is believed when she states that she was forced. For in addition [to what has been cited above] many authorities are of the opinion that even in the city, and even in the absence of witnesses, a woman is believed when she claims "I was forced."

Far be it from anyone to cast aspersion on these honorable Jewish women. On the contrary, it is our duty to proclaim the reward that they will be granted by "the One who hears the plea of the destitute." . . . He will heal their sorrow and bestow upon them the blessings of womanhood. . . . We must avoid causing them sorrow and anguish. There are instances in which women in similar circumstances were divorced by their husbands. Alas for us that such a thing has happened in our time.

In my opinion there is no need to make any effort to remove the contemning legend from the bodies of such women. On the contrary, it should be preserved. It should be considered not a sign of disgrace and shame but a symbol of honor and courage . . . and an enduring reminder that we shall yet see the defeat of the transgressors from whose face is blotted any human semblance. They are like beasts of the forest and voracious wolves, hastening to spill innocent blood and to put to death the pious and the upright. This legend upon the arms of innocent and pure souls will always remind us of that which is written in the Torah of Moses, the man of God, "Sing aloud, O you nations, of His people; for He avenges the blood of His servants, and renders vengeance to His adversaries" [Deut. 32:43].[51]

Here is the text of the wedding ceremony. In Jewish law anyone may perform a wedding, for Jews are essentially married by consent. The passing of a ring, or any object of value, from groom to bride represents a contract which is valid if it is witnessed by two other adult male Jews. The prayers which surround this act represent the ancient engagement rituals, before it, and seven blessings said on behalf of the congregation afterward, if a *minyan* (a minimum quorum of ten male adults) is present. Nowadays the wedding ritual is conventionally read by a rabbi.

> You who come are blessed in the name of the Lord.
> May He who is supreme in might, blessing and glory bless this bridegroom and this bride.

> *A cup of wine is filled and held by the officiant who recites:*
> Praised are You, Lord our God, King of the universe who creates the fruit of the vine.
> Praised are You, Lord our God, King of the universe whose mitzvot [commandments] add holiness to our lives, who commanded us concerning forbidden marriages, who forbade us those to whom we are not married, and permitted us those married to us by means of the bridal canopy and the wedding ceremony. Praised are You, Lord who sanctifies His people Israel through the wedding ceremony beneath the bridal canopy.

> *The first cup of wine is presented first to the bridegroom and then to the bride. The bridegroom then places the ring on the right forefinger of his bride and says:*
> By this ring you are consecrated to me as my wife in accordance with the law of Moses and the people Israel.

> *The second cup of wine is held by the officiant and/or other participants who recite:*
> Praised are You, Lord our God, King of the universe who creates the fruit of the vine.
> Praised are You, Lord our God, King of the universe who created all things for His glory.
> Praised are You, Lord our God, King of the universe, Creator of mortals.
> Praised are You, Lord our God, King of the universe who created man and woman in His image, fashioning woman in the likeness of man, preparing for man a mate, that together they might perpetuate life. Praised are You, Lord, Creator of mortals.
> May Zion, once barren, rejoice as her children are gathered

to her in joy. Praised are You, Lord who causes Zion to rejoice in her children.

Grant joy to these loving companions, as You did for Your first creatures in the Garden of Eden. Praised are You, Lord who grants joy to bride and groom.

Praised are You, Lord our God, King of the universe who created joy and gladness, bride and groom, pleasure, song, delight and happiness, love and harmony, peace and companionship. Lord our God, may there always be heard in the cities of Judah and in the streets of Jerusalem voices of joy and gladness, voices of bride and groom, the jubilant voices of those joined in marriage under the bridal canopy, the voices of young people feasting and singing. Praised are You, Lord who causes the groom and bride to rejoice. [52]

GENDER

In rabbinic Judaism, the law (halakhah) makes a fundamental distinction between men and women. Men are obligated to obey all the commandments, both negative and positive; women must obey the negative commandments but they are relieved of all of the positive commandments which are to be performed at a set time. So, the daily prayers, which are recited morning, afternoon, and evening, must be said by men; women may say them if they wish, but the busy wife and mother need not, for she is not free to stop from her duties at the exact times of prayer. Through the ages the effect of this distinction was to create great insistence on the religious education of boys and much less on that of girls. Women who were learned in the law existed in every century, but they were always exceptional.

A second element in the Talmudic and medieval definitions of the status of women was the fear that free mingling with men would lead to sexual transgressions. Men ought to have their minds on the study of Torah; easy association with women would distract them. The separation of sexes in prayer is an ancient restriction, even though there is evidence that there was not complete separation on all occasions in the laymen's section of the Temple in Jerusalem. Every synagogue building that has survived in Europe, including those built in medieval Spain before the expulsion, contains a separate gallery or section for women.

Perhaps the most serious distinction between men and women is in their status before the law. With very few exceptions, women are not accepted as witnesses. In the marriage relationship, the husband was commanded to love and honor his wife more than himself and to treat her with gentleness, but ultimately his wishes prevailed. In the law of the Talmud, income from the wife's labor, or even from her dowry, belongs to the husband. The most painful of all the restrictions for women is in the law of divorce. The *get*, the bill of divorce, is given by the husband to the wife and not in reverse. Even if a civil divorce has been granted, the wife cannot claim a *get* as her due. The husband must agree, and if he refuses, her remarriage is permanently blocked in Orthodox halakhah. In Talmudic and medieval times, wherever rabbinic tribunals had some powers of constraint, they might jail the husband to force him to initiate a *get*. In contemporary Israel, where rabbinic courts control matters of personal status for Jews, such action is taken on occasion. But in the Diaspora, where rabbinic tribunals have no powers of enforcement, the inequality of women in cases of divorce has remained an acute problem for those who are obedient to the halakhah.

In modern times, the role of women in society began to change even among the Orthodox. Girls were attending public schools, and women were working outside the home. The imbalance between increasing secular education and the little that girls were being taught about the Jewish religion became a problem, even for the most Orthodox believers. Rabbi Yehiel Weinberg, in permitting bat-mitzvah celebrations (see above, in the section on Bar Mitzvah, Confirmation, and Bat Mitzvah), was not the first Orthodox authority to justify new action in a changing world. Rabbi Issacher Dov Rokeah, who was the Rebbe of Belz in the first decades of this century, was notable even among the religious leaders of Polish Jewry for his uncompromising opposition to any change. Nonetheless, he approved of the initiative of Sarah Schenirer to found schools for the intensive education of girls. She began with one school in Krakow, and from it grew the network of Beth Jacob schools:

I went back to Krakow in 1917 and invited a small group of observant women to listen to my plan. They approved. I was afraid that even if adults were excited about my idea, the younger generation would laugh at it. But I persisted. One Saturday afternoon I lectured to about forty girls on *Pirke Avot* ("The Sayings of the Fathers"). Dwelling on the passage "and make a hedge about the Torah," I spoke about the hedges and fences with which our sages surrounded the commandments. The girls, I could see, were amused. I could see their ironic smiles. My talk was received coldly, mockingly. I knew how hard was the road I had marked out for myself, but I did not give up. . . .

The days turned into weeks; my plan began to take shape. The girls' organization I had founded began to grow; yet I feared it would not bring the results I hoped for. Was it possible to influence grown girls who had ideas of their own? I decided to move in another direction. One must begin with little children. A young shoot bends more easily. Orthodox schools should be organized, in which girls could be educated in the spirit of the ancient Jewish people. The idea preoccupied me. I wrote my brother, asking advice. At first he cautioned that I would become involved in disputes with the Jewish parties already operating their own school systems. But he suggested that I come to him in Marienbad, where we could visit the Belzer rebbe and ask his advice. Though I could ill afford the trip, my joy was so great I went. My brother took me to the rebbe, to whom he submitted a note explaining: "My sister would like to guide and teach Jewish girls in the ways of Judaism and Torah." Then the rebbe gave me his blessing and his wishes for my success. It was as though new energy poured into me.

In 1917 I finally had my own school. Who could understand how I felt with twenty-five beaming little faces before me? Once I had sewn clothing for many of them. Now I was giving them spiritual raiment. The school expanded from day to day. Soon I had forty pupils. The children were choice material; they had not yet tasted sin. They learned that man does not live by bread alone and that everything comes from God's mouth. They came to know that only by serving God sincerely could they live truly happy lives.

As for me, I am so absorbed in my work nothing else exists. I do not notice how the hours, the days, the weeks pass. But this is only the beginning.[53]

This opinion of the Rebbe of Belz was accepted by most of the Orthodox Jewish leaders. In Lithuania, Rabbi Israel Meir Kagan, known as the Hafetz Hayyim, expressed his opinions about teaching Jewish texts to women in a letter written in 1933 (the last year of his life):

> When I heard that pious and God-fearing people have organized themselves to found Beth Jacob schools to teach Torah, the fear of God, and good conduct to Jewish girls, I was moved to respond to this good work with warmest congratulations and with prayers that they succeed in their task. This effort is particularly important in our day when heresy, God save us, dominates everywhere, and all kinds of secular ideologies are capturing Jewish souls. Everyone who harbors the fear of God in his heart is commanded to enroll his daughter in these new schools. All of the concerns and supposed implications which are evoked by the prohibitions against teaching one's daughter Torah have no force in our day. . . . But this is not the place to explain at length. Our present generation is unlike previous generations. In older days, every Jewish home was suffused with tradition; fathers and mothers followed the ways of the Torah and of the faith and [the women] read the *Tz'enah U-r'enah* [the translation into Yiddish of the Five Books of Moses, with pious additions]. Alas, in this sinful time, it is no longer so. Therefore, we must use all of our spiritual energy and resolve to increase such schools, to attract everyone whom we can possibly save.[54]

In the next half-century, intensive religious education of girls became the norm among all the Orthodox. Some remained unwilling to teach girls the Talmud, for they were not obligated by all of its laws, but even that barrier began to fall. The Rebbe of Lubavitch, Rabbi Menahem Mendel Schneerson, has argued that women need to know the classic texts because their obligations include not only the commandments which are incumbent upon them, but also, most fundamentally, the inner spiritual essence of the divine teaching.

> When G-d told Moshe to prepare the Jews to receive the Torah, He commanded him, "This is what you shall say to the House of Ya'akov and speak to the children of Israel" [*Shemos* 19:3]. Our Sages explain that the "House of Ya'akov" refers to Jewish women, and the "the children of Israel," to the men [*Mechilta*, quoted

by Rashi in his commentary to the above verse.]; i.e. G-d told Moshe to approach the women first.

This order implies a sense of priority. For Torah to be perpetuated among the Jewish people, precedence must be given to Jewish women. Giving such prominence to women may appear questionable in view of several traditional attitudes. Those attitudes, however, are narrow and restrictive when judged by the objective standard of Torah law and certainly may be considered so within the context of the application of these standards to contemporary society.

Torah law requires a woman to study all the laws and concepts necessary to observe the mitzvos which she is obligated to fulfill [Shulchan Aruch HaRav, Hilchos Talmud Torah 1:14]. This encompasses a vast scope of knowledge, including the laws of Shabbos, Kashrus, Taharas HaMishpochoh [the code governing sexual relations], and many other areas of Jewish law. Indeed, many men would be happy if their Torah knowledge would be as complete.

Also, among the subjects which a woman must know is P'nimiyus HaTorah, Torah's mystic dimension. A woman is obligated to fulfill the mitzvos of knowing G-d, loving Him, fearing Him, and the like. Indeed, the obligation to fulfill these mitzvos is constant, incumbent upon us every moment of the day [See the introductory letter to Sefer HaChinuch]. The fulfillment of these mitzvos is dependent on the knowledge of spiritual concepts as implied by the verse, "Know the G-d of your fathers and serve Him with a full heart [I Chronicles 28:9]." The study of P'nimiyus HaTorah is necessary to achieve this knowledge.

Throughout the generations, we have seen women with immense Torah knowledge. The Talmud mentions Bruriah, the daughter of Rabbi Chaninah ben Tradyon and the wife of Rabbi Meir [Pesachim 62b]. Throughout the Middle Ages, we find records of many women who corrected their husbands' Torah texts [Letters of the Previous Rebbe, Vol 5, p. 336]. In his memoirs, the Previous Rebbe describes how the Alter Rebbe's family put a special emphasis on women's Torah knowledge and the Previous Rebbe educated his own daughters in this spirit.[55]

The new attitude among the Orthodox to the education of girls was a break of precedent with the customs of past centuries. But, no injunctions of the halakhah were being nullified. The situation in Jewish law remained unchanged even for women, many of whom, even among the pious, were leading very modern lives. The inequity in the law of divorce was especially rankling. It was first confronted in the "middle-of-the-road" traditionalist circles of Conservative Judaism. One of the most learned Conservative rabbis, Louis M. Epstein (1887–1949), a notable Talmudist who possessed Orthodox ordination, suggested a premarital agreement which would give protection to the *agunah*, the Jewish woman who was denied a *get*.

> . . . It is not unthinkable that a daring, progressive rabbinate, basing itself on Talmudic precedent, will some day once and for all declare Biblical marriage at an end and usher in a well regulated marriage that is free from the encumbrances of the present Jewish marriage.
>
> But who can wait for that day? The *agunot* cannot afford to wait. And evidently they do not wait. They defy Jewish law, and the purity of the Jewish family is being broken down. Needless to say that something must be done immediately, lest we lose the last thread of respect for Jewish law.
>
> We have applied ourselves to this problem, keeping in mind one objective, to invest a court with the power of granting a divorce to the wife without the consent and in the absence of the husband. We find that this is possible on the basis of the existing halakhah. It may be achieved by the husband's making out an instrument at the time of the marriage authorizing the court to grant his wife a divorce in his absence and appointing the necessary witnesses and agents for the purpose.
>
> This requires a brief and simple ceremony which must take place prior to the marriage. . . . If at any time later the wife is deserted, she goes to the *Bet-Din* (rabbinic court) named in the instrument and presents that document and the *Bet-Din* causes the divorce to be given to her without consulting the husband, if the case merits such action.[56]

Epstein's suggestion was rejected by almost all Orthodox authorities, not because it was unsound in Talmudic law, but because a rabbinic court of Conservative rabbis had no standing in the mind of the Orthodox. The Conservative rabbis reconsidered the issue of the *agunah* at a convention a generation later, in 1951. Rabbi David Aronson (1894–1988) made a more radical suggestion, that rabbinic courts make use of the power which the Talmud had once ascribed to them, the right to dissolve marriages. Indeed, he even cited a medieval precedent, in an opinion by Rabbi Isaac ben Sheshet, allowing the dissolution of marriages by community elders, if a couple was married without their consent and against their will.

> There is a rabbinic concept which is of prime importance to the consideration of our problem. The principle, "whosoever betroths a wife himself does so with the implicit understanding that his act is in agreement with the rabbinical enactments and acceptable to the rabbis," is applied not to annul a marriage by validating a bill of divorce. The implication is that the rabbinic authority to regulate the conditions of Kiddushin, of betrothal, contains *ipso facto* the authority to regulate the forms and conditions of the *Get*. . . .
>
> We must interpret [this principle] to mean that it is the accepted principle of the rabbis today that when a man marries he ought to be and wants to be fair to the woman, and that he, therefore, agrees to extend to her the same rights and freedom and protection that he wants for himself. In other words, if the marriage does not work out, he subjects himself to the same rabbinic binding and unbinding authority, and that the *Bet-Din* may free the woman under the same conditions as it does him. This becomes binding upon the man and woman who enter into the marriage union according to the law of Moses and the people of Israel, in two ways:
>
> a) It becomes a condition of the marriage, giving the *Bet-Din* the authority to dissolve the marriage when in their opinion conditions make this process best. (There's no reflection on them or children.)
>
> b) It implies the power of a *Bet-Din* to arrange for the writing of the *Get*, when this process is deemed best. [57]

The renewed concern in the Conservative movement over the question of the *agunah* evoked a proposal by Professor Saul Lieberman (1898–1983), the senior Talmudic authority on the faculty of the Jewish Theological Seminary. He suggested a premarital agreement in which bride and groom both agree to abide by the decisions of a rabbinic tribunal. This pre-marital agreement was supposedly enforceable in civil law as a contract between the parties, who could be ordered by civil judges to abide by its terms. This addition to the ancient *Ketubah*, the pre-marital agreement between groom and bride which has existed since Talmudic times (in which the groom promises, essentially, to support the bride and not to divorce her without financial compensation), was adopted by the Conservative movement in 1954:

> And in solemn assent to their mutual responsibilities and love, the Bridegroom and Bride have declared: As evidence of our desire to enable each other to live in accordance with the Jewish law of marriage throughout our lifetime, we, the Bride and Bridegroom, attach our signatures to this Ketubah, and hereby agree to recognize the *Bet-Din* of the Rabbinical Assembly and the Jewish Theological Seminary of America, or its duly appointed representatives, as having authority to counsel us in the light of Jewish Tradition which requires husband and wife to give each other complete love and devotion, and to summon either party at the request of the other, in order to enable the party so requesting to live in accordance with the standards of the Jewish law of marriage throughout his or her lifetime.[58]

Within the Orthodox community, there had been some stirrings towards a comparable solution to the problems raised by halakhic practice in the matter of divorce. Rabbi Eliezer Berkovits, of Chicago and Jerusalem, took the lead in proposing a pre-marital agreement not essentially different from the Lieberman proposal, to be enforced by Orthodox rabbinic tribunals, but that suggestion has not been accepted. The discomfort over the status of women in Jewish law has, however, been growing among the Orthodox, especially among those elements where women play an equal role in all aspects of life, including politics and even religious thought. Berkovits was among those who spoke for this attitude at a conference of the progressive wing of the religious Zionists in Israel in 1983:

> It appears to me that there are two decisions of Maimonides which very nearly summarize woman's position in society during the era of the Talmud and, after that, during the Middle Ages. He writes, in the section on Gender Relations in his legal code: "It is a dishonor for a woman to keep appearing in public, sometimes outside her door and sometimes walking in the street. Her husband must forbid such conduct and not allow her to leave the house more than once or twice a month, as needed. The real beauty of the woman is to sit in a corner of her house, as it is

written, 'All the honor of the king's daughter is within.' " Maimonides' second injunction is: "Every woman is to wash her husband's face, hands, and legs, to pour his drink, and to make his bed. She must serve her husband in such tasks as giving him water, or implements, or removing them, as necessary. She is not, however, compelled to offer such services to his father or his son."

Clearly, in our day we have no sympathy or understanding for such injunctions. It indeed is important to know that the Rabbis of the Talmud were themselves aware that this definition of gender relations was unjust. They knew that the command to woman to sit at home was equivalent to jailing her and that thus her status was no higher than that of a slave to her husband. In various ways the Rabbis of the Talmud tried to improve her lot, but basically the Rabbinic attitude remained that "women are lightheaded" and that neither their word nor their judgment is dependable.

I think that apologetics will not help us here. We have reached the point where we must face the truth: this [Rabbinic] attitude is not based on the Torah. The stories about Sarah and Rebecca [in the Bible] describe clever women who possessed great force of character. . . . The negative judgments in Talmudic and medieval sources on the nature of women are rooted in social realities that are different from those of our time. What we regard as offensive to the dignity of women was not so regarded in Talmudic times. . . . It is nonetheless important to understand that these views and the laws that were based upon them (such as the rulings by Maimonides) are not the judgment of the Torah on woman and her nature, but the opinions of past ages. Now that those ages are gone, the reasons for such negative judgments are no more, and the restrictions based on vanished social circumstances are null.[59]

Nevertheless, all elements of the Orthodox community have continued to insist upon separation of the sexes in the synagogue. The Orthodox position has become firmer and more univocal in recent decades. In 1951, a quarrel began in a synagogue in Cincinnati, Adath Israel. For at least a half-century, men and women had been separated by an aisle at prayer, but there was no partition (*mehitzah*) as prescribed by Orthodox practice. A large majority of the congregation voted to introduce mixed seating, by amending the original constitution of the congregation, which had defined it as Orthodox. The minority insisted that congregational traditions were unalterable, and it sued the majority in civil court. Depositions by rabbinic experts were introduced by both sides. Rabbi Jacob Agus, arguing for family seating, said "that in a [medieval] society where so strict a code [of separation] governs the social relations between men and women, it is quite natural to have a balcony or partition in the synagogue; and, by the same token, it is unnatural to retain such practice in the synagogue when the other practices constituting its social context no longer prevail." Those who opposed change were supported by two major rabbinic leaders of the Orthodox community, Rabbi Eliezer Silver and Rabbi Joseph Soloveitchik. Both declared the mingling of sexes in the synagogue to be an infraction of Jewish law, though they agreed that the lack of a physical barrier (*mehitzah*) between the sexes did not put Adath Israel "in the class of a Reform temple."

The majority of Adath Israel won in court and was given the right to amend the practices of the congregation. But, the issues that were ventilated in this quarrel were becoming moot. Among the Orthodox, there was ever less tolerance of anything other than complete separation of the sexes with a *mehitzah*. This was the view of Rabbi Moshe Feinstein who declared in 1949 that a synagogue with a partition less than four and one-half feet high is unfit for Orthodox worship. The Union of Orthodox Rabbis of the United States and Canada ruled as follows in a widely distributed pamphlet (as cited in *Conservative Judaism* of Fall, 1956, pp. 15–16):

> A synagogue that does not have a proper *mehitzah* is not a kosher synagogue, and it is not permitted to pray there. It is not allowed to give any support, moral or financial, to any synagogue which has no proper *mehitzah*. If a person lives in an area where there is only a synagogue without a *mehitzah*, he should endeavor to organize a *minyan* in a private home, and if this is impossible, he should pray without a *minyan* rather than attend services in a non-kosher synagogue.

The Orthodox were not unique in moving to create small, private prayer circles, rather than worship in unacceptable synagogues. In the 1960s and the 1970s, an increasing number of younger people in the Conservative movement were forming *havurot* (associations) to pray and study together away from the formalism of large synagogues. Sitting together at services was no longer enough for them, for all the roles in the conduct of services were still monopolized by men. Almost all of the *havurot* insisted on total equality of both genders in the conduct of religious services. These innovations reflected the feminism of the 1960s and 1970s, which had affected many Jewish women. Some had simply abandoned the Jewish religion as hopelessly patriarchal; others had remained, to remake Judaism and the Jewish community in a more egalitarian mode. These women were aware that all the other religious traditions, and the existing secular society, were just as patriarchal in their basic structures. The feminist struggle needed to be conducted on all fronts.

Some of the Jewish feminists, such as Blu Greenberg, were trying to remain Orthodox. Others, such as Susan Weidman Schneider, came from the more liberal wings of Judaism. Greenberg hoped that Orthodoxy itself could find ways of responding to feminism:

. . . How, in fact, can we transmit messages about sexual identity if not through distinct functions? Just when I concluded that it borders on obscenity not to count a woman as part of a *mezuman* (the quorum for grace after meals)—a woman who has organized, prepared and served a meal to her family—I would find my own teenage sons, who are (mostly) models of filial love and respect, vehemently disagreeing.

All this makes me quite vulnerable. In fact, I find it hard to resist writing my own critique of the work. It's an easy enough task, given the inconsistencies: calling for equality and freedom of choice, yet maintaining that there are primary and secondary models of behavior for men and women; calling for specific mitzvot for male and female without satisfactorily fleshing them out; calling for a love for halakhah and tradition, yet subtly tearing away at parts of its intricate tapestry, perhaps weakening other threads in the process. And yet . . .

Perhaps this is the only legitimate response one can make at this time: a series of tentative remarks. If feminism is a revolution, as I believe it is, and Judaism is and always has been the rock-bottom source of a Jew's values, thoughts, feelings, actions, mores, laws, and loves—how else can one respond to and be part of that turbulent encounter but with a stammer, one step forward and half a step backward. I envy those who can say, "This is halakhah. That's it!" Or, "These are the absolute new truths, and nothing less will do!" I envy, but I also suspect, their unexamined complacency. I suspect that their fear is even greater than mine; therefore, they must keep the lid on even tighter and show no ambivalence, no caution, and no confusion. . . .

. . . Transition women, like myself, are taking everything less for granted and finding each step more exhilarating.[60]

Susan Weidman Schneider was much less restrained in her criticism of the inherited Jewish tradition, but she too remained indissolubly linked to that heritage:

Interpretation of these texts and, indeed, rulings on how to live a Jewish life on a day-to-day basis have until now been made exclusively by Jewish men in a setting usually closed to women: a house of study, court of law, synagogue, or boardroom. These interpretations have direct bearing on the lives of women, yet we were systematically denied the right to participate when decisions were made. Some women believe that our foremothers, strong Jewish women that they must have been, must surely have contributed to this process in ways unrecorded by male historians, as they cared for the rabbis or scholars or scribes who were their fathers or brothers or husbands, offering a slice of women's experience along with the chicken soup. If this informal participation did exist, we have been denied the knowledge of what is male and what is female contribution to formal Judaism as it has come down to us. Lacking this knowledge, we must assume, as most Jews have, that women were excluded from the process of creating Judaism as we know it today, and therefore were excluded from the partnership with the Divine which Jews believe will bring about the repair of the world. . . .

With the concept of women's essential otherness so ubiquitous in Jewish law and practice, the tension (and the source of inspiration) for those who are evaluating women's role comes from the desire *not* to cast aside all aspects of Judaism but to move beyond its limited view of women, so that our lives and Jewish life can be richer and fuller. It isn't easy for us to reconcile feminist strivings for equality with the patriarchal historical core of Judaism. A woman feeling herself bound by tradition might choose to deny her feminism, while a more radical feminist might want to move away from Judaism altogether. But for women morally committed to self-determination, yet at the same time feeling inexorably linked to something in the very tradition they fault, reinterpreting the tradition itself is the alternative to self-denying acceptance or wholesale rejection.[61]

The ultimate issue of gender equality is the ordination of women as rabbis. The Reform movement had insisted, from its very beginnings in the middle of the nineteenth century, that men and women have the same status in the synagogue. The question of the ordination of women was first debated in 1922 at a meeting of the Central Conference of American Rabbis. The outcome was negative. The words of one representative from each side of the debate follow, excerpted from the presentations of Rabbi Jacob Z. Lauterbach and Rabbi David Neumark, respectively:

. . . traditional principles debarring women from the rabbinate were not formulated in an illiberal spirit by the Rabbis of old or out of a lack of appreciation of women's talents and endowments. Indeed the Rabbis of old entertained a high opinion of womanhood and frequently expressed their admiration for woman's ability and appreciated her great usefulness in religious work. Thus, e.g., they say, "God has endowed woman with a finer appreciation and a better understanding than man" (Niddah 45b); . . . "It was due to the pious women of that generation that the Israelites were redeemed from Egypt (Sotah)." . . . These and many other sayings could be cited from Rabbinic literature in praise of woman, her equality to man and, in some respects, superiority to him. . . . But with all their appreciation of woman's fine talents and noble qualities, the Rabbis of old have also recognized that man and woman have each been assigned by the Torah certain spheres of activity, involving special duties. . . .

[The fact that the woman] was exempt from certain obligations and religious duties necessarily excluded her from the privilege of acting as the religious leader or representative of the congregation (sheliach tzibbur). She could not represent the congregation in the performance of certain religious functions since, according to the Rabbinic principle, one who is not personally obligated to perform a certain duty cannot perform that duty on behalf of others and certainly cannot represent the congregation in the performance of such duties. . . .

Shall we adhere to this tradition, or shall we separate ourselves from Catholic Israel and introduce a radical innovation which would necessarily create a distinction between the title Rabbi as held by a Reform rabbi and the title Rabbi in general? . . . We are still carrying on the activity of the Rabbis of old who traced their authority through a chain of tradition to Moses and the Elders associated with him, even though in many points we interpret our Judaism in a manner quite different from theirs. . . . The ordination which we give to our disciples carries with it, for our time and generation, the same authority which marked the ordination given by [Rabbi] Judah Hanasi to Abba Areka or the ordination given by any teacher in Israel to his disciples throughout all the history of Judaism. We should therefore not jeopardize the hitherto indisputable authoritative character of our ordination. . . .

It has been rightly said that the woman who enters a profession must make her choice between following her chosen profession or the calling of mother and home-maker. . . .

In [the] important activity of the rabbi—exercising a wholesome influence upon the congregation—the woman rabbi would be deficient. The woman in the rabbinical office could not expect the man to whom she was married to be merely a helpmate to her, assisting her in rabbinical activities. And even if she could find such a man, willing to take a subordinate position in the family, the influence upon the families in the congregation of such an arrangement in the home and in the family life of the rabbi would not be very wholesome. . . . And there is, to my mind, no injustice done to woman by excluding her from this office. There are many avenues open to her if she chooses to do religious or educational work. I can see no reason why we should make this radical departure from traditional practice except the specious argument that we are modern men and, as such, we recognize the full equality of women to men. . . .

(Neumark:) . . . the traditional functions of the rabbi have nothing to do with representation of the congregation in the performance of certain religious duties from which women are freed. There are certain categories of men, such as those who are deformed and afflicted with certain bodily defects, who could not act as readers but could be rabbis for decisions in ritual matters and questions of law. . . .

. . . women are not free from the duties of prayer, grace after meals, and Kiddush, and they can read for others (cf. Mishnah and Gemara, *Berakhot* 20a–b). . . . Thus, even in our modern conception of the function of the rabbi, which includes reading [the service], a woman can act as representative according to traditional law.

. . . If a woman is to be debarred from the rabbinate in Orthodox Judaism because she cannot serve as a reader, then the only logical consequence would be that Reform Judaism, which has decided in favor of the woman reader, should disregard the Orthodox attitude, and admit women to the rabbinate. . . .

The entire question reduces itself to this: women are already doing most of the work that the ordained woman rabbi is expected to do, but they do it without preparation and without authority. I consider it rather a duty of the authorities to put an end to the prevailing anarchy by giving women a chance to acquire adequate education and an authoritative standing in all branches of religious work. The practical difficulties cannot be denied. But they will be worked out the same way as in other professions, especially in the teaching profession, from the kindergarten to post-graduate schools. . . . You cannot treat the Reform rabbinate from the Orthodox point of view. . . .[62]

The ordination of women in the Reform movement did not begin until 1972. The debate on this issue soon began within the Conservative movement, where women were increasingly being permitted to occupy all of the other roles in the synagogue. The ordination of women was accepted by the Jewish Theological Seminary in 1984. The attitude which led to this decision was best defined by the senior member of the faculty of the Seminary, Rabbi Simon Greenberg:

The Conservative approach affirms, among other things, that although the roots of Jewish law are planted in Heaven, its branches and its fruits grew and are growing on earth, and that their form and their rationale are determined by the sages and interpreters of each generation. "Jephthah in his generation is like Samuel in his generation" (*Rosh Hashanah* 25b). They are influenced by the time and the place in which they function. . . .

We are living at a time and in an environment when generalizations such as "women's intellect is of little account" are not accepted by the overwhelming majority of the literate population. I assume that there is no one on the Seminary Faculty who accepts them. The process of equating the rights of women in all areas of life to the rights of men in Western democratic society has to the best of our knowledge reached a level unprecedented in human history, and we must decide whether our tradition is capable of assimilating this process, and whether we should encourage, slow down or reject its assimilation. In the time and place in which we live the wall excluding women from the multifaceted activities in our society is almost totally destroyed. First and foremost, we live in a society in which it is usual for boys and girls, and men and women, to be found in each other's company from their earliest years until old age, in kindergarten, at the university, on the street, at work, in economic and political life, in the theatre, at resorts, at sport stadiums, and so forth. History does not know of a society like ours in which women not only participate in every profession but also play a role in them as equals among equals. . . . The presence of women under all sorts of conditions and in all circumstances is among the most common experiences of our lives. Even though their appearance as rabbis will be unusual for a time, their presence as women among men will not be unusual at all. I assume that the tradition is capable of assimilating the process since its traces have been prominent in the tradition from its beginnings, from God's words to Abraham—"Whatever Sarah tells you, listen to her voice" (Genesis 21:12)—to the establishment of the "Shulamis" schools [for girls]. . . .

It seems to me that not one of the members of the Seminary Faculty believes that the present status of women in Jewish law adds honor and dignity to Jewish law. Not one of them would point to these laws as a proof that we are "a great nation which has just statutes and laws" (Deut. 4:8). And I cannot accept the idea that the present legal status of women must remain as it is until the appearance of Elijah. Neither my mind nor my heart is able to accept a legal system which has no way of correcting its own apparent shortcomings.[63]

The last word in this discussion of gender belongs properly to one of the most eloquent contemporary Jewish women, the novelist and essayist Anne Roiphe:

In Jewish life it seems that the forces that separate male and female, that mark them as different creatures, that distort the common humanness of both, have won ancient victories; only now, post-Holocaust, with the new threat of assimilation at the doorstep, with the infiltration of ideas from Socialists, Zionists, the mavericks of the Jewish and non-Jewish world, are there the beginnings of a fight being made to change the status of women within the Jewish religion. The loss of women scholars, the loss of female poets and psalm-makers, of a female Rashi or Maimonides, can never be replaced, but perhaps now at a point when a new covenant can be drawn . . . women can be given justice.[64]

HOMOSEXUALITY

Jewish texts since the Bible have prohibited homosexual behavior. Homoerotic conduct by women was thought to be minimal, and was treated with lenience, as an offense against public policy, but not as a mortal sin. The texts, therefore, deal largely with men. Some of the specific rulings have changed from time to time. For example, in the second century Rabbi Judah the Prince, in his legal code, the Mishnah, forbade two males from sharing one blanket [*Kiddushin*, 4:14]. Yet the Gemara, the elaboration of that code, sees no reason to forbid such behavior since Jews "are not under the suspicion of homosexuality" [*Kiddushin*, 82a]. Both these clashing views were reasserted by later authorities in the Middle Ages. The first known modern responsum about a homosexual's standing in the *halakhah* was written by Rabbi Abraham Isaac Kook in the second decade of this century, in what was then Palestine. A man who had been appointed to be a ritual slaughterer *(shochet)* was in danger of losing his position because of a rumor that he had been involved in a homosexual act. Some thought that this should disqualify him. Rabbi Kook permitted the man to remain in his position, arguing that homosexuality is unrelated to the qualifications required of a *shochet*, and that the man probably had repented from an uncharacteristic act.

Rabbi Norman Lamm (who was then the rabbi of a congregation in New York and has since become the president of Yeshiva University) suggested in the *Encyclopedia Judaica* yearbook of 1974 that the community should orient itself to viewing homosexuals as patients rather than as criminals. Rabbi Lamm urged that we should "attempt to help the homosexual," though "we do not condone the act." Rabbi Lamm proposed that medical and psychological assistance be offered to those "whose homosexuality is an expression of pathology . . . and are willing to seek help." He also urged that jail sentences be abolished for all homosexuals except for those who are "guilty of violence, seduction of the young or public solicitation." He declared that while all laws against homosexual behavior should remain on the books, they should not be enforced. The precedent that he cited is the occasional suggestion in Talmudic literature that some conduct might be forbidden, but no punishment need be enforced.

Rabbi Solomon Freehof was asked in the early 1970s by the president of the Union of American Hebrew Congregations, Rabbi Alexander M. Schindler, whether his representative on the West Coast was acting properly in organizing a congregation of homosexuals. Is such an effort "in accordance with the spirit of the Jewish tradition?" Here is Rabbi Freehof's response:

> There is no question that Scripture considers homosexuality to be a grave sin. The rabbi who organized this congregation said, in justifying himself, that being Reform, we are not bound by the Halacha of the Bible. It may well be that we do not consider ourselves bound by all the ritual and ceremonial laws of Scripture, but we certainly revere the ethical attitudes and judgments of the Bible. In Scripture [Leviticus 18:22] homosexuality is considered to be "an abomination." So, too, in Leviticus 20:13. If Scripture calls it an abomination, it means that it is more than a violation of a mere legal enactment; it reveals a deep-rooted ethical aversion. How deep-rooted this aversion is can be seen from the fact that although Judaism developed in the Near East, which is notorious for the prevalence of homosexuality, Jews keep away from such acts, as is seen from the Talmud [Kiddushin 82a] which states that Jews are not "under the suspicion of homosexuality." In other words, the opposition to homosexuality was more than a Biblical law; it was a deep-rooted way of life of the Jewish people, a way of life maintained in a world where homosexuality was a widespread practice. Therefore homosexual acts cannot be brushed aside, as the rabbi on the West Coast is reported to have done, by saying that we do not follow Biblical enactments. Homosexuality runs counter to the sancta of Jewish life. There is no sidestepping the fact that from the point of view of Judaism, men who practice homosexuality are to be deemed sinners.

But what conclusion is to be drawn from the fact that homosexual acts are sinful acts? Does it mean, therefore, that we should exclude homosexuals from the congregation and thus compel them to form their own religious fellowship in congregations of their own? No! The very contrary is true. It is forbidden to segregate them into a separate congregation. The Mishna [*Megilla* IV, 9], says that if a man in his prayer says, "Let good people bless Thee, O Lord," the man who prays thus must be silenced. Bertinoro explains why we silence the man who says, "Let the *good* praise Thee." He says it is a sin to say so because the man implies that only righteous people shall be in the congregation. The contrary is true. He adds that the chemical "chelbena" (Galbanum) has an evil odor; yet it is included in the recipe of the sacred incense offered in the Temple in Jerusalem. . . .

To sum up: Homosexuality is deemed in Jewish tradition to be a sin, not only in law but in the Jewish way of life. Nevertheless it would be a direct contravention of Jewish law to keep sinners out of the congregation. To isolate them into a separate congregation and thus increase their mutual availability is certainly wrong. It is hardly worth mentioning that to officiate at a so-called "marriage" of two homosexuals and to describe their mode of life as Kiddushin (i.e., sacred in Judaism) is a contravention of all that is respected in Jewish life.[65]

A few years later, in 1983, Rabbi David M. Feldman, a Conservative rabbi whose Talmudic learning is widely respected, was equally firm in insisting that only heterosexual unions can be blessed:

From the standpoint of Judaism . . . the "illness" attitude has served as a welcome device enabling the rabbi or Jewish law to be compassionate rather than judgmental. This can be said to accord with the Talmud's extra-halachic observation that "a man does no sin unless he is possessed by a spirit of madness." But the illness theory has come under fire from various sources. Gay militants reject it not only as scientifically invalid but also as oppressively paternalistic. The claim is that continued oppression of homosexuals is legitimized by psychiatry in order to safeguard a sexual caste system. On the other hand, Thomas Szasz has been militating for years against the notion of illness for most disorders. There is no such thing as mental sickness, he insists. "We are all a little more or less adjusted to certain norms than the next person." The concept of mental illness is an evil concept; it makes us patronizing and judgmental, and even permits us to institutionalize those whom we judge. . . .

Much of the Jewish sexual code . . . has as its purpose—to the extent that we can speak of the law's purpose—the preservation of the marriage bond and the family unit. In an age of family dissolution it is all the more urgent to assert the stance of halakhah against an antithetical life-style.

Appropriate here is another Talmudic reference to the subject, in a passage which sought to evaluate the decadent heathenism of the surrounding society. Those heathens might indulge in homosexual liaisons, says the Talmud, but they are not so far gone, or so cynical, as to arrange a marriage contract for the purpose! This remark is applied to the problem of corruption, generally, by the great moralistic tract of the 18th century, *Mesillat Yesharim*: even in the worst degeneration there is a redeeming feature that offers hope—namely, that moral lapses are not made respectable. However, while sincere, even non-patronizing, empathy may be called for, condonation of homosexuality as an alternate way of life is not.[66]

In 1990, at its annual convention, the Rabbinical Assembly, the association of Conservative rabbis, declared utmost sympathy for the plight of gays and lesbians. The rabbis pleaded for understanding and help, especially for the unfortunate people with AIDS:

Whereas Judaism affirms that the Divine image reflected by every human being must always be cherished and affirmed, and
Whereas Jews have always been sensitive to the impact of official and unofficial prejudice and discrimination, wherever directed, and
Whereas gay and lesbian Jews have experienced not only the constant threats of physical violence and homophobic rejection, but also the pains of anti-Semitism known to all Jews and, additionally, a sense of painful alienation from our own religious institutions, and
Whereas the extended families of gay and lesbian Jews are often members of our congregations who live with concern for the safety, health and well-being of their children, and
Whereas the AIDS crisis has deeply exacerbated the anxiety and suffering of this community of Jews who need in their lives the

compassionate concern and support mandated by Jewish tradition, Therefore Be It Resolved that we, the Rabbinical Assembly, while affirming our tradition's prescription for heterosexuality,

1. Support full civil equality for gays and lesbians in our national life, and

2. Deplore the violence against gays and lesbians in our society, and

3. Reiterate that, as are all Jews, gay men and lesbians are welcome as members in our congregations, and

4. Call upon our synagogues and the arms of our movement to increase awareness, understanding and concern for our fellow Jews who are gay and lesbian.[67]

At their annual convention in 1990, the rabbis of the Reform movement, the Central Conference of Rabbis, debated the report presented by an Ad Hoc Committee on Homosexuality and the Rabbinate. A minority at the convention wanted to go as far as permitting marriage ceremonies *(Kiddushin)* for stable homoerotic relationships. The majority would not agree, but it did identify with the position of the Reform rabbinical seminary, the Hebrew Union College, that a gay or lesbian was not automatically to be barred from the rabbinate:

The committee is acutely aware that the inability of most gay and lesbian rabbis to live openly as homosexuals is deeply painful. Therefore, the committee wishes to avoid any action that will cause greater distress to our colleagues. As a result, the committee has determined that a comprehensive report is in the best interest of our Conference and the Reform movement as a whole.

Publicly acknowledging one's homosexuality is a personal decision that can have grave professional consequences. Therefore, in the light of the limited ability of the Placement Commission or the CCAR to guarantee the tenure of the gay or lesbian rabbis who "come out of the closet," the committee does not want to encourage colleagues to put their careers at risk. Regrettably, a decision to declare oneself publicly can have potentially negative effects on a person's ability to serve a given community effectively. In addition, the committee is anxious to avoid a situation in which pulpit selection committees will request information on the sexual orientation of candidates. The committee urges that rabbis, regardless of sexual orientation, be accorded the opportunity to fulfill the sacred vocation that they have chosen.

All human beings are created *betselem Elohim* ("in the divine image"). Their personhood must therefore be accorded full dignity. Sexual orientation is irrelevant to the human worth of a person. Therefore, the Reform movement has supported vigorously all efforts to eliminate discrimination in housing and employment. The committee unequivocally condemns verbal and physical abuse against gay men and lesbian women or those perceived to be gay or lesbian. We reject any implication that AIDS can be understood as God's punishment of homosexuals. We applaud the fine work of the gay and lesbian outreach synagogues, and we, along with the UAHC, call upon rabbis and congregations to treat with respect and to integrate fully all Jews into the life of the community regardless of sexual orientation.

The committee's task was made particularly difficult because the specific origin of sexual identity and its etiology are still imperfectly understood.

Scholars are not likely to come to an agreement anytime soon about the causes of sexual orientation, or its nature. Various disciplines look at sexuality in different ways and rarely confront each other's ideas. . . . Short of definitive evidence, which no theory has thus far received, the disagreement is likely to continue. Cognitive and normative pluralism will persist for the indefinite future.

The lack of unanimity in the scientific community and the unanimous condemnation of homosexual behavior by Jewish tradition adds to the complexity of the question. It is clear, however, that for many people sexual orientation is not a matter of conscious choice but is constitutional and therefore not subject to change. It is also true that for some, sexual orientation may be a matter of conscious choice. The committee devoted considerable time in its discussion to the significance of conscious choice as a criterion for formulating a position on the religious status of homosexuality. The majority of the committee believes that the issue of choice is crucial. For some on the committee the issue of choice is not significant.

In Jewish tradition heterosexual, monogamous, procreative marriage is the ideal human relationship for the perpetuation of the species, covenantal fulfillment, and the preservation of the Jewish people. While acknowledging that there are other human relationships which possess ethical and spiritual value and that there are some people for whom heterosexual, monogamous, procreative marriage is not a viable option or possibility, the majority of the committee reaffirms unequivocally the centrality of this ideal and its special status as *kiddushin*. To the extent that sexual orientation is a matter of choice, the majority of the committee affirms that heterosexuality is the only appropriate Jewish choice for fulfilling one's covenantal obligations.

A minority of the committee dissents, affirming the equal possibility of covenantal fulfillment in homosexual and heterosexual relationships. The relationship, not the gender, should determine its Jewish value—*Kiddushin*.

The committee strongly endorses the view that all Jews are religiously equal regardless of their sexual orientation. We are aware of loving and committed relationships between people of the same sex. Issues such as the religious status of these relationships as well as the creation of special ceremonies are matters of continuing discussion and differences of opinion. . . .

The acceptance by our congregations of gay and lesbian Jews as rabbis was a topic of discussion. We know that the majority of Reform Jews strongly support civil rights for gays and lesbians, but the unique position of the rabbi as spiritual leader and Judaic role model make the acceptance of gay or lesbian rabbis an intensely emotional and potentially divisive issue. While we acknowledge that there are gay and lesbian rabbis who are serving their communities effectively, with dignity, compassion, and integrity, we believe that there is a great need for education and dialogue in our congregations. . . .

One of the original issues that brought the committee into existence was the concern about the admissions policy of the College-Institute. President Alfred Gottschalk has recently set forth the admissions policy of HUC-JIR. The written guidelines state that HUC-JIR considers sexual orientation of an applicant only within the context of a candidate's overall suitability for the rabbinate, his or her qualifications to serve the Jewish community effectively, and his or her capacity to find personal fulfillment within the rabbinate. The committee agrees with this admissions policy of our College-Institute. . . .

The CCAR has always accepted into membership, upon application, all rabbinic graduates of the HUC-JIR. The committee reaffirms this policy of admitting upon application rabbinic graduates of the HUC-JIR. . . .[68]

Contemporary Jewish authorities are, thus, in basic agreement that homosexuals should be treated with compassion. There is a consensus in opposition to the demands by gay and lesbian activist that their sexual preferences be treated as an equally valid lifestyle. Among the Orthodox, blanket condemnation of homosexuality has been replaced, at least among many, by stretching the term "illness" to make the forgiveness possible. Conservative rabbis insist on equality in society for homosexuals, but they are unwilling even to consider the possibility of an avowed homosexual as rabbi. The Reform will not debar a gay or a lesbian from being ordained, on that ground alone, though most rabbis of the Reform movement continue to insist that heterosexual marriage is the preferred role model. Attitudes have clearly been changing, but will they continue to change?

PARENTS AND CHILDREN

That children must love and honor their parents is undoubted. However, the sources emphasize that, patriarchal though ancient Jewish society was, the duty to honor parents applied in equal measure to the father and the mother. The parent-child relationship was not one way, for parents have specified duties toward their children.

> Honor your father and your mother, that your days may be long in the land which the Lord your God gives you.[69]

> Cursed be he who dishonors his father or his mother.[70]

> There are three partners in a human being: The Holy One, praised be He, a father and a mother. When a child honors parents, the Holy One says: It is as though I were dwelling among them and they were honoring Me. Rabbi Judah the Prince says: He-who-spoke-and-the-world-was-created knows that a child honors a mother more than a father. Therefore [Ex. 20:12], the Holy One, praised be He, preceded honoring one's father to honoring one's mother. He-who-spoke-and-the-world-was-created knows that a child fears a father more than a mother. Therefore [Lev. 19:3] the Holy One, praised be He, preceded the fear of one's mother to fear of one's father. When a child pains his father and

his mother, the Holy One, praised be He, says: I did well in not dwelling among them for had I done so, they would have caused Me pain.[71]

They asked Rav Ulla: To what degree must one honor one's parents? He told them: Go and see how a non-Jew named Dama ben Netinah treated his father in Ashkelon. The sages once sought to conclude a business transaction with him, through which he would gain 600,000 gold *denarii*. But the key to his vault was under the pillow of his sleeping father, and he refused to disturb him.[72]

The disciples of Rabbi Eliezer the Great asked him to give an example of honoring one's parents. He said: Go and see what Dama ben Netinah did in Ashkelon. His mother was feeble minded and she used to strike him with a shoe in the presence of the council over which he presided, but he never said more than "It is enough, mother." When the shoe fell from her hand he would pick it up for her, so that she would not be troubled.[73]

Rabbi Simeon ben Johai said: Great is the duty of honoring one's parents, for the Holy One, praised be He, gave it status greater than the duty of honoring Him. Concerning the Holy One it is written "Honor the Lord with your substance" [Prov. 3:9]. How is this done? By leaving grain in the field for the poor, giving priestly and poor tithes, observing the commandments of *Sukkah* and *Lulav*, *Shofar*, *Tefillin* and *Tzitzit*, feeding the hungry, giving drink to the thirsty, and clothing the naked. If you have the means to do these, then you are obligated to do them, but if you do not have the means you are not obligated. However, when it comes to honoring your parents, whether you are a person of substance or not, you are obligated to "honor your father and your mother" [Ex. 20:12]—even if you have to beg from door to door.[74]

It is written "Honor your father and your mother" [Ex. 20:12] and it is written "Honor the Lord with your substance" [Prov. 3:9]. Scripture compares honoring one's parents with honoring God.[75]

"Each of you shall revere his mother and his father, and you shall observe My Sabbaths; I am the Lord your God" [Lev. 19:3]. One might think that honoring one's parents could have precedence over Sabbath observance. Therefore the verse is written in this way, to state that "all of you are obligated to honor me."[76]

Scripture everywhere speaks of the father before the mother. Does the honor due the father exceed the honor due the mother? Therefore Scripture states: "Each of you shall revere his mother and his father" [Lev. 19:3], to teach that both are equal. However, the sages have said: Scripture everywhere speaks of the father before the mother because both the child and the mother are bound to honor the father. So too in the study of Torah. If the son has gained much wisdom while he sat before his teacher, his teacher becomes his father, since both he and his father are bound to honor the teacher.[77]

A father is obligated to see that his son is circumcised, to redeem him [if he is the first-born], to teach him Torah and a craft and to find a wife for him. Some say that he must teach his son to swim. Rabbi Judah said: Whoever does not teach his son a craft is considered as having taught him thievery.[78]

Rav said: A father should never favor one son more than the others, for because of a little extra silk which Jacob gave to Joseph, his brothers became jealous, sold him into slavery and it came about that our ancestors went down to Egypt.[79]

Whoever hears a section of the Torah from his grandson is considered as hearing it at Mount Sinai on the day of Revelation, as it is written ". . . make them known to your children and your children's children . . . on the day that you stood before the Lord your God at Horeb" [Deut. 4:9–10].[80]

Rabbi Hiyya bar Abba did not eat breakfast before he reviewed the previous day's verse with his child and taught a new verse. Rabbi bar Rav Huna did not eat breakfast before he took his child to school.[81]

". . . and teach them to your children, to speak of them" [Deut. 11:19]. From this it is said: When a child begins to speak, his father should speak with him in the holy tongue and teach him Torah. If he does not do so, it is as though he buries him.[82]

KASHRUTH (DIETARY LAWS)

The most pervasive of Jewish rituals, for they are observed by the faithful in the very act of eating to sustain life, are the laws of kashruth, the regulations about forbidden and permitted foods. There have been many attempts through the ages to "explain" these rules. There are several such remarks to be found in the section below, culminating in the concluding three paragraphs, written by Maimonides. Essentially the traditional writings have produced two basic reasons for kashruth: that these laws represent a curbing of animal appetites and that they were ordained as a way of setting the Jews apart in their day to day life, so that they might be conscious of their responsibility as members of a priest-people. Contemporary Reform Judaism has rejected these laws, though at least one of its leaders, Kaufmann Kohler, knew that this left it with the problem of finding "other methods to inculcate the spirit of holiness in the modern Jew, to render him conscious of his priestly mission." Ultimately, the laws of kashruth cannot be rationalized. The believer accepts them as part of a total system, the Jewish way to holiness, ordained by God. The non-believer may cling to kashruth out of sentiment or attachment to a cultural past, but this clinging has demonstrably seldom outlasted one generation of disbelief.

Therefore to this day the Israelites do not eat the sciatic muscle on the hip socket, because Jacob's hip socket was wrenched at the sciatic muscle.[83]

You shall be consecrated to Me. Therefore you shall not eat flesh that is torn by beasts in the field; you shall cast it to the dogs.[84]

You shall not boil a kid in its mother's milk.[85]

These are the animals which you may eat of all the beasts of the earth. Whatsoever divides the hoof and is wholly cloven-footed, and chews the cud, among the beasts, you may eat. But among those that chew the cud or divide the hoof, you shall not eat these. The camel, which chews the cud but does not divide the hoof, is unclean to you. The rock-badger, which chews the cud but does not divide the hoof, is unclean to you. The hare too, which chews the cud but does not divide the hoof, is unclean to you. And the swine, which divides the hoof but does not chew the cud, is unclean to you. The flesh of these you shall not eat, nor shall you touch their carcasses, because they are unclean to you.[86]

These you may eat of all that are in the waters: Everything in the waters that has fins and scales, whether in the seas or in the rivers, you may eat. But anything that is in the sea or the rivers that has no fins and scales . . . is an abomination to you. . . . Of their flesh you shall not eat.[87]

If any one of the house of Israel or of the strangers who dwell among them should eat blood I will set My face against him, and will cut him off from among His people. For the life of the flesh is in the blood, and I have given it to you, that you may make atonement with it for your lives upon the altar; for it is blood that makes atonement by reason of the life. Therefore I have said to the children of Israel: No person among you, nor of the strangers who dwell among you, shall eat blood. If any one of the children of Israel or of the strangers who dwell among them hunts down any beast or fowl which is lawful to eat, he shall pour out its blood and cover it with earth. For the life of all flesh is in the blood; therefore I have said to the children of Israel: You shall not eat the blood of any flesh, because the life of all flesh is in the blood, and whoever eats it shall be cut off.[88]

You shall not eat anything that dies of itself. You may give it to the alien that is in your towns, to eat, or you may sell it to a foreigner. For you are a people holy to the Lord your God.[89]

The following signs disqualify cattle [making it *trefah* and so unfit for consumption]: if the gullet is pierced or the windpipe torn; if the membrane of the brain is pierced; if the heart is pierced through to the cells; if the spine is broken and the spinal cord severed; if the liver is completely missing; if the lung is pierced or defective (Rabbi Simeon says it is not *trefah* unless its bronchial tubes are pierced); if the maw is pierced, or the gall-bladder or the intestines; if the inner stomach is pierced or if the greater part of its outer coating is torn (Rabbi Judah says a handbreadth in larger cattle, or the greater part in smaller cattle); if the third stomach or the second stomach is pierced on its outermost side; if the beast has fallen from a roof or has most of its ribs broken; if it has been mauled by a wolf (Rabbi Judah says: if small cattle have been mauled by a wolf, large cattle by a lion, small birds by a hawk and larger birds by a vulture). This is the general rule: If the animal could not have remained alive for twelve months in like state, it is *trefah*.[90]

No flesh may be cooked in milk [to avoid the possibility of transgressing the law against boiling a kid in its mother's milk: Ex. 23:19; 34:26; Deut. 14:21], excepting the flesh of fish and locusts. No flesh may be served on the table together with cheese, excepting the flesh of fish and locusts. . . . One may tie up meat and cheese in the same cloth provided that they do not touch one another. . . . If a drop of milk fell upon a piece of meat that was cooking in a pot and there was enough to give its flavor to that piece, that piece cannot be eaten. If one stirred the pot and there was enough to give the flavor of the milk to everything in it, none of it can be eaten.[91]

"These are the living things which you may eat" [Lev. 11:2]. . . . "The way of God is perfect, the promise of the Lord proves true. He is a shield for all who take refuge in Him" [II Sam. 22:31; Ps. 18:31]. The ways of the Holy One praised be He are perfect. What can it matter to Him whether an animal is slaughtered according to prescribed ritual or whether it is simply stabbed with no regard to ritual, before it is eaten? Does it benefit Him or does it harm Him in any way? What can it matter to Him if one eats forbidden or permitted foods? "If you are wise, you are wise for yourself, and if you scoff you alone will bear the consequences" [Prov. 9:12]. The commandments have been given for the purpose of purifying mortals.[92]

The commandment concerning the killing of animals is necessary, because the natural food of man consists of vegetables and of the flesh of animals. . . . Since, therefore, the desire of procuring good food necessitates the slaying of animals, the Law enjoins that the death of the animal should be the easiest. It is not allowed to torment the animal by cutting the throat in a clumsy manner, by poleaxing, or by cutting off a limb while the animal is alive.

It is also prohibited to kill an animal and its young on the same day [Lev. 22:28], in order that people should be restrained and prevented from killing the two together in such a manner that the young is slain in the sight of the mother; for the pain of the animals under such circumstances is very great. There is no difference in this case between the pain of man and the pain of other living beings. . . .

The same reason applies to the law which enjoins that we should let the mother [bird] fly away when we take the young. . . . If the Law provides that such grief should not be caused to cattle or to birds, how much more careful must we be that we should not cause grief to our fellowmen.[93]

VEGETARIANISM

In a perfect world, in the Garden of Eden, before the fall, Adam and Eve ate no meat. After the fall, human beings, in their sinful state, began to slaughter animals for food. Indeed the Talmud prescribes flesh as food at the holiday table, to complete the "rejoicing" which is enjoined for all the major festivals. Nonetheless, some Jews have insisted on being vegetarians throughout the centuries. Joseph Albo, the medieval philosopher argued their case:

. . . aside from the fact that [expressions of] cruelty, rage, anger, and the acquisition of a bad disposition to shed blood freely, are involved in the slaughter of animals, eating the flesh of some animals will lead to coarseness, foulness, and dullness. . . . Even though the flesh of some animals is good food and suitable for human consumption, God wanted to deprive people of the slight good which lies in eating meat in order to prevent the enormous evil which might result from it. That is why He forbade Adam to eat the flesh of animals. To replace what would be lacking [in his diet] He ordained for Adam the consumption of appropriate, nourishing foods such as wheat and barley and all other seed-bearing plants whose seeds can be sown, and all trees whose fruit bears seeds. To the other animals He gave for food all green grass that has no seed which can be planted. The purpose of this was to show the superiority of the human animal to the other animals.[94]

Struggling with the same problem, Rabbi Shneur Zalman of Liady (1745–1813) justified the eating of animal flesh as a form of communion with God. The flesh that is consumed can be made holy, if it is eaten in piety:

The entire world exists for the glory of the Creator. If a God-fearing person eats . . . meat or drinks wine . . . for the sake of expanding his heart to God and His Torah, or for the sake of fulfilling the mitzvah of enjoyment on the Sabbath and on the Festivals . . . then that flesh [which is consumed] has been affected by a measure of radiance, and it ascends to the Almighty as a sacrifice.[95]

In the end of days, so the mystic Rabbi Abraham Isaac Kook (1865–1935) asserted, our world will again be the Garden of Eden. Animals will not be harmed or destroyed for food.

. . . In time to come, the effect that knowledge brings will be spread even to the animals [they too will then have a perception of God that knowledge brings and will be able to draw near to God]. "They will not harm or destroy on all My holy mountain, for the land will be filled with knowledge of the Lord . . ." Sacrifices offered at that time will be limited to grain offerings and vegetation, and that will be pleasing to God as [animal sacrifices were] in days of old, in ancient times.[96]

CHARITY

Caring for others is not merely a generalized moral commandment in Judaism. It is spelled out in specific, legally binding obligations which everyone must heed. In all ages Jews were supremely conscious of the need to aid and succor one another. This has been strongly ingrained by the innumerable persecutions they have suffered since the beginning of the Exile in the year 70 and which have not ceased even in our own generation, which has witnessed Nazism. The immense efforts of present-day Jewry to help Jews in need all over the world are in the line of this most ancient tradition.

For six years you shall sow your land and gather in its yield; but the seventh year you shall let it rest and lie fallow, that the poor of your people may eat; and what they leave the wild beasts may eat. You shall do likewise with your vineyards, and with your olive groves.[97]

When you reap the harvest of your land, you shall not reap your field to its very borders, neither shall you gather the gleanings of your harvest. And you shall not strip your vineyard bare, neither shall you gather the fallen grapes of your vineyard; you shall leave them for the poor and for the stranger: I am the Lord your God. [98]

At the end of every three years you shall bring forth all the tithe of your produce of that year, and lay it up within your towns. Then the Levite, because he had no portion or inheritance, as you have, and the stranger, the fatherless, and the widow, who are within your towns, shall come and eat and be filled; that the Lord your God may bless you in all the work of your hands that you undertake. [99]

If there is among you a poor man, one of your brethren who dwells within the gates of any of your towns in the land which the Lord your God gives you, you shall not harden your heart or close your hand against your poor brother but you shall open your hand to him and you shall lend him enough for what he needs. Beware lest there be a base thought in your heart, saying, "The seventh year, the year of release, draws near" and you turn your eye away from your poor brother, giving him nothing, and he cry against you to the Lord, and it be a sin in you. But you shall give to him, and your heart shall not be grieved when you give to him, that the Lord your God may bless you at all times, and in all things to which you put your hand. For the poor shall never cease in the land; therefore I command you to open your hand to your poor and needy brother who lives in the land. [100]

The ear that heard me blessed me, and the eye that saw me gave witness to me, because I had delivered the poor man who cried out, and the orphan who had no helper. The blessing of him that was ready to perish came upon me, and I comforted the heart of the widow. I was clad with justice, and I clothed myself with righteousness as with a robe and a diadem. I was eyes to the blind and feet to the lame. I was a father to the poor, and the cause of the stranger I searched out most diligently. I broke the jaws of the wicked, and from his teeth I took the prey. [101]

The passage below is a letter written by the Jews of Alexandria in the eleventh century to a nearby community in Fostat, asking for help in the ransoming of captives.

You are the supporters of the poor and the aid of the men in need, you study diligently, you rouse the good against the evil impulse. You walk in the right way and practise justice. We let you know that we always pray for you. May God grant you peace and security.

We turn to you today on behalf of a captive woman who has been brought from Byzantium. We ransomed her for 24 denares besides the governmental tax. You sent us 12 denares; we have paid the remainder and the tax. Soon afterwards sailors brought two other prisoners, one of them a fine young man possessing knowledge of the Torah, the other a boy of about ten. When we saw them in the hands of the pirates, and how they beat them and frightened them before our own eyes, we had pity on them and guaranteed their ransom. We had hardly settled this when another ship arrived carrying many prisoners. Among them were a physician and his wife. Thus we are again in difficulties and distress. And our strength is overstrained, as the taxes are heavy and the times critical. . . .[102]

Maimonides summarized the legal obligation to give charity in his code of Jewish law, the *Mishneh Torah*, in the section entitled "The Laws of Giving to the Poor."

If the poor asks of you and you have nothing in your hand to give him, soothe him with words. It is forbidden to rebuke a poor man or to raise one's voice against him in a shout, for his heart is shattered and crushed and it is written, "A broken and contrite heart, O God, You will not despise" [Ps. 51:19]. And it is written, "I dwell in the high and holy place and also with him who is of a contrite and humble spirit, to revive the spirit of the humble and to revive the heart of the contrite" [Isa. 57:15]. Alas for anyone who has humiliated a poor man, alas for him. He should rather be like a father both with compassion and with words, as it is written, "I was a father to the poor" [Job 29:16]. . . .

There are eight degrees in the giving of charity, each one higher than that which follows it:

1. The highest degree, exceeded by none, is giving a gift or a loan or taking one as a partner or finding him employment by which he can be self-supporting. . . .

2. Giving charity to the poor without knowing to whom one gives, the recipient not knowing the donor's identity, for this is a good deed of intrinsic value, done for its own sake. An example of this is the Hall of Secret Donations which was maintained in the Temple. The righteous would donate in secret and the

poor would be supported from it in secret. Approximating this is giving to a charity fund. One should not give to a charity fund unless he knows the collector is trustworthy and wise and conducts himself properly, like Rabbi Hananiah ben Tradyon.

3. Giving to one whose identity one knows, although the recipient does not know the donor's identity. An example of this would be the action of those great sages who would walk about in secret and cast coins at the doors of the poor. It is fitting to imitate such a custom and it is a high degree indeed, if the charity collectors [through whom one can give impersonally] do not conduct themselves properly.

4. Giving without knowing to whom one gives, although the recipient knows the donor's identity. An example of this would be the action of those great sages who would wrap up coins in a bundle and throw it over their shoulder. The poor would then come to take it without suffering any embarrassment.

5. Giving before being asked.

6. Giving only after being asked.

7. Giving inadequately, though graciously.

8. Giving grudgingly.

The great sages would give a coin for the poor before each prayer service and then pray, as it is written, "I shall behold Your face in righteousness" [Ps. 17:5]. Giving food to one's older sons and daughters (though one is not obligated to do so) in order to teach the males Torah and to direct the females on the proper path, and giving food to one's father and mother, is considered to be charity. And it is a great degree of charity, for relatives should have precedence. . . .

One should always press himself and suffer rather than be dependent upon others; he should not cast himself upon the community as a responsibility. Thus the sages commanded: "Rather make your Sabbath like a week day than be dependent upon others" [*Pesahim* 112a]. Even if a man was learned and respected and then became poor he should occupy himself with a trade, even a lowly trade, rather than be dependent upon others. It is better to strip the hide of dead animals than to say "I am a

great sage, I am a priest; support me." Among the great sages
there were wood choppers, those who watered gardens and those
who worked with iron and charcoal. They did not ask the community for money and they did not take it when it was offered to
them. [103]

The paragraphs which follow are a selection from a more recent
code of Jewish law, the *Shulhan Arukh*. Its author was Rabbi
Joseph Caro (1488–1575), of Safed in Palestine, and the code
that he wrote is to this day the recognized authority in Jewish
law for those who follow the halakhah, the law as defined by
rabbinic Judaism.

The ransom of captives takes precedence over the act of sup-
porting and clothing the poor, and there is no commandment
which is as great as that of ransoming captives. Therefore, any
religious object may be converted into cash for the purpose of
using that money to ransom captives, even if this involves the use
of monies designated for the restoration of the Temple. . . .

Whoever tarries in ransoming captives when it is possible to
do so is considered as one who sheds blood.

Captives are not to be ransomed for exorbitant sums, for the
sake of social order, lest enemies devote themselves to capturing.
But one may ransom himself with whatever sum he desires. . . .

We should not help captives escape, for the sake of the social
order, lest enemies make life more difficult for them and increase
the regulations for guarding them. . . .

A woman is to be ransomed before a man; if the place of
captivity is one where the practice of homosexuality is common,
the men are to be ransomed first.

If one is in captivity along with his father and his teacher, he
is to be ransomed before his teacher, and his teacher before his
father. However, if his mother is also there, her being ransomed
has first priority.

If a man and his wife are both in captivity, she is to be shown
preference, and a court may take possession of and administer his
property in order to ransom her, even if he strongly states that
she should not be ransomed with his property. He is not to be
obeyed in such a case.

If a man is in captivity and he has property but does not want
to ransom himself, he is ransomed against his will. [104]

HEALTH, HEALING, AND HUMAN DIGNITY

The Torah exists to make life possible, not to shorten or destroy it. "And I have given them My laws, and I have informed them of My judgments, which man shall keep, and he shall live by them" (Ezekiel 20:11). This is an oft-quoted injunction. Any activity which endangers your own life, or shortens it, is forbidden. The basic ruling is summarized by Maimonides:

> Whether it be one's roof or anything else potentially dangerous which could cause a person's death—for example, if one has a well or a pit in his yard, containing water or not—the owner has an obligation to build an enclosure ten handbreadths high, or else to make a cover for the well or pit to prevent a person's falling to his death. So it is with any life-threatening obstacle—there is a commandment to remove and to beware of it, and to be especially cautious about it, as it is stated in Scripture: "Take care of yourself and watch yourself carefully" (Deut. 4:9). One who does not remove potentially dangerous obstacles, letting them remain, disregards a commandment and transgresses the prohibition against bringing blood-guilt upon one's house (Deut. 22:8).
>
> The Sages forbade many things because they are life-threatening. If anyone ignores them, saying, "Look, if I endanger myself, of what concern is it to others?" or, "I am not cautious about such things," he is to be flogged because of rebelliousness. And these are the prohibited acts: One shall not place his mouth on a pipe flowing with water and drink from it, and one shall not drink at night from rivers or ponds, lest he swallow a leech because he is unable to see it. And one shall not drink water which is uncovered, lest he die because a snake or another poisonous creature drank from it first. . . . One should not place a dish of food underneath his seat during a meal, lest something harmful fall into it unnoticed. Likewise, one should not leave a knife stuck into a citron or a radish, lest someone fall on the point of the knife and be killed. Likewise, one should not walk close to a leaning wall or on a shaky bridge, or enter a ruin, or pass through any other such dangerous place.[105]

Rabbi Moses Isserles (1525?–1572) adds another cautionary note in his gloss on a passage in the *Shulhan Arukh* (*Yoreh Deah* 116:5):

> . . . One should be cautious about everything which is potentially life-threatening. . . . [A listing of potentially dangerous situations follows.] . . . Anyone who is concerned for his life avoids them. And it is forbidden to rely upon a miracle.

In a presentation urging people not to squander on insignificant activities time which could be spent profitably in Torah study, Rabbi Israel Meir Kagan, known as the Hafetz Hayyim (1838–1933), forbade the smoking of tobacco:

> . . . In addition to the known fact that they [cigarettes and pipes] are harmful to the body, they cause damage to the soul through squandering time that should be spent in Torah study, for the smoker spends at least one-half hour daily preparing them and smoking them, and once he becomes accustomed to this it is hard to stop. And it sometimes happens that he lacks the paper for cigarettes, so he spends time going from one person to another asking for paper until he finds it, thus squandering even more time. And so it goes that during the year he will squander hundreds of hours which should have been spent in Torah study. Of course I am certainly aware that many will respond, "We were forced into it; we didn't have the strength to stop." The question, however, is: Who forced you into it? Are you yourselves not to blame? Had you not fallen into the habit in the first place, it would be easy for you to stop. You yourselves must bear the onus.[106]

A generation later, the eminent Orthodox authority, Rabbi Moshe Feinstein, forbade even "passive smoking."

> . . . The law is plain and simple . . . it is forbidden for people to smoke in a house of study so long as there is even one nonsmoker there who is disturbed by it, even though he may not be harmed or fall ill because of it. This is truer still when one could be apprehensive about the sickness or harm which could be caused by it, even when there are smokers who claim that this ruling will lead them to squandering time which should be spent in Torah study. . . . Wherever there are non-smokers who say that smoking harms them, even if that harm is limited to their anguish, it is forbidden to smoke in a house of study.[107]

Autopsies

The halakhic principle that the law exists to further life provided no unequivocal answers on the question of autopsies. This injunction conflicted with a near absolute in the halakhah, that the remains of the dead must be shown respect, that they must be buried intact, and that no benefit may be derived from them. As we shall soon see, a decision was rendered two centuries ago by Rabbi Ezekiel Landau to permit autopsies only if the information gained from such investigation would help in the immediate treatment of an existing patient. They were forbidden simply to gain medical knowledge, even of rare diseases. This view has become increasingly untenable as a restriction on contemporary medical research. Knowledge that is gained about a specific disease helps, or will help, to cure some patient, if only by increasing the statistical evidence for various forms of treatment. In this spirit, the Sephardi chief rabbi of Israel from 1939 to 1953, Rabbi Ben Zion Meir Hai Ouziel (1880–1953), wrote an advisory opinion:

> I have been asked by one of my friends if the Torah or Rabbinic ordinances forbid autopsies carried on carefully and precisely, for the purpose of gaining knowledge about a specific disease and the manner of its cure. . . . It seems to me that permission may be given, as I will explain. Nevertheless, as I responded to my questioner, a general question which touches all Jews throughout the world will be the object of divided opinions. Therefore it would be better if this question were presented to the Chief Rabbinate in Jerusalem, from which office there will come instruction from outstanding authorities of our generation. But I thought that I would express my opinion on this topic, as an exercise in theory and not as a legal decision. . . .
>
> . . . Rabbi Ezekiel Landau [1713–1793, Poland and Bohemia] was asked by the physicians of a patient who died, for permission to perform an autopsy in order to discover the source of the illness, to learn from this case about [the healing of] others. Rabbi Landau responded: "In the case before us, when there is no patient [here and now] who is in need [of their investigation] they simply want to learn what they can in the event that a patient should appear who would need [what they learn]. Surely permission for an au-

topsy cannot be given. . . . Even non-Jewish doctors who are not bound by our laws perform such experiments only on the corpses of those who were executed by a court of law or of those who had sold their bodies for this purpose while alive. A more lenient decision will open the door, Heaven forbid, to autopsies upon all of our dead for the purpose of learning the structure and function of the internal organs. . . ."

In my humble opinion, I have not found in any of the stated reasons a basis for forbidding [autopsies]. Concerning the argument that there is no patient before us in immediate need, and that an autopsy should not be performed for the benefit of some possible patient in the future, I say that . . . there always will be many people afflicted with the same illness. If we know of none at this time, they will appear in the future. . . . [And timing is important.] If the autopsy is not performed at once, it will never be performed, and the knowledge that could have been gained will be lost to us forever. This certainly will be the cause of many deaths.

But if this decision should lead to autopsies for all of the dead, routinely, then I would feel constrained to withdraw this lenient opinion. The dead must not be treated as public property for use by anyone who wants to learn medicine. But when doctors do not know the cause of a disease and they want to use the opportunity of an autopsy to add to their knowledge . . . the saving of lives is involved. In such cases an autopsy should certainly be allowed, [provided that it proceeds] with special care to avoid causing the dead indignity or dishonor.

Therefore I disagree with the even greater stringency of Rabbi Moses Schreiber [1762–1839, Hungary] who went beyond Rabbi Landau's decision. Rabbi Schreiber wrote that even when we have before us a patient with a disease similar to that of the patient who has just died, and an autopsy would therefore have a chance of saving a life, an autopsy is forbidden, because of the prohibitions against benefitting from the dead and against disfigurement. . . . I agree with my contemporary, Rabbi Yehudah Leib Graubart, may His Creator and Redeemer protect him, that the prohibition against benefitting from the dead does not apply when learning is involved. . . .[108]

Rabbi Ouziel's advisory opinion was written against the background of serious controversy over autopsies in the State of Israel. The basic law of the state was passed in 1953, permitting dissections of the body when the deceased had agreed before his death, in writing, that his body could be used for such purposes. In all other cases, physicians were empowered to perform an autopsy either to establish the cause of death, if it were unknown, or to use one of the organs of the dead body as a transplant to help someone who is desperately ill. This law left unclear whether it was physicians or the family who had the last word in deciding whether an autopsy was to be performed. After many years of debate, no agreement could be found in Israel to define the boundary between the often clashing wishes of families and physicians. In 1966, the chief rabbinate of Israel formally forbade autopsy in any form "except in a matter of immediate danger to life, and then only with the approval in each instance of an authoritative rabbi who is commissioned to make such decisions." As a result of the quarrel, fewer autopsies were being performed because many families went so far as to keep watch on the hospitals, to make sure that the remains of a recently deceased member of the family would not be disturbed. And yet, the view of Rabbi Ouziel to broaden permission of autopsies wherever a reasonable case can be made that the autopsy contributes to the saving of life is shared by Rabbi Immanuel Jakobovits, the former chief rabbi of the United Synagogue of England. Orthodox opinion is divided between those who would be no more permissive than Rabbi Ezekiel Landau was two centuries ago, and those who would essentially forbid only routine autopsies. Here is Rabbi Jakobovits's opinion:

> While no general sanction can be given for the indiscriminate surrender of all bodies to postmortem examinations, the area of sanction should be broadened to include tests on new drugs and cases of reasonable suspicion that the diagnosis was mistaken; for autopsies under such conditions, too, may directly result in the saving of life. . . .
>
> Any permission for an autopsy is to be given only on condition that operation is reduced to a minimum, carried out with the greatest dispatch in the presence of a Rabbi or religious supervisor if requested by the family, and performed with the utmost reverence and with the assurance that all parts of the body are returned for burial.
>
> Just as it is the duty of rabbis to urge relatives not to consent

to an autopsy where the law does not justify it, they are religiously obliged to insure that permission is granted in cases where human lives may thereby be saved, in the same way as the violation of the Sabbath laws in the face of danger to life is not merely optional but mandatory.[109]

Transplants

The transplantation of organs does involve disturbing the dead, but the major contemporary Orthodox interpreters of the halakhah have had little problem agreeing that such action is permissible and even praiseworthy. Rabbi Isser Yehudah Unterman (1886–1976), who was the Ashkenazi chief rabbi of Israel from 1954 to 1976, permitted corneal transplants. The essential logic of his decision applied to all other transplants which helped prolong life. The Orthodox halakhists almost unanimously forbid cosmetic operations, because the risk of the procedure, in their view, outweighs the psychological benefits to the patient. Even if it did not, Orthodox halakhists were very leery of tampering with the body for purposes of vanity. More liberal decisors, almost all of them Conservative and Reform rabbis, are willing to allow such operations if the patient is severely disturbed by his or her present situation. What follows immediately below is some of the text of Rabbi Unterman's decision in the matter of corneal transplants:

. . . Does the law allow transplanting from a corpse to a living person . . . a cornea which will become an organic part of that person?

This is a questionable matter because of the law that it is forbidden to derive benefit from a corpse; as a result of a transplant operation the living will derive benefit from a corpse. Another problem is that it is strictly forbidden to disfigure the dead, or to do anything which shows disrespect to the dead. . . . It is clear to me that this injunction does not apply to operations which lead to saving an endangered life, because strict prohibitions of the Torah are set aside when saving a life is at stake. Operations undertaken to save lives are certainly to be permitted. . . .

Corneal transplant is very common today. It is an operation in which the cornea of a corpse is removed (a short while after death) and attached to the eye of someone who is unable to see because of a defective cornea. Sight is restored as a result of this procedure. But can this procedure be subsumed under the legal category of a life-saving technique? A person's very life is not endangered when he cannot see. . . . And the [Rabbinic] statement that "a blind person is considered to be like the dead" [merely] suggests that a person who cannot see the sun is denied life's pleasures. It is similar to the saying that one who is childless is like the dead. . . .

But it can perhaps be argued that blindness is life-endangering, since it could cause one to fall into a pit or to be in peril whenever he is walking about. . . . The blind cannot always remain at home, and when they cross the street, dangers lie in wait for them. When they enter or leave their home, or visit the home of a friend, they usually have to go up and down stairs, which can be dangerous. Therefore being blind should be considered as life-endangering. However, what would the law be if one is blind in only one eye? Is corneal transplant to be permitted in such an instance?

. . . Upon reflection, it seems to me that there is a basis for allowing all corneal transplants. The absence of any precedent in the Rabbinic sources is apparently due to the fact that in ancient times such operations were unknown. Surely according to the principles of halakhah one should seek ways to permit them. In any case, I have not found any contradiction to such a decision either in the Talmud or in later Rabbinic literature.

The basis for granting permission is that [using] part of a corpse is forbidden only so long as it is dead. . . . Even though the body from which the part has been taken is still dead, this is not a determining factor. The prohibition against using a corpse for advantage applies only when the part itself remains dead. But when it is attached to the body of the living and is infused with vitality as blood courses through it, the transplanted cornea is now alive. . . .

But the prohibition against disfiguring the dead surely poses a difficulty. One could argue that this rule is not absolute. Dissection (when required by the law and in similar instances) is not defined as disfigurement if the dissected part is used for purposes of healing. . . .

It seems to me that since the cornea is not outwardly visible, and since the eyes of the dead are always closed, one may declare that no disfigurement is involved. And I would think that if a blind person (blind in one eye or in both eyes) with a healthy cornea would be asked [while alive] to donate his cornea, for which he has no need, to cure the blindness of someone whose cornea is defective, and the doctors assure him that the operation would be neither dangerous nor painful—[his positive response] would fulfill, with his very body, the commandment to perform an act of kindness for others by healing someone else with a part of his body which is of no use to him.

Should this be the case, one could assume that the dead would also be pleased with such use of their corneas. And even though it is written that the dead are freed of [obligations to fulfill] the commandments, great merit and satisfaction would accrue to the soul of the dead whose body is used for such a great *mitzvah*. Such considerations should not be taken lightly. . . .

And may God instruct us in wonders from His Torah, a life-giving Torah, and grant us the merit of giving proper instruction on the basis of principles established in our holy Torah.[110]

In recent years, the question of transplants in general was broadly considered by Rabbi Eliezer Waldenberg (1917–), who was head of the Rabbinic High Court in Jerusalem. The question before him was not the use of organs from the dead, but the permissibility of transplanting organs, such as kidneys, from a live donor. He forbade anyone to volunteer one of his organs if such action might endanger his own life. Waldenberg ruled that the prohibition against such a procedure applies also to the physician performing the operation. Waldenberg added that no one could be compelled to take such action. Organ transplants could be allowed even when there is substantial danger to the life of the donor only to save lives of especial value, such as that of a scholar of great importance, or of a young person to whom his aging father wanted to donate an organ. This discussion revolves around the question of whether a volunteer may be permitted ever to donate an organ. But Waldenberg was aware that such judgments about the comparative value of individual lives put those who make them on a moral "slippery slope." The most contemporary question—"by what standard does one allocate scarce medical resources?"—is on the horizon in this decision, but it is not yet faced (*Tzitz Eliezer*, Vol. 10, 25:7). The dominant view, in all wings of Judaism, is that the use of medical resources may not be determined by any assessments of the value of one life as compared to another. This is particularly true of economic differences. The poor should not be the last in the queue. "What proves that your blood is redder than someone else's?" is a basic principle of Rabbinic law.

Abortion

On what grounds the decision to abort a fetus may be made was already an issue in the Talmud. The fundamental ruling in the Talmud is that a fetus which endangers the life of the mother must be destroyed; otherwise, even though the fetus is not regarded as a human person, it is forbidden to kill it at will. And yet, there is substantial disagreement among the authorities as to what might constitute an acceptable reason for an abortion. The most severe view is that of Rabbi Moshe Feinstein, written in 1977:

> . . . Maimonides *(Laws of Murder* 1:9) states explicitly that killing the fetus is actually murder . . . It is permitted to dismember the fetus in the womb of a pregnant woman who is in hard labor, in order to save her life, for the fetus [in this case] is like a pursuer who seeks to kill her. The Torah obligates every Jew to save the one who is pursued, even if it means taking the life of the pursuer, even when the pursuer is a minor, even when the pursuer himself is operating out of coercion. Though one who does this [who takes the life of the fetus] is not to be punished, it is actually a form of murder; the pursuer may be killed only because of the obligation to save a life, even at the cost of the pursuer's life. . . .
>
> . . . There is a difficulty with Maimonides' statement, for if the fetus has the status of a pursuer, we should permit [taking its life] even when its head has emerged [and Maimonides does not allow that]. Rav Hisda raised this problem in the Talmud [recalling the teaching that once the head of the fetus has emerged it may not be harmed, since one independent life may not be taken to save another independent life] *(Sanhedrin 72b).* We should be guided by Rav Huna's explanation that the latter case is different, since the mother is being pursued from Heaven, and therefore the fetus [whose head has emerged] is not considered to be a pursuer [but is a separate, independent life]. . . .

. . . The Mishnah (*Ohalot* 7:6) is specific in its language, [teaching] that if a woman is in hard labor, with her life in danger, the fetus must be dismembered while it is still in the womb and removed limb by limb, since the life of the mother has priority over the life of the fetus. If the greater part of the child has already emerged it may not be touched, since the claim of one independent life cannot override the claim of another independent life. . . . The fetus [which has emerged] is considered to be a living creature [whose life is on a par with the life of the mother] and it is forbidden to kill it . . . However, it is permitted to do so [when it is totally in the womb], because the mother's life has priority over the life of the fetus.

. . . To kill the fetus is forbidden until doctors have made an evaluation that it is almost certain that the mother would otherwise die . . . It must be established that the fetus is a pursuer. But no distinctions are to be made among fetuses in other circumstances. Fetuses with a [predictably] short life expectancy, as determined by physicians, such as those who are born with Tay-Sachs disease, even when examinations show that the child to be born will have such a problem, may not be destroyed. Such a fetus poses no danger to the mother's life; it is not a "pursuer." This fetus may not be destroyed even though it is a source of great anguish for both parents. Because of this I have instructed Torah-observant physicians that they should not conduct such examinations, which can serve no good purpose. Since they are forbidden to abort the fetus, the knowledge that it has the Tay-Sachs disease will only be causing anguish for the parents. Moreover, [as a consequence of the examination] the parents might choose to go to a non-Jewish doctor, who does not observe laws of the Torah, for an abortion. . . .

I have written at length on the matter of this great breach in the world, since the ruling powers in many countries, including Prime Ministers of the State of Israel, have allowed the killing of fetuses. There is need now to make a fence to protect the Torah. Lenient decisions must be avoided, especially when they touch on the most serious of all prohibitions, against killing. Therefore, I was amazed by a responsum written by a sage in the Land of Israel to the Director of the Shaarei Tzedek Hospital [in Jerusalem], published in the journal *Assia* (#13) which permits aborting a fetus over three months old which has been found to have the Tay-Sachs disease. He prefaced [his decision] by saying that many decisors hold that the killing of embryos is a law traced to the

Rabbis [rather than to the Torah, and therefore is of lesser weight and is flexible]. . . . But he cites the responsa of Rabbi Joseph Treni [1500–1580] and of Rabbi Jacob Emden [1697–1776] incorrectly. . . . It is plain and simple, as I have written, that the clear halakhah according to the early Rabbis, commentators, and decisors forbids the killing of any embryo, whether properly conceived or a *mamzer*, whether ordinary embryos or those known to have the Tay-Sachs disease. Killing them is forbidden, and one should not err by depending upon the responsum of that sage [whom I have mentioned] . . . Everyone is obliged to pay respect to the Torah and true judgment (*v'din emet*).[111]

The opinion that was the object of Feinstein's vehement denunciation had been stated by Rabbi Eliezer Waldenberg. He had permitted abortion of a fetus known to bear Tay-Sachs disease, on the grounds that the mother's anguish would be unbearable. "In this specific case, where birth will bring with it terrible consequences, one can permit abortion up to seven months, on condition that the abortion will present no danger to the mother. . . . After seven months, the fetus is in most respects already formed." Waldenberg knew that he was dealing with a new situation, for Tay-Sachs disease had not been known to those who had considered the question of abortion in earlier rabbinic literature. He based his view on a reading of the earlier sources contrary to that of Rabbi Feinstein. In Waldenberg's opinion, killing a fetus is not murder, for the fetus does not belong to the category of "living beings" (*Tzitz Eliezer*, Vol. #13, 102). Waldenberg's view was not essentially different from that of the Reform authority, Rabbi Solomon Freehof. He held that the anguish of the mother is grounds for an abortion:

It is rather remarkable that the whole question of abortion is not discussed very much (in actual cases) in the traditional law. . . . The first responsum is by a great authority, Yair Chaim Bachrach, of Worms, seventeenth century. In his responsum ("Chavos Yair" 31) he was asked the following question: A married woman confessed to adultery and, finding herself pregnant, asked for an abortion. Bachrach was asked whether it is permissible by Jewish law to comply. . . . He concludes from the discussion of the Tosfos to Chullin, that a Jew is not permitted to destroy a foetus, that it is forbidden for him to do so, even though he would not be convicted for it.

Yet in the next century the opposite opinion is voiced, and also by a great authority, namely Jacob Emden ("Yabetz" I, 43). He is asked, concerning a pregnant adulteress, whether she may have an abortion. He decides affirmatively, on the rather curious ground that if we were still under our Sanhedrin and could inflict capital punishment, such a woman would be condemned to death and her child would die with her anyway. Then he adds boldly (though with some misgivings) that perhaps we may destroy a foetus even to save a mother excessive physical pain.

Solomon Skola, in his Responsa, "Beth Shelomo" (Lemberg, 1878, Choshen Mishpot 132), says that if it is within the first forty days of the pregnancy, there is no possible objection to an abortion; but even if it is older, the danger to the mother's life and health determines if an abortion may be performed. . . .

A much more thorough, affirmative, and intelligent opinion is given by Ben Zion Ouziel, the late Sephardic Chief Rabbi (in "Mishp'tey Uziel" III, 46 and 47). He concludes, after a general analysis of the subject, that an unborn fetus is actually not a *nefesh* at all and has no independent life. It is part of its mother, and just as a person may sacrifice a limb to be cured of a worse sickness, so may this fetus be destroyed for the mother's benefit. Of course, he reckons with the statement of the Tosfos to Chullin 33a, that a Jew is not permitted *(lo shari)* to destroy a fetus, although such an act is not to be considered murder. Ouziel says that of course one may not destroy it. One may not destroy anything without a reason. But if there is a worthwhile purpose, it may be done. The specific case before him concerned a woman who was threatened with permanent deafness if she went through with the pregnancy. Ouziel decided that since the fetus is not an independent *nefesh* but is only part of the mother, there is no sin in destroying it for her sake.

In the case which you are considering, I would therefore say that since there is strong preponderance of medical opinion that the child will be born imperfect physically, and even mentally, then for the *mother's* sake (i.e. her mental anguish now and in the future) she may sacrifice this part of herself. This decision thus follows the opinions of Jacob Emden and Ben Zion Ouziel against the earlier opinion of Yair Chaim Bachrach.[112]

In recent years, Reform Judaism has moved wholeheartedly, and the Conservative movement with some reluctance, to the view that an unwanted baby is, *ipso facto*, a cause of anguish for the mother; therefore, the decision whether to have an abortion is to be left in her hands. The Orthodox community, even at its most liberal, continues to insist that "abortion on demand" is forbidden. The fetus may not be a human person, but it can be denied life only if it presents clear danger to the life of the mother. Such a determination can be made only by competent authority, that is, rabbis after hearing the views of physicians.

Death and Life Support

In the halakhah, the definition of death is the cessation of breathing. Contemporary medical technology has made it possible for patients to breathe, and for their hearts to beat, with the help of machines even after all brain function is gone. Rabbi Moshe Feinstein, who was usually a strict constructionist of Talmudic precedent, came to surprisingly "liberal" conclusions on the question of the definition of death. He was helped by the medical and Talmudic expertise of his son-in-law, Rabbi Moshe Tendler. Together, in 1976, they reached the conclusion that death is defined by the end of brain activity, and that breathing by machine need not be continued:

If debris from a collapsing building has fallen on someone [and it is not known whether he is dead or alive] you must clear away the debris until you reach his nose, even on the Sabbath, in order to examine him (*Yoma* 85). The ruling is given in Maimonides (*Hilkhot Shabbat* 2:19) and in the *Shulhan Arukh* (329:4). If there is the slightest sign of breathing [discerned by holding a feather or a thin piece of paper beneath his nose], he is considered to be alive. If the feather or the paper does not move, he is assumed to be dead. But this procedure must be followed a number of times, as I have explained elsewhere (*Igrot Moshe, Yoreh Deah,* part 2, *siman* 174, section 2) in explaining the words of Maimonides (4:5), who wrote that one should wait a while lest the person simply had fainted, waiting for the amount of time after which it is not possible for a person to live without taking a breath, observing him all of the time, without being distracted for a moment, and noticing no breathing during all of that time. . . .

. . . I have heard from my son-in-law, the distinguished Rabbi Moshe David Tendler [a scientist], that physicians can inject substances into the veins by which they can determine whether the connection between the brain and the rest of the body [including the flow of blood to the brain] has been broken. If this connection no longer exists and if there is decay of the brain [cells], the situation is parallel to decapitation [and the patient is therefore clearly dead]. This leads us to be stringent when considering the case of someone in a coma who is unresponsive and cannot breathe without a respirator; he is not to be considered dead until this test is taken. If the test reveals that the connection between the brain and the rest of the body is being maintained, even though he is not breathing independently he should remain attached to the respirator even for a long period of time. Only when the test reveals that there is no longer a connection between the brain and the rest of the body is he to be considered dead.

And my son-in-law has also noted that in the case of those who have taken toxic substances such as large numbers of sleeping tablets, no determination [concerning death] can be made until the toxic substances are no longer in the body, as seen through blood tests. Such a patient who is unable to breathe independently must be attached to an artificial respirator until tests show that there are no toxic substances in the body. Then, if he is not breathing independently the respirator need not be attached again, for he is dead. But if he is breathing even slightly with difficulty he is alive and he should be attached to the respirator again.[113]

Even though Rabbi Feinstein is willing to accept brain-death as the end of life, he nonetheless forbade actively turning off respirators. He ruled that when the oxygen tanks needed to be replaced, one could wait fifteen minutes—that is, sufficient time to establish that the patient could breathe on his own—and not reattach the machines. Rabbi Eliezer Waldenberg suggested putting respirators on time clocks, so that one could reevaluate the patient at regular periods and decide not to restart the respirators if the patient could not breathe without them:

This is a response to a question from Dr. David Meir who was then Director of the Shaarey Tzedek Hospital in Jerusalem.

[We begin with Rabbi Waldenberg's summary of the question which was directed to him by the doctor.] . . . A man is brought to an emergency room after a terrible traffic accident. His skull may be crushed. The doctors, attempting to save him, quickly set up life-support systems and connect him to an artificial respirator since he is not breathing and it is also possible that his heart cannot beat independently.

After several hours, or days, it is clear that the patient lacks all independent signs of life. The question is whether the life-support mechanism, in this situation, is to be considered an instrument which is 'preventing' [the death] of the patient, in which case it would be permitted to remove the respirator. While a medical staff cares for a patient in an emergency room, it is not possible for them to evaluate with precision the patient's condition; every effort must be made there to save him, using all available medical equipment. Only later when in the course of treatment it becomes clear, for example, that the skull of the patient is crushed or that his spinal cord is broken, does the doctor confront the problem of stopping active treatment. It is emphasized that the question arises when the medical evaluation reveals that the patient's condition is incurable, hopeless. The purpose [of stopping active treatment] would be to prevent his suffering from continuing: to make it possible for the patient to die peacefully, to experience death with dignity, without having the degradation of being transformed into a creature attached to many tubes, to no avail, which destroys the divine image which is in him. . . .

. . . In The Book of the Pious (Sefer Hasidim, ¶ 723) it is written that if the sound of wood-chopping heard by a dying person is preventing the soul's departure, the person chopping wood is to be removed from the vicinity.

. . . We come now to my response. Every ailing person brought to an emergency room after an accident, or an incident of poisoning or the like, even including those whose skulls have been crushed, must be treated immediately with all possible life-saving equipment and therapies, including attachment to all available medical machinery. This machinery should be attached to special clocks with regulators, similar to those used on the Sabbath. They should be set for short periods of time, for twelve or twenty-four hours, for example. During this time the doctors will be able to conduct clinical tests with the available equipment to decide if the patient has any chance at all to live. If that is so, when the equipment stops, it should be restarted at once. However, if it becomes clear, for example, that the brain is crushed, and that there is no hope that the patient will live, or that the spine is broken and there is no connection between the brain and the body, the doctor will not be obligated to restart the respirator. . . .

. . . Indeed, it is forbidden for the doctor to do so, for reconnecting the patient to life support systems will at the most lead to [mechanical] bodily movements and will not at all lead to restoring him to life. Restoring the respirator will cause only immeasurable suffering and anguish. . . .

. . . It should be added that one should not disregard the additional factor which you [the questioner, the doctor] mention, namely the large expenditures which the family must make, which drives many families to the threshold of poverty, to no good purpose.

And may it be His will that Scripture be applied to us, as it is written: "Rescue me . . . from men, O Lord, with Your hand, from men whose share in life is fleeting" (Ps. 17:14), understood as in the commentary of Rashi as a plea that we be among those whose death in bed results from Your hand because their allotted time has ended through advanced age, and among those who have a portion in the life of the world to come.[114]

Note: Elsewhere (vol. 14, #80) Waldenberg maintains that blood transfusions, oxygen, antibiotics, intravenous fluids, nutrition, and pain relief medications must always be maintained for a patient who is terminally ill.

Orthodox halakhists refused to pass the barrier between not restarting the respirator and actively turning it off. To end life by active human intervention, even for the most merciful of reasons, is repugnant to Jewish scholars of all persuasions: man is not permitted to play God. This feeling is particularly strong in this century, which has witnessed so much murder, and especially of Jews by Nazis, in the name of purifying the human race. And yet there is a well-established principle in the halakhah that suffering must be alleviated, especially in the case of a *gosses*, someone who is in the throes of dying. To Rabbi Waldenberg's quotation from *The Book of the Pious*, that a woodchopper can be ordered to cease if the irritation caused by the noise keeps the soul of a *gosses* from departing, one can add a tale from the death bed of Rabbi Judah the Prince. His disciples were praying for him, and thus they kept him from dying. His servant disturbed their prayers, to end Rabbi Judah's suffering (*Ketubot* 104a).

The weight of contemporary halakhic opinion is on the side of the view that medicine may be given to relieve suffering in extreme situations, even if its side effect is to shorten life, and especially if there is any small chance that such medicine might actually help to alleviate the disease. Euthanasia is forbidden. Withholding medicine in hopeless situations "to let nature take its course" is, arguably, within the parameters of Jewish religious law. But what is the rule about withholding nourishment? There is no doubt that a patient who can still be fed by mouth must be fed. Patients being fed intravenously are in a different situation. Some authorities on contemporary medical ethics, including physicians and moral philosophers who are committed Jews, assert that intravenous solutions of food and water are as much medicine as substances which are given to patients intravenously. Therefore, they may be stopped for the same reason for which medicines might no longer be given. Rabbinic opinion is preponderantly, without regard to denomination, on the other side of this argument. To take away food and water, even if they come through a feeding tube, is not the same—most of the authorities insist—as ending medical treatment.

As medical technology keeps advancing, the questions that have been discussed in this section, and new ones which will be occasioned by future advances, will continue to be debated. The underlying principles of Judaism about life and death will be interpreted anew, and by scholars of differing outlooks. The fundamentals will remain the same: the Jewish tradition enjoins respect for life; acts which enhance life have a presumption in their favor. One dare not participate in euthanasia, but people must be helped to die in peace. Maimonides ruled that the essence of man is in his intellect, with the implication that when the intellectual capacity is gone, life should be allowed to end (*Mishneh Torah, Hilkhot Yesodei Ha-Torah* 4:8). This thought guided Rabbi Seymour Siegel (1927–1988), of the Conservative movement, in his permitting a "living will" in which the patient leaves instructions limiting what might be done in treating him in extreme situations:

It is clear that where death is imminent and where the procedure cannot bring a cure or even a significant amelioration of pain, what is best for the individual (especially if he expresses his opinion through a will) is to allow him to die naturally. . . . What the Living Will makes possible is the giving of the privilege to the patient himself to stop those things "that delay the soul's leaving the body." The developments of medical technology have caused problems which our ancestors could hardly have foreseen. We must not forget, in our loyalty to tradition, the welfare of the suffering patient who, when the Giver of Life has proclaimed the end of his earthly existence, should be allowed to die in spite of our machines.[115]

LOVE YOUR NEIGHBOR

The well-known passage from rabbinic teaching with which this section begins is expanded on in turn by Samuel Laniado, a rabbi in Aleppo in the second half of the sixteenth century, Moses Luzatto, a mystic and an ethicist in eighteenth-century Italy, and by four Hasidic teachers of the eighteenth and nineteenth centuries.

A heathen once came to Shammai and said, "I will become a proselyte on the condition that you teach me the entire Torah while I stand on one foot." Shammai chased him away with a builder's measuring stick. When he appeared before Hillel with the same request, Hillel said, "Whatever is hateful to you, do not do to your neighbor. That is the entire Torah. The rest is commentary; go and learn it."[116]

". . . you shall love your neighbor as yourself; I am the Lord . . ." [Lev. 19:18].

"I am the Lord." This explains two things. First, since the souls that are as they should be are all a part of God, and since the soul of one man and the soul of his neighbor are both carved out of the same throne of Splendor, therefore "love for your neighbor as for yourself" is meant literally, for he is as you. Since I, God, am He who created your soul and the soul of your neighbor, he is as you. And, second, if your love for your neighbor is as the love for yourself, this is considered love for Me, because "I am the Lord." Since your love for him is like the love for yourself, even for him who is an infinitesimal part of Me—how much more will you love Me! For the love of your neighbor will be considered as if I, God, had Myself received it.[117]

The practice of lovingkindness is essential to piety. The [Hebrew] word for piety or saintliness is derived from the same root as the word for kindness [chesed]. According to our sages, the world is based upon three things, one of them being the practice of lovingkindness. . . . Raba preached that whoever possesses the following three traits is obviously a descendant of our father Abraham: compassion, modesty, and the practice of lovingkindness. . . . Our sages said, "In three respects lovingkindness is superior to giving charity. Charity entails the giving of one's property, while the practice of lovingkindness entails the giving of one's self. Charity is given only to the poor, while lovingkindness may be shown both the poor and the rich. Charity can be given only to the living, while lovingkindness can be shown to both the living and the dead" (Sukkah 49b). . . . Lovingkindness demands that we not cause pain to any human being, not even to an animal. We must be merciful and compassionate to animals. Thus is it written, "A righteous man has regard for the life of his beast" [Prov. 12:10].[118]

A minor saint is capable of loving minor sinners. A great saint loves great sinners. The Messiah will see the merit of every Jew.[119]

Falsehood imitates truth and it seems impossible to know which is which. What, therefore, is the difference between the upholders of truth and the champions of falsehood? This is the unfailing sign: men of truth are especially dedicated to the task of redeeming captives. They hate slavery. This is the test by which you can tell the difference.[120]

A disciple of Rabbi Menachem Mendel of Kotzk, a man of large affairs, once came to him and complained that he was so involved in business that he could find no time to study even a bit of the Torah. The master asked him: "How many people do you employ in your business?" "A hundred and fifty," was the answer. "So. You provide a living for a hundred and fifty families. This is worth while enough that you should suffer for it both in this world and in the world to come."[121]

It is written of Joseph's brothers that "They saw him afar off, and before he came near unto them, they conspired against him to slay him" [Gen. 37:18]. The reason why the brothers wanted to kill Joseph is that they saw him only from afar. Had they seen him in true nearness, they would have understood his essence, and they would have loved him.

In every man there is a spark of the Divine Soul. The power of evil in man darkens this flame and almost puts it out. Brotherly love among men rekindles the soul and brings it closer to its source. [122]

4

THE CYCLE OF THE YEAR

THE SABBATH

In a basic Rabbinic image, mortals are God's partners in the work of creation. God labored and then He rested; human beings labor to perform their creative tasks and they, too, must rest. The Five Books of Moses ordain absolute abstention from work on the Sabbath. The Prophets emphasized that the ritual restrictions are necessary for attaining the spiritual state which is the purpose and meaning of the Sabbath.

The heavens and the earth were finished, and all their host. And on the seventh day God finished His work which He had done, and He rested on the seventh day from all His work which He had done. So God blessed the seventh day and hallowed it, because on it God rested from all His work which He had done in creation.[1]

Remember the Sabbath day, to keep it holy. Six days you shall labor, and do all your work; but the seventh day is a Sabbath to the Lord your God; on it you shall not do any work, you or your son, or your daughter, your manservant or your maidservant, or your cattle, or the stranger who is within your gates; for in six days the Lord made heaven and earth, the sea and all that is in them, and rested on the seventh day; therefore the Lord blessed the Sabbath day and hallowed it.[2]

Wherefore the children of Israel keep the Sabbath, to observe the Sabbath throughout their generations, for a perpetual covenant. It is a sign between Me and the children of Israel forever, for in six days the Lord made heaven and earth, and on the seventh day He ceased from work and rested.[3]

Observe the Sabbath day to keep it holy, as the Lord your God commanded you. Six days you shall labor and do all your work; but the seventh day is a Sabbath to the Lord your God; on it you shall not do any work, you or your son, or your daughter or your manservant or your maidservant, or your ox or your ass or any of your cattle or the stranger who is within your gates, that your manservant and your maidservant may rest as well as you. You shall remember that you were a servant in the land of Egypt, and the Lord your God brought you out from there with a mighty hand and an outstretched arm; therefore the Lord your God commanded you to keep the Sabbath day.[4]

Thus says the Lord: Maintain justice, and do what is right, for My salvation is soon to come, and My deliverance will be revealed. Blessed is the one who does this, the mortal who holds fast by it, who keeps the Sabbath and does not profane it, who keeps his hands from doing any evil. Let not the alien who adheres to the Lord speak, saying, "The Lord will surely separate me from His people." . . . And the aliens who adhere to the Lord, who serve Him and who love His name, everyone who keeps the Sabbath from profaning it, and who holds fast to My covenant, will I bring to My holy mountain, and I will make joyful in My house of prayer. Their burnt offerings and their sacrifices shall be acceptable upon My altar, for My house shall be called a house of prayer for all peoples.[5]

If you cease trampling the Sabbath, from doing your business on My holy day, and call the Sabbath a delight, and the holy day of the Lord glorious, and honor it, not going your own ways, nor pursuing your business, nor speaking thereof, then you shall be delighted in the Lord, and I will lift you up above the high places of the earth, and will feed you with the heritage of Jacob your father; for the mouth of the Lord has spoken.[6]

And it shall come to pass, if you will hearken to Me, says the Lord, and bring in no burdens by the gates of this city on the Sabbath day, and if you will sanctify the Sabbath day, doing no work therein, then shall there enter through the gates of this city kings and princes who sit upon the throne of David, riding in chariots and on horses, they and their princes, the men of Judah, and the inhabitants of Jerusalem, and this city shall be inhabited for ever. . . . But if you will not hearken to Me, to sanctify the Sabbath day, bringing in no burdens through the gates of Jerusalem on the Sabbath day, then I will set its gates on fire and it shall devour the houses of Jerusalem, and it shall not be extinguished. [7]

In those days I saw in Judah some treading wine presses on the Sabbath, and others carrying sheaves and loading them onto asses with wine and grapes and figs, and all manner of goods, and bringing them into Jerusalem on the Sabbath day. I warned them about selling food on that day. Some men of Tyre who lived there brought fish and all manner of wares, and they sold them on the Sabbath to the children of Judah in Jerusalem. I rebuked the nobles of Judah, and said to them, "What is this evil thing that you do, profaning the Sabbath day? Did not your ancestors do these things for which God brought all this evil upon us and upon this city? And you bring more wrath upon the people Israel by violating the Sabbath. [8]

The Mishnah, the code of Jewish law edited by Rabbi Judah the Prince in the second century, is next to the Bible the most sacred of Jewish books. It is the kernel of the Talmud, which is the record of three centuries of exegesis of the Mishnah. The rules for the Sabbath that appear next are primarily from the Mishnah, with a comment or two included from its interpretation in the Talmud (the *Gemara*).

The rules about the Sabbath, Festal offerings and sacrilege are like mountains hanging by a hair, for there is scanty teaching about them in Scripture while the rules are many. [9]

The principal categories of work [which are forbidden on the Sabbath] are forty less one: sowing, plowing, reaping, binding sheaves, threshing, winnowing, cleansing crops, grinding, sifting, kneading, baking, shearing, washing, beating or dyeing wool, spinning, weaving, making two loops, weaving two threads, separating two threads, tying a knot, loosening a knot, sewing two stitches, ripping in order to sew two stitches, hunting a gazelle [or similar beast], slaughtering or flaying or salting it or curing its hide, scraping it or cutting it up, writing two letters, erasing in order to write two letters, building, pulling down, putting out a fire, lighting a fire, striking with a hammer and taking anything from one domain to another [e.g. from private domain to public domain or vice versa]. These are the principal categories of work: forty less one.[10]

They sat and pondered: We have learned that the principal categories of work [forbidden on the Sabbath] are forty less one. To what do these categories correspond [i.e. on what basis have they been selected]? Rabbi Hanina bar Hama told them that they correspond to the categories of work in the building of the Tabernacle. [NOTE: Because of the juxtaposition of the commandments not to work on the Sabbath, Ex. 35: 1-3, and the description of the work involved in the construction of the Tabernacle, Ex. 35: 4ff., it was construed that every type of work which went into the construction of the Tabernacle is the type of work which is forbidden on the Sabbath. The Hebrew word for "work" is the same in both passages: *melakhah*.]. . . It has been taught: Liability is incurred [for working on the Sabbath] only for work which comes under one of those categories which were involved in the construction of the Tabernacle. They sowed; therefore you must not sow on the Sabbath. They reaped; therefore you must not reap on the Sabbath. [NOTE: Certain crops had to be sown and reaped in the process of producing dyes for the hangings in the Tabernacle.] They lifted planks from the ground [public domain] to a cart [private domain]; therefore you must not carry from a public to a private domain on the Sabbath. They lowered planks from the cart to the ground; therefore you must not carry from a private to a public domain on the Sabbath. They transferred planks from cart to cart; therefore you must not carry from one private domain to another on the Sabbath. But, you may ask, what wrong is done by that? Abaye and Rava, and some say Rav Adda bar Ahavah, explained that this would entail passing through public domain [the air between the carts is held to be public domain].[11]

Whenever there is doubt as to whether a life may be in danger, the laws of the Sabbath may be suspended.[12]

One may warm water for a sick person on the Sabbath. . . . We do not wait until the Sabbath is over, on the assumption that he will get better, but we warm the water for him right away, because whenever there is doubt as to whether or not a life may be in danger, the laws of the Sabbath may be suspended. . . . And this [violation of the Sabbath laws, whatever it might have to be] is not to be done by Gentiles or by minors [who are not obligated to observe the Sabbath law anyway] but by Jewish adults.[13]

"Call the Sabbath day a delight" [Isa. 58:13]. How do you make it a delight? Rav Judah, the son of Rav Samuel bar Shilat, said in the name of Rav: With a dish of vegetables [spinach or beets] and a large fish and garlic. Rav Hiyya ben Ashai said, quoting Rav: Even something very small, if it was prepared specifically in honor of the Sabbath, is a delight. What is an example of this? Rav Papa said: A pie of fish-hash and flour.[14]

"God blessed the seventh day and He hallowed it" [Gen. 2:3]. He blessed it with man's countenance, for man's countenance on the Sabbath day is unlike that of any other day of the week.[15]

The Emperor asked Rabbi Joshua ben Hananiah, "What gives your Sabbath-meal such an aroma?" He replied, "We have a spice called Sabbath, which is added to each dish we serve." The Emperor said, "Give me some of this spice." Rabbi Joshua replied, "If you observe the Sabbath, the spice works; but if you do not observe it, the spice does not work."[16]

Rabbi Levi said: If the Jewish people would observe the Sabbath properly even once, the son of David [the Messiah] would come. Why? Because observing the Sabbath is equal to all the other commandments in importance.[17]

This brief excerpt from Judah Halevi's *Kuzari* summarizes the classic themes of the Sabbath.

God commanded cessation of work on the Sabbath and holy days, as well as in the culture of the soil, all this "as a remembrance of the exodus from Egypt," and "remembrance of the work of creation." These two things belong together, because they are the outcome of the absolute divine will, but not the result of accident or natural phenomena. It is said, "For ask now of the days that are past . . . whether such a great thing as this has ever happened or was ever heard of. Did any people ever hear the voice of God speaking out of the midst of the fire, as you have heard, and still live? Or has any god ever attempted to go and take a nation for himself from the midst of another nation . . ." [Deut. 4:32 *ff.*]. The observance of the Sabbath is itself an acknowledgment of His omnipotence, and at the same time an acknowledgment of the creation by the divine word. He who observes the Sabbath because the work of creation was finished on it acknowledges the creation itself. He who believes in the creation believes in the Creator. He, however, who does not believe in the creation falls prey to doubts of God's eternity and to doubts of the existence of the world's Creator. The observance of the Sabbath, therefore, brings one nearer to God than monastic retirement and asceticism.[18]

Rabbi Judah the Pious (1150-1207), one of the saintliest figures of medieval German Jewry, is the author of the *Sefer Hasidim* ("The Book of the Pious"), a compendium of spiritual practices and tales. The two paragraphs that follow are excerpted from his discussion of the Sabbath.

"Remember the Sabbath day, to keep it holy" [Ex. 20:8]. But is one liable to forget the Sabbath day? For it does recur every seventh day. The verse means to imply that one must remember to remove those things which would make him forget to remember the Sabbath. For example, one should not be sad on the Sabbath. . . . Each Sabbath, one should do those things which remind him that it is Sabbath: One should bathe on Sabbath eve and dress in his best clothes and arrange for an *oneg shabbat* ("joy of the Sabbath") celebration, and read those things which are suitable for the Sabbath day. . . .

"On the sixth day they shall prepare" [Ex. 16:5]. One must very diligently prepare for the Sabbath in advance. He must be diligent and quick in this as one who has heard that the Queen is going to lodge at his home, or as one who has heard that a bride and all her company are coming to his home. What would he do in such instances? He would greatly rejoice and say: "They do me great honor by staying under my roof." He would say to his servants: "Make the house ready, set it in order, sweep it out and make the beds in honor of those who are coming. I shall go to buy as much bread, meat and fish as I can, in their honor." What, for us, is greater than the Sabbath? The Sabbath is a bride, a Queen; the Sabbath is called a delight. Therefore, we surely must take pains to prepare for the Sabbath; each person himself must prepare, even though he has one hundred servants.[19]

The modern religious philosopher, Abraham Joshua Heschel (1907–1973), is the author of this prose-poem about the Sabbath.

The Bible is more concerned with time than with space. It sees the world in the dimension of time. It pays more attention to generations, to events, than to countries, to things; it is more concerned with history than with geography. To understand the teaching of the Bible, one must accept its premise that time has a meaning which is at least equal to that of space; that time has a significance and sovereignty of its own. . . .

Judaism teaches us to be attached to *holiness in time*, to be attached to sacred events, to learn how to consecrate sanctuaries that emerge from the magnificent stream of a year. The Sabbaths are our great cathedrals; and our Holy of Holies is a shrine that neither the Romans nor the Germans were able to burn; a shrine that even apostasy cannot easily obliterate: the Day of Atonement. According to the ancient rabbis, it is not the observance of the Day of Atonement, but the Day itself, the "essence of the day," which, with man's repentance, atones for the sins of man. . . .

One of the most distinguished words in the Bible is the word *qadosh*, holy; a word which more than any other is representative of the mystery and majesty of the divine. Now what was the first holy object in the history of the world? Was it a mountain? Was it an altar?

It is, indeed, a unique occasion at which the distinguished word *qadosh* is used for the first time: in the Book of Genesis at the end of the story of creation. How extremely significant is the fact that it is applied to time: "And God blessed the seventh *day* and made it *holy*" [Gen. 2:3]. There is no reference in the record of creation to any object in space that would be endowed with the quality of holiness.

This is a radical departure from accustomed religious thinking. The mythical mind would expect that, after heaven and earth have been established, God would create a holy place—a holy mountain or a holy spring—whereupon a sanctuary is to be established. Yet it seems as if to the Bible it is *holiness in time*, the Sabbath, which comes first. . . .

The meaning of the Sabbath is to celebrate time rather than space. Six days a week we live under the tyranny of things of space; on the Sabbath we try to become attuned to *holiness in time*. It is a day on which we are called upon to share in what is eternal in time, to turn from the results of creation to the mystery of creation; from the world of creation to the creation of the world. [20]

Jewish liturgy prescribes special prayers for the Sabbath, some of which find their place at this point in our volume. First, two passages from the prescribed prayers for the Sabbath day; then, Kiddush, the prayer over wine, the symbol of joy, with which the Friday night meal, the feast of the Sabbath, begins; and then, *Havdalah*, the prayer over wine, spices, and fire with which the end of the Sabbath is marked—wine in remembrance of the joy of the Sabbath that has just gone, spices to uplift the spirit which is saddened by its end, and fire to mark the fact that now the workaday week begins, and fire may again be kindled.

Those who celebrate the Sabbath rejoice in Your kingship, hallowing the seventh day, calling it delight. All of them truly enjoy Your goodness. For it pleased You to sanctify the seventh day, calling it the most desirable day, a reminder of Creation.

Our God and God of our ancestors, accept our Sabbath offering of rest. Add holiness to our lives with Your mitzvot [commandments] and let Your Torah be our portion. Fill our lives with Your goodness and gladden us with Your triumph. Cleanse our hearts and we shall serve You faithfully. Lovingly and willingly, Lord our God, grant that we inherit Your holy gift of the Sabbath forever, so that Your people Israel who hallow Your name will always find rest on this day. Praised are You, Lord who hallows the Sabbath.[21]

Praised are You, Lord our God, King of the universe who creates fruit of the vine.

Praised are You, Lord our God, King of the universe whose mitzvot [commandments] add holiness to our lives, cherishing us through the gift of His holy Sabbath granted lovingly, gladly, a reminder of Creation. It is the first among our days of sacred assembly which recall the Exodus from Egypt. Thus You have chosen us, endowing us with holiness, from among all peoples by granting us Your holy Sabbath lovingly and gladly. Praised are You, Lord who hallows the Sabbath.[22]

Behold, God is my deliverance; I am confident and unafraid. The Lord is my strength, my might, my deliverance. With joy shall you draw water from the wells of deliverance. Deliverance is the Lord's; He will bless His people. *Adonai tzeva'ot* [the Lord of Hosts] is with us; the God of Jacob is our fortress. *Adonai tzeva'ot,* blessed the one who trusts in You. Help us, Lord; answer us, O King, when we call.

Everyone recites the following two lines together.

Grant us the blessings of light, of gladness, and of honor which the miracle of deliverance brought to our ancestors.

I lift the cup of deliverance and call upon the Lord.

Blessing over wine:

Praised are You, Lord our God, King of the universe who creates the fruit of the vine.

Blessing over spices:

Praised are You, Lord our God, King of the universe who creates fragrant spices.

Blessing over flames of havdalah *candle:*

Praised are You, Lord our God, King of the universe who creates the lights of fire.

Praised are You, Lord our God, King of the universe who has endowed all creation with distinctive qualities, distinguishing between sacred and secular time, between light and darkness, between the people Israel and other people, between the seventh day and the six working days of the week. Praised are You, Lord who distinguishes between sacred and secular time.[23]

THE FESTIVALS

The Sabbath is of course the most frequent of Jewish holidays, but there are others. In Biblical times, when the Temple still stood in Jerusalem, there were three pilgrim festivals when all male adults were required to visit the Temple, "to appear before the Lord." As we shall soon see, historical explanations are given for these festivals in the Bible; that is, each is related to a major event in Jewish history. Biblical Judaism, however, knew their agricultural origins as equally important. They marked the stages of the harvest, and were therefore celebrated with a special joy. In contemporary practice there are many reminiscences of their agricultural character.

You shall rejoice in your feast, you and your son and your daughter, your manservant and your maidservant, the Levite, the stranger, the fatherless and the widow who are in your towns.[24]

Three times a year all your males shall appear before the Lord your God at the place which He will choose: at the feast of unleavened bread, at the feast of weeks and at the feast of booths. They shall not appear before the Lord empty-handed, but each with his own gift, according to the blessing of the Lord your God which He has given you.[25]

Everyone is required to fulfill the commandment to appear before the Lord [at the three festivals of the year; see Ex. 23: 14–17] with the exceptions of a deaf-mute, an imbecile, and a child [none of whom is obliged to fulfill any of the commandments], a person of doubtful sex, a person of double sex, women, slaves who have not been completely freed, one who is either lame, blind, sick, or aged and one who can not go up to Jerusalem by foot.[26]

Rabbi Eliezer said: On a holiday one can either eat and drink or sit and study. Rabbi Joshua said: He should divide the day, devoting half to eating and drinking and half to the House of Study. And Rabbi Johanan said: Both of them [Rabbi Eliezer and Rabbi Joshua] were expounding Scripture. One verse says "a solemn assembly for the Lord your God" [Deut. 16:8]. Another verse says a "a solemn assembly for you" [Num. 29:35]. Rabbi Eliezer held that the day should be either completely "for the Lord" or completely "for you." And Rabbi Joshua held that it should be divided, one half "for the Lord" and one half "for you."[27]

Our sages taught: A man is obligated to see that his wife and the other members of his household enjoy the festivals, as it is written, "You shall rejoice in your festivals, you and your son and your daughter, your manservant and your maidservant . . ." [Deut. 16:14]. How do you see that they enjoy the festival? By giving them wine. But Rabbi Judah says that men and women should each be provided for according to what is suitable for them. Men should be provided for with wine. And what of women? Rav Joseph taught: In Babylonia they should be provided for with many-colored garments, and in Palestine with garments of polished flax.[28]

A non-Jew asked Rabbi Akiva in Sepphoris [in the upper Galilee]: Why do you celebrate the festivals, since God has told you "My soul despises your New Moons and your appointed festivals" [Isa. 1:14]? Rabbi Akiva answered him: Had He said "My New Moons and My appointed festivals" I would have to agree with you. However, He said "your New Moons and your appointed festivals," referring to festivals like those which Jeroboam the son of Nevat [who split the ten northern tribes into a separate kingdom after the death of Solomon] celebrated, as it is written "Jeroboam celebrated a festival on the fifteenth day of the eighth month . . . that he had devised in his own heart, and he ordained a festival for the people of Israel . . ." [I Kings 12:32-33]. But those festivals and New Moons which are decreed in the Torah will never be abolished. How do I know? Because their source is the Holy One, praised be He, as it is written: "These are the appointed festivals of the Lord . . ." [Lev. 23:4].[29]

PASSOVER

The miracle of the exodus from Egypt is an event which Judaism has never ceased to remember. References to it pervade the prayer book. God Himself, personally and not through the agency of an angel, redeemed His people from bondage. They left Egypt so quickly at the moment of redemption that the Jews had no time to allow their dough to leaven. Hence they baked flat cakes, the matzoth which are eaten to this day during the Passover holiday in commemoration of the exodus.

And this day shall be for a remembrance to you, and you shall keep it a feast to the Lord throughout your generations by ordinance for ever. Seven days shall you eat unleavened bread. On the first day there shall be no leaven in your houses; whoever eats anything leavened, from the first day until the seventh day, that person shall be cut off from Israel. The first day shall be a holy convocation, and the seventh day shall be a holy convocation; you shall do no work on them, except what must be done to provide food for everyone. You shall observe the feast of unleavened bread, for on this same day I brought your hosts out of the land of Egypt. Therefore you shall observe this day throughout your generations by ordinance for ever. In the first month, from the fourteenth day of the month in the evening, you shall eat unleavened bread, until the twenty-first day of the same month in the evening. Seven days there shall be no leaven in your houses. Whoever eats what is leavened, that person shall be cut off from the congregation of Israel, whether he be a stranger or one who was born in the land. You shall eat nothing leavened; in all your habitations you shall eat unleavened bread.[30]

On the night preceding the fourteenth of Nisan [Passover begins on the fifteenth] the *hametz** must be searched out by the light of a candle. Any place into which *hametz* is never brought need not be searched.[31]

Rabbi Meir says: *Hametz* may be eaten through the fifth hour [i.e. eleven A.M.] on the fourteenth of Nisan, but at the start of the sixth hour it must be burned. Rabbi Judah says: It may be eaten through the fourth hour, held [neither eaten nor burned] during the fifth hour, and it must be burned at the start of the sixth hour.[32]

So long as *hametz* may be eaten, one may give it as fodder to cattle, wild animals and birds, or sell it to a non-Jew, and one is permitted to derive benefit from it in any fashion. But when the time is past [and *hametz* may no longer be eaten], it is forbidden to derive benefit from it, nor may one light an oven or a stove with it. Rabbi Judah says: Removal of the *hametz* [Ex. 12:15] may be accomplished by burning. But the sages say: *Hametz* may be crumbled and scattered to the wind or thrown into the sea.[33]

If [on the fourteenth of Nisan] a man was on his way to slaughter his Passover offering or to circumcise his son or to participate in the wedding banquet at the home of his father-in-law and he remembered that he had left *hametz* in his house, he may return and remove it, if he has time to do so and yet fulfill his religious obligation; otherwise, he may annul the *hametz* in his heart [thus decreeing that it be considered as dirt, and as not in his possession]. If he was on his way to help those endangered by soldiers, a flood, thieves, a fire, or a falling building, he should annul the *hametz* in his heart [and not try to return by any means, since quick action may save a life]. However, if he was on his way to celebrate Passover at a place of his own choosing, he must return home at once to remove the *hametz*.[34]

Where it is the custom to do work until noon on the day before Passover, people may do so. Where it is the custom not to do

---

Hametz—anything, edible or not, made from or containing grain, flour, or bran of wheat, barley, spelt, goat-grass, or oats, which, due to contact with water or other liquid containing water, has fermented or is in the process of fermenting. Ex. 12:19 forbids *hametz* throughout the seven days of Passover (15-21 of Nisan).

work, people may not work. If one went from a place where they do work to a place where they do not, or from a place where they do not work to a place where they do, we apply the more stringent custom of both the place which one has left [in the event of a return] and the place to which one has gone. Let no one act in a manner different from local custom, lest it lead to conflict.[35]

Rabban Gamaliel used to say: Whoever has not said the verses concerning the following three things at Passover has not fulfilled his obligation. "Passover, unleavened bread and bitter herbs." "Passover," because God passed over the houses of our ancestors in Egypt. "Unleavened bread," because our ancestors were redeemed from Egypt [and there was no time, when they left, for their dough to ferment]. "Bitter herbs," because the Egyptians embittered the lives of our ancestors in Egypt. In each generation every individual is obliged to feel as though he or she personally came out of Egypt, for it is written, "You shall tell your child on that day 'It is because of what the Lord did for me when I came out of Egypt' " [Ex. 13:8].[36]

Three references to rejoicing are found [in the Pentateuch] concerning the festival of Sukkot. "You shall rejoice in your festival" [Deut. 16:14], ". . . you shall be altogether joyful" [Deut. 16:15] and "you shall rejoice before the Lord your God seven days" [Lev. 23:40]. However, there is not one such reference concerning Passover. Why not? . . . Because that season of the year was a time of death for many Egyptians. [When Israel came out of Egyptian slavery, many Egyptians died at the Sea of Reeds and, in addition, the Egyptian first-born had already died during the plagues.] Thus indeed is our practice: All seven days of Sukkot we recite the prayer of Hallel [joyous praise of the Lord] but on Passover we recite the prayer of Hallel in its entirety only on the first day. Why? Because of the verse, "Do not rejoice in the fall of your enemy, and let not your heart be glad when he stumbles" [Prov. 24:17].[37]

They mix him the second cup [of the four cups of wine which are drunk at the Passover table]. Then the child asks the father— and if the child does not understand the procedure, the father teaches the child how to ask—"Why is this night different from other nights? On all other nights we may eat either leavened or unleavened bread, but on this night we eat only unleavened bread. On all other nights we may eat all types of herbs, but on this night we eat only bitter herbs. On all other nights we eat meat roasted, stewed or cooked, but on this night we eat only roasted meat. On all other nights we dip but once, but on this night we dip twice." The father instructs the child according to the child's understanding. He begins with the disgrace and ends with the glory. And he expounds, beginning with "A wandering Aramean was my father . . ." [Deut. 26:5] continuing until he finishes the entire section.[38]

On the night of Passover Jews sit down to a ceremonial meal at which the ritual symbols described just above, the bitter herb and the matzoth, are eaten as an act of symbolic remembering. A stylized version of the story of the exodus is told; it begins by having the youngest member of the family ask four ritualized questions (quoted above) about the meaning of the feast. Here are a few excerpts from the Passover ritual (the Haggadah), representing some of the "answers" that are given.

We were slaves to Pharaoh in Egypt, but the Lord our God brought us out of there with a mighty hand and an outstretched arm. If the Holy One, praised be He, had not brought our ancestors out of Egypt, then we, our children and our children's children would be slaves to Pharaoh in Egypt.

Though all of us might be wise, all of us learned and all of us elders, though all of us might know the Torah well, it is still our duty to tell the story of the exodus from Egypt. And whoever elaborates upon the story of the Exodus deserves great praise. . . .

At first our ancestors were idol worshipers, but then God brought us near to His service, as it is written, "Joshua said to all the people: thus says the Lord, God of Israel, 'In olden times your ancestors lived beyond the river [Terah the father of Abraham and of Nahor] and they served other gods. But I took your father Abraham from there and led him throughout the land of Canaan and I increased his descendants. I gave him Isaac, and to Isaac I gave Jacob and Esau. I gave to Esau Mount Seir as his inheritance, but Jacob and his children went down into Egypt.' "

Praised is He who keeps His promise to Israel, praised is He. . . .

In each generation every individual is obliged to feel as though he or she personally came out of Egypt, as it is written, "You shall tell your child on that day saying, It is because of what the Lord did for me when I came out of Egypt." It was not our ancestors alone whom the Holy One, praised be He, redeemed, but He redeemed us as well, along with them, as it is written, "He brought *us* out of there, in order to lead us to, and give us, the land which He promised to our ancestors."

Therefore we are obliged to thank, praise, laud, glorify, and exalt, to honor, bless, extol and adore Him who performed all these wonders for our ancestors and for us: He brought us out of slavery into freedom, out of sorrow into joy, out of mourning into a holiday, out of darkness into daylight and out of bondage into redemption. Let us then sing before Him a new song: Halleluyah![39]

SHABUOT

In the ancient agricultural calendar this festival was marked by bringing the first fruits of the harvest to the Temple. In the cycle of Jewish historical memory, Shabuot is the day of the encounter at Sinai, when God revealed Himself to Moses and the Jewish people. The Voice was heard speaking the Ten Commandments. Jewish piety has embroidered on the meaning of this encounter in a myriad of ways. One of the most imaginative and poetic among the many is the idea that at Sinai God and Israel were "married" (the essential image, as we have seen earlier, of the Rabbinic commentary on the Song of Songs). There are a number of examples in Jewish literature of "marriage contracts" between God and Israel, with heaven and earth "signing" as witnesses.

You shall count seven weeks. Begin to count the seven weeks from the time you first put the sickle to the standing grain. Then you shall keep the Feast of Weeks for the Lord your God with the tribute of a freewill offering from your hand, which you shall give as the Lord your God blessed you. And you shall rejoice before the Lord your God, you and your son and your daughter. . . .[40]

I am the Lord your God who brought you out of the land of Egypt, out of the house of bondage. You shall have no gods besides Me.

You shall not make for yourself a graven image, or the likeness of anything that is in heaven above or on the earth beneath, or in the waters under the earth. You shall not bow down to them, or serve them, for I, the Lord your God, am an impassioned God, visiting the iniquity of the fathers upon the children to the third and fourth generations of those who hate Me, and showing mercy to the thousandth generation of those who love Me and keep My commandments.

You shall not take the name of the Lord your God in vain, for the Lord will not hold guiltless the one who takes His name in vain.

Remember the Sabbath day, and keep it holy. Six days shall You labor, and do all your work, but the seventh day is the Sabbath of the Lord your God. You shall do no work on it, You or your son or your daughter, your manservant or your maidservant, or your cattle, or the stranger who is within your gates. For in six days the Lord made heaven and earth, the sea and all that is in them, and He rested on the seventh day. Therefore the Lord blessed the seventh day and hallowed it.

Honor your father and your mother, that You may live long upon the land which the Lord your God is giving You.

You shall not murder.

You shall not commit adultery.

You shall not steal.

You shall not bear false witness against your neighbor.

You shall not covet your neighbor's house, or his wife, or his manservant or his maidservant, or his ox, or his ass, or anything that is your neighbor's.[41]

"Your two breasts are like two fawns, twins of a gazelle . . ." (Song of Songs 4:5). This alludes to the two tablets upon which were inscribed the Ten Commandments, each tablet the "twin" of the other. The five commandments on the first tablet correspond to the five commandments on the second tablet. "I am the Lord your God" corresponds to "You shall not murder," for the murder diminishes the image of the Holy One, praised be He, [as human beings are created in the image of God]. "You shall have no gods besides Me" corresponds to "You shall not commit adultery," for one who whores after idolatrous worship is like an "adulterous wife, who receives strangers instead of her husband" [Ezek. 16:32]. "You shall not take the name of the Lord your God in vain" corresponds to "You shall not steal," for the thief will be led to taking a false oath. "Remember the Sabbath day" corresponds to "You shall not bear false witness," for whoever desecrates the Sabbath bears false witness against the Creator, declaring [by that declaration] that He did not rest on the seventh day, after Creation. "Honor your father and your mother" corresponds to "You shall not covet," for one who is covetous [of his neighbor's wife] will in the end beget a son who will treat him with disrespect and who will honor one who is not his father.[42]

SUKKOT

To discuss the Sukkot festival here is to step somewhat out of chronological order, for in the calendar of the Jewish year this festival occurs after the High Holy Days, Rosh Hashanah and Yom Kippur. Nonetheless, Sukkot belongs together with Passover and Shabuot, for it is the last of the three "pilgrim festivals." Like them, it has a dual significance. In the ancient Palestinian agricultural calendar it was the end of the harvest, when everybody moved out into the field, living in tents, in order to complete the work before the winter rains began. The Bible also gives us a historical reason for prescribing that one must live in a temporary abode specially erected for the festival; it is a way of remembering the forty years of wandering by the Jews in the wilderness on their way to the Promised Land.

From the fifteenth day of this seventh month shall be kept the feast of tabernacles, seven days to the Lord. The first day shall be a holy convocation; you shall not work at your occupations. Seven days you shall bring offerings by fire to the Lord. On the eighth day you shall observe a holy convocation, and bring an offering made by fire to the Lord. It is a day of solemn assembly; you shall not work at your occupations.[43]

From the fifteenth day of the seventh month, when you shall have gathered in all the fruits of the land, you shall celebrate the festival of the Lord seven days; on the first day and on the eighth day there shall be complete rest. On the first day you shall take the fruit of goodly trees, branches of palm trees, and boughs of leafy trees, and willows of the brook, and you shall rejoice before the Lord your God seven days. And you shall observe it as a festival of the Lord seven days in the year. It shall be a statute forever throughout your generations. In the seventh month you shall celebrate this festival. You shall dwell in booths seven days;

all that are native-born in Israel shall dwell in booths, that your posterity may know that I made the children of Israel dwell in booths when I brought them out of the land of Egypt; I am the Lord your God.[44]

A *Sukkah* [the temporary shelter erected for the Sukkot holiday] more than twenty cubits high is not valid; though Rabbi Judah declares it valid. If it is not ten handbreadths high or does not have three sides, or if the unshaded area is larger than the shaded area, it is not valid. The School of Shammai declare an old *Sukkah* invalid, and the School of Hillel declare it valid. What is deemed an "old" *Sukkah?* One that was built thirty days before the holiday. However, if it was made specifically for the holiday, even at the beginning of the year [i.e. immediately after the preceding Sukkot holiday], it is valid.[45]

Our sages taught: "You shall dwell in booths seven days" [Lev. 23:42]. This means that you should consider the booth as a fixed dwelling for these days. This statement led them to say that one should consider a *Sukkah* [booth] permanent and a home temporary for these seven days of Sukkot. How? He should transfer the finest furniture and beds to the *Sukkah*, eat and drink in the *Sukkah* and study in the *Sukkah*.[46]

If a palm branch [or a *lulab**] was acquired by robbery or was withered, it is not valid. If it came from an *asherah* [a tree worshiped by idolators] or from an apostate city [*see* Deut. 13:16], it is not valid. If its tip was broken off or if its leaves were split, it is not valid. If its leaves were spread apart, it is valid. Rabbi Judah says: It may be tied up at the end. The thorn-palms of the Oron Mount [near Jerusalem] are valid. A palm-branch three handbreadths in length is valid if it is long enough to shake.[47]

Rabbi Eleazar said: Why were seventy bullocks offered in the Temple at Sukkot? [This is a comment to Mishnah *Sukkah* 5:6. Biblical law in Num. 29:13-32 ordains that thirteen bullocks be offered on the first day of Sukkot. During the remaining six days the number of bullocks was reduced by one each day.] Seventy were offered for the sake of the seventy nations of the world [to

---

*The ritual prescription is to take the palm branch *(lulab)* together with the branches of myrtle *(hadas)* and willow *(aravah)* in the right hand, and the citron *(etrog)* in the left hand, and to hold the hands close together during part of the liturgy on the festival of Sukkot [Lev. 23:40].

atone for them]. Why was a single bullock offered on the eighth day? For the single nation [i.e. Israel]. . . . Rabbi Johanan said: Alas for the idolaters! They have suffered a great loss without even knowing what they have lost. While the Temple stood, the altar could atone for them; but now [since the Temple has been destroyed] what will atone for them?[48]

This interpretaton of the meaning of the "four species" is from the *Sefer HaHinukh* ("The Book of Education"), the first medieval volume of Jewish religious instruction. It was composed by Aaron Halevi of Barcelona, a Spanish Talmudist who lived at the end of the thirteenth century.

. . . Since the rejoicing [on the holiday of Sukkot] might cause us to forget the fear of God, He, praised be He, has commanded us to hold in our hands at that time certain objects which should remind us that all the joy of our hearts is for Him and His glory. It was His will that the reminder be the four species . . . for they are all a delight to behold. In addition, the four species can be compared to four valuable parts of the body. The *etrog* [citron] is like the heart, which is the temple of the intellect, thus alluding that man should serve his Creator with his intellect. The *lulav* is like the spinal cord, which is essential for the body, alluding that one should direct one's entire body to His service, praised be He. The myrtle is like the eyes, alluding that one should not be led astray after his eyes on a day when his heart rejoices. The willow branch is like lips. We complete our actions through speech, and thus the willow branch alludes to the fact that we should control our mouth and the words that issue from it, fearing God, praised be He, even at a time of rejoicing.[49]

Jonathan Eibeschütz (1690-1764) was essentially a product of East European Jewry, though he served as rabbi in Metz, France, and Hamburg, Germany. A master of all fields of Jewish learning, including the kabbala, he was also a great preacher.

On Sukkot, the end of the Days of Repentance, the Torah advises us to accept the exile and to consider all the world as a void, as a shadow. Therefore we are told to leave permanent dwellings for a temporary dwelling, to teach that we are strangers on the earth, without permanance, and that our days are like a shadow lasting a night, blown away by a wind. What does man profit from all his labors under the sun? All his days let his eyes be on high to the One who dwells in the heavens. Therefore one must use twigs and branches for the roof of the *Sukkah* [booth], that the stars be clearly visible from inside it, that one might direct his heart to heaven. The Holy One, praised be He, will have compassion for the afflicted and the poor, for He knows man's low state. . . . What man can escape the afflictions and alterations of time? . . . It is profound advice to observe the seven days of Sukkot, for the verdict of the judgment of the Day of Atonement is not definitely set until Shemini Atzeret [at the end of the Sukkot festival]. We must then rejoice, trusting in the lovingkindness of the Lord, that He will judge our cause. Thus for the seven days of the festival. But the man who fears the word of the King of the universe will have a booth [*Sukkah*] not only during the festival of Sukkot. During the whole year, everything for him will be a temporary dwelling, and he will sleep in the shadow of the *Sukkah* and leave his permanent dwelling. [50]

A comparable thought is expressed in a twentieth-century sermon.

Sukkot is the harvest festival. At the conclusion of the harvest in ancient Israel, the tithes were due. The Jewish farmer had then to exercise his generosity by setting aside a portion of the harvest for the priesthood and some of it for the support of the poor. Obviously, at the moment when the farmer found himself confronted by the commandment to give some of his crop to charity, there was danger that the spirit of perversity would arise within him. He might reason: why should I give away to others that for which I have labored, which I have earned? Therefore, it was ordained that men live in the *Sukkah*, in a temporary dwelling, during this festival. Its purpose was to suggest that man himself is but a temporary sojourner in this world, that his home is his but for a moment, that nothing really belongs to anyone permanently, for the earth is the Lord's. This sobering thought is a bar to selfishness and a spur to charity. [51]

The Sukkot festival ends with an additional day "of solemn assembly." In contemporary Jewish practice this holiday is marked primarily by the festival of the Rejoicing in the Law (*Simchat Torah*). Throughout the year, in the prescribed synagogue ritual, the Five Books of Moses are read consecutively as the weekly Sabbath lesson from the Bible. The cycle of readings ends and begins again on this day. It is marked by joyous processions and dancing with the Torah Scrolls, which are taken from the ark in which they rest, and by the calling of everyone in the synagogue who normally is called plus small children to say a blessing at the reading desk over a passage from the Torah Scroll.

Seven days [of Sukkot] you shall present offerings by fire to the Lord. On the eighth day you shall hold a holy convocation and present an offering by fire to the Lord. It is a solemn assembly; you shall not work at your occupations.[52]

"On the fifteenth day of the seventh month you shall have a holy convocation . . . you shall observe a festival to the Lord seven days. . . . On the eighth day you shall have a solemn assembly . . ." [Num. 29:12, 35]. This might be compared to a king who invited his children to a banquet for seven days. When it was time for them to leave, he said to them: My children, please stay with me one more day. It is difficult for me to part with you.[53]

ROSH HASHANAH

Rosh Hashanah, the New Year, is the beginning of the annual cycle of the Jewish religious year. It falls on the first of the lunar month Tishri, which usually occurs in September. The ten days from Rosh Hashanah (literally, the "head of the year") through Yom Kippur (the Day or Atonement) are known as the "Ten Days of Repentance." These are the most solemn days of the year, for this is the period in which, in the image of the tradition, all the world is judged before God's heavenly throne. Nonetheless, solemn and serious as Rosh Hashanah is, it is not somber. It is the season of repentance—and of the faith that God forgives the contrite heart.

In the seventh month, on the first day of the month, you shall observe a day of complete rest, a holy convocation proclaimed with loud blasts. You shall not work at your occupation and you shall present an offering by fire to the Lord.[54]

Nehemiah the Tirshatha [governor], Ezra the priest and scribe, and the Levites who taught the people, said to all the people: "This is a holy day to the Lord your God; do not mourn or weep."

For all the people wept when they heard the words of the Torah. And he also said to them, "Go, eat your choice foods and drink sweet wine, and send portions to whoever has nothing prepared, for this day is holy to our Lord. Be not sad, for rejoicing in the Lord is your strength." And the Levites stilled all the people, saying, "Hold your peace, for the day is holy; be not sad." Then all the people went to eat and drink, and to send portions, and to make great mirth, because they understood the words that he had told them. [55]

Rabbi Abbahu said: Why is the horn of a ram sounded on Rosh Hashanah? The Holy One, praised be He, said, "Sound before Me the horn of a ram, that I might be reminded of the binding of Isaac, the son of Abraham, and thus consider your fulfillment of this commandment [of sounding a horn] as though you had bound yourselves upon an altar before Me. [See Gen. 22, where the ram is sacrificed in place of Isaac.][56]

Rabbi Kruspedai said, quoting Rabbi Johanan: On Rosh Hashanah [when the world is judged], three books are opened in the heavenly court; one for the wicked, one for the righteous, and one for those in between. The fate of the righteous is inscribed and sealed then and there: Life. The fate of the wicked is inscribed and sealed then and there: Death. The fate of those in between lies in doubt from Rosh Hashanah until Yom Kippur. If, during those days, they show their worth through their deeds, they are inscribed and sealed for Life; and if not, they are inscribed and sealed for Death. [57]

Rabbi Pinhas and Rabbi Hilkiah said in the name of Rabbi Simon: Each year, all of the ministering angels appear before the Holy One, praised be He, and ask, "Lord of the Universe! When does Rosh Hashanah occur this year?" And He answers them, "Why do you ask Me? Let us inquire of the earthly court" [which in ancient times set the date of each new month and thus the entire calendar].

Rabbi Hoshayah taught: When the earthly court decrees "Today is Rosh Hashanah," the Holy One, praised be He, tells the ministering angels, "Set up the court room, and let the attorneys for defense and prosecution take their places, for My children have stated 'Today is Rosh Hashanah.' " But if the earthly court should reconsider and decide that the following day should be declared the first of the year, the Holy One, praised be He, tells the ministering angels, "Set up the court room and let the attorneys for prosecution and defense take their places on the morrow, for My children have reconsidered and decided that tomorrow is to be declared the first of the year."

What is the reason for this? "For it is a statute in Israel, an ordinance of the God of Jacob" [Ps. 81:5]. However, if it is not a statute in Israel, it is not an ordinance [for] the God of Jacob.[58]

Let not a repentant sinner imagine that he is remote from the estate of the righteous because of the sins and misdeeds that he has done. This is not true, for he is beloved and precious to God as if he had never sinned. Indeed, his reward is great, because he has tasted of sin and separated himself from it, having conquered his evil inclination. It is written in the Talmud that "In the place where repentant sinners stand perfect saints cannot stand" (*Berakhot* 34b); their estate is higher than that of those who never sinned because they have had to struggle more fiercely to subdue their evil inclination.[59]

With the help of God, the eve of the holy Sabbath, 5591 [1831].

To my beloved son, Isaac, may his light shine;

I received your letter this very hour and I have no time at all to answer it properly. May the Almighty strengthen your heart and move you on the great and fearful day of Rosh Hashanah which is approaching, that you may make it your purpose henceforth to renew yourself each day for good. Do not lose a day without a period of solitary meditation, during which you will contemplate your ultimate purpose. Snatch each day as much study of Torah, prayer and good deeds as you will be able to steal from this passing shade, this vanity of vanities, this evanescent cloud. Remember well that all our days are nothing. Every man can snatch in them some piece of eternity on some level. More than this I am not free to write now.

The words of your father, who seeks your peace and prays for you,

Nathan of Nemirov[60]

The selections that follow, to the end of the section on Rosh Hashanah, are taken from the prescribed prayers of the Rosh Hashanah liturgy.

We acclaim this day's pure sanctity, its awesome power. This day, Lord, Your dominion is deeply felt. Compassion and truth, its foundations, are perceived. In truth do You judge and prosecute, discern motives and bear witness, record and seal, count and measure, remembering all that we have forgotten. You open the Book of Remembrance and it speaks for itself, for every man has signed it with his deeds.

The great shofar is sounded. A still, small voice is heard. This day even angels are alarmed, seized with fear and trembling as they declare: "The day of judgment is here!" For even the hosts of heaven are judged. This day all who walk the earth pass before You as a flock of sheep. And like a shepherd who gathers his flock, bringing them under his staff, You bring everything that lives before You for review. You determine the life and decree the destiny of every creature.

On Rosh Hashanah [New Year's Day] it is written and on Yom Kippur [The Day of Atonement] it is sealed. How many shall leave this world and how many shall be born into it, who shall live and who shall die, who shall live out the limit of his days and who shall not, who shall perish by fire and who by water, who by sword and who by beast, who by hunger and who by thirst, who by earthquake and who by plague, who by strangling and who by stoning, who shall rest and who shall wander, who shall be at peace and who shall be tormented, who shall be poor and who shall be rich, who shall be humbled and who shall be exalted.

But penitence, prayer and good deeds can annul the severity of the decree.

Your glory is Your nature: slow to anger, ready to forgive. You desire not the sinner's death, but that he turn from his path and live. Until the day of his death You wait for him. Whenever he returns, You welcome him at once. Truly You are Creator, and know the weakness of Your creatures, who are but flesh and blood.

Man's origin is dust and his end is dust. He spends his life earning bread. He is like a clay vessel, easily broken, like withering grass, a fading flower, a passing shadow, a fugitive cloud, a fleeting breeze, scattering dust, a vanishing dream.

But You are King, eternal God.

Your years have no limit, Your days have no end. Your sublime glory is beyond comprehension. Your mysterious name is beyond explanation. Your name befits You as You befit Your name. And You have linked our name with Yours.[61]

Today the world is born. Today all creatures everywhere stand in judgment, some as children and some as slaves. If we merit consideration as children, show us a father's mercy. If we stand in judgment as slaves, grant us freedom. We look to You for compassion when You declare our fate, awesome, holy God.[62]

O Lord our God, let all Your creatures sense Your awesome power, let all that You have fashioned stand in fear and trembling. Let all mankind pledge You their allegiance, united whole heartedly to carry out Your will. For we know, Lord our God, that Your sovereignty, Your power and Your awesome majesty are supreme over all creation.

Grant honor, Lord, to Your people, glory to those who revere You, hope to those who seek You and confidence to those who await You. Grant joy to Your land and gladness to Your city. Kindle the lamp of Your anointed servant, David, by fulfilling our prayers for the days of the Messiah soon, in our days.

Then the righteous will be glad, the upright rejoice, the pious celebrate in song. When You remove the tyranny of arrogance from the earth, evil will be silenced, all wickedness will vanish like smoke.[63]

YOM KIPPUR

One day a year Jews attempt to serve God as if they were angels, not mortals. Angels neither eat nor drink; their sole daily task is to praise God. So on Yom Kippur (the Day of Atonement) the Jew neither eats nor drinks anything at all, observing the strictest of fasts, spending every waking hour in prayer and introspection. On that day, the conclusion of the Ten Days of Repentance, the fate of each human being for the year to come is finally decided. It was legal procedure in the ancient Jewish law courts that the accused sat in the dock in an attitude of mourning; such an attitude is prescribed for all Jews on this most solemn day. But with all its solemnity, even on Yom Kippur the sense of at-homeness with God continues to prevail. Note in particular the story of Rabbi Elimelekh of Lizhensk (died in 1787), one of the founders of Hasidism, in the section following.

The tenth day of this seventh month shall be the Day of Atonement. It shall be a holy convocation for you, and you shall practice self-denial, and you shall bring an offering by fire to the

Lord. You shall do no work on this day for it is a day of atonement, to atone for you before the Lord your God. Every person who does not practice self-denial on this day shall be cut off from his people. And whoever does any work will I cause to perish from among his people. You shall do no work on that day; it is a statute forever throughout your generations, in all your dwellings. It is a Sabbath of complete rest and you shall practice self-denial beginning on the ninth day of the month at evening, from evening until evening you shall keep your Sabbath.[64]

Seven days before Yom Kippur they escorted the High Priest [kohen gadol] from his own house to a special chamber on the Temple grounds [where he stayed until Yom Kippur]. Another priest [kohen] was prepared to take his place lest something happen to render him unfit [by becoming ritually unclean or by suffering certain bodily defects] to perform his duties.[65]

The High Priest placed both hands upon the bullock and made confession for himself and for his household. And thus did he say: O God, I have committed iniquity, I have transgressed, I have sinned against You, I and my household. I beseech You, O God, to forgive the iniquities and the transgressions and the sins which I have committed against You, I and my household, as it is written in the Torah of Moses, Your servant, "For on this day atonement shall be made for you, to cleanse you. Of all your sins before the Lord . . ."

And when they heard the glorious, awesome Name expressly pronounced as it was only on Yom Kippur and only by the High Priest, in a way we no longer know, the priests and all the people standing in the Temple Court would bow and kneel and fall prostrate to the ground, saying: "Praised be His glorious sovereignty throughout all time!"

The High Priest would prolong his utterance of the Name until the people had completed their praise, whereupon he would complete the verse he had begun, saying: ". . . you shall be cleansed."[66]

[Later in the Service, the High Priest followed a similar procedure on behalf of the priestly House of Aaron (Mishnah Yoma 4:2) and then on behalf of the entire House of Israel (Mishnah Yoma 6:2).]

On Yom Kippur, eating, drinking, washing, anointing with oil, wearing of sandals and sexual intercourse are forbidden. A king or bride may wash their faces, and a woman after childbirth may wear sandals, according to Rabbi Eliezer. But the sages forbid it.[67]

Young children are not to fast on Yom Kippur. But one or two years before they come of age they should be trained [by fasting part of the day], that they may become well versed in the commandments.[68]

If a pregnant woman smells food and craves it on Yom Kippur, she may be fed until she recovers. One who is ill may be fed at the word of experts [i.e. medical advisers]. If no experts are readily available, one who is ill may be fed at his own demand, until he says "Enough."[69]

The numerical value of the letters in the word "Satan" [Hebrew: *Hasatan*] is 364, the total number of days in a year, less one. Satan can accuse the Jewish people and lead them astray every day of the year, with the exception of Yom Kippur. On that day the Holy One, praised be He, says to Satan, "You have no power over them today. Nevertheless, go and see what they are doing." When Satan finds them all fasting and praying, clothed in white garments like angels, he immediately returns in shame and confusion. The Holy One asks him, "How are My children?" Satan answers, "They are like angels, and I have no power over them." Thereupon the Holy One, praised be He, puts Satan in chains and declares to His people, "I have forgiven you."[70]

One who says, "I will sin and repent, and sin and repent again" will be given no chance to repent. For one who says, "I will sin and Yom Kippur will effect atonement," Yom Kippur effects no atonement. Yom Kippur effects atonement for one's transgressions against God; but it effects atonement for one's transgressions against other human beings only if the offended has first been appeased.[71]

Rabbi Simeon ben Gamliel said: There were no happier days for the people Israel than the fifteenth of Ab and Yom Kippur, on which the young girls of Jerusalem would venture forth. All of them would dress in simple white garments, borrowed from each other, so that even the poorest among them need not be embarrassed. . . . They would venture forth to dance in the vineyards. What would they sing as they danced? "Lift up your eyes, young man, and look around, that you might make your choice.

Look not for beauty, but look for family. 'Charm is deceitful and beauty is vain, but a God fearing woman is much to be praised' [Prov. 31:30]."[72]

Rabbi Elimelekh of Lizhensk once sent his disciples on the eve of the Day of Atonement to observe the actions of a tailor. "From him," he said, "you will learn what one should do on this holy day." From a window the disciples saw the tailor take a book from his shelf in which was written all the sins that he had committed throughout the entire year. Book in hand, the tailor addressed God: "Today, the day of forgiveness for all Israel, the moment has come for us—You, God, and myself—to settle our account. Here is the list of all my sins, but here also is another volume in which I have written down all the sins that You have committed: the pain, the woe and the heartache that You have sent me and my family. Lord of the universe, if we were to total the accounts exactly, You would owe me much more than I would owe You! But it is the eve of the Day of Atonement, when everyone is commanded to make peace with his fellow. Hence, I forgive You for Your sins if You will forgive me for mine." The tailor then poured himself a cup of wine, pronounced the blessing over it, and then exclaimed: "*L'hayyim!* [To life!], Master of the world. Let there now be peace and joy between us, for we have forgiven each other, and our sins are now as if they never were."

The disciples returned to Rabbi Elimelekh, recounted the tale of what they had seen and heard and complained that the tailor's words were overly impudent before Heaven. Their master answered that God Himself and His heavenly court had come to listen to what the tailor had said, in great innocence, and that the tailor's words had caused great joy in all the heavenly spheres.[73]

It is written in the liturgy of Rosh Hashanah:
"And the angels will hasten, and fear and trembling will seize them, and they will say, Behold it is the Day of Judgment, to judge the hosts of heaven in justice." Why quote the hosts of heaven? When God sits as Judge over the people Israel, He also judges the angels. The angels themselves were created only so that they may elevate the prayers of the people Israel on high. The Almighty desires that on this day they should be defenders of Israel before His judgment seat. He scrutinizes the angels to determine whether they are carrying out their responsibility. When Rosh Hashanah comes, the angels begin to trem-

ble, for fear that they are not carrying out the will of their Creator.[74]

On the Day of Atonement it is the custom to wear a shroud, which is a white and clean garment used as the last raiment of the dead. This custom acts to implant in man's heart humility, and submission to the Divine will. (Gloss of Rabbi Moses Isserlin, *Orah Hayyim*, 510).

Rabbi Moses Teitelbaum once commented on this passage on the night of Yom Kippur, as follows: "Brethren, heed well that these garments which we are now wearing will be our apparel when we go to the next world, to account to the King of kings. Let us therefore imagine that we are now standing in these robes before the heavenly throne. Would we not be completely repentant? But repentance does not help after death. It does help now; therefore let us be remorseful with all our heart for our sins, and truly resolve not to sin again."[75]

The most famous of Jewish prayers is *Kol Nidre* (All Vows), the prayer with which the evening service of Yom Kippur [the Day of Atonement] begins. (All Jewish holy days and holidays as well as the Sabbath begin at sundown, for the "day" of the religious calendar is from sundown to sundown.) It is a declared and unalterable view of Judaism that one's prayers even on Yom Kippur can atone only for one's sins against God. Yom Kippur does not atone for sins against another human being until one has placated the person offended. *Kol Nidre* came into the ritual in the early Middle Ages as a formal annulment of those vows one had made to God, *not* whatever obligations one might have assumed to another human being. In Jewish sentiment the *Kol Nidre* prayer has been associated with the secret synagogues of the Marranos in medieval Spain. These forced converts to Christianity supposedly made it possible for themselves to say the Yom Kippur prayers with a clear conscience by first annulling the vows to another faith that they had taken under duress. The haunting melody of *Kol Nidre* is the best-known chant in all of Jewish liturgy.

By the authority of the court on high and by the authority of the court below, with divine consent and with the consent of the congregation, we hereby declare that is is permissible to pray with those who have transgressed.

All vows and oaths that we take, all promises and obligations that we make, vowing, swearing and binding ourselves [to God] from this Yom Kippur to the next Yom Kippur, may it come to us with blessing, we hereby retract. They shall be absolved, released, annulled, made void, and of no effect; they shall not be binding, nor shall they have any force. Our vows shall not be vows, our promises shall not be promises, our oaths shall not be oaths.[76]

Ten times on Yom Kippur the liturgy prescribes the saying of a confession. It is characteristic of Judaism that the confession obviously includes more sins than perhaps the greatest of sinners could have committed. The confessionals are couched not in the first person singular but in the first person plural. For in the deepest sense, we are each responsible for the sins of all.

Our God and God of our ancestors, let our prayer come before You; hide not from our supplication. For we are neither so brazen nor so arrogant to claim before You, Lord our God and God of our ancestors, that we are righteous and have not sinned, for indeed we have sinned.

We have trespassed, we have betrayed, we have robbed, we have spoken slander. We have perverted what is right, we have wrought wickedness, we have been presumptuous, we have done violence, we have forged lies. We have given evil counsel, we have spoken falsely, we have scoffed, we have revolted, we have blasphemed, we have been rebellious, we have been perverse, we have transgressed, we have oppressed, we have been stiff-necked. We have acted wickedly, we have acted corruptly, we have committed abominations, we have gone astray, we have led others astray.

We have turned away from Your good commandments and judgments and it has not profited us. You are just in all that has befallen us, for You have acted faithfully while we have been unrighteous.

What can we say to You, who dwell on high, and what can we tell You, who abide in the heavens? You know everything, hidden and revealed.

You know the mysteries of the universe, and the hidden secrets of everyone alive. You probe our innermost depths. You examine our thoughts and desires. Nothing escapes You, nothing is hidden from Your sight.

May it therefore be Your will, Lord our God and God of our ancestors, to forgive us all our sins, to pardon all our iniquities, and to grant us atonement for all our transgressions.[77]

We must mention here the more important minor festivals and fast days of the Jewish religious calendar. These are the eight days of Hanukkah, which commemorates the deliverance of the Maccabees from their Syrian and Greek oppressors; its chief ritual is the kindling of candles for eight days. Purim marks the triumph of Mordecai and Esther over the wicked Haman in Persia. The story of that event as told in the Book of Esther is read in the synagogue. The most solemn of non-Biblical fasts is the Ninth of Ab, which was ordained by the Rabbis in memory of the destruction of the Temple. Indeed, according to Rabbinic tradition, both the First and the Second Temples were destroyed on the Ninth of Ab. This fast is as complete as that of Yom Kippur. It is a day of mourning, and the Book of Lamentations is read. But on the Sabbath immediately following this somber fast the ecstatic words of Isaiah, "Comfort ye, comfort ye, My people . . . speak to the heart of Jerusalem and cry out to it . . . that its sin is forgiven," are chanted as part of the synagogue service.

New Observances

In recent decades there have been numerous stirrings toward formally remembering the destruction of European Jewry during the Second World War. The twenty-seventh day of Nissan in the Hebrew calendar, when the revolt against the Nazis by the Jews in the Warsaw ghetto in 1943 was finally crushed, has been set aside, in Israel and in the Diaspora, as a day of remembrance. The forms of observance generally include the lighting of candles and the saying of prayers in memory of the dead, but these commemorative events are usually public meetings rather than synagogue services. In ultra-Orthodox, non-Zionist circles, this most recent "destruction" during the Nazi years has been added to the solemn fast day of the Ninth of Ab, which was instituted in ancient times to mark the destruction of the First Temple by the Babylonians and the Second Temple by the Romans.

The creation of the State of Israel has been celebrated in liturgy for the synagogue. Immediately after Israel was founded, the Chief Rabbinate ordained a prayer in the synagogues on the Sabbath and the Festivals in which this historic event was described as "the first sprouting of our redemption." This theology was contested by the ultra-Orthodox, and even by many more liberal believers who were Zionists, on the ground that we cannot know the Divine intention; the redemption will come when He wills it. Soon, various proposals were made in Israel to make its Independence Day, the fifth of Iyyar, into a religious festival, complete with special prayers parallel to those of the biblically ordained holy days. The Religious Kibbutz movement published a prayerbook which includes the following instructions:

On the eve of Independence Day one should leave work early, before sunset.

People should bathe and dress in holiday attire in honor of the day.

People should get shaved and have their hair cut in honor of the day.

There are to be no eulogies, and no fasting, on Independence Day.

People gather in the synagogue for a service which begins with two chapters from the Book of Psalms to stimulate an awareness of the holiday [following the decision of the Chief Rabbinate].

The one who chants the service begins it [with *barkhu*, the formal call to prayer] in the musical setting appropriate for a Festival . . .

Some add the [special, for Independence Day] *al hanissim* prayer of gratitude for miracles to the text of the Silent Prayer and to the text of the Blessings after Meals.

After the Silent Prayer of the Evening Service, the entire Hallel [the prayer which responds to miracles] is recited, with the appropriate formal blessings preceding and following it. The same practice is followed in the Morning Service.

After prayers [in the morning] people gather for raising the national flag. . . . All who are gathered there should begin by singing "When the Lord restored the exiles to Zion we were like dreamers" [Psalm 126]. After the flag is raised it is lowered to half staff for the memorial prayer, and then raised once more. Chapter 62 of Isaiah is read aloud, with other passages appropriate to the day. We conclude with the singing of *Hatikvah*.[78]

This introductory section ends by encouraging visits to hitherto unfamiliar locales throughout the country and in one's own community and area. Visits to War of Independence battle sites are also recommended, "in order to transmit the magnitude of the miracle." And this is the blessing to be recited at such sites: "Praised are You, Lord our God, King of the universe who performed a miracle for us at this place." Special liturgies for Israel's Independence Day exist in various forms in many synagogues in Israel, and in some in the Diaspora, but such prayers have not become the norm. Almost everyone in the Jewish world agrees that Israel's existence is a fact of transcendent importance, but there continues to be political and religious controversy over what this modern "miracle" means and how it is to be celebrated.

5

LAND

THE HOLINESS OF THE LAND

There is hardly a major passage in the Five Books of Moses which fails to reflect and to reiterate the promise that God made to Abraham, that the land of Canaan would be his inheritance and that of his descendants. Judah Halevi expressed the classic view of Jewish faith that the people Israel is the heart of humanity (*see above*, Chapter I); a few paragraphs below, in this section, there is a comparable image from Rabbinic literature, that the Holy Land is the navel of the world. This land was fashioned by God for a particular service to Him, that its very landscape should help mold the character and spirit of His beloved people.

The Bible itself was already aware of the problem that the land was inhabited by others and that they might therefore claim ownership. It offers two answers: that the tribes living in the land were guilty of many sins, thus defiling it, and that no people could claim ultimate ownership in any land, for the earth is the Lord's. The comment of Rashi on the first verse of Genesis, with which we begin this section, expands on the second argument to "explain" why the Bible needed to begin with the story of creation. This argument has had a long history; it recurs in so modern a writer as Martin Buber in a letter he wrote in 1939 defending Zionism to Mahatma Gandhi: "It seems to me that God does not give any one portion of the earth away. . . . The conquered land is, in my opinion, only lent even to the conqueror who has settled on it—and God waits to see what he will make of it."

God dwells particularly in the Holy Land, and yet He is present everywhere, for the heavens and the heavens of the heavens cannot contain Him. In other words, everything that can be said about the doctrine of the chosenness of the people applies to His choice of the land. It is ultimately a mystery. Like the doctrine of the chosenness of the people, it has been and remains a powerful and impassioned motif of Jewish faith.

"In the beginning God created the heavens and the earth" [Gen. 1:1]. Rabbi Isaac said: The Torah [which is the book of Law for the Jewish people] should have commenced with the verse "This month shall be unto you the first of the months" [Ex. 12:2], for that is the first commandment in the Bible to the Jewish people as a whole. Why, then, does it commence with the account of Creation? Because of the following: "He has told His people the power of His works [i.e. an account of the work of Creation] in order that He might give them the heritage of the nations" [Ps. 111:6]. Should the people of the world tell the Jewish people, "You are robbers, because you took the land of the seven nations of Canaan by force," they could reply, "All the earth belongs to the Holy One, praised be He. He created it and gave it to whom He pleased. When He willed, He gave it [the Land] to them, and when He willed He took it from them and gave it to us."[1]

I will give to you, and to your descendants after you, the land of your sojournings, all the land of Canaan, for an everlasting possession; and I will be their God.[2]

And when the time drew near for Israel [Jacob] to die, he called for his son Joseph and said to him, "If now I have found favor in your sight, put your hand under my thigh as a pledge of your steadfast loyalty. Do not bury me in Egypt, but let me lie with my fathers. Take me out of Egypt and bury me in their burying place.[3]

Now when all of these things befall you, the blessing and the curse which I have set before you, and you take them to heart amidst all the nations among whom the Lord your God shall have driven you, and you return to the Lord your God, and obey His commandments, as I command you this day, you and your children, with all your heart and with all your soul, then the Lord your God will restore your fortunes and will have compassion upon you. He will gather you again from all of the nations where the Lord your God has scattered you. Even if your outcasts are at the ends of the world, the Lord your God will gather you and bring you back from there. And the Lord your God will bring you into the land which your ancestors possessed, and you shall possess it, and He shall make you more prosperous and more numerous than your ancestors were.[4]

Is it then to be thought that God will indeed dwell on earth? For if heaven and the heaven of heavens cannot contain You, how much less this house which I have built. But have regard for the prayers and supplications of Your servant. O Lord my God, hearken to the cry and the prayer which Your servant offers before You this day. May Your eyes be open toward this house day and night, toward the place of which You have said, "My name shall abide there." May You hearken to the prayer which Your servant will offer toward this place. And when You hear the supplications that Your servant and Your people Israel offer toward this place, hearken in Your heavenly abode, and when You hear, forgive.[5]

Just as the navel is found at the center of a human being, so the Land of Israel is found at the center of the world, as it is stated: "Who dwell at the center of the earth" [Ezek. 38:12], and it is the foundation of the world. Jerusalem is at the center of the Land of Israel, the Temple is at the center of Jerusalem, the Holy of Holies is at the center of the Temple, the Ark is at the center of the Holy of Holies and the Foundation Stone is in front of the Ark, which point is the foundation of the world.[6]

Even after the destruction of the Temple in Jerusalem and the Exile of Jewry from the land, its holiness remained. The Rabbis of the Talmud enacted this doctrine into law.

One may compel his entire household to go up with him to the Land of Israel, but none may be compelled to leave it. All of one's household may be compelled to go up to Jerusalem [from any other place in the Land of Israel], but none may be compelled to leave it.[7]

One should live in the Land of Israel, even in a city the majority of whose people are not Jews, rather than live outside of the Land, even in a city the majority of whose people are Jews. Whoever lives in the Land of Israel is considered to be a believer in God. . . . Whoever lives outside of the Land is considered to be in the category of one who worships idols. . . . Whoever lives in the Land of Israel lives a sinless life, as it is written, "The people who dwell there will be forgiven their iniquity" [Isa. 33:24]. . . . Whoever is buried in the Land of Israel is considered as though he were buried beneath the Altar. . . . Whoever walks a distance of four cubits in the Land of Israel is assured of a place in the world to come.[8]

Living in the Land of Israel equals in import the performance of all the commandments of the Torah.[9]

Rabbi Zeira said: Even the conversation of those who live in the Land of Israel is Torah.[10]

Ten measures of wisdom came into the world. The Land of Israel took nine, and the rest of the world took one.[11]

The Land of Israel is holier than all other lands.[12]

The atmosphere of the Land of Israel makes men wise.[13]

The Holy One, praised be He, said: A small group of men in the Land of Israel is dearer to Me than the Great Sanhedrin outside of the Land.[14]

A man may enter into a contract [verbally, with a nonJew] for the purpose of acquiring a house in the Land of Israel, even on the Sabbath [on which day such a transaction is usually forbidden].[15]

Jerusalem is the light of the world, as it is stated: "Nations shall walk by your light" [Isa. 60:3]. Who is the light of Jerusalem? The Holy One, praised be He, as it is written: "The Lord will be your everlasting light" [Isa. 60:19].[16]

Ten measures of beauty came into the world; nine for Jerusalem and one for the rest of the world.[17]

In every age, even when persecution was at its worst, some Jews clung to the Holy Land. The Romans and their successors, the Byzantine rulers, never were able to push all the Jews out of the Land. Some remained under the Arab conquerors in the eighth century. Even during the dangerous days of the Crusades, there were pietists who obeyed the commandment to dwell in the Holy Land. The Jewish community in Palestine was often few in number, but some always came to replenish it. The prayer book abounds in expressions of longing for the Land, but the tie through the ages was not only emotional and spiritual. Even in the unlikeliest circumstances some Jews continued to "ascend" (for to go to the Holy Land means to ascend in degree). Here is a letter written by one such pietist who went to Palestine, Isaiah Hurwitz (1555–1630), a distinguished Talmudist who was born in Prague and ended his days in Safed.

> Although Jerusalem lies in ruins now, it is still the glory of the whole earth. There is peace and safety, good food and delicious wine. . . . The Sephardim also increase much in Jerusalem, even in the hundreds, and they build big houses here. We consider all this a sign of deliverance, may it come speedily. Within a short time, you will hear, with the help of the Lord, that the community of the Ashkenazim is great indeed and venerable. For I know that many will come there who are desirous of joining me. May the Lord grant me life and health. I shall develop a wonderful activity for the study of the Torah which so far has been without a right guidance. That is why, because of our sins, ruin came. I wish to become a faithful shepherd to those who would study our sacred Law. It is also my intention to report the state of affairs here to the leaders of our people in Poland, to the sages among the leaders in Bohemia and to spread truth and confidence in every respect. . . .
>
> My beloved children, tell everybody who intends to go to the Holy Land to settle in Jerusalem. Let nobody assume that I give this advice because I shall settle there. Far be this from me! But I give this advice in all sincerity because all is good there and nothing is lacking. The city is enclosed and surrounded by a wall. It is as big as Lwow [the capital city of southeastern Poland], but the most important point is that it is particularly holy and the gate of heaven. I have firm confidence that the Lord will let much knowledge of Torah spread through me, so that the word may be fulfilled that out of Zion shall go forth the Law.[18]

Among the Hasidim, a sect which was founded in the eighteenth century, the Baal Shem Tov himself attempted to go to the Holy Land but failed. Legend has it that Satan opposed the plan, fearing that the encounter between the holiest man of the generation and the sacred soil of the Promised Land would produce such holiness that the Messiah would come. The Baal Shem Tov's great-grandson, Rabbi Nahman of Bratslav (1772–1811), did succeed in reaching the Holy Land, but did not stay there more than a few months. The story of his journey, too, has been embellished with many legends. One such tale relates that he remained in the Holy Land less than one day, just enough to perform his mysterious kabbalistic "Torah" there. Upon his return Rabbi Nahman told his disciples that he had been reborn and that his true teaching could only be that which he would say after the refreshment of his soul in the Holy Land. The version below is from the authorized account of Rabbi Nahman's teachings, as written down by his faithful disciple, Rabbi Nathan of Nemerov.

Rabbi Nahman of Bratslav lived in the Land for only six months, and most of this time he spent in Tiberias, engaged in the study of *kabbalah* and mystic discipline. He made haste to return to his disciples, in order to bring the message of the Land to them. From this time forth, Rabbi Nahman was another man.

His disciples have borne witness that all the life which he possessed came only from his having lived in the Land of Israel. Every thought and opinion which was his came only from the power of his having lived in the Land of Israel, for the root of all power and wisdom is in the Land of Israel. It was his wish that all teachings which he had disclosed before he was in the Land of Israel not be recorded in his books. It was necessary to record only those new teachings which he propounded after he was in the Land of Israel, and it was necessary to write all of these, every single word.[19]

GALUT (EXILE)

The Jewish people was exiled from the Holy Land into Babylonian captivity in Biblical days. Why did this happen? The Bible has a simple answer, that it was punishment for the sins of the people. The "chosen people" had even less right than the original inhabitants of the land to defile the soil of the Holy Land. But would God forsake them utterly on foreign soil? No, is the answer of prophets and psalmists. The God of all the world is present in Babylonia, too. After the term of their punishment is over they will be restored. But the exile wore on, especially the Second Exile after the year 70, and the most self-critical of peoples could not really believe that its suffering was entirely the result of its own sins. The doctrine of the "suffering servant" was invoked and expanded, that the people of Israel was bearing not only its own sins but the sins of others. The Exile was a time of testing, a prolonged corporate trial, like God's trial of Abraham. The task of the people was to remain faithful and to remember Zion.

> Who is so wise as to understand this? To whom has the mouth of the Lord spoken, that he can explain it? Why is the land in ruins, wasted like a wilderness, so that no one passes through? And the Lord said: Because they have forsaken the Torah which I gave them, and have not hearkened to My voice and have not followed it, but have followed the perverseness of their own heart, and the Baalim, which their ancestors had taught them. Therefore, thus says the Lord of Hosts, the God of Israel: Behold I will feed this people with wormwood, and give them gall to drink. I will scatter them among nations whom their ancestors never knew, and I will send the sword after them, until I have consumed them. [20]

> By the rivers of Babylon, there we sat and wept
> When we remembered Zion.
> There on the willows we hung up our lyres,
> For there our captors asked us for songs,
> Our tormentors for amusement:
> "Sing us one of the songs of Zion."

> How can we sing the Lord's song
> In an alien land?
> If I forget you, O Jerusalem,
> Let my right hand forget its cunning,
> Let my tongue cleave to my palate
> If I remember you not,
> If I set not Jerusalem above my greatest joy. [21]

The wicked emperor Hadrian, who conquered Jerusalem, boasted, "I have conquered Jerusalem with great power." Rabbi Johanan ben Zakkai said to him, "Do not boast. Had it not been the will of Heaven, you would not have conquered it." Rabbi Johanan then took Hadrian into a cave and showed him the bodies of Amorites who were buried there. One of them measured eighteen cubits [approximately thirty feet] in height. He said, "When we were deserving, such men were defeated by us, but now, because of our sins, you have defeated us."[22]

Whenever Israel is enslaved, the *Shekhinah* [God's immediate Presence in the world], as it were, is enslaved with them. . . . For it is written, "In all their affliction, He was afflicted" [Isa. 63:10]. This teaches that He shares in the affliction of the group. But what of the affliction of the individual? Scripture states, "He will call upon Me and I will answer him; I will be with him in trouble" [Ps. 91:15]. . . . It is written, "From before Your people, whom You did redeem to Yourself out of Egypt, the nation and its God" [after II Sam. 7:23]. . . . Rabbi Akiva said: Were it not written in Scripture, it would be impossible to say such a thing. Israel said to God: You have redeemed Yourself, as it were. Likewise, you find that whenever Israel was exiled, the *Shekhinah*, as it were, went into exile with them, as it is written, "I exiled Myself to the house of your ancestors when they were in Egypt" [after I Sam. 2:27]. When they were exiled to Babylon, the *Shekhinah* went into exile with them, as it is written, "For your sake I was sent to Babylon" [after Isa. 43:14]. When they were exiled to Elam, the *Shekhinah* went into exile with them, as it is written, "I will set My throne in Elam" [Jer. 49:38]. . . . And when they return in the future, the *Shekhinah*, as it were, will return with them, as it is written, "Then the Lord your God will return with your captivity" [Deut. 30:3]. This verse does not state "The Lord will bring back" [Hebrew: *v'heshiv*], but "He will return" [Hebrew: *v'shav*].[23]

Judah Halevi lived in Spain and longed for Zion, to which he went toward the end of his life. This poem is part of the liturgy for the fast of the Ninth of Ab, which commemorates the destruction of the Temple.

My heart is in the east, and I in the uttermost west.
How can I savour food? How shall it be sweet to me?
How shall I render my vows and my bonds, while yet

Zion lies beneath the fetters of Edom, and I in Arab
chains?
A light thing would it seem to me to leave all the good
things of Spain—
Seeing how precious in mine eyes it is to behold the dust
of the desolate sanctuary.[24]

Hasdai ibn Shaprut (915–970) was the principal minister in
the court of the caliph of Cordova and the leader of all Jewry
in the Iberian peninsula. The letter below to the King of the
Khazars is remarkable in its longing for the Holy Land, and
equally remarkable is the answer that he received, which is here
printed after Hasdai's letter.

I, Hasdai, son of Isaac, may his memory be blessed, son of
Ezra, may his memory be blessed, belonging to the exiled Jews
of Jerusalem, in Spain, a servant of my lord the King, bow to
the earth before him and prostrate myself towards the abode of
your Majesty, from a distant land. I rejoice in your tranquility
and magnificence, and stretch forth my hands to God in heaven
that He may prolong your reign in Israel. . . . We, indeed, who
are of the remnant of the captive Israelites, servants of my lord
the King, are dwelling peacefully in the land of our sojourning,
for our God has not forsaken us. . . . He who tries the heart and
searches the reins knows that I did none of these things [in trying
to communicate with you] for the sake of my own honor, but
only to know the truth, whether the Israelitish exiles anywhere
form one independent kingdom and are not subject to a foreign
ruler. If, indeed, I could learn that this was the case, then, de-
spising all my glory, abandoning my high estate, leaving my
family, I would go over mountains and hills, through seas and
lands, till I should arrive at the place where my lord the King
resides, that I might see not only his glory and magnificence, and
that of his servants and ministers, but also the tranquility of the
Israelites. On beholding this my eyes would brighten, my reins
would exult, my lips would pour forth praises to God who has
not withdrawn His favor from His afflicted ones. Now, therefore,
let it please your Majesty, I beseech you to have regard to the
desires of your servant, and to command your scribes who are at
hand to send back a reply from your distant land to your servant

and to inform me fully concerning the condition of the Israelites and how they came to dwell there. . . .

One thing more I ask of my lord, that he would tell me whether there is among you any computation concerning the final redemption [i.e. Messianic redemption] which we have been awaiting so many years, while we went from one captivity to another, from one exile to another. How strong is the hope of him who awaits the realization of these events, and Oh! how can I hold my peace and be restful in the face of the desolation of the house of our glory and remembering those who, escaping the sword, have passed through fire and water, so that the remnant is but small. We have been cast down from our glory, so that we have nothing to reply when they say daily unto us, "Every other people has its kingdom, but of yours there is no memorial on the earth." Hearing, therefore, the fame of my lord the King, as well as the power of his dominions, and the multitude of his forces, we were amazed, we lifted up our head, our spirit revived, and our hands were strengthened, and the kingdom of my lord furnished us with an argument in answer to this taunt. May this report be substantiated, for that would add to our greatness. Blessed be the Lord of Israel who has not left us without a kinsman as defender nor suffered the tribes of Israel to be without an independent kingdom. May my lord prosper for ever.[25]

The Reply:

With reference to your question concerning the miraculous end of days, our eyes are turned to the Lord our God and to the wise men of Israel who dwell in Jerusalem and Babylon. Although we are far from Zion, we have heard that because of our iniquities the computations are erroneous; nor do we know aught concerning this. But if it please the Lord, He will do it for the sake of His great name; nor will the desolation of His house, the abolition of His service and all the troubles that have come upon us be lightly esteemed in His sight. He will fulfil His promise, and "the Lord whom you seek shall suddenly come to His temple, even the messenger of the Covenant in whom you delight says: behold, he shall come, saith the Lord of hosts" [Mal. 3:1]. . . . May God hasten the redemption of Israel, gather together the captives and dispersed, you and me and all Israel that love His name, in the lifetime of us all.[26]

Each of the documents that follow, from various centuries, expresses the theme of mourning for Zion and the desire to return.

The first is from a letter of Rabbi Obadiah of Bartinoro, a distinguished Italian Talmudist of the second half of the fifteenth century, who left his home to settle in the Holy Land. He is here writing to his father in Italy.

> On Tuesday morning . . . we left Hebron, which is a day's journey distant from Jerusalem, and came on as far as Rachel's tomb, where there is a round, vaulted building in the open road. We got down from our asses and prayed at the grave, each one according to his ability. On the right hand of the traveller to Jerusalem lies the hill on which Bethlehem stands. . . .
>
> From Bethlehem to Jerusalem is a journey of about three miles. The whole way is full of vineyards and orchards. The vineyards are like those in Romagna, the vines being low, but thick. About three-quarters of a mile from Jerusalem, at a place where the mountain is ascended by steps, we beheld the famous city of our delight, and here we rent our garments, as was our duty. A little farther on, the sanctuary, the desolate house of our splendor, became visible, and at the sight of it we again made rents in our garments.[27]

The next piece dates from the eleventh century. It is part of a letter of recommendation written by the community of Salonica and addressed to the Jewish communities on the route to Palestine.

> . . . We send greetings to you and feel it is our duty to inform you about the request of Mr. N. N. He is a Jew from Russia and stayed with us here in Salonica, where he met his relative, Mr. X. Y., who returned recently from the holy city of Jerusalem, may it be restored by the Lord for ever. When he was told about the splendor of Palestine, Mr. N. N. too became very desirous of going there and prostrating himself on the sacred spot. He asked us to give him these few lines in order to use them as a means of introduction.
>
> Please help him to reach his goal by the proper route, with the support of reliable men, from town to town, from island to island. For he knows neither Hebrew nor Greek nor Arabic but only Russian, the language of his homeland.
>
> At all times the house of Israel, our brethren . . . excelled in the strength of righteousness and the power of charity, and you know their reward.[28]

Here is another letter, written around 1550, by Jews of Salonica.

The two Hebrew men, the two good messengers whom you have sent to seek out a refuge for you, have arrived here, and we rejoiced when we saw them, but we were deeply afflicted in our hearts on hearing of the yoke which the nations are about to let fall on you, and of the sufferings of exile which have been heaped up and placed upon your neck. And even this does not satisfy the nations, their hand is stretched out to strike at you once more, as they say: "Let us drive out the Jews!" Because of this our heart is faint, and we are sorry for you because the enemy has prevailed. The only thing which comforts us by the mercy of the Lord, the Master of pity, praise to Him and to His gracious deeds, is that He has made us come hither to this vast place where we eat bread which is our own, to a land which the Lord cares for from the beginning of the year even unto its end, and where nothing is lacking. . . .

Therefore, our esteemed brethren, who combine judgment with energy, do not hesitate to come hither and to enjoy the best of this land, and do not wait until the Count-Palatine tells you: "Rise up, and get you forth from among my people" [Ex. 12:31], lest the Egyptians become urgent upon you and send you out of the land in haste. You might not be able to spare the time necessary for the preparation of the departure, and the name of the Lord might, unfortunately, be profaned, as happened with the painful expulsion of the unfortunate Jews, descendants of Jacob, driven from Castile and Portugal, who, pressed by time, were forced to change their faith, on account of our great sins.

May the supreme Lord reunite the whole of Israel in the one place which has been elevated from the beginning, the place of our sanctuary; may your eyes and ours see Zion, the peaceful abode, when the Lord will bring back the captives of Jacob, and when it will again be said: "The Lord will be magnified from the border of Israel" [Mal. 1:5], because He will break the yoke of the nations which weighs heavily on your neck, according to the desire of your heart, full of the fear of God, and according to the desire of us who are making vows for your welfare and for your deliverance, and who invoke the Lord every day in favor of the remnant of Israel.[29]

This prayer about the Exile is very famous indeed. It was composed late in the eighteenth century by a great Hasidic master, Rabbi Levi Yitzhak of Berditshev (1740–1810).

> Good morning to You, Lord of the World!
> I, Levi Yitzhak, son of Sarah of Berditshev, am coming to
>   you in a legal matter concerning Your people of Israel.
> What do You want of Israel?
> It is always: Command the children of Israel!
> It is always: Speak unto the children of Israel!
> Merciful Father! How many peoples are there in the world?
> Persians, Babylonians, Edomites!
> The Russians—what do they say?
>   Our emperor is the emperor!
> The Germans—what do they say?
>   Our kingdom is the kingdom!
> The English—what do they say?
>   Our kingdom is the kingdom!
> But I, Levi Yitzhak, son of Sarah of Berditshev, say:
>   "Glorified and sanctified be His great name!"
> And I, Levi Yitzhak, son of Sarah of Berditshev, say:
> I shall not go hence, nor budge from my place
> until there be a finish
> until there be an end of exile—
> "Glorified and sanctified be His great name!"[30]

Why the pain of the Exile? Spanish Jewry in the fifteenth century, the community which suffered intense persecution and, finally, expulsion in 1492, faced this question with particular sharpness. Solomon ibn Verga, a Spanish Jew who lived through the expulsion, gives poignant expression to the mood of that generation.

> Surely from of old You are my holy God. We shall not die though fire consume us. With regularity our troubles appear, the last in their severity causing earlier troubles to be forgotten. The happy of heart moan, the joy of our proudly exulting ones has ceased. In days to come, Jacob shall take root, all our enemies shall march forth to scatter us; the light is darkened by the clouds

of our time; they have driven us to the final border; we have not retained strength and there is no breath left.

O God, You have expelled me time after time, but I have said that I shall bear the wrath of the Lord, for I have sinned. Defend, now, my cause, bring me out into light. Behold, new troubles I declare; we look for brightness but we walk in gloom. Lions roar at us, fiercer than the evening wolves.

. . . answer me, O Lord my God; preserve our remnant, for if You oppose us, what can our latter end be? . . .

I remember days of old. You set our nest among the stars and the splendor of Your glory was upon us, but now You have brought us down from there. . . .

Send forth Your hand on high, O Lord God, for there is no worm on earth as low as we are in our humiliation, like one forsaken among the dead. . . . If they increase the weight of his tombstone, he will not know it, and if they attempt to trouble him, he will not understand. But the living takes his own continual troubles and confusions to heart; his soul is bitter day and night, like ours at this time. If our transgressions have increased . . . pray increase Your power as You have promised, shepherd Your people with Your staff; do not deliver up our survivors with mortal staff, merciful and compassionate God.

How can You tolerate more when You have witnessed the evil which has befallen Your people, how can You, when you have witnessed the destruction of the homeland of Your servants' children? Belittle not our troubles; regard us from Your holy habitation. In spite of all the persecutions we have followed You. Speedily robe Yourself with lovingkindness and deliver us, for Your sake.[31]

Rabbi Jacob Emden (1697–1776) and Rabbi Jonathan Eibeshütz were fierce antagonists, but they agreed on the hope of the return to Zion as a central theme of Jewish piety. The first paragraph just below is by Emden, and the second, by Eibeshütz.

We do not mourn properly over Jerusalem. Were we guilty of this transgression alone, it would be sufficient reason for the extension of the period of our Exile. In my opinion this is the most likely, most apparent and the strongest reason for all of the dreadful terrifying persecutions which have befallen us in Exile, in all the places of our dispersion. We have been hotly pursued. We have not been granted rest among the nations with our humiliation, affliction and homelessness, because this sense of mourning has left our hearts. While being complacent in a land not ours, we have forgotten Jerusalem; we have not taken it to heart. Therefore, "Like one who is dead have we been forgotten," from generation to generation sorrow is added to our sorrow and our pain.[32]

One must weep ceaselessly over the rebuilding of Jerusalem and the restoration of the glory of King David, for that is the object of human perfection. If we do not have Jerusalem and the kingdom of the House of David, why should we have life? . . . Since our many transgressions have led to the Destruction and to the desolation of our glorious Temple and the loss of the kingdom of the House of David, the degree to which we suffer the absence and the lack of good is known to all. Surely have we descended from life unto death. And the converse is also true: "When the Lord restores the captivity of Zion," we shall ascend from death unto life. Certainly the heart of anyone who possesses the soul of a Jew is broken when he recalls the destruction of Jerusalem.[33]

TENSION BETWEEN GALUT AND RETURN

After the destruction of the First Temple, Jeremiah was convinced that the Exile would not end immediately. He therefore counseled the Jewish people to make peace with the condition that would last some generations by settling down into the civic life of Babylonia. Six centuries later, after the destruction of the Second Temple, Babylonia became a greater center of Jewish population and of Jewish learning than Palestine. There are therefore echoes in Rabbinic writings of the notion that Babylonia is as good a place for the Jew to live in as Palestine. Medieval rabbis quieted their conscience for failing to fulfill the commandment to go to the Holy Land by emphasizing the difficulty of the journey and the fact that the laws of tithing and other such obligations which applied in the Holy Land could no longer be obeyed there.

Thus says the Lord of Hosts, the God of Israel, to the whole community whom I have caused to be exiled from Jerusalem to Babylon: Build homes, and dwell in them; plant orchards, and eat their fruit. Take wives, and beget sons and daughters, and take wives for your sons and give your daughters to husbands, that they may bear sons and daughters. Multiply there, be not diminished. Seek the welfare of the city to which I have caused you to be exiled, and pray to the Lord on its behalf, for in its prosperity shall you prosper. . . .

For thus says the Lord: After seventy years are concluded in Babylon, I will visit you, and I will fulfill My favorable promise to you, to bring you back to this place. For I know the plans I have made for you, says the Lord, plans for well being, not for affliction, to give you a hopeful future. When you call upon Me, and when you come to pray to Me, I shall hearken to you. You will seek Me and you will find Me when you seek Me whole-heartedly. And I will be found by you, says the Lord, and I will restore your fortunes. I will gather you from all the nations, and from all the places to which I have driven you, says the Lord. And I will bring you back to the place from which I sent you into exile.[34]

Whoever lives in Babylon is considered as though he lived in the Land of Israel.[35]

Rabbi Berokia and Rabbi Eliezer were once walking by a gate outside of Tiberias, when they saw a coffin being brought into Israel from outside the Land. Rabbi Berokia said: Of what use is this? He lived and died outside of the Land, and now he has come to be buried in it! I would quote Scripture to him: In your life "you made My heritage an abomination" [Jer. 2:7] and in your death "you have come to defile My land" [ibid]. Rabbi Eliezer said to him: Since he will be buried in the Land of Israel, the Holy One, praised be He, will grant him atonement, as it is written, "He makes expiation for the land of His people" [Deut. 32:43].[36]

This law [emphasizing the importance of living in the Land of Israel] is no longer enforced due to the risks inherent in a journey to the Land of Israel. Rabbenu Hayyim maintains that living in the Land of Israel is no longer a religious obligation because of the difficulty and impossibility of fulfilling many of the precepts involving the soil.[37]

Mordecai Kaplan defined a widely accepted contemporary view. He argued that those Jews living in lands of freedom are not in Exile, while maintaining that the state of Israel has a particular importance for a present-day revival of Jewish culture and spiritual values. For him Israel was a social, political and cultural necessity for the creative survival of his this-worldly version of Judaism. Absent from his thinking is the mystery of the divine choice of a people and of the land for it. Peace, freedom and Jewish survival were his Messiah, not the Messiah of the traditional vision, who will appear in the world as the dramatic culmination of human history.

Jews in the Diaspora will continue to owe exclusive political allegiance to the countries in which they reside. The tie that binds Diaspora Jewry to Eretz Israel is a cultural and religious one. Culture and socioeconomic life are so closely interrelated that it is difficult for Diaspora Jewry to create new Jewish cultural values, since there is no possibility in the Diaspora of an autonomous Jewish social and economic life.

American Judaism is needed, and will long continue to be needed as a force to inspire and motivate our participation in the establishment of a Jewish commonwealth. . . .

. . . We have a part in the social, economic, and cultural life of America, and, unless we give to the common welfare of the American people the best that is in our power to give, we are not doing our full duty to our country. But as Jews, the very best we have to give is to be found in Judaism, the distillation of centuries of Jewish spiritual experience. As convinced Jews and loyal Americans, we should seek to incorporate in American life the universal values of Judaism, and to utilize the particular sancta of Jewish religion as an inspiration for preserving these universal values. To fail to do so would mean to deprive Judaism of universal significance and to render Jewish religion a mere tribalism that has no relevance to life beyond the separate interests of the Jewish group. The attitude of Jewish isolationists or the negators of the Diaspora, which would keep American Jewry with its loins perpetually girt for a hasty departure for Eretz Israel, is not likely to inspire our neighbors with confidence in the Jew, or with respect for Judaism.

Those of our young people who possess the abilities that are needed now in Eretz Israel to build there a productive economy for the rising Jewish Commonwealth, an economy based on the socialized exploitation of natural resources instead of on the exploitation of the weak by the strong, should by all means be encouraged to go to Eretz Israel. The colonizing and constructive effort in Eretz Israel should enlist those of our youth who possess the kind of pioneer spirit essential to nation-building. Our Jewish young men and women ought to be made to feel that their going to Eretz Israel to serve their own people would be as legitimate and noble an adventure as for other Americans to serve the various peoples in the Far East in a missionary or cultural capacity. But students who plan to go to Eretz Israel, with the expectation of engaging in some white-collar profession, would not render any specially needed service there, and only deprive American Jewish life of some needed service they might render here. We American Jews need desperately every available person who has the ability to transmute the cultural and religious values of our tradition into a living creative force.

. . . Those who despair of Jewish survival in the Diaspora, by maintaining that only in Eretz Israel can Judaism survive, evade the urgent task of rendering Judaism viable in America. Long-distance building of Eretz Israel is no less important than building it on the spot, but it cannot serve as a substitute for living a Jewish life here. Until Jews realize that the Jewish problem in the Diaspora and the Jewish problem in Eretz Israel are one, they are running away from reality and defeating their own purpose. Only as we assume the responsibility for having Judaism live wherever Jews are allowed to live are we likely to succeed in any of our Jewish undertakings.

There can be no question that in the Diaspora we Jews lack the spirit of dedication that goes with our people's renascence in Eretz Israel. We are without the magic power that comes with the spoken and creative Hebrew word. We are far from the land where the Jewish spirit is being reborn. But given the will, the intelligence and the devotion, it is feasible so to relive and to re-embody, within the frame of a democratic American civilization, the vital and thrilling experience of our people in Eretz Israel that, in the long run, we might achieve in our way as great and lasting a contribution to human values as they are achieving in theirs.[38]

THE RETURN

The ultimate return of Jewry to the Holy Land and the Messianic age are related to each other. The faith in God's promise is the ground for the sure and certain hope that the return will take place.

> Thus says the Lord: Keep your voice from weeping and your eyes from tears; for your work shall be rewarded, says the Lord. Your children will come back from the land of the enemy. There is hope for your future, says the Lord. Your children shall return to their own land.[39]

> An ancient tradition states that Jerusalem will not be rebuilt until the ingathering of all the exiles. If anyone should tell you that all the exiles have been gathered but Jerusalem is not rebuilt, do not believe it. For the Psalmist first stated "The Lord builds up Jerusalem" and then "He gathers the dispersed of Israel" [Ps. 147:2].[40]

> As for the principle of the redemption itself, that is something that must be accepted for several reasons. Among these are the validation presented by the miracles performed by Moses, who was the first to speak of these things. There are also the signs produced for the prophet Isaiah and other prophets who announced the redemption as well as the fact that He that sent them would undoubtedly carry out His promise, as is stated by Scripture: "That confirms the word of His servant, and performs the counsel of His messengers" [Isa. 44:26].

> Another (reason why Israel's ultimate redemption must be accepted as a matter of course) is that God is just, doing no injustice, and He has already subjected his nation to a great and long protracted trial, which undoubtedly serves partly as punishment and partly as a test for us. Whichever happens to be the case, however, there must be a limitation of time, for (such operations) cannot proceed endlessly. . . .

A (third) reason is that God is trustworthy in His promise, His utterance standing firm and His command enduring forever, as it is said in Scripture: "The grass withers, the flower fades, but the word of our God shall stand forever" [Isa. 40:8].

A (fourth) reason (for believing in our people's final redemption) is the parallel we can make between the promises concerning it and God's first promise, the one He had made to us at the time when we were in Egypt. He had then promised us only two things; namely, that He would execute judgment upon our oppressor and that He would give us great wealth. That is the import of His statement: "And also that nation, whom they shall serve, will I judge; and afterward they shall come out with great substance" [Gen. 15:14]. Yet our eyes have seen what He has done for us besides that; namely, the cleaving of the sea, and the Manna and the quail [to feed the Israelites in their forty years of wandering in the desert], and the assembly at Mount Sinai, and the arresting of the sun and other such things. All the more certain, therefore (must the ultimate redemption be). For God has made us great and liberal promises of the well-being and bliss and greatness and might and glory that He will grant us twofold (in return) for the humiliation and the misery that have been our lot. Thus it is said in Scripture: "For your shame which was double . . . therefore in their land they shall possess double" [Isa. 61:7].

Furthermore, what has befallen us has been likened by Scripture to a brief twinkling of the eye, whereas the compensation God will give us in return therefore has been referred to as His great mercy. For it says: "For a small moment have I forsaken you; but with great compassion will I gather you" [Isa. 54:7]. . . .

Therefore, also, do you find us patiently awaiting what God has promised us, not entertaining any doubts concerning it, nor worrying or despairing. On the contrary, our courage and tenacity increase constantly, as is expressed in Scripture: "Be strong, and let your heart take courage, all you that wait for the Lord" [Ps. 31:25].[41]

Everyone in Israel [i.e., every Israelite] must in his heart steadfastly resolve to go to Eretz Yisrael and to remain there. But if he cannot go himself, he should, if his circumstances permit—whether he be a craftsman or a merchant—support some person in that country, and so do his part in restoring the Holy Land, which has been laid waste, by maintaining one of its rightful inhabitants.

He must feel the desire to pray there before the King's palace, to which the Divine Presence still clings, even in destruction. Therefore he who does not live in that country cannot give perfect service to God.

You shall not plan, God forbid, to settle in a place not in that country. The mistake our parents made was that of ignoring this precious land, and thereby they caused much suffering in the generations that came after them. The thought of this land was our solace in our bitter exile, when many rose against us, for we could never find peace and rest. But when we forgot our yearning for that land, we ourselves were forgotten like the dead. Not one in a thousand fared forth to settle there, perhaps only one from a whole country, and two out of a whole generation. No heart longed for its love or was concerned with its welfare and no one yearned to behold it. Whenever we found a little rest, we thought we had come upon a new land of Israel and a new Jerusalem. And misfortune befell us because Israel lived in peace and enjoyed honors in Spain and in other countries, for more than a thousand years after the destruction of the Temple, and no son of Israel remained in the Holy Land. God is just. They were no longer aware that exile is their lot, and they mixed with the people among whom they lived, and learned their ways. No one at all yearned for Zion; it was abandoned and forgotten. We did not think of returning to our home. The city that contained the graves of our fathers was not our goal. We shared the joys of others.

We asked, "Who is the wise man that he may understand this? Wherefore is the land perished and laid waste like a wilderness?" And the Lord said: "Because they have forsaken My law" [Jer. 9:11-12]. For Israel is called God's heritage, and the land is His heritage, and the Torah [Law] is connected with both, with the people of God and the heritage of God, and whoever leaves the one has also abandoned the other. [42]

Eretz Israel and the Torah are one and the same thing. And had the land not previously been in the hands of the Canaanites, it would have spewed out Israel, those who sinned against the Torah, and never would they have been allowed to return. That was why the sheath had to be in existence before the core of the fruit, and the land had to remain in the hands of the Canaanites, for many years. But in reality, it was holy even then, for holiness was innate in it from time immemorial, save that then it was well hidden and none knew of it until our father Abraham came and began to reveal the holiness of the land. For he was a man of love. Love that seeks no return was the quality with which he sustained the world before the Torah was given, and it was this very love that was hidden in Eretz Israel: it was the hidden Torah, for Eretz Israel and the Torah are one and the same thing. Then, when Israel received the Torah, and came to Eretz Israel, they were able to continue in the revelation of holiness, and to lift hidden holiness into the open. And so, even though later on they offended the holiness that had been made apparent, and were lax in the fulfillment of the Torah, they could still long endure in Eretz Israel, because of the strength of that love which seeks no return, and because of that hidden Torah which is implicit in the holiness of the Land. And even now that we are exiled from our land for the vast number of our transgressions, Eretz Israel still persists in holiness because of the strength of the hidden Torah and the love that seeks no return, the love that was hidden in the land even when it was still in the hands of the Canaanites. That is why we are always waiting to return to our land, for we know that in secret it is ours.[43]

Modern Zionism was nurtured in the soil of the religious doctrines about the Holy Land and the return to it. In its contemporary expression, however, it represents on the surface a blending of three other things: the pain of the Exile, in its modern manifestation in anti-Semitism; the example of the national revivals in Europe and the world as a whole in the past century or so; and a secularized version of the Messianic ideal, either by making an end to the peculiarities of the situation of the Jew in the world by gathering Jews into a nation of their own or, after the creation of that state, by setting for it tasks of larger importance for humanity than those a small people would normally set for itself.

The passages below are from Leo Pinsker (1821–1891), an early figure of Russian Zionism; from Theodor Herzl (1860–1904), the greatest figure of modern Zionism; and from Solomon Schechter. The first two were primarily secular thinkers; the third, a modern religionist of conservative bent.

The Jews are not a living nation; they are everywhere aliens; therefore they are despised. The civil and political emancipation of the Jews is not sufficient to raise them in the estimation of the peoples.

The proper and the only remedy would be the creation of a Jewish nationality, of a people living upon its own soil, the auto-emancipation of the Jews; their emancipation as a nation among nations by the acquisition of a home of their own.

We should not persuade ourselves that humanity and enlightenment will ever be radical remedies for the malady of our people. The lack of national self-respect and self-confidence, of political initiative and of unity, are the enemies of our national renaissance.

In order that we may not be constrained to wander from one exile to another, we must have an extensive and productive place of refuge, a gathering place which is our own.

The present moment is more favorable than any other for realizing the plan here unfolded.

The international Jewish question must receive a national solution. Of course, our national regeneration can proceed only slowly. We must take the first step. Our *descendants* must follow us with a measured and unhurried pace.

A way must be opened for national regeneration of the Jews by a congress of Jewish notables.

No sacrifice would be too great in order to reach the goal which will assure our people's future, everywhere endangered.

The financial accomplishment of the undertaking can, in the nature of the situation, encounter no insuperable difficulties.

Help yourselves, and God will help you![44]

I have been occupied for some time with a work which is of immeasurable greatness. I cannot tell today whether I shall bring it to a close. It has the appearance of a gigantic dream. But for days and weeks it has filled me, saturated even my subconsciousness; it accompanies me wherever I go, broods above my ordinary daily converse, looks over my shoulder and at my petty, comical journalistic work, disturbs me, and intoxicates me.

What it will lead me to it is impossible to surmise as yet. But my experience tells me that it is something marvelous, even as a dream, and that I should write it down—if not as a memorial for mankind, then for my own delight or meditation in later years. And perhaps for something between both these possibilities: for the enrichment of literature. If the romance does not become a

fact, at least the fact can become a romance. Title: The Promised
Land![45]

. . . Zionism is an ideal, and as such is indefinable. It is thus
subject to various interpretations and susceptive of different aspects. . . . That each of its representatives should emphasize the
particular aspect most congenial to his way of thinking, and most
suitable for his mode of action, is only natural. On one point,
however, they all agree, namely, that it is not only desirable, but
absolutely necessary, that Palestine, the land of our fathers, should
be recovered with the purpose of forming a home for at least a
portion of the Jews, who would lead there an independent national
life. . . . The great majority of Zionists remain loyal to the great
idea of Zion and Jerusalem, to which history and tradition, and
the general Jewish sentiment, point. It is "God's country" in the
fullest and truest sense of the words. It is the "Promised Land"
still maintaining its place in every Jewish heart, excepting those,
perhaps, with whom Jewish history commences about the year
1830.
    . . . Zionism declares boldly to the world that Judaism means
to preserve its life by *not* losing its life. It shall be a true and
healthy life, with a policy of its own, a religion wholly its own,
invigorated by sacred memories and sacred environments, and
proving a tower of strength and of unity not only for the remnant
gathered within the borders of the Holy Land, but also for those
who shall, by choice or necessity, prefer what now constitutes the
Galut.
    . . . I belong to that class of Zionists that lays more stress on
the religious-national aspects of Zionism than on any other feature peculiar to it. The rebirth of Israel's national consciousness,
and the revival of Israel's religion, or, to use a shorter term, the
revival of Judaism, are inseparable. When Israel found itself, it
found its God. When Israel lost itself, or began to work at its self-
effacement, it was sure to deny its God. The selection of Israel,
the indestructibility of God's covenant with Israel, the immortality
of Israel as a nation, and the final restoration of Israel to Palestine,
where the nation will live a holy life on holy ground, with all
the wide-reaching consequences of the conversion of humanity
and the establishment of the Kingdom of God on earth—all these
are the common ideals and the common ideas that permeate the
whole of Jewish literature extending over nearly four thousand
years.[46]

The concluding selection is from Rabbi Abraham Isaac Kook. He was very aware of the announced secular ideals in the name of which most of modern Zionism was conceived. Kook, perhaps the most significant modern Jewish thinker in the classical mold, was at once enough of a believer and enough of a radical thinker to assert that Jewish destiny yet proceeded in the ancient categories of divine election, sin, exile and redemption. It was clear to Kook that laboring for Zion was holy and part of the divine plan, the necessary human preparations for the coming of the Messiah. Men might think that they were laboring for socialism or secular nationalism but they were doing God's holy work, for whatever contributed to making an end to the Exile was a divinely appointed preamble to the Messiah.

Eretz Yisrael is not something apart from the soul of the Jewish people; it is no mere national possession, serving as a means of unifying our people and buttressing its material, or even its spiritual, survival. Eretz Yisrael is part of the very essence of our nationhood; it is bound organically to its very life and inner being. Human reason, even at its most sublime, cannot begin to understand the unique holiness of Eretz Yisrael; it cannot stir the depths of love for the land that are dormant within our people. What Eretz Yisrael means to the Jew can be felt only through the Spirit of the Lord which is in our people as a whole, through the spiritual cast of the Jewish soul, which radiates its characteristic influence to every healthy emotion. This higher light shines forth to the degree that the spirit of divine holiness fills the hearts of the saints and scholars of Israel with heavenly life and bliss.

To regard Eretz Yisrael as merely a tool for establishing our national unity—or even for sustaining our religion in the Diaspora by preserving its proper character and its faith, piety and observances—is a sterile notion; it is unworthy of the holiness of Eretz Yisrael. A valid strengthening of Judaism in the Diaspora can come only from a deepened attachment to Eretz Yisrael. The hope for the return to the Holy Land is the continuing source of the distinctive nature of Judaism. The hope for the Redemption is the force that sustains Judaism in the Diaspora; the Judaism of Eretz Yisrael is the very Redemption.

Jewish original creativity, whether in the realm of ideas or in the arena of daily life and action, is impossible except in Eretz Yisrael. On the other hand, whatever the Jewish people creates in Eretz

Yisrael assimilates the universal into characteristic and unique Jewish form, to the benefit of the Jewish people and of the world. . . .

Deep in the heart of every Jew, in its purest and holiest recesses, there blazes the fire of Israel. There can be no mistaking its demands for an organic and indivisible bond between life and all of God's commandments; for the pouring of the spirit of the Lord, the spirit of Israel which completely permeates the soul of the Jew, into all the vessels which were created for this particular purpose; and for expressing the word of Israel fully and precisely in the realms of action and idea. . . .

An outsider may wonder: How can seeming unbelievers be moved by this life force, not merely to nearness to the universal God but even toward authentic Jewish life—to expressing the divine commandments concretely in image and idea, in song and deed. But this is no mystery to anyone whose heart is deeply at one with the soul of the Jewish people and who knows its marvelous nature. The source of this Power is the Power of God, in the everlasting glory of life.[47]

ALL THE LAND?

In June 1967 the State of Israel won the Six Day War against its Arab neighbors. It was suddenly in possession of all Jerusalem, including the Temple Mount, and all the land between the Mediterranean Sea and the Jordan River. It was said that the war was a miracle, a clear sign of Messianic times. Some believers who had long hoped for Jewish possession of "the undivided land of Israel" insisted that the territories which had just been captured could never be given back. Mercaz Harav, a yeshiva in Jerusalem, was the seed-bed of the doctrine that all of the land of Israel had to be redeemed, and that no risk should stand in the way of the Divinely ordained purpose. After the Six Day War, the leader and mentor of this academy, Rabbi Tzvi Yehuda Kook, soon issued a public declaration utterly forbidding the return of any part of the land:

There is not the slightest possibility of permitting that which the Torah forbade absolutely again and again. It is forbidden to turn over any part of our land to non-Jews, and it is most certainly against the Torah to allow them permanent possession. Therefore all Jews, and especially the spiritual authorities, the Cabinet Ministers and the men of the army, are commanded to prevent such action [to return any of the land] with all the strength that he can muster. And those who act to prevent return of the land will be helped from heaven. . . . Whatever will be done in this illegal cause [of return of territory], which is against the true teaching of the Torah and endangers Israel's security—whether it be done by the mistake of statesmen or the faint-heartedness of rabbinic scholars—is hereby nullified, now and forever. Such action contradicts the historic purposes and the actual situation of the Jewish people. . . . There is no validity, either in law or in life, to such policy.[48]

The Bible prohibits the transfer of any part of the Land of Israel into gentile hands for two reasons: to preclude a gentile foothold in the Land and to prevent the consequent annulment of the precepts relating to the Land. This prohibition undoubtedly applies to all of the soil of the Land of Israel, for all of it is pledged to the Jewish people and consecrated to the *mitzvot*. . . .

No Biblical basis can be adduced for an irrevocable renunciation of territory in favor of a foreign nation, when the result is total abolition of the Jewish presence. Far from being in the "interest" of Jews, the severing of our bonds with any part of the Holy Land is a national misfortune of the highest order.

Further light on this Biblical ban is thrown by the writings and comments of that outstanding champion and "father of Israel," Ramban (Nachmanides). Drawing on the Jerusalem Talmud, Ramban writes as follows: " 'The land shall not be sold in perpetuity' (Leviticus 25:23) to such as would take possession of it, but who would fail to implement the regulations of the Jubilee incumbent upon the Jews; that is, the land cannot be sold to the gentiles. Indeed, we must ensure that any land sold will definitely revert to Jewish ownership. On no account must we allow any soil of the Land of Israel to remain in alien hands. The Land is the Lord's, and we are but residents and tenants. It is the will of God that the Land be occupied by none other than ourselves, that we regain this Land and hold on to it for good."

From the comments of the early Rabbinic scholars, the Rishonim, it emerges distinctly that if a Jew commit an offense by handing over any part of the territory of the Land of Israel to a non-Jew, his act will lack any legal force, having contravened a dictate of the Torah. . . . Thus, it is as if the transaction had never been undertaken.[49]

Rabbi Tzvi Yehuda Kook and his disciples read the conquest of the West Bank and Gaza as the manifestation of God's will in history, certain that we are living in Messianic times and that Jewish ownership of the whole of the Land of Israel is a necessary stage of the Redemption. Here is a characteristic passage from the writings of one of the leading figures among these Messianic believers, Rabbi Shlomo Aviner:

> The sensitive will be alive to the promptings of the Divine and will naturally respond and rally to the cause of the God of Israel. There must, in the first place, be an unqualified readiness for the sacrifice of body and soul in this cause; we must respond with all the natural means at our disposal. We may then expect the miraculous to enhance our own earthly efforts, thus fusing the natural and the supernatural into an integrated, light-emitting power source. We have it on the authority of the Talmud (*Berakhot* 20a) that readiness for sacrifice evokes the intervention of Heaven. Doubts have arisen on the propriety of planning, acting and risking on a semi-natural and semi-miraculous basis, seeing that our sages have explicitly rejected reliance on miracles. This query might carry greater force if passivity on the Messianic plane was likely to ensure success. This problem was presented to the author of *Kol ha-Tor*, the so-called "Manual of Redemption" attributed to the towering Gaon of Vilna. In his reply we are instructed that "the footsteps of the Messiah" denote a substantially transformed situation. This meant that all action in this context would draw Heavenly assistance even a thousand times greater than the customary measure-for-measure reward. . . .
>
> Just as the Divine commandment to conquer the Land overrules the principle of "that he may live by them" (Leviticus 18:5), so also does it transcend the human notions of national rights to the Land. This follows from the fundamental Jewish ideal that human ethics, and the universal sense of justice found in man, derive their reality solely from the word of God. Such is the message transmitted to the world in the account of the Binding of Isaac, wherein the categorical superiority of the Divine over human morality is dramatically exposed. Man is, no doubt, instructed to act justly and righteously, but this too has no other

meaning but that grounded in the will of the Creator. Thus, ours is not an autonomous scale of values, the product of human reason, but rather an heteronomous or, more correctly, "theonomous" scale rooted in the will of the Divine architect of the universe and its moral order.

Maimonides, whose monumental Code encompasses all aspects of life, provided us with a classic definition of kingship and the Messianic era that served as a prototype for all subsequent treatment of this theme. There we have the explicit Halakhic ruling disqualifying the demand for the performance of miracles as a precondition to our acceptance of the Messiah. Thus, says Maimonides, Rabbi Akiva and all his fellow sages at no time required Bar Kochba to corroborate his title by supernatural evidence. They "deemed" him to be the "Anointed," the "presumed" if not necessarily the "undisputed" Messiah, until he was killed and it was evident that he was not the expected one. From this we may definitely infer that all national-territorial developments bearing a Messianic imprint ought to be recognized as such, even on the basis of mere "presumption," unless there arises distinct evidence to the contrary. [50]

The major rabbinic authority who is quoted and requoted by Rabbi Tzvi Yehuda Kook and his disciples is Nachmanides (1194–1270). In his listing of the 613 commandments, Nachmanides specified that dwelling in the Land of Israel remained an obligatory commandment even after the Jews had been exiled from the Holy Land. Nachmanides himself had obeyed this rule; he had gone from Spain to spend his last years in the Holy Land. Thus, it has been argued that possessing all of the Holy Land is a continuing commandment which must be fulfilled whenever there is sufficient power in Jewish hands to hold on to the land, and that relinquishing any of the land for reasons of diplomatic prudence is forbidden by religious authority. This view was radically challenged by the former Sephardi Chief Rabbi of Israel, Rabbi Ovadiah Yosef. He maintained that the principle of saving lives, by lessening the possibility of bloodshed, overrides all other considerations:

> The halakhah (law) is incontrovertible that saving a life takes precedence over every commandment in the Torah except for the prohibitions against idolatry, forbidden sexual unions, and murder. The Jerusalem Talmud rules (*Yoma* 8:5) that if one stops to

ask a rabbi whether it is permissible to desecrate the Sabbath and
Yom Kippur in order to save a life, this delay is a form of murder.
While he is busy asking the question, the patient might die. When
a life is at stake, haste is required. Maimonides, too, wrote in the
Mishneh Torah (*Hilkhot Shabbat* 2:3) in this spirit, and he added
that such a rule establishes that the laws of the Torah exist not
to wreak vengeance but to spread mercy, love and peace in the
world. . . .

[As for the right of non-Jews to dwell in the land of Israel]
Nachmanides wrote . . . that idolaters are not permitted to dwell
in the Holy Land, lest Jews be tempted by their practices, but it
is clear that this prohibition applies only to idolaters. . . . In the
view of most early authorities, this prohibition does not apply to
Muslims, who are not idolaters. . . .

But what of the view of Nachmanides that we remain commanded to inherit the land, that any war to regain and to keep
it in our possession is divinely commanded, and that such a war
is not to be avoided because of danger to life? Even according to
Nachmanides, there is no religious obligation to engage in war
and to endanger lives in order to retain control of territories . . . which have been conquered by us. We have no king
and no Sanhedrin today, nor do we possess the *Urim ve Tumim*
without which a divinely commanded war cannot take place.
Nachmanides wrote in his *Sefer ha-Mitzvot* that the king and the
Sanhedrin may declare war only after they have posed the question
to the *Urim ve Tumim*, the oracular stones on the breastplate of
the high priest, and have received an answer. . . . If a question
were to come before us whether it is correct to sacrifice one life
to bring the Messiah, we would certainly rule that the Messiah
cannot come at the cost of the life of even one Jew. The saving
of a life takes precedence over all the commandments in the
Torah, even the commandment to bring the Messiah and achieve
the redemption. . . . Therefore there is no bar to returning territory in order to avoid a probable war.[51]

The sharpest attack on religio-political Messianism was leveled
by Professor Isaiah Leibovitz. He had long denied that there was
any religious significance to the Jewish State. Holiness is a religious category, and it cannot be applied to any political or social
purposes, not even to the Zionist State:

About the "beginning of the Redemption" only one who is in
direct communication with heaven has a right to speak. . . . We

have no such communication and, therefore, none of us is permitted to say that we are moving towards Redemption. . . . The
Messiah is always on the way . . . The Messiah who actually
appears is a false Messiah. . . .

Nationalism and patriotism are not in themselves religious
values. The prophets of Israel in the period of the First Temple,
and the scholars of the Second Temple were, most of them,
"traitors" from the perspective of secular nationalism and patriotism. The rabbis who are demanding today that the territories
be kept "for religious reasons" are not continuing the tradition of
the prophet Elijah, but of the 850 priests of Baal and Ishtar "who
ate at the table of Jezebel."[52]

The formulas which point toward the realization of messianic
purposes . . . are actually a cover for secular ultra-nationalism.
Under existing conditions, the religious interests are not in territory, but rather in guarding of the Jewish character of the State
of Israel and in maintaining its links with the Jewish people as a
whole. Both of these preconditions of our existence will be destroyed if the State is transformed into an organ of Jewish domination over an Arab near-majority. . . . Our security does not
depend on the specific boundaries. . . . We must root ourselves
in our Jewish State . . . and continue to live within it a life of
universal and Jewish values.[53]

A religious counterattack on Tzvi Yehuda Kook and Gush
Emunim was mounted, also, by the most prominent of ultra-
Orthodox, non-Zionist religious leaders in Israel, Rabbi Eliezer
Menahem Shach. Speaking at a public meeting in the spring of
1979 in Rehovot, Rabbi Shach denied that the recent conquests
had Messianic significance:

The Jewish people is not like all other peoples . . . Most of
the years of our existence we had no land at all, except for the
relatively short time that we possessed the land of Israel. . . . Even
today we are not quite as sovereign as we pretend. We still depend
on the good will of the nations, and we have no reason to preen
ourselves with the territory that is in our control. It makes no
difference whether we control more or less space. What is important for us are "wells of living water," places where the Torah
is taught, and its precepts are observed. How did our people
remain alive to this day? What explains the fact that we have
remained one people, even though we were scattered to the four

corners of the earth? We have not disappeared among the people, but rather we have guarded our uniqueness. How did we do this? What kept us separate from them? Only our holy Torah. . . . We do not have to pay any attention to territories, to how much land might remain in our hands, but only to the true source of our existence. [54]

Those committed to the "undivided land of Israel" are not all religious believers. Many secular nationalists insist that Jews have an historic right to all of the land that their ancestors inhabited. Other secular nationalists among the Zionists insist that compromise with the Arabs is more important, both practically and morally, than any ideology about the inalienability of territory. Over this Jewish debate there hovers, inevitably, the question of the national and religious interests of others, and especially of the Arabs. If the Messiah is coming, soon, in our day, the moral and political problems which plague the present will be resolved—but what if He is not imminent? Neither the theologians nor the political thinkers have yet said their last word on the subject of the "undivided land of Israel."

6

DOCTRINE

W hen God resolved upon the creation of the world, He took counsel with the Torah—that is Divine Wisdom. She was skeptical about the value of an earthly world on account of the sinfulness of man, who would be sure to disregard her precepts. But God dispelled her doubts. He told her that Repentance had been created long before and sinners would have the opportunity to mend their ways. Besides, good work would be invested with atoning power, and Paradise and Hell were created to dispense reward and punishment. Finally, the Messiah was appointed to bring salvation, which would put an end to all sinfulness.[1]

The preceding quotation is from *Sefer Raziel*, a volume of secret mystic writings of uncertain date and authorship. The themes mentioned above are the major foci of doctrinal concern in Judaism. It should be added here again, for emphasis, that Judaism knows no accepted catechism. It is nonetheless untrue to maintain that the Jewish religion is a set of legal commandments divorced from faith. Jewish faith is indefinable in Western theological categories, which are alien to its essence, and by nature it permits variation in belief. There is, however, an immanent logic of its own that will appear to the careful reader of this volume and especially of the selections that follow in this section.

HUMAN DIGNITY AND POTENTIAL

Mortals are created in the image of God—this is the essential Biblical doctrine of humanity. God loves justice and mercy; people must therefore be true to their divinely ordained character by practicing these virtues. To be like God in the Jewish view means to be His partner in ruling the world and in carrying forward the work of making order, a just order, in the world. Man can descend to great depths, but he is not by nature irretrievably sinful. There are temptations to evil in the world, but the path of piety is not to renounce the world. Man's task is to hallow life, to raise the workaday world in which he eats, labors and loves, to its highest estate so that his every act reflects the divine unity of all being. Note in particular the last three selections in this section, by Judah Halevi and Nahman of Bratslav.

God created man in His own image, in the image of God He created him.[2]

Thus says the Lord: "Let not the wise man glory in his wisdom, let not the mighty man glory in his might, let not the rich man glory in his riches; but let him who glories glory in this, that he understands and knows Me, that I am the Lord who acts with kindness, justice, and righteousness in the world; for in these things I delight, says the Lord."[3]

When I look at Your heavens, Your handiwork, the moon and the stars which You have set in place, what are mortals that You should be mindful of them, mere mortals, that You should take note of them, that You have made them little less than divine, adorning them with glory and majesty? You have given them dominion over other creatures, placing all creation at their feet.[4]

Long ago when the world with its inhabitants was not yet in existence, You conceived the thought, and commanded with a word, and at once the works of creation stood before You. You said that You would make for Your world man an administrator of Your works, that it might be known that he was not made for the sake of the world, but the world for his sake.[5]

How are witnesses admonished in capital cases? They would bring them in and admonish them as follows: Perhaps you will offer mere assumption or hearsay or second hand information; or you might say to yourselves that you heard it from one who is trustworthy. Or perhaps you do not know that we shall test your statements with subsequent examination and inquiry. Know, therefore, that capital cases are not like civil cases. In civil cases, one may make atonement by paying a sum of money, but in capital cases the witness is answerable for the blood of any person who is wrongfully condemned and for the blood of his descendants who would have been born to him generation after generation to the end of time. For thus have we found it to be with Cain, who slew his brother. It is written, "The bloods of your brother cry to Me from the ground" [Gen. 4:10]. It says not "the blood of your brother" but "the *bloods* of your brother"—his blood and the blood of his descendants.

Therefore a single human being, Adam, was created as the ancestor of all, to teach that whoever destroys a single life is considered by Scripture as having destroyed an entire world, that whoever saves a single life is considered by Scripture as having saved an entire world.

And a single human being was first created to instill peace among all, since no one can say to another, "My father was greater than your father." . . .

And a single human being was first created to proclaim the greatness of the Holy One, praised be He, for man casts many coins with one die and they are all alike, while the King of kings, the Holy One, praised be He, casts every human being with the die of Adam yet no person is like any other. Therefore every human being is obliged to say: For my sake the world was created.[6]

Man is beloved, for he was created in the divine image. Man is especially dear to God in that it was made known to him that he was created in the divine image, as it is written, "In the image of God He made man" [Gen. 9:6].[7]

Let all your deeds be for the sake of heaven. They once asked Hillel where he was going. He answered, "I am going to perform a religious act (*mitzvah*)." "Which one?" "I am going to the bath house." "Is that a religious act?" "Yes. . . . Those who are in charge of the images of kings which are erected in theaters and circuses scour them and wash them and are rewarded and honored for it. How much more should I take care of my body, for I have been created in the image of God, as it is written, 'In the image of God He created man' " [Gen. 5:1].[8]

Why was man created on the sixth day [after the creation of all other creatures]? So that, should he become overbearing, he can be told "The gnat was created before you were."[9]

"Consider the work of God; who can make straight what He has made crooked?" [Eccles. 7:13]. When the Holy One, praised be He, created Adam, he showed him all the trees in the Garden of Eden, telling him "Behold, My works are beautiful and glorious; yet everything which I have created is for your sake. Take care that you do not corrupt or destroy My world."[10]

Rabbi Simon said: When the Holy One, praised be He, was about to create Adam, the angels were divided into two different groups. Some said, "Let him not be created," while others said, "Let him be created." "Love and Truth met together; Righteousness and Peace kissed each other" [Ps. 85:10]. Love said, "Let him be created, for he will do loving deeds" but Truth said, "Let him not be created, for he will be all lies." Righteousness said, "Let him be created, for he will do righteous deeds," but Peace said, "Let him not be created, for he will be all argument and discord." What did the Holy One, praised be He, do? He seized Truth and cast it to the ground, as it is written, "Truth was cast down to the ground" [Daniel 8:12]. Then the angels said to the Holy One: Lord of the Universe! How can you despise Your angel Truth? Let Truth rise from the ground, as it is written, "Truth will spring up from the ground" [Ps. 85:11].[11]

One day Elijah the prophet appeared to Rabbi Baruka in the market of Lapet. Rabbi Baruka asked him, "Is there any one among the people of this market who is destined to share in the world to come?" . . . Two men appeared on the scene and Elijah said, "These two will share in the world to come." Rabbi Baruka asked them, "What is your occupation?" They said, "We are merry-makers. When we see a man who is downcast, we cheer him up. When we see two people quarrelling with one another, we endeavor to make peace between them."[12]

When the Holy One, praised be He, was about to create men, the angels said, " 'What is man, that You are mindful of him?' [Ps. 8:5.] Why do You need man?" The Holy One, praised be He, answered, "Who, then, shall fulfill My Torah and commandments?" The angels said, "We shall." God answered, "You cannot, for in it is written 'This is the law when a man dies in a tent . . .' [Num. 19:14], but none of you die. In it is written 'If a woman conceives, and bears a male child . . .' [Lev. 12:2], but none of you give birth. In it is written 'This you may eat . . .' [Lev. 11:21], but none of you eat."[13]

In our view, a servant of God is not one who detaches himself from the world, lest he be a burden to it, and it to him; or hates life, which is one of God's bounties granted to him. . . . On the contrary, he loves the world and a long life, because it affords him opportunities of deserving the world to come. The more good he does the greater is his claim to the next world. . . .

The pious man is nothing but a prince who is obeyed by his senses, and by his mental as well as his physical faculties, which he governs corporeally, as it is written, "He who rules his spirit is better than he who takes a city" [Prov. 16:32]. He is fit to rule, because if he were the prince of a country he would be as just as he is to his body and soul. He subdues his passions, keeping them in bonds, but giving them their share in order to satisfy them as regards food, drink, cleanliness, etc.[14]

The capacity to see is a high and lofty power. The eyes always see great and marvelous things. If man would only attain the merit of having pure eyes, he would know important things by the power of his eyes alone. His eyes are always seeing but they do not know what they are seeing.[15]

There are unbelievers who maintain that the world is eternal, but this view is baseless. The truth is that the world and all that it contains can exist, but it need not necessarily; only God *must* exist and He creates all the worlds *ex nihilo*. When Israel obeys the will of God, it becomes rooted in the Highest Source which is eternal and thereby the whole world is raised into the realm of eternal existence.

Man can become part of God's unity, which is eternal, only by forgetfulness of self; he must forget himself completely in order to partake of the Divine Unity. One cannot reach such an estate except in aloneness. By withdrawing into intimate dialogue with God, man can attain the complete abandonment of his passions and evil habits, i.e. he can free himself from the claims of his flesh and return to his Source. The best time for such withdrawal is at night, when the world is free of the claims of earthly existence. During the day men chase after the concerns of this world. This atmosphere is disturbing even to the man who is personally de-tached from such concerns, for the worldly bustle of others makes it harder for him to attain to the state of self-forgetfulness. Such withdrawal is best attained in a place which people do not pass by.

When man attains his level, his soul becomes an existential necessity, i.e. he ascends from the realm of the possible to that of the eternal. Once he himself has become eternal, he sees the whole world in the aspect of its eternity.[16]

HUMAN RESPONSIBILITY

God is omnipotent, yet mortals must be responsible. Everything is foreseen, yet mortals have free will. These are the classic contradictions of theistic faith, and they appear very early in Judaism. There is no attempt at philosophic resolution, only the assertion that human beings know that they have choices to make and that they are morally responsible for those choices. Mortals cannot help but know that there is a God who judges them and upon whom they cannot place the responsibility for their own misdeeds.

People are not responsible for themselves alone. Each individual is responsible to society for the well-being of all. There must therefore be law in society and respect for government, unless society itself transgresses the moral law. The rights of individuals are absolute, for every individual is created in the divine image. Each has his or her particular virtue and capacity for service.

The proper response to life is piety and reverence, not only before God but before other people.

> I call heaven and earth to witness against you this day, that I have set before you life and death, blessing and curse; therefore, choose life, that you may live, you and your descendants.[17]

> Behold, I set before you this day blessing and curse: blessing if you obey the commandments of the Lord your God which I command you this day, and curse if you do not obey the commandments of the Lord your God but turn from the path which I command you this day to follow other gods which you do not know.[18]

There are six things which the Lord hates,
Seven which are an abomination to Him:
Haughty eyes, a lying tongue,
Hands that shed innocent blood,
A mind that devises wicked plots,
Feet that are swift to run to mischief,
A false witness uttering lies,
And one who incites brothers to quarrel.[19]

Ben Azzai taught: Hasten in pursuit of the slightest commandment, and flee from sin; for one commandment leads to another and one sin leads to another. The reward of a commandment is another to be fulfilled and the reward of one transgression is another.[20]

Everything is foreseen by God, and freedom of choice is given; the world is judged with goodness, and all depends upon the preponderance of good or evil deeds.[21]

Everything is in the hands of heaven, except the fear of heaven.[22]

The world is judged according to the preponderance of good or evil, and the individual is judged in the same way. Therefore, one who fulfils one commandment is truly blessed, for he has tipped the balance to the side of merit for himself and for the entire world. However, if he commits one transgression, woe is he, for he has tipped the balance to the side of guilt for himself and for the entire world, as it is said, "One sinner destroys much good" [Eccles. 9:18]. One sin of an individual destroys much good for himself and for the entire world.[23]

"And the Lord spoke to Moses and Aaron, saying, 'Separate yourselves from this congregation, that I may consume them in a moment.' And they fell upon their faces and said, 'O God, the God of the spirit of all flesh, shall one man sin and will You be wroth with all the congregation?' " [Num. 16:20–22]. Rabbi Simeon ben Johai said: Several men were sitting in a boat. One of them began boring a hole beneath himself with an auger. His companions said, "What are you doing?" He replied, "What business is it of yours? Am I not boring a hole under myself?" They answered, "It is our business because the water will come in and swamp the boat with all of us in it."[24]

For two and one half years the Schools of Hillel and Shammai debated the question whether it would have been better had man never been created. Finally they agreed that it would have been better had man not been created. However, since man had been created, let him investigate his past deeds, and let him give due consideration to what he is about to do. [25]

When Rabbi Johanan ben Zakai was ill, his disciples visited him. . . . They said to him, "Bless us, master!" He said to them, "May it be His will that the fear of heaven be as great for you as the fear of flesh and blood." His disciples asked, "Only as great?" He answered, "If it only *would* be as great! You know that one who commits a sin is saying, 'No one will see me.' "[26]

"You make men like the fish of the sea" [Hab. 1:14]. Just as in the sea the larger fish swallow up the smaller fish, so it is among human beings. Were it not for fear of the government, every one who is more powerful than another would swallow up the other. This is what Rav Hanina said: Pray for the welfare of the government, for were it not for fear of the government, everyone would swallow up his neighbor alive. [27]

Rabbah bar bar Hana brought a case against some laborers who, during their work, had broken a cask of wine. He took away their clothing. The laborers complained against Rabbah to Rav, who told him to return their clothing to them. When Rabbah asked, "Is this the law?" Rav answered, "Yes, as it is written, 'That you may walk in the way of the good' " [Prov. 2:20]. He returned their clothing to them. The laborers then said, "We are poor men and have worked all day and have nothing to eat." Rav said, "Pay them their wages." When Rabbah asked again, "Is this the law?" Rav answered, "Yes, as it is written, 'Keep the path of the righteous' " [*ibid.*]. [28]

RULES OF CONDUCT

The essential rule of conduct is *imitatio Dei*, the imitation of God. No matter what the circumstances, people can organize their lives around this basic principle. The rule does not require asceticism, but it does ask that we live every waking moment in the awareness that we are never alone, for God is always present.

The selections below span the centuries, from early Rabbinic writings of the second century, through various medieval and early modern "rules" laid down by distinguished fathers for their children, to the concluding passages of insights from the classic early generations of Hasidim in the eighteenth century.

Rabbi Hama ben Rabbi Hanina said: What does this verse mean?—"You shall walk after the Lord your God" [Deut. 13:5]. Is it possible for a human being to walk after the *Shekhinah?* Is it not written, "The Lord your God is a consuming fire" [Deut. 4:24]?—It means that we should follow the attributes of the Holy One, praised be He.

He clothes the naked, as it is written, "The Lord God made for Adam and for his wife garments of skins and clothed them" [Gen. 3:21]. Thus you should clothe the naked.

The Holy One, praised be He, visited the sick, as it is written, "The Lord appeared to him [Abraham] by the oaks of Mamre" [Gen. 18:1]. [According to Rabbinic tradition, the elderly Abraham was recuperating from his circumcision, narrated in the seventeenth chapter.] Thus you should visit the sick.

The Holy One, praised be He, comforted mourners, as it is written, "After the death of Abraham, God blessed Isaac his son" [Gen. 25:11]. Thus you should comfort mourners.

The Holy One, praised be He, buried the dead, as it is written, "He buried him [Moses] in the valley in the land of Moab" [Deut. 34:6]. Thus you should bury the dead. . . .

Rabbi Simlai expounded: The Torah begins with an act of lovingkindness and it ends with an act of lovingkindness. It begins with an act of lovingkindness, as it is written, "The Lord God made for Adam and for his wife garments of skins and clothed them" [Gen. 3:21]. It ends with an act of lovingkindness, as it is written, "He buried him [Moses] in the valley in the land of Moab" [Deut. 34:6]. [29]

This was a favorite saying of the Rabbis of Javneh: I am a creature of God and my neighbor is also His creature; my work is in the city and his in the field; I rise early to my work and he rises early to his. As he cannot excel in my work, so I cannot excel in his. You might say that I do great things while he does small things. However we have learned that it matters not whether a man does much or little, if only he directs his heart toward Heaven. [30]

The Holy One, praised be He, daily proclaims the virtues of a bachelor who lives in a large city and does not sin, a poor man who restores a lost object to its owners, and a rich man who gives a tithe of his profits in secret.[31]

The Holy One, praised be He, loves three: Whoever does not become angry, whoever does not become drunk, and whoever does not insist upon reprisals. The Holy One, praised be He, hates three: Whoever says one thing with his mouth and another thing in his heart, whoever knows of evidence in favor of someone but does not testify, and whoever sees a disgraceful thing in another and testifies against that person as a single witness [since a minimum of two witnesses is needed to bring about a formal conviction, one witness merely gives the defendant a bad reputation].[32]

Rav said: At judgment day everyone will have to give an accounting for every good thing which he (or she) might have enjoyed and did not enjoy.[33]

Whoever abstains from drinking wine is called a sinner [the Nazirite, who had vowed, among other mortifications of the flesh, not to drink wine, was required to bring a sin offering]. All the more, then, is one who painfully abstains from everything to be called a sinner. It was concluded from deep analysis of Biblical texts, that one who fasts habitually is called a sinner.[34]

Akavya ben Mahalalel attested to four things [which he held in opposition to the majority of the contemporary sages]. The sages told him "Akavya! Reverse your opinion on these four matters and we will appoint you President of the Court of Israel." He answered "I prefer to be called a fool all my life rather than become wicked for one hour before God."[35]

These Rabbinic values find expression in medieval and early modern "ethical wills."

. . . My son, be zealous in visiting the sick, for a visitor lightens pain. Urge the patient to return in repentance to his Maker. Pray for him, and go. Do not burden him with a long visit, for the burden of his illness is enough to bear. When you enter a sickroom, enter cheerfully, for his heart and eyes are on those who enter to visit him.

My son, be zealous in participating in the burial of the dead, delivering them into the hand of your Maker, for this is an important duty. Whoever performs a kind act with the knowledge that he who benefits cannot repay will receive unmerited kindness from the Holy One, praised be He.

My son, be zealous in comforting mourners and speak to their heart. Job's companions were deserving of punishment because they reproached him when they should have consoled him. . . .

. . . My son, be zealous in helping to bring the bride to the bridal canopy and in gladdening the groom. . . .

My son, do not crush the poor with your words, for the Lord will plead his cause. Such sinful conduct would cause many accusers to rise on high, to reveal your sins to your detriment, and there will be no one to defend you. But whoever treats the poor with generosity acquires intercessors on high who will proclaim his cause to his benefit.[36]

Devote yourself to science and religion; habituate yourself to moral living, for "habit is master over all things." As the Arabian philosopher holds, there are two sciences, ethics and physics. Strive to excel in both. . . .

Show respect to yourself, your household, and your children, by providing decent clothing, as far as your means allow; for it is unbecoming for any one, when not at work, to go shabbily dressed. . . .

If the Creator has mightily displayed His love to you and me, so that Jew and Gentile have thus far honored you for my sake, endeavor henceforth so to add to your honor that they may respect you for your own self. This you can effect by good morals and by courteous behavior; by steady devotion to your studies and your profession. . . .

Let your countenance shine upon the sons of men: tend their sick, and may your advice cure them. Though you take fees from the rich, heal the poor gratuitously; the Lord will requite you. Thereby shall you find favor and good understanding in the sight of God and man. Thus you will win the respect of high and low among Jews and non-Jews, and your good name will go forth far and wide. You will rejoice your friends and make your foes envious. . . .

Examine your Hebrew books at every new moon, the Arabic volumes once in two months, and the bound codices once every quarter. Arrange your library in fair order, so as to avoid wearying yourself in searching for the book you need. Always know the case and chest where it should be. . . .

Never refuse to lend books to anyone who has no means to purchase books for himself, but only act thus to those who can be trusted to return the volumes. . . .Cover the bookcases with rugs of fine quality; and preserve them from dampness and mice, and from all manner of injury, for your books are your good treasure. . . .

Make it a fixed rule in your home to read the Scriptures and to peruse grammatical works on Sabbaths and festivals, also to read Proverbs and the Ben Mishle [a popular work of aphorisms by Samuel Ha-nagid (993–1055)]. . . .

My son, honor your comrades, and seek opportunities to benefit them by your wisdom, in counsel and deed.[37]

"Hear, my son, your father's instruction, and forsake not your mother's teaching" [Prov. 1:8]. Become accustomed to speaking gently to all men, at all times. Thus you will be delivered from anger, which causes man to sin. . . . When you are delivered from anger, there will arise in your heart the quality of humility, the best of all good things, for it is written, "The reward of humility is the fear of the Lord" [Prov. 22:4]. Reverence results from humility, for humility makes you to consider always whence you came and where you are going. Humility reminds you before whom you must give account in the future—the King of glory.

So I will explain how you should accustom yourself to the quality of humility and how to practice it continually. Let all your words be gentle and let your head be bowed; let your eyes be directed to the ground and your heart on high. Do not look at the face of one with whom you speak. Let every man be greater than you in your eyes. If he be wise or wealthy you must honor him. If he is poor and you are rich or if you are wiser than he, take it to your heart that you are the guiltier and he the more innocent. If he sins, it is in error but if you sin it is with intent to do so.

In all your actions, words and thoughts, and at all times, think of yourself as standing before God, with His *Shekhinah* resting upon you, for His glory fills the universe. Speak in reverence and in respect, as a servant addressing his master. Conduct yourself with modesty in dealing with every man. If a man should call to you, do not answer him in a loud voice, but gently and in a subdued voice, as one standing before his superior.

Be zealous to read in the Torah regularly, so you will be able to fulfill its precepts. After you study, examine in your mind what you have learned, to ascertain if it contained some principle which you can fulfill. Examine your deeds in the morning and in the evening, and thus all your days will be spent in repentance.

When you pray, remove all worldly matters from your heart. Set your heart right before God. Cleanse your thoughts and meditate before uttering a word. Act in this way all the days of your life, in all things, and you will not sin. Thus will all your deeds be upright, and your prayer pure, clean, devout and accepted before God. For it is written "Lord, You will hear the desire of the humble; You will strengthen their heart, You will incline Your ear" [Ps. 10:17].[38]

These are the things which a man must do to escape the snares of death and to bask in the light of life:

Do not rush into an argument. Beware of oppressing other men, whether by money or by word; neither envy nor hate them. Keep far from oaths and from the iniquity of vows, from frivolity and anger which confuse both the spirit and the mind of man. Do not use the name of God for vain purposes or in foul places. Do not rely upon the broken reed of human support and do not set up gold as your hope, for that is the beginning of idolatry. Distribute your money according to God's will. He is able to cover your deficit. It is good and upright to belittle your good deeds in your own sight and to magnify your transgressions; to increase the mercies of your Creator, who formed you in the womb and gives you food in due season. Do not serve for the sake of being rewarded when you perform His commandments, and do not avoid sin out of fear of punishment. Serve in love. Let expenditure of your money be of less value to you than utterance of your words. Do not rush to utter a bad word until you have weighed it in the scales of your judgment. Bury in the walls of your heart whatever is said to you even though it is not said in secrecy. If you hear the same thing from someone else, do not say "I have already heard it."

Accustom yourself to awaken at dawn and to rise from your bed at the song of the birds. Do not rise as a sluggard, but with eagerness to serve your Creator. Do not be a drunkard or a glutton, lest you forget your Creator and thus be led to sin. Do not set your eyes upon one who is richer than you but upon one who is poorer. Do not look to one who is your inferior in the service and fear of Heaven, but to one who is your superior. Rejoice when you are reproved; listen to advice and accept instruction. Do not be haughty, but be humble and like dust upon which everyone treads. Do not speak with insolence, and do not raise your forehead, rejecting the fear of Heaven. Never do privately what you would be ashamed to do publicly. Do not say "Who will see me?"

Do not raise your hand against your neighbor. Neither slander nor give false reports of any person. Do not rush to give an insolent answer to those who say unpleasant things to you. Do not shout in the street, do not bellow like an animal; let your voice be soft. Do not make your neighbor blush in public. The first of all precautions is the avoidance of covetousness. Do not consider it a small matter if you have but one enemy. Do not tire of seeking a faithful friend; do not lose him. Do not try to make your friendship attractive through flattery and hypocrisy and do not speak with a double heart. Do not maintain your anger against your neighbor for a day, but humble yourself and ask forgiveness. Do not be haughty, saying "He has harmed me. Let him ask forgiveness of me." Every night, before you retire, forgive whoever has harmed you with words. If men curse you, do not answer. Be counted among the insulted (and not among the insulters).

Keep your feet on the path, firmly maintaining yourself in the middle of the road in regard to eating and drinking. Be neither accessible to all nor a recluse from all. Turn neither to the left nor to the right. Do not rejoice too much; remember that your life is a breath. You are formed from the dust and your end is the worm. Do not be easily offended, lest you gather needless enemies. Do not pry into the secrets of others. Do not be overbearing to the people of your city, and yield to the will of others. Will that which your Creator wills. Rejoice in your lot, whether it be large or small. Pray continually before Him to incline your heart toward His testimonies. Do not be an ingrate. Honor everyone who opened a door for you to earn life's necessities. Do not speak falsehoods. Be faithful to every man. Do not be slow in greeting every man, whether Jew or Gentile. Do not anger another person. . . .

Pursue justice [i.e. in this context, contribute to charity]. Do not give less than half a shekel each year and at one time. Every month and every week give what you can. On every day let there not be lacking a small donation before prayer. Contribute the "continual offering" each Friday. When your income reaches a titheable amount, set aside the tithe. Thus you will have something at hand whenever you would give, whether to the living or the dead, whether to the poor or the rich.

Enjoy neither food nor drink without reciting a blessing before and after. Be zealous to praise your Creator for satisfying you. Cover your head when you mention God. Let your innermost self be stirred when you speak of Him. Do not be among those of whom Scripture says "They honor Me with their lips, while their hearts are far from Me" [Isa. 29:13]. Wash your hands before praying and before eating. Sanctify yourself in all things. Do not behave with levity; let the fear of Heaven be upon you. Before eating and before sleeping set regular times for studying the Torah. Speak of its words at your table. Direct the members of your household according to the Torah, in all matters which need direction.

Be of proper intent when you pray, for prayer is service of the heart. If your child speaks to you and does not speak from his heart, will you not be angry? How, then, insignificant droplet, should you act in the presence of the King of the universe? Do not be like a servant who was given an important object for his own good and spoiled it. How could such a one face the King? How good it would be to ask forgiveness for saying "Forgive us" without sincere intent. Do not be lax in confessing your sins morning and evening, or in mentioning Zion and Jerusalem with a broken heart and in tears. When you recite the verse "You shall love the Lord your God with all your heart, with all your soul, and with all your might," speak as one who is ready to offer his life and his wealth to sanctify Him. Thus will you fulfill the verse "For Your sake we are slain every day" [Ps. 44:23]. Yet trust in the Lord with all your heart and have faith in His providence, for His eyes scan the entire earth and He sees all the ways of each man. Make mention of Him day and night. When you lie down, think of His love and in your dreams you will find it. When you awake, you will delight in Him and He will set your paths straight. Fulfill your good deeds in the spirit of humbly walking before Him, for this is the preferred service of the Lord, the service acceptable to Him.[39]

The sin of taking interest is so great that whoever commits it is considered as though he denied the God of Israel, God forbid. "If he lends at interest, and takes increase, shall he live? He shall not live" [Ezek. 18:13]. In commenting upon this verse our sages said that "He shall not live" means that such a man will not be resurrected, for usury and the like are abominable in the sight of the Lord. I see no need in elaborating upon this, since every Jew already dreads it.[40]

Most people are not outright thieves, taking their neighbors' property and putting it in their own premises. However, in their business dealings most of them have a taste of stealing, whenever they permit themselves to make a profit at the expense of someone else, claiming that profit has nothing to do with stealing. . . .

Rabbi Judah forbade merchants to distribute parched corn and nuts to children as an inducement for them to come to his shop. The other sages permitted it, but only because his competitors could do the same [*Baba Metzia* 60a]. Our sages said, "Defrauding a human being is a graver sin than defrauding the Sanctuary" [*Baba Batra* 88b]. . . . When Abba Hilkiah was working for an employer, he would not even return the greetings of men of learning, considering it wrong to use the time belonging to his employer for his own purposes [*Ta'anit* 23a–b]. . . . Even if a man should perform a commandment during the time when he should be working, it is not accounted to his credit, but it is accounted as a transgression. . . . If a man should steal some wheat, grind it, bake it and then recite a benediction over it, he blasphemes, as it is written, "The greedy, though he bless, condemns the Lord" [Ps. 10:3].[41]

If you will delve into the matter, you will realize that the world was created for man's use. Surely the fate of the world depends upon the conduct of man. If a man is attracted by things of this world and is estranged from his Creator, he is corrupted and he can corrupt the entire world along with him. However, if he controls himself, cleaves to his Creator and makes use of the world only to the degree that it helps him in serving his Creator, he raises himself to a higher level of existence and the world rises with him. For it is of great significance to all things created when they serve the perfect man who is sanctified with the holiness of God, praised be He.[42]

The wise man who is completely detached from the masses cannot ever raise the level of his generation. If a man is lying in a ditch, he who would drag him out must come close to him and get a bit dirty. It is impossible to get someone else out of a ditch by standing still in your own proper place.

A teacher of public morality is like a broom which can sweep the dirt out of the house only if it becomes somewhat soiled itself. [43]

"Who is wise? He who learns from every man" [Mishnah *Avot* 4:1], even from the lowest of the low. Even in such a man there is a spark of the good which can serve as an example. So, when Jethro came to his son-in-law Moses, he said to him: "Indeed, you are a prophet and a sage, but you may still learn something from me." This was an example for all future generations. [44]

SIN AND REPENTANCE

Sin is rebellion against God, but more seriously yet, Judaism considers it the debasement of man's proper nature. Punishment is therefore not primarily retribution; it is chastisement, as a father chastises his children, to remind them of their proper dignity and character. Repentance is therefore in Hebrew *teshuvah*, returning, man's turning back to his truest nature.

An ancient Rabbinic perspective on the motivation for proper behavior is articulated at the beginning of the collection of teachings known as *Pirkei Avot* ("Teachings of the Sages" 1:3). We read there a favorite teaching of the sage known as Antigonus of Sokho: "Do not be like servants who serve their master expecting to receive a reward. Be rather like servants who serve their master unconditionally, with no thought of reward. And let the fear of God determine your actions."

Perhaps the Jewish attitude toward sin was expressed at its loftiest by the Hasidic master Rabbi Menahem Mendel of Kotzk (1787–1859): "My hope is that you do not sin, not because it is forbidden, but because there is not enough time."

The evil inclination is to be compared to a conjurer who runs around among people with a closed hand daring them to guess what is in it. At that moment each one thinks that the conjurer has what each one desires for himself hidden in the clenched hand. Everyone therefore runs after him. Once the conjurer stops for a moment and opens his hand, it becomes clear to everyone that it is completely empty; there is nothing in it.

Exactly so does the evil inclination fool the whole world. Everyone rushes after him, for all imagine, in their error, that he has in his hand what they want and desire. In the end the evil inclination opens his hand and everyone sees that there is nothing in it. The very one who said to each man "open your mouth and I will fill it," he himself is completely empty.[45]

Regret is a great art in which few are expert. The chief purpose of regret is not to feel sorry for evil actions but to uproot evil from its very source. Whoever is not expert in this art tends to use his power of regret to strengthen the evil within him and not to weaken it.

The wicked are as full of regrets as a pomegranate is full of seeds; nonetheless they do not know what regret is. Precisely because they have so many regrets, they tend to grow hardened in their wickedness. What I mean is best expressed by the image of two wrestlers: when one sees that the other is about to subdue him, he summons up strength with which to withstand the attack—and so it goes from round to round. By the same token, improper regrets, which are based in the human passion for conquest, represent a form of wrestling with evil and can therefore become a way of evoking redoubled efforts by the "Evil One."[46]

There is no righteous man on earth whose deeds are good and who does not sin.[47]

Therefore, House of Israel, I will judge each one of you according to his ways, says the Lord God. Return, and turn back from all your transgressions; let them not be a stumbling block of sin for you. Cast away from you all the transgressions which you have committed, and make yourselves a new heart and a new spirit, that you die not, House of Israel. For I desire not the death of anyone, says the Lord God; therefore, return and live.[48]

The righteous descendants of Adam upon whom death has been decreed . . . approach Adam and say, "You are the cause of our death." Adam replies: "I was guilty of one sin, but there is not a single one among you who is not guilty of many sins."[49]

The First Temple was destroyed because of the sins of idolatry, sexual licentiousness and murder. . . . But during the time of the Second Temple, the people were engaged in the study of Torah, and the performance of commandments and deeds of loving-kindness. Why, then, was the Second Temple destroyed? Because the people were guilty of groundless hatred. This teaches that the sin of groundless hatred is considered to be as grave as the sins of idolatry, sexual licentiousness and murder. [50]

Rav Immi said, "There is no death without sin, and there is no suffering without transgression. There is no death without sin, as it is written, 'The person who sins shall die. A child shall not bear the sins of a parent, nor shall a parent bear the sins of a child. The righteousness of the righteous shall be accounted to him alone, and the wickedness of the wicked shall be accounted to him alone' [Ezek. 18:20]. And there is not suffering without transgression, as it is written, 'I will punish their transgressions with the rod and their iniquity with scourges [i.e. suffering]' " [Ps. 89:33].

The angels said to the Holy One, praised be He, "Lord of the universe! Why did You punish Adam with death?" He answered them: "I gave him one simple commandment to observe, and he transgressed it." The angels said, "But Moses and Aaron fulfilled the entire Torah and they died!" He said to them, "One fate comes to all, to the righteous and to the wicked . . . as is the good man so is the sinner" [Eccles. 9:2]. . . .

Rabbi Simeon ben Eleazar said: "Moses and Aaron also died because of their sin, as it is written 'because you did not believe in Me, to sanctify Me in the eyes of the people Israel' [Num. 20:12]. Had you believed in Me, you would still be alive." . . .

On the other hand, there is death without sin, and there is suffering without transgression. [51]

"There was a small city with few people in it, and a great king came against it and besieged it, building mighty works against it. But there was found in it a poor wise man who by his wisdom saved the city" [Eccles. 9:14–15]. Rabbi Ammi bar Abba explained these verses in the following way: "There was a small city"—this is the body. ". . . with few people in it"—these are the parts of the body. ". . . and a great king came against it and besieged it"—this is the evil impulse. ". . . building mighty works against it"—these are sins. "But there was found in it a poor wise man"—this is the good impulse. ". . . who by his wisdom saved the city"—this refers to repentance and good deeds.[52]

May it be Your will, O Lord my God and God of my ancestors, to shatter and bring to an end the yoke of the evil impulse from our heart; for You have created us to do Your will and we are under obligation to do Your will. You desire it and we desire it. What, then, hinders? The leaven in the dough [i.e. the evil impulse]. It is well known to You that there is within us no power to resist it. May it be Your will, my God and God of my ancestors, to cause it to cease from dominating us and to subjugate it. Then shall we do Your will as our own, with a perfect heart.[53]

"Open to me, my sister, my love, my dove" [Song of Songs 5:2]. Rabbi Issi said: The Holy One, praised be He, said to the Israelites, "Open to Me the gates of repentance as much as the eye of a needle, and I will open for You gates wide enough for carriages and wagons to pass through.[54]

Repentance is greater than prayer, for Moses' prayer to enter the land of Canaan was not accepted and the repentance of Rahab the harlot [who helped Joshua enter Jericho, and begin the conquest of the Holy Land] was accepted.[55]

"Teach us to number our days" [Ps. 90:12]. Rabbi Joshua said: If we knew the exact number of our days, we would repent before we die. Rabbi Eleazar said: "Repent one day before your death." His disciples asked him, "Who knows when he will die?" Rabbi Eleazar answered, "All the more then should one repent today, for one might die tomorrow. As a result of this, all of one's life will be spent in repentance."[56]

Scripture states, "Let the wicked forsake his ways and the sinful man his plans. Let him return to the Lord [i.e. repent] who will have mercy upon him" [Isa. 55:7]. God desires repentance. He does not desire to put any creature to death, as it is said, "I do not desire the death of the wicked, but only that the wicked turn from his way and live" [Ezek. 33:11].[57]

How do we know that one who repents is regarded as having gone up to Jerusalem, built the Temple and the altar, and offered upon it all the sacrifices mentioned in the Torah? It is written, "The sacrifice acceptable to God is a contrite spirit, a crushed and broken heart" [Ps. 51:127].[58]

Five categories of people will not be forgiven: Those who repent repeatedly, those who sin repeatedly, those who sin in a righteous generation, those who sin with the intention of repenting, and those who profane God's name.[59]

Judaism does have, as the next passage reflects, a strong tendency to stress the sinfulness of human nature, but this is never made into an absolute. There is a divinely appointed remedy which one can and must apply to oneself: the life of Torah.

The Torah is the only remedy for the evil impulse. Whoever thinks that he can be helped without it is mistaken and will realize his error when he dies for his sins. Man's evil impulse is truly very strong. Unbeknown to him it gradually prevails over and dominates him.[60]

SUFFERING

Why do the righteous suffer? The question was asked in its most famous and searing form by Job. Job's friends attempted to provide him with answers, but he rejected them all. In the end Job could only affirm, in the image of God's speaking to him out of the whirlwind, that God's plans are beyond human knowing and that people cannot condemn God in order to justify themselves. The believer cannot really stretch his faith to its uttermost limit and condemn himself so utterly as to assert that all his sufferings are direct punishment for his sins. Some are; some suffering is borne by those who carry part of the burden of the sin of their generation, or of past generations. But ultimately the believer can only say, in the words of a poignant Hasidic prayer, "God, do not tell me why I suffer, for I am no doubt unworthy to know why, but help me to believe that I suffer for Your sake." That suffering is not meaningless, though its meaning is often hidden from us, and that it is not wasted, is the response of faith to tragedy.

Rava said: When one experiences suffering, let him scrutinize his past deeds, as it is written, "Let us search and examine our ways and return to the Lord" [Lam. 3:10]. If one has scrutinized his past deeds without discovering the cause of his suffering, let him attribute it to the neglect of Torah, as it is written, "Blessed is the one whom You chasten, O Lord, and whom You teach out of Your Torah" [Ps. 94:12]. If he has attributed his suffering to the neglect of the Torah without discovering any justification, it is certain that his suffering is a chastening out of love, as it is written, "For whom the Lord loves He chastens, as a father the son in whom he delights" [Prov. 3:12].[61]

A calf being led to slaughter ran away and buried its head between the knees of Rabbi Judah. He said to the calf, "Go! For this have you been created." Since he was not compassionate, he was visited with great sufferings. . . . Once, when Rabbi Judah's housemaid was about to sweep away some newborn kittens, he said to her, "Don't harm them! It is written, 'The Lord is good to all, and His compassion is over all that He has made' " [Ps. 145:9]. Since he now showed compassion, compassion was extended to him [and his sufferings ceased].[62]

Rav Judah said in the name of Rav: When Moses ascended on high, he found the Holy One, praised be He, engaged in adding coronets to the letters of the Torah [three small strokes are added to the tops of certain Hebrew letters when they are written in a Torah scroll]. Moses said, "Lord of the universe! Does the Torah lack anything, that these additions are necessary?" He answered, "After many generations, a man by the name of Akiva ben Joseph will arise, and he will expound heaps and heaps of laws based upon each jot and tittle." Moses said, "Permit me to see him." God replied, "Turn around." Moses then sat down behind eight rows of Rabbi Akiva's disciples and listened to the discourses upon the Torah. He was ill at ease, for he was unable to follow their arguments. However, during a discussion of a certain subject, when the disciples asked the master, "How do you know that to be so?" and Rabbi Akiva replied, "It is a law given to Moses at Sinai," he was comforted. When he returned to the Holy One, praised be He, he said, "Lord of the universe! You have such a man and yet You give the Torah through me?!" God replied: "Be silent. Such is My decree." Moses then said, "Lord of the universe! You have shown me his Torah; show me his reward." "Turn around," He said. Moses turned around and saw merchants weighing out Rabbi Akiva's flesh in a marketplace. [Rabbi Akiva died the death of a martyr during the persecutions at the hands of the Romans after they had crushed the Bar Kochba rebellion of the years 131 to 135.] Moses cried out, "Lord of the universe! Such Torah and such a reward?!" God replied, "Be silent. Such is My decree."[63]

When Rabbi Gamaliel, Rabbi Eleazar, Rabbi Joshua and Rabbi Akiva were once travelling, they heard the great tumult of the city of Rome in the distance. The first three wept, but Rabbi Akiva laughed. When they asked "Why do you laugh?" he asked "Why do you weep?" They said, "These heathen, who worship and burn incense to idols, live here in peace and security, while our Temple, the footstool at the Throne of God, is destroyed by fire. How should we not weep?" Rabbi Akiva replied, "That is why I laugh. If this is the lot of those who transgress His will, how much more glorious shall be the lot of those who perform His will."[64]

God has also informed us that during our entire sojourn in this workaday world He keeps a record of everyone's deeds. The recompense for them, however, has been reserved by Him for the second world, which is the world of compensation. This latter world will be brought into being by Him when the entire number of rational beings, the creation of which has been decided upon by His Wisdom, will have been fulfilled. There will He requite all of them according to their deeds. This is borne out by the statement of the saint, "I said in my heart: 'The righteous and the wicked God will judge' " [Eccles. 3:17]. He said also, "For God shall bring every work into judgment concerning every hidden thing, whether it be good or whether it be evil" [Eccles. 12:14]. . . .

Notwithstanding this, however, God does not leave His servants entirely without reward in this world for virtuous conduct and without punishment for iniquities. For such requitals serve as a sign and an example of the total compensation which is reserved for the time when a summary account is made of the deeds of God's servants. . . .

It is, therefore, only a specimen and a sample of these rewards and punishments that is furnished in this world, while the totality of their merits is stored for the virtuous like a treasure. Thus Scripture says: "O how abundant is Your goodness, which You have laid up for them that fear You" [Ps. 31:20]. Similarly the totality of their demerits is laid up and sealed for the wicked, as Scripture says elsewhere: "Is not this laid up in store with Me, sealed up in My treasuries?" [Deut. 32:34].[65]

The good is that which is closer to God and the evil is that which is farther from Him. Evil is therefore a lower degree of good.

Evil is the footstool of good, and there is no absolute evil.

"Open for us the treasury of the good" [from the Liturgy]. There no doubt is good in all the bitter woes that come upon us, because evil cannot proceed from God. We, however, do not understand the good that is hidden within it. Therefore we beg of you, our Creator, "Open for us the treasury of the good, that is, open our eyes that we may understand the good that is hidden within evil."[66]

Know that man has to walk on a very narrow bridge. The chief rule is that he should never fear. A spiritually mature person does not fear.

The truth is that the world is full of woes. There is no one who really possesses this world. Even the greatest magnates and princes do not truly possess this world, because their days are filled with upsets and pain, with disturbances and sadness, and every one has his own particular woe.

It is strange that everyone says that both this world and the world to come exist. In respect to the world to come, yes, we believe that it exists. Perhaps there is even a this world in some universe, but here on earth it is clearly hell itself, for all men are ever laden with great woe.[67]

A man once came to Rabbi Menahem Mendel to pour out his bitter heart. His wife had died in childbirth, leaving him with seven young children including the newly born infant. He had other woes too and did not know where to turn.

Rabbi Menahem Mendel listened to him, but while listening the rabbi kept his eyes lowered. After a moment of deep meditation Rabbi Menahem Mendel raised his head, looked straight into the eyes of the petitioner and said: "I am not equal to the task of consoling you after such cruel suffering. Only the true Master of mercy is equal to that. Turn to Him."[68]

Postbiblical thinkers have pondered how the freedom of the human will and the resultant indetermination of the future can be reconciled with divine foresight and predetermination. Outstanding among all that has been said in the effort to overcome this contradiction is the well-known saying of Rabbi Akiva ("All is surveyed, and the power is given"), whose meaning is that to

God, Who sees them together, the times do not appear in succession but in progress-less eternity, while in the progression of times, in which man lives, freedom reigns, at any given time, in the concrete moment of decision; beyond that, human wisdom has not attained. In the Bible itself, there is no pondering; it does not deal with the essence of God but with His manifestation to mankind; the reality of which it treats is that of the human world, and in it, the immutable truth of decision applies.

For guilty man, this means the decision to turn from his wrong way to the way of God. Here we see most clearly what it means in the biblical view that our answering-for-ourselves is essentially our answering to a divine address. The two great examples are Cain and David. Both have murdered (for so the Bible understands also David's deed, since it makes God's messenger say to him that he "slew Uriah the Hittite with the sword"), and both are called to account by God. Cain attempts evasion: "Am I my brother's keeper?" He is the man who shuns the dialogue with God. Not so David. He answers: "I have sinned against the Lord." This is the true answer: If one becomes guilty against anyone, in truth one becomes guilty against God. David is the man who acknowledges the relation between God and himself, from which his answerability arises, and realizes that he has betrayed it.

The Hebrew Bible is concerned with the terrible and merciful fact of the *immediacy* between God and ourselves. Even in the dark hour after he has become guilty against his brother, man is not abandoned to the forces of chaos. God Himself seeks him out, and even when He comes to call him to account, His coming is salvation.[69]

This passage concludes *The Last of the Just*, André Schwarz-Bart's novel (originally published in French in 1959) about Jewish suffering through the ages, culminating in the Nazi death camps.

The building resembled a huge bathhouse. To left and right large concrete pots cupped the stems of faded flowers. At the foot of the small wooden stairway an S.S. man, mustached and benevolent, told the condemned, "Nothing painful will happen! You just have to breathe very deeply. It strengthens the lungs. It's a way to prevent contagious diseases. It disinfects." Most of them went in silently, pressed forward by those behind. Inside, numbered coathooks garnished the walls of a sort of gigantic cloakroom where the flock undressed one way or another, encouraged by their S.S. cicerones, who advised them to remember the numbers carefully. Cakes of stony soap were distributed. Golda begged Ernie not to look at her, and he went through the sliding door of the second room with his eyes closed, led by the young woman and by the children, whose soft hands clung to his naked thighs. There, under the showerheads embedded in the ceiling, in the blue light of screened bulbs glowing in recesses of the concrete walls, Jewish men and women, children and patriarchs were huddled together. His eyes still closed, he felt the press of the last parcels of flesh that the S.S. men were clubbing into the gas chamber now, and his eyes still closed, he knew that the lights had been extinguished on the living, on the hundreds of Jewish women suddenly shrieking in terror, on the old men whose prayers rose immediately and grew stronger, on the martyred children, who were rediscovering in their last agonies the fresh innocence of yesteryear's agonies in a chorus of identical exclamations: "*Mama! But I was a good boy! It's dark! It's dark!*" And when the first waves of Cyclon B gas billowed among the sweating bodies, drifting down toward the squirming carpet of children's heads, Ernie freed himself from the girl's mute embrace and leaned out into the darkness toward the children invisible even at his knees, and he shouted with all the gentleness and all the strength of his soul, "Breathe deeply, my lambs, and quickly!"

When the layers of gas had covered everything, there was silence in the dark room for perhaps a minute, broken only by shrill, racking coughs and the gasps of those too far gone in their agonies to offer a devotion. And first a stream, then a cascade, an irrepressible, majestic torrent, the poem that through the smoke of fires and above the funeral pyres of history the Jews—(who for two thousand years did not bear arms and who never had either missionary empires or colored slaves) traced in letters of blood on the earth's hard crust—that old love poem unfurled in the gas chamber, enveloped it, vanquished its somber, abysmal snickering: "SHEMA YISRAEL ADONOI ELOHENU ADONOI ECHOD . . . Hear, O Israel, the Lord is our God, the Lord is One. O Lord, by your grace you nourish the living, and by your great pity you resurrect the dead, and you uphold the weak, cure the sick, break the chains of slaves. And faithfully you keep your promises to those who sleep in the dust. Who is like unto you, O merciful Father, and who could be like unto you . . . ?"

The voices died one by one in the course of the unfinished poem. The dying children had already dug their nails into Ernie's thighs and Golda's embrace was already weaker, her kisses were blurred when, clinging fiercely to her beloved's neck, she exhaled a harsh sigh: "Then I'll never see you again? Never again?"

Ernie managed to spit up the needle of fire jabbing at his throat, and as the woman's body slumped against him, its eyes wide in the opaque night, he shouted against the unconscious Golda's ear, "In a little while, *I swear it!*" And then he knew that he could do nothing more for anyone in the world, and in the flash that preceded his own annihilation he remembered, happily, the legend of Rabbi Chanina ben Teradion, as Mordecai had joyfully recited it: "When the gentle rabbi, wrapped in the scrolls of the Torah, was flung upon the pyre by the Romans for having taught the Law, and when they lit the fagots, the branches still green to make his torture last, his pupils said, 'Master, what do you see?' And Rabbi Chanina answered, 'I see the parchment burning, but the letters are taking wing.' " . . . "*Ah, yes, surely, the letters are taking wing,*" Ernie repeated as the flame blazing in his chest rose suddenly to his head. With dying arms he embraced Golda's body in an already unconscious gesture of loving protection, and they were found that way half an hour later by the team of *Sonderkommando* responsible for burning the Jews in the crematory ovens. And so it was for millions, who turned from *Luftmenschen* into *Luft.* I shall not translate. So this story will not finish with some tomb to be visited in memoriam. For the smoke that rises from crematoriums obeys physical laws like any other: the particles come together and disperse according to the wind that propels them. The only pilgrimage, estimable reader, would be to look with sadness at a stormy sky now and then.

And praised. *Auschwitz.* Be. *Maidanek.* The Lord. *Treblinka.* And praised. *Buchenwald.* Be. *Mauthausen.* The Lord. *Belzec.* And praised. *Sobibor.* Be. *Chelmno.* The Lord. *Ponary.* And praised. *Theresienstadt.* Be. *Warsaw.* The Lord. *Vilna.* And praised. *Skarzysko.* Be. *Bergen-Belsen.* The Lord. *Janow.* And praised. *Dora.* Be. *Neuengamme.* The Lord. *Pustkow.* And praised . . .

Yes, at times one's heart could break in sorrow. But often too, preferably in the evening, I can't help thinking that Ernie Levy, dead six million times, is still alive somewhere. I don't know where. . . . Yesterday, as I stood in the street trembling in despair, rooted to the spot, a drop of pity fell from above upon my face. But there was no breeze in the air, no cloud in the sky. . . . There was only a presence.[70]

THE HOLOCAUST

The murder of six million Jews by the Nazis, and their helpers, during the Second World War, was the greatest of all tragedies that the Jewish people have ever endured. How could a merciful God permit these unspeakable horrors? What purpose of His could the mass murder of a million and a quarter children, and nearly five million adults, possibly serve? Schwarz-Bart had contemplated all of the woes of Jewish existence with cosmic resignation. The Yiddish poet Jacob Glatstein (1896–1971) rebelled, and called God to account.

The Dead Do Not Praise God

We received the Torah at Sinai,
and in Lublin we gave it back.
The dead do not praise God,
the Torah was given to life.
And as we together, all of us together,
stood at the giving of the Torah
so we all together died at Lublin.

I will introduce the wonder of
the brambly head, the pious eyes,
the trembling mouth of a little Jewish child
into this fearful tale.
For him will I fill a Jewish sky with stars,
and to him speak thus:
The Jewish people is a fiery sun
from beginning to beginning to beginning.
Learn this, little one, dear Jewish little one,
from beginning to beginning to beginning.

Our whole dream-like people stood at Mount Sinai
and received the Torah:
the dead, the living, the yet unborn.
All Jewish souls answered:
We will obey and hearken.
And you, the saddest Jewish little one of all generations,

were also standing at Mount Sinai.
Your nostrils caught the raisin-almond smell
of each word in the Torah.
You were wrapped in a piece of the mountain as in a *tallis*.
It was *Shavuos*, the holiday of greenery.
You joined in singing like a songbird:
I will obey and hearken, hearken and obey,
from beginning to beginning to beginning.

Jewish little one, your life is engraved
in the star-filled Jewish sky;
you were never absent,
you dared not be absent.
We hoped and prayed you into being.
Always, when we were, you were too.
And when we vanished,
you vanished along with us.

And as we together, all of us together,
stood at the giving of the Torah
so we all together died at Lublin.
From all sides precious souls came flying,
those who lived out their lives, those who died young,
those who were tortured, tested in every fire,
those yet unborn, all of the dead Jews,
from old grandfather Abraham on,
were in Lublin at the great disaster,
all those who had stood at Mount Sinai
and received the Torah
took upon themselves these holy deaths.
"We want to die together with our whole people,
we want once more to die,"
the souls wailed.
Mama Sarah, Mother Rachel,
Miriam, and Deborah the prophet,
perished with prayers and songs.
Moses our teacher, who so much did not want to die,
when his time came, died once again.
And his brother Aaron,

and King David,
and the Rambam, and the Vilna Gaon,
and the Maharam and the Maharshal,
the Seer and Abraham Eiger.
And with every holy soul
that perished in pain
died hundreds of souls
of precious dead Jews.

And you, cherished little one, were also there.
You, engraved against the star-filled Jewish sky,
were there too, and died there.
Sweet as a dove you stretched your neck
and sang with the patriarchs and the matriarchs.
From beginning to beginning to beginning.

Close your eyes, beloved Jewish little one,
and remember how the Baal-Shem rocked you in his arms,
when your whole dream-like people
perished in the gas chambers of Lublin.

And above the gas chambers
and the holy dead souls
there smoldered a desolate extinguished Sinai.

Little one with a brambly head,
pious eyes and trembling mouth,
you were the quiet, small, forlorn
Torah which was being given back.
You were standing at Sinai and weeping,
weeping your tears into a dead world.
From beginning to beginning to beginning.

And this is what you wept:
We received the Torah at Sinai,
and in Lublin we gave it back.
The dead do not praise God,
The Torah was given to life.[71]

In the liturgy for the festivals, the explanation for the destruction of both Temples is "because of our sins, You exiled us from

our land." In the face of the Holocaust, some Rabbinic theologians attempted to follow this path, to justify the ways of God by suggesting that the Jewish people had indeed sinned and that the Holocaust was punishment. It was a painful call for God's people to mend its ways. Two Hungarian rabbis insisted on totally opposing identifications of the dreadful sin for which the Jewish people was being punished. Rabbi Yoel Teitelbaum (1888–1979), a fierce anti-Zionist, who was a major Hasidic leader in Hungary before and during the war, wrote later that God had punished the Jews for having become Zionists. They were forcing His hand to bring the redemption, when the proper attitude was to wait; worse still, the Zionists were secular nationalists rather than Orthodox believers:

> In every generation before this one, whenever trying times came upon the people of Israel, they sought to discover why this was so, what sin had caused it, so that they could repent and return to God, blessed be He, as we have learned in the Bible and the Talmud. . . . But now in this our generation, there is no need to seek out the sin which has brought the trouble upon us, for it is stated explicitly and openly by the [Talmudic] Sages. They told us specifically what they had learned in the Bible, that breaking the oath not to "climb the wall" and not to try and hasten the redemption would cause God to let the Jews be fair game for all their enemies, just as the wild deer and antelope are fair game to all hunters. And because of our many sins, this is what happened. The sectarians and heretics made all kinds of attempts to break that oath. They "climbed the wall" and demanded for themselves sovereignty and freedom before the appointed time, which is equivalent to hastening the redemption, and they convinced many Jews to support the profane idea. . . . It is not surprising therefore that we have witnessed this immense manifestation of God's anger . . . and during the destruction even the most saintly and pious people were killed on account of those who had sinned and caused others to sin . . . and the divine wrath was most fearsome and terrible to behold. . . .[72]

> And those of the Children of Israel whom God let remain alive, in accordance with His oath that He will never totally destroy them, were also punished with a bitter and trying punishment, with that creation of Satan which has succeeded in acquiring impious sovereignty; this He has done in order to put

the people of Israel to a great test. . . . We have not yet realized that all the troubles and tribulations which have come upon us were the result of those wicked people's sin. . . . And now whoever has a brain in his head can recognize the truth: that it is the transgression of those who lead others astray with the impure idea of Zionism, and it is all the deeds done for the sake of that impure idea which have brought down on us all troubles and suffering. . . .[73]

And because of our many sins, now too, this abomination is being done in Israel—that there are those who think and say that there were miracles and wonders performed as it were by God, just like the miracles accompanying the Exodus from Egypt, and they do not see that these things only increase the impure strength of the Zionists, who are a thousand times worse than the Golden Calf, inasmuch as the Golden Calf did not constitute complete heresy and Zionism does.[74]

During the war years in Hungary, another former anti-Zionist, Rabbi Issachar Teichthal, changed his mind most radically. He was now convinced that these horrors were the result of the refusal of the Jews to labor for their redemption. The Holocaust was punishment not for Zionism but for anti-Zionism:

And after I have placed before you, my brother—the reader of this book, the words of the Sages and holy men of former times, you will see that already eighty years ago the Holy Spirit awoke . . . that we should return to the bosom of our mother [the land of Israel] and embrace the stranger no more, but rather devote all our strength and money and possessions to buy holy land in order to raise it up from the dust, build it up and improve it and raise the prestige of our kingdom . . . and to awaken our brethren the children of Israel to purchase property in the land of Israel from the Arabs. A special opportunity arose when the Sultan was involved in the [First World] War and in need of money, and was ready to sell the land of Israel, Transjordan and Syria for nearly nothing . . . if only they had influenced the people of Israel and persuaded them to participate in it—then how many thousands of Jews would have settled in the land of Israel, and how the land would have developed! How many Jews would have been saved thus from death, and, given life, could have saved more Jews, thereby fulfilling the injunction 'to save those escaped from death'! But because they opposed it—and not only opposed it but awakened such hate for the building of our land in the hearts of simple, pious Jews, that anyone who opened his mouth to speak of it or became excited about it himself, was considered disgusting and despicable. Thus they truly sowed hatred and disgust for our precious land . . . and fell into the sin of the twelve spies [whom Moses sent to spy out the land, Numbers 12–13] about whom it was said [Psalms] they spoke rebelliously against their God and despised the holy land. And what was their fate?—that they caused generations to lament their deed. And these [who oppose Zionism] have caused even more lamentation; [because of their opposition] we have arrived at the situation we are in today and have stressed this abomination in the house of Israel, endless trouble and sorrow upon sorrow—all because we despised our precious land.[75]

Now we, the Children of Israel, are in great distress, God save us quickly, and suffering has become a matter of course; new troubles appear not from day to day but from hour to hour, so that if I were to recount them, all the pages in the world would not suffice, and I leave it to those who will write of it later. . . . But the main thing, to my mind, is to remember that we are in great trouble, with each new day's trouble greater than the day before—therefore now, certainly, we need the merit of our holy land to protect us and preserve us and save us from these straits. . . . Our holy land will plead our cause so that He will remember us speedily with words of salvation and mercy, because our strength is failing. . . .[76]

Speaking in Jerusalem in 1944, when the news of the murders had become known, Judah Leon Magnes (1877–1948) refused to suggest that he could ascribe any meaning to this genocide. But he would not stop believing in God:

I have said that I do not know *what* the meaning is of this desert of thick darkness that shuts us in. But by means of this religious approach I find myself facing in the positive direction, and not the reverse. It is as though two men were together standing on a narrow, obscure path. This path is the pessimism common to both. Then the one turns with all his might in the direction of No, and there he remains standing, while the other turns with all his might in the direction of Yes,—yes, there is a meaning to all this.

Thus turned, this man cannot stand still. He has started on a long and weary road. He wants with all his will to be among those who seek the Face and pursue righteousness. But from that man God hides His Face. An opaque screen holds him asunder from the living God. For all his trying to come nearer and to touch the outer fringe, he cannot. It will not be given him to appear before the presence, to hear the voice, or to understand the meaning of these massacrings, this wanton butchery. Yet he can do no other than to persist in his quest to the last, to keep on inquiring, struggling, challenging. He will not be granted tranquility of soul. But if it be given him to renew the forces of his being day to day and constantly to be among the seekers, the rebellious—that is the crown of his life and the height of his desire.

It is said of Rabbi Levi Isaac of Berdichev that he spoke thus: *"I do not ask, Lord of the world, to reveal to me the secrets of Thy ways—I could not comprehend them. I do not ask to know why I suffer, but only this: Do I suffer for Thy sake?"*

For us, too, it would be enough to ask, not *what* is the meaning of this anguish, but that it *have* a meaning; and that our need of asking be so sincere that it becomes a prayer:

Teach us only this: Does man suffer for *Thy sake*, O Lord?[77]

Martin Buber, the philosopher and theologian, suggested the metaphor of the "eclipse of God"—that the destruction of the Nazi years had happened because some dark force was interposed between God and His creatures, so that His light did not reach us in those years:

Eclipse of the light of heaven, eclipse of God—such indeed is the character of the historic hour through which the world is passing. But it is not a process which can be adequately accounted for by instancing the changes that have taken place in man's spirit. An eclipse of the sun is something that occurs between the sun and our eyes, not in the sun itself. Nor does philosophy consider us blind to God. Philosophy holds that we lack today only the spiritual orientation which can make possible a reappearance 'of God and the gods,' a new procession of sublime images. But when, as in this instance, something is taking place between heaven and earth, one misses everything when one insists on discovering within earthly thought the power that unveils the mystery. He who refuses to submit himself to the effective reality of the transcendence as such . . . contributes to the human responsibility for the eclipse.

Assume that man has now fully brought about 'the elimination
of the self-subsisting suprasensual world,' and that the principles
and the ideals which have characterized man in any way, to any
extent, no longer exist. His true *vis-a-vis*, which, unlike principles
and ideals, cannot be described as It, but can be addressed and
reached as Thou, may be eclipsed for man during the process of
elimination; yet this *vis-a-vis* lives intact behind the wall of darkness. Man may even do away with the name "god," which after
all implies a possessive, and which, if the possessor rejects it, i.e.,
if there is no longer a "God of man," has lost its *raison d'etre:*
yet He who is denoted by the name lives in the light of His
eternity. But we, "the slayers," remain dwellers in darkness, con-
signed to death.[78]

My father, Rabbi Zvi Elimelekh Herzberg, was much closer
in outlook to Magnes than to Buber. His faith in God was un-
shakable. Therefore, for him, the Holocaust was an awful mystery
to be contemplated only in silence. In this view, he was at one
with the Rebbe of Belz, Rabbi Aaron Rokeach, who had survived
the Holocaust—and never spoke of it. Here are some of my
father's reflections:

> When a man sees that everything is lost, and that even children
> are slaughtered, there is only one way to continue—the way of
> silence. This is the ultimate heroism. Only Moses could hear the
> voice of the Lord as He spoke, delivering judgments of fire and
> water. Only Moses could understand why. But we are not equal
> to hearing that voice. We can at least be silent, and not rebel
> against Heaven. This is what Rabbi Isaac Napaha meant when
> he declared [in *Ethics of the Fathers*], "A hero is he who overcomes
> his nature."
>
> When terrible trials come upon the Jewish people, there is a
> danger that many will turn to heresy and disbelief, and challenge
> God's providence and His justice. We must be firm in our faith,
> lest we be swept away. One of the greatest figures in the Talmud,
> Elisha ben Abuyah, left the faith during the Roman persecutions
> in the second century after he saw the tongue of Rabbi Hutzpit
> lying in the garbage. Elisha challenged God: "How can You
> condemn a tongue which scattered pearls of wisdom to lick the
> dust?" And so Elisha left the faith.
>
> Elisha ben Abuyah became known as "the other" because he
> had questions which he did not hesitate to ask, and complaints

against Heaven which he dared to utter. People like ourselves must overcome our impulse to rebel against God. Silence is not a simple matter. It is a sacrifice, even more than those which were once brought on the altar in Jerusalem. Silence, awesome silence, is in these days the essence of heroism.[79]

My father never spoke in the past tense of the Jews who had been murdered. He willed the familiar towns and villages of Eastern Europe to be alive and still present for him. After 1945, he and my mother devoted themselves to evoking these Jewish towns by helping many survivors rebuild their lives. The words that I wrote in 1989 reflect their teaching:

And so, in expiation of the sins of the fathers, whose quiet interventions in Washington did little good, this generation of American Jewish leaders is largely confrontationist with enemies and critics. Holocaust consciousness has created a sense of Jews as an embattled bastion in the very America of today which is free and open enough for Jews to enshrine their most painful memory in museums in very public places. But there is a deep truth to this paradox. Somewhere within men and women of my generation remains the question I ask myself in my darkest thoughts about each of those friends who are not Jews: who among them would risk his life, if Hitler ever came again, to hide my grandchildren? But that fearful doubt is always accompanied by another: how would I behave inside Auschwitz if it were ever built in Scarsdale, or in Idaho, or near Camp David? I cannot answer either of these questions with certainty. I must hope—and work to increase the hope—that these questions will never be asked again.

And so, after a half-century of thinking about the Holocaust, of hearing many stories, and of reading many books, I am left with a lifelong quarrel with God, and ambivalent relationships with the Gentile world, with Jews—and with myself. Even though I was once overwhelmed by the silence of the Rebbe of Belz, I cannot join him. I must light candles in memory of my family, and I continue to grieve over the horror of their deaths—but it is their lives that I want to remember. Let the barracks remain in Auschwitz, untouched, as a warning to the world, that mankind should never again pollute the earth with such buildings. The Jew within me cannot forget the gas chambers but what I most want to remember are the children who published a daily newspaper in Theresienstadt, the inmates of Auschwitz who held forbidden prayer services, and the heroes of the Warsaw Ghetto, in the years before the revolt, who conducted schools in defiance of Nazi edicts. This is what I have learned from rereading the Book of Job on the aftermath of the Holocaust. After his disaster Job begat a new family, recreated his flocks and herds and did good again to all who came into his sight. Job remembered what he had lost, but he did not simply continue to scream; he lived on.

During Passover week Jews remember the revolt in the Warsaw Ghetto. The rising began on April 19, 1943, on the eve of Passover, that year, and the last of the resistance was not crushed by the Nazis until May 16. This hopeless revolt has become a great symbol; these were Jews who died fighting. In recent years, the passive Jews, those who supposedly went too quietly to their deaths, are being "pardoned." The gruesomeness of the tortures are now at the center of concern, "lest we forget." One cannot be like the Rebbe of Belz and be silent. One must remember— but what are we to remember? Only how six million Jews died, or how they lived?

The survivors did not dwell on death; they rebuilt life. This was the lesson they were teaching: a people must remember but it cannot live on by making a cult of its woes. The faith of the Jews is not simply remembering the Holocaust; it is the Jewish religion, which—before and after the Nazis—reasserts the verse in Psalms [118:17], "I will not die, for I will live." Those who remained after the Holocaust, and their children and grandchildren, must live all the harder, and all the more decently, to carry on for every one of the unfinished lives.[80]

DEATH AND THE WORLD TO COME

In the Bible itself the arena of human life is this world. There is no doctrine of heaven and hell, only a growing concept of an ultimate resurrection of the dead at the end of days. The doctrine of the resurrection was debated in post-Biblical times. The normative view became that held by the Pharisees, that there will be a resurrection of the dead. Concurrently, the notion of judgment of the individual in the afterlife beyond the grave, his consignment to heaven or to hell, began to arise.

For a tree there is hope; if it should be cut down it will renew itself; its shoots will not stop sprouting. Though its roots be old in the earth and its stump be dead in the ground, at the scent of water it will bud and bring forth leaves, as a sapling. But mortals languish and die. Man perishes and where is he? As the waters of the sea fail, and the river dries up and is parched, so mortals lie down to sleep, never to rise. When the heavens are no more he will awake, only then will he be aroused out of his sleep.[81]

In death there is no remembrance of You; in Sheol, who can give You praise?[82]

And there will be a time of trouble, such as there has never been since the nation came into being. At that time your people will be delivered. . . . And many of those who sleep in the dust of the earth will awake, some to everlasting life and some to shame and everlasting contempt.[83]

All of the people Israel have a share in the world to come, for it is written, "Your people shall all be righteous; they shall possess the land [interpreted here as referring to the world to come] forever, the shoot of My planting, the work of My hands, that I might be glorified" [Isa. 60:21]. The following have no share in the world to come: Whoever says that resurrection of the dead is not derived from the Torah, whoever says that the Torah is not from Heaven, and an Epicurean [in the mind of the Rabbis, a philosopher who says that the world is eternal and not created by God].[84]

How do I know that the resurrection of the dead is derived from the Torah? It is written, "The Lord said to Moses, you shall say to the Levites 'When you take the tithe from the people Israel . . . you shall give the Lord's offering to Aaron the priest. . . .' " [Num. 18:25–28]. Did Aaron live forever? He did not even enter the Land of Israel. How, then, could this verse apply? We must therefore infer that this verse teaches that Aaron will live in the future and that Israel will then give him the offering. This teaches that the resurrection of the dead is derived from the Torah. . . . Rabbi Simlai said: How do we know that the resurrection of the dead is derived from the Torah? It is written, "I established My covenant with them [the patriarchs], to give them the land of Canaan . . ." [Ex. 6:4]. The verse states not "to give you" but "to give them" [the patriarchs themselves]. This teaches that the resurrection of the dead is derived from the Torah.

The Sadducees asked Rabban Gamaliel: What evidence do you have that the Holy One, praised be He, revives the dead? He answered: I have proof from the Torah, the Prophets and the Writings; but they did not accept his proof. In the Torah it is written, "Then the Lord said to Moses: You will sleep with your fathers, and will rise . . ." [Deut. 31:16]. The Sadducees objected: It may mean that this people will rise up and go whoring after the strange gods of the land. In the Prophets it is written, "Let your dead revive, let dead bodies arise. Awake and sing, you who dwell in dust, for your dew is a dew of light, and on the land of the shades you will let it fall" [Isa. 26:19]. But the Sadducees replied that this may refer to the dead whom Ezekiel revived [Ezek. 37]. In the Writings it is written, "Your palate is like finest wine that glides down smoothly for my beloved, moving gently the lips of those who are asleep [i.e. in the tomb]" [Song of Songs 7:10]. The Sadducees replied that this may refer to an ordinary movement of the lips while one sleeps. . . . Finally, Rabban Gamaliel quoted the verse ". . . the land which the Lord swore to give to your fathers, to give to them . . ." [Deut. 11:9]. It is not said "to you" but "to them." This proves the resurrection of the dead [for since the patriarchs died before the occupation of the land, God's promise could be fulfilled only by raising them from the dead]. Others say that he cited the verse "You who hold fast to the Lord your God are all alive this day" [Deut. 4:4].[85]

Rabbi Eliezer said: The nations [i.e. non-Jews] will have no share in the world to come, as it is written "The wicked shall depart to Sheol, and all the nations that forget God" [Ps. 9:17]. The first part of the verse refers to the wicked among Israel. However, Rabbi Joshua said to him: If the verse had stated "The wicked shall depart to Sheol, and all the nations," I would agree with you. But the verse goes on to say "that forget God." Therefore it means to say that there are righteous men among the other nations of the world who do have a share in the world to come.[86]

When Rabbi Johanan ben Zakai was ill, his disciples visited him. When he saw them, he began to weep. They said to him, "Lamp of Israel, pillar on the right, mighty hammer! Why do you weep?" He answered them, "If I were being led before a king of flesh and blood, I would weep, even though his anger, if he were angry with me, would not be everlasting, though his prison, if he imprison me, would not hold me for eternity, though he could not sentence me to eternal death, and though I could appease him with words and bribe him with money. And now I am being led before the King of kings, the Holy One, praised be

He, who lives and endures to all eternity. If He is angry with me, His anger is eternal. If He imprisons me, His prison will hold me eternally. He could sentence me to eternal death. And I cannot appease Him with words or bribe Him with money. Furthermore, two paths lie before me, one to the Garden of Eden, and one to Gehinnom [Hell] and I know not in which I will be led. Should I then not weep?"[87]

We have learned that the judgment of the wicked in Gehinnom lasts twelve months. Rabbi Eliezer asked Rabbi Joshua, "What should one do to escape the judgment of Gehinnom?" He replied, "Let him occupy himself with good deeds." . . . "Better is a poor man who lives blamelessly . . ." [Prov. 19:1]. Whoever walks in blamelessness before his Creator in this world will escape the judgment of Gehinnom in the world to come.[88]

Everything which the Holy One, praised be He, has caused to be injured in this world will be healed in the world to come. The blind will be healed, as it is written, "then the eyes of the blind shall be opened" [Isa. 35:5]. The lame will be healed, as it is written, "then shall the lame leap as the hart" [Isa. 35:6]. Everyone will be healed. However, everyone will rise with the defects he had in life. The blind will rise blind, the deaf will rise deaf, the lame will rise lame, and the dumb will rise dumb. They will rise clothed as they were in life. . . . Why will each one rise with the defects which they had in life? That the wicked of the world might not say, "After they died God healed them and then brought them here," implying that these were actually others. The Holy One, praised be He, said, "Let them rise with the defects they had in life, and then I shall heal them, as it is written, 'That you may know and believe Me and understand that I am He. Before Me there was no God formed, and after Me none shall exist' " [Isa. 43:10]. Later, even the animals will be healed, as it is written, "The wolf and the lamb will feed together, and the lion will eat straw like the ox" [Isa. 65:25]. However, the one that brought injury to everyone shall not be healed, as it is written, "and dust shall be the serpent's food" [ibid.]. Why? Because he brought everything to dust.[89]

Rav used to say: In the world to come, there is neither eating nor drinking nor procreation, nor business dealings nor jealousy nor hatred nor competition. Righteous men sit with their crowns on their heads and enjoy the splendor of the *Shekhinah*.[90]

Rabbi Hiyya bar Abba said, quoting Rabbi Johanan: All of the prophecies of consolation and of good things to come uttered by the prophets apply only to the days of the Messiah. As for the world to come, "no eye has ever seen, O God, only You have seen" [*after* Isa. 64:3].[91]

"You shall keep My statutes and My ordinances, by doing which a man shall live; I am the Lord" [Lev. 18:5]. This implies that man shall live in the world to come. In this world, man's end is death. How, then, can it be said "by doing which a man shall live"? This "living" must refer to the world to come. "I am the Lord"; faithful to reward.[92]

Saadia in the tenth century concluded that the doctrine of resurrection was accepted by all Jews, most of whom identified that event with the end of time, when the Messianic redemption will come.

The author of this book declares that, as far as the doctrine of the resurrection of the dead is concerned—which we have been informed by our Master will take place in the next world in order to make possible the execution of retribution—it is a matter upon which our nation is in complete agreement. The basis of this conclusion is a premise mentioned previously in the first treatises of this book: namely, that man is the goal of all creation. The reason why he has been distinguished above all other creatures is that he might serve God, and the reward for his service is life eternal in the world of recompense. Prior to this event, whenever He sees fit to do so, God separates man's spirit from his body until the time when the number of souls meant to be created has been fulfilled, whereupon God brings about the union of all bodies and souls again. . . .

We consequently do not know of any Jew who would disagree with this belief. Nor is it hard for him to understand how his Master can bring the dead to life, since he has already accepted as a certainty the doctrine of *creatio ex nihilo*. The restoration by God of aught that has disintegrated or decomposed should, therefore, present no difficulty to him.

Furthermore God has transmitted to us in writing the fact that there would be a resurrection of the dead at the time of the Messianic redemption, which has been borne out by means of miraculous proofs. It is in regard to this point that I have found a difference of opinion to exist: namely, as to whether there will be a resurrection of the dead in this world. For the masses of our nation assert that it will come about at the time of the redemption. They interpret all verses of the Bible in which they find references to the resurrection of the dead in their exoteric sense and set the time to which they refer as being unquestionably that of the redemption.

I have noted, moreover, that some few of the Jewish nation interpret every verse in which they find mention made of the resurrection of the dead at the time of the redemption as referring to the revival of a Jewish government and the restoration of the nation. Whatever, on the other hand, is not dated as taking place at the time of the redemption is applied by them to the world to come. . . .

I have inquired and investigated and verified the belief of the masses of the Jewish nation that the resurrection of the dead would take place at the time of the redemption.[93]

Maimonides defined the world to come, the world beyond the grave, as a place where pure spirits engage in purely spiritual exercise.

The good which is stored up for the righteous is life in the world to come, life unaccompanied by death, good unaccompanied by evil. This is written in the Torah: "That it may be good with you and that you may live long" [Deut. 22:7]. We learn from tradition that the phrase "that it may be good with you" refers to the world which is all good, and that the phrase "that you may live long" refers to the world which is certainly long, the world to come. The reward of the righteous is that they will merit this pleasantness and goodness. The punishment of the wicked is that they will not merit such life but will be utterly cut off in their death. Whoever does not merit such life is a dead being who will never live but is cut off in his wickedness and perishes like an animal. . . .

In the world to come there are no bodies, but only the souls of the righteous alone, without bodies, like the angels. Since there are no bodies in the world to come, there is neither eating nor drinking nor anything at all which the bodies of men require in this world. Nothing occurs in the world to come, but the righteous sit there with their crowns on their heads, enjoying the splendor of the *Shekhinah* (*Berakhot* 17a). Clearly there are no bodies there, for there is neither eating nor drinking there, and the statement of the sages that "the righteous sit there" was stated as a parable.

The righteous there neither work nor strain. The statement that their crowns are on their heads means to say that the knowledge they possessed, on account of which they merited life in the world to come, is there with them and this knowledge is their crown. . . . ". . . enjoying the splendor of the *Shekhinah.*" This means that they know and derive from the Truth of the Holy One, praised be He, what they do not know in this world, confined by a dull and lowly body.[94]

Whatever may be the doctrine of heaven and hell, the central emphasis of Judaism has remained on this world, from the beginning. It is here and not in any world to come that people have the possibility to choose, and to justify their life by choosing the good.

> King Solomon said: "Whatever is in your power to do, do with all your might, for there is no action or thought or knowledge or wisdom in Sheol, where you are going" [Eccles. 9:10; Rabbinic tradition identifies Solomon as the author of Ecclesiastes]. Whatever one does not do while he has the power granted him by his Creator, the power of freedom of the will, which is his all the days of his life when he is free and responsible, he will not be able to do in the grave or in Sheol, where he will not have this power. Whoever does not perform many good deeds during his lifetime can not perform them after his death. Whoever has not taken account of his deeds will not have time to do so in the world to come. Whoever has not gained wisdom in this world will not gain wisdom in the grave.[95]

On the deathbed, if one is conscious, this is the prayer prescribed for recitation. The pious have always regarded it as a mark of particular mercy from God if one dies uttering the last two lines of the confession.

> My God and God of my ancestors, accept my prayer; do not ignore my supplication. Forgive me for all the sins which I have committed in my lifetime. I am abashed, and ashamed of those wicked deeds and sins which I committed. Please accept my pain and suffering as atonement, and forgive my wrongdoing, for against You alone have I sinned.
>
> May it be Your will, Lord my God and God of my ancestors, that I sin no more. With Your great mercy cleanse me of my sins, but not through suffering and disease. Send a perfect healing to me and to all who lie sick in their beds.

Unto You, Lord my God and God of my ancestors, I acknowledge that both my healing and my death depend upon Your will. May it be Your will to heal me. Yet if You have decreed that I shall die of this affliction, may my death atone for all the sins and transgressions which I have committed before You. Shelter me in the shadow of Your wings and grant me a share in the world to come.

Father of orphans and Guardian of widows, protect my beloved family, with whose soul my soul is bound.

Into Your hand I commit my soul. You have redeemed me, O Lord God of truth.

Hear O Israel, the Lord our God, the Lord is One.

The Lord, He is God. The Lord, He is God.[96]

This prayer is prescribed for recitation by mourners at public services for eleven months immediately after the death of a parent, immediate blood relative, or spouse. It is the Kaddish, sanctification of God's name. Noteworthy and characteristic is the fact that the departed is not mentioned nor is his or her soul prayed for. Its theme is public praise of the glory of God at a time when hard questions of faith often are raised.

Hallowed and enhanced may He be
throughout the world of His own creation.

May He cause His sovereignty soon to be accepted,
during our life and the life of all the people Israel.
And let us say: Amen.

May He be praised throughout all time.

Glorified and celebrated, lauded and worshiped,
acclaimed and honored, extolled and hallowed
may the Holy One be,
praised beyond all song and psalm,
beyond all tributes which mortals can utter.
And let us say: Amen.

Let there be abundant peace from Heaven,
with life's goodness for us and for all the people Israel.

And let us say: Amen.

He who brings peace to His universe
will bring peace to us and to all the people Israel.
And let us say: Amen.[97]

THE MESSIAH

There are two countertendencies in the Jewish vision of the Messiah. The ecstatic poetry of the prophets tended to suggest that the Messiah would come as the result of cataclysms and cosmic miracles. There are, however, more sober views in the Bible which identify the Messiah with real political events, like the restoration of the Jews from Babylonian captivity by their deliverer, the Persian King Cyrus. Each of these notions has continued throughout the history of Jewish faith. Rabbi Akiva in the second century hailed Bar Kochba, the leader of the revolt against Rome in 131–5, as the Messiah; other Rabbis held to the ecstatic view.

> And it shall came to pass in the end of days
> That the mountain of the Lord's House
> Shall stand firm above the mountains,
> And it shall tower above the hills,
> And all the nations shall flow unto it.
> Many peoples shall go and say:
> "Come, let us go up to the mountain of the Lord,
> To the House of the God of Jacob,
> That He will teach us His ways,
> And that we will walk in His paths."
> For Torah shall come forth from Zion,
> The word of the Lord from Jerusalem.
> He will judge among the nations,
> And will arbitrate for the many peoples.
> They shall beat their swords into plowshares,
> And their spears into pruning hooks.
> Nation shall not lift up sword against nation,
> and they shall never again experience war.[98]

Behold, the days are coming, says the Lord, when I will raise up for David a true branch. He shall reign as king and shall prosper, and he shall do what is just and right in the land. In his days Judah shall be saved and Israel shall dwell securely. . . .[99]

Behold, I send you Elijah the prophet before the coming of the awesome, fearful day of the Lord. He shall turn the heart of fathers to the children and the heart of children to their parents, lest I come and smite the land with destruction.[100]

Rabbi Joshua ben Levi came upon Elijah the prophet standing at the entrance of Rabbi Simeon ben Johai's cave. . . . He asked Elijah, "When will the Messiah come?"
Elijah replied, "Go and ask him yourself."
"Where is he?"
"At the city gates."
"How will I recognize him?"
"He sits among the diseased poor. All of the others loosen every one of their bandages at the same time and then bind them up again. But he loosens and binds the bandages over his sores one by one. For he thinks: Perhaps I will be needed; I must be ready to go at once."
Rabbi Joshua ben Levi went to see him. "Shalom to you, my teacher."
Said the Messiah, "Shalom to you, ben Levi."
"When will his lordship come?"
"Today!"
Rabbi Joshua returned to Elijah, who asked, "What did he tell you?" . . .
"Surely he deceived me, for he said that he is coming today and he has not come."
Replied Elijah, "You misunderstood him. He was citing Scripture for you. Surely he had in mind a verse from Psalms—Today shall I come, if only all of you would listen to His voice" [Ps. 95:7].[101]

Rabbi Johanan ben Zakai said: If you should have a sapling in your hand when they tell you that the Messiah has arrived, first plant the sapling and then go to greet the Messiah.[102]

Here are some echoes in the writings of Saadia of the proliferating legends about the cataclysms and wars that would usher in the coming of the Messiah.

. . . it has been transmitted by the traditions of the prophets that God would cause misfortunes and disasters to befall us that would compel us to resolve upon repentance so that we would be deserving of redemption. That is the sense of the remark of our forbears: "If the Israelites will repent, they will be redeemed. If not, the Holy One will raise up a king whose decrees will be even more severe than those of Haman, whereupon they will repent and thus be redeemed" (*Sanhedrin* 97b).

Our forbears also tell us that the cause of this visitation will be the appearance in Upper Galilee of a man from among the descendants of Joseph, around whom there will gather individuals from among the Jewish nation. This man will go to Jerusalem after its seizure by the Romans and stay in it for a certain length of time. Then they will be surprised by a man named Armilus, who will wage war against them and conquer the city and subject its inhabitants to massacre, captivity, and disgrace. Included among those that will be slain will be that man from among the descendants of Joseph.

Now there will come upon the Jewish nation at that time great misfortunes, the most difficult to endure being the deterioration of their relationship with the governments of the world who will drive them into the wilderness to let them starve and be miserable. As a result of what has happened to them, many of them will desert their faith, only those purified remaining. To these Elijah the prophet will manifest himself and thus the redemption will come. [103]

Maimonides reflects the more realistic tendency. The Messiah will indeed be a king from the house of David who will gather the scattered of Israel together, but the order of the world will not be radically changed by his coming. There will be a world of peace and justice, a world perfected to the level that Jewish teaching imagined for a humanity that is truly obedient to the teachings of the Torah. Thus the Messianic era is conceived as the result of natural processes.

The Anointed King [the Messiah] will in time arise and establish the kingdom of David in its former position and in the dominion it originally had. He will build up the sanctuary and gather the scattered of Israel. In his day, the laws will become what they were in olden times. . . .

Do not think, however, that the Anointed King must give signs and miracles and create new things in this world, or bring the dead back to life, and the like. It will not be so. For see: Rabbi Akiva, who was a great sage among the sages of the Mishnah, it was he who carried arms for ben Koziba, the king, and it was he who said of him that he was the Anointed King. [The reference is to Bar Kochba, the leader of the revolt in 131 to 135.] He and all the sages of his generation thought that this was the Anointed King, until he was slain in his guilt. And after he was slain, they all knew that he was not the Anointed King. But never had the sages asked him for a sign or for miracles. The root of these things is the following: This Torah, its statutes and its laws, is for all times. There is nothing one could add to it, and nothing one could take away. . . .

Do not think in your heart that in the days of the Anointed something will be changed in the ways of the world, or that an innovation will appear in the work of creation. No. The world will go its ways as before, and that which is said in Isaiah, "The wolf shall dwell with the lamb, and the leopard shall lie down with the kid" [Isa. 11:6], is but a parable, and its meaning is that Israel will dwell in safety with the wicked among the heathen, and all will turn to the true faith; they will not rob nor destroy, and they will eat only what is permitted, in peace, like Israel, as it is written, "The lion shall eat straw like the ox" [Isa. 11:7]. And everything else like this that is said concerning the Anointed, is also a parable. In the days of the Anointed all will know what the parable signifies and what it was meant to imply.

The sages said: "Nothing, save the cessation of the servitude to the nations, distinguishes the days of the Anointed from our time" (*Sanhedrin* 91b). From the words of the prophets, we see that in the early days of the Anointed a battle will take place "against Gog and Magog," and that before this battle against Gog and Magog, a prophet will arise who will make straight the people of Israel and prepare their hearts, as it is written, "Behold, I will send you Elijah the prophet before the coming of the great and terrible day of the Lord" [Mal. 3:23]. But he comes only to bring peace into the world, as it is written, "And he shall turn the hearts of the fathers to the children" [Mal. 3:24].

Among the sages there are some who say Elijah will come before the Anointed. But concerning these things and others of the same kind, none knows how they will be until they occur. For the prophets veil these things, and the sages have no tradition concerning them, save what they have deduced from the Scriptures, and so herein their opinion is divided. At any rate, neither the order of this event nor its details are the foot of faith. A man must never ponder over legendary accounts, nor dwell upon interpretations dealing with them or with matters like them. He must not make them of primary importance, for they do not guide him either to fear or to love God. Nor may he seek to calculate the end. The sages said: "Let the spirit of those breathe its last, who seek to calculate the end" (Sanhedrin 97b). Rather let him wait and trust in the matter as a whole, as we have expounded.

The sages and the prophets did not yearn for the days of the Anointed in order to seize upon the world, and not in order to rule over the heathen, or to be exalted by the peoples, or to eat and drink and rejoice, but to be free for the Torah and the wisdom within it, free from any goading and intrusion, so that they may be worthy of life in the coming world.

When that time is here, none will go hungry, there will be no war, no zealousness and no conflict, for goodness will flow abundantly, and all delights will be plentiful as the numberless motes of dust, and the whole world will be solely intent on the knowledge of the Lord. Therefore those of Israel will be great sages, who know what is hidden, and they will attain what knowledge of their Creator it is in man's power to attain, as it is written, "For the earth shall be full of the knowledge of the Lord, as the waters cover the sea" [Isa. 11:9].[104]

Rabbi Zvi Hirsch Kalischer (1795–1874), a rabbi in the classic mold who was one of the forerunners of modern Zionism, reiterated the view of Maimonides in order to justify human effort as preparation for the day of the Messiah.

The redemption of Israel, for which we long, is not to be imagined as a sudden miracle. The Almighty, praised be His name, will not suddenly descend from on high and command His people to go forth. He will not send His Messiah from heaven in a twinkling of an eye, to sound the great trumpet for the scattered of Israel and gather them into Jerusalem. He will not surround the Holy City with a wall of fire or cause the Holy Temple to descend from the heavens. The bliss and the miracles that were promised by His servants, the prophets, will certainly come to pass—everything will be fulfilled—but we will not run in terror and flight, for the redemption of Israel will come by slow degrees and the ray of deliverance will shine forth gradually.

My dear reader! Cast aside the conventional view that the

Messiah will suddenly sound a blast on the great trumpet and cause all the inhabitants of the earth to tremble. On the contrary, the Redemption will begin by awakening support among the philanthropists and by gaining the consent of the nations to the gathering of some of the scattered of Israel into the Holy Land. . . .

Can we logically explain why the Redemption will begin in a natural manner and why the Lord, in His love for His people, will not immediately send the Messiah in an obvious miracle? Yes, we can. We know that all our worship of God is in the form of trials by which He tests us. When God created man and placed him in the Garden of Eden, He also planted the Tree of Knowledge and then commanded man not to eat of it. Why did He put the Tree in the Garden, if not as a trial? . . . When Israel went forth from Egypt, God again tested man's faith with hunger and thirst along the way. . . . Throughout the days of our dispersion we have been dragged from land to land and have borne the yoke of martyrdom for the sanctity of God's name; we have been dragged from land to land and have borne the yoke of exile through the ages, all for the sake of His holy Torah and as a further stage of the testing of our faith.

If the Almighty would suddenly appear, one day in the future, through undeniable miracles, this would be no trial. What straining of our faith would there be in the face of miracles and wonders attending a clear and heavenly command to go up and inherit the land and enjoy its good fruit? Under such circumstances, what fool would not go there, not because of his love of God, but for his own selfish sake? Only a natural beginning of the Redemption is a true test of those who initiate it. To concentrate all one's energy on this holy work and to renounce home and fortune for the sake of living in Zion before "the voice of gladness" and "the voice of joy" are heard—there is no greater merit or trial than this. . . .

For all this to come about there must first be Jewish resettlement in the Land; without such settlement, how can the ingathering begin?[105]

The thirteen articles of faith presented by Maimonides in his commentary to the Mishnah are as close as Judaism ever came to a catechism. Despite the author's immense prestige, they have never been completely accepted. These articles appear in the Prayer Book in rhymed form. They serve as part of an introduction to the daily morning service and are often sung at the end of Friday evening services (*Yigdal*). Nonetheless, this formulation of the faith has been challenged by other theologians throughout the centuries. This text is profoundly important as the most famous statement of the Orthodox faith, and yet even as such it is not binding on the conscience of the believing Jew.

I believe with perfect faith that the Creator, praised be He, is the Creator and the Guide of all creation, and that He alone has made, does make and will make all things.

I believe with perfect faith that the Creator, praised be He, is a Unity, and that there is no unity like His in any manner, and that He alone is our God, who was, is, and will be.

I believe with perfect faith that the Creator, praised be He, is not a body, and that He is free from all attributes of a body, and that He has no form whatsoever.

I believe with perfect faith that the Creator, praised be He, is the first and the last.

I believe with perfect faith that to the Creator, praised be He, and to Him alone is it proper to pray, and that it is not proper to pray to any besides Him.

I believe with perfect faith that all the words of the prophets are true.

I believe with perfect faith that the prophecy of Moses our great teacher, may he rest in peace, was true, and that he was the father of the prophets, both those who preceded and who followed him.

I believe with perfect faith that the entire Torah now in our possession is the same that was given to Moses our teacher, may he rest in peace.

I believe with perfect faith that this Torah will never be replaced, and that there will never be another Torah from the Creator, praised be He.

I believe with perfect faith that the Creator, praised be He, knows every deed of men and all their thoughts, as it is written, "He fashions the hearts of them all and observes all their deeds" [Ps. 33:15].

I believe with perfect faith that the Creator, praised be He, rewards those who keep His commandments and punishes those who transgress His commandments.

I believe with perfect faith in the coming of the Messiah, and though he tarry I will wait daily for him.

I believe with perfect faith that there will be a revival of the dead at a time when it shall please the Creator, praised be He, and exalted be His fame for ever and ever. [106]

MODERN DOCTRINES AND DENOMINATIONS

The movement for the "reform" of Judaism began in the first years of the nineteenth century with initiatives to make changes in public worship, and in the aesthetics of the synagogue. In 1810, Israel Jacobson built the synagogue is Seesen with a steeple, in the manner of a church. He insisted on decorum, and preached in German. By 1817, a group of Jews in Hamburg formed the "New Israelite Temple Association" to establish an unprecedented form of Jewish worship. The founders of this temple were very consciously entering a new age.

Since public worship has for some time been neglected by so many, because of the ever decreasing knowledge of the language in which alone it has until now been conducted, and also because of many other shortcomings which have crept in at the same time—the undersigned, convinced of the necessity to restore public worship to its deserving dignity and importance, have joined together to follow the example of several Israelitish congregations, especially the one in Berlin. They plan to arrange in this city also, for themselves as well as others who think as they do, a dignified and well-ordered ritual according to which the worship service shall be conducted on Sabbath and holy days and on other solemn occasions, and which shall be observed in their own temple, to be erected especially for this purpose. Specifically, there shall be introduced at such services a German sermon, and choral singing to the accompaniment of an organ. [107]

The founding of the temple at Hamburg occasioned fierce debate. Only one Orthodox rabbi, Aaron Chorin (1766–1844), defended these innovations.

I knew well the yen which some zealots have for persecuting others, which does not rest until it has done harm, which is deaf to all reason, insensitive to all progress, and resistant to all ennoblement. But after mature thought my reason returned. What, I thought, shall truth remain repressed because weak people dislike it? Shall the sun hide its light because the night owl cannot bear it? No, I thought, I will publicly testify to the truth and not shrink back from the hatred which would likely descend on me.

And so I issued my treatise *Kin'at Ha-emet* [Zeal for Truth, published in Dessau, 1818], in which I hoped to deal with the above-mentioned questions in simple, unambiguous terms. I stated that it was not only permissible, but obligatory, to free the worship ritual from its adhesions, to hold the service in a language understandable to the worshiper, and to accompany it with organ and song.[108]

The innovations were otherwise widely and vehemently denounced by the leaders of Orthodoxy. The central theme of the many objections was that change is forbidden. Perhaps the sharpest statement was by Rabbi Moshe Schreiber, writing in reply to an open letter from Rabbi Baruch ben Meir, of Hamburg.

Re your complaint that the temple of the reformers is closed during the week and is only open on Sabbath: I wish it would be closed on Sabbath, too, since they changed the liturgy that has come down from the men of the Great Synagogue, from the sages of the Talmud, and from our sainted fathers . . . and also omitted the reference to the coming of the Messiah, the restoration of Zion and Jerusalem . . . and employ Christians to play the harp and the organ . . . on the Sabbath, which is prohibited to us; and most of their prayers are in German. . . .

With respect to the use of non-Hebrew in public worship service! This is totally impossible. The statement of the Mishnah (*Sotah* 7:1) that the Tefilah (silent) prayer can be said in any language. . . . this can be done only occasionally . . . but a permanent reader must not use a foreign language in a public service . . . for an accurate translation into another language is impossible. . . . As to the objection that ordinary people do not understand what they say in Hebrew . . . it is better to introduce the requirement of learning the meaning of the prayers than introducing that they be said in a foreign language. . . . (Nachmanides, beginning of *Ki Tisa* in Exodus); and our sages said that the world was created by using the holy language. God gave us the Torah in Hebrew; therefore we cannot talk to Him in our ordinary (non-Hebrew) language.

Therefore, what you said with respect to the holy synagogue is law. . . . It is a law that it is prohibited to use their (the Reform) prayerbooks, which are written in a foreign language. The text has to be Hebrew and the versions have to be old (i.e. traditional), as printed long ago. The organ must not be used, certainly not on a Sabbath . . . and I agree to prohibit (the above innovations) to every Jew. . . .[109]

As Rabbi Moshe Schreiber intimated in his opinion, the fundamental break between the Orthodox and the "Reformers" was not over synagogue practice, but over doctrine. The "Reformers" were welcoming the new age by declaring themselves to be at home, no longer "exiles" from the land of their ancestors, or waiting for the Messiah to come and redeem them. They were redefining Judaism as a universal religion which teaches morality, and for which the ritual commandments were essentially irrelevant. The "Reformers" of Hamburg were soon echoed in the United States in Charleston, South Carolina, where a group seceded from the local congregation to organize the "Reform Society of Israelites." In 1826, this society published its creed. After a number of passages about the One God, Creator of the universe, the authors of the catechism equated the specifics of Judaism, as they wanted to perpetuate it, with universal morality.

I believe, with a perfect faith, that the laws of God, as delivered by Moses in the Ten Commandments, are the only true foundations of piety towards the Almighty and of morality among men.

I believe, with a perfect faith, that morality is essentially connected with religion, and that good faith towards all mankind is among the most acceptable offerings to the Deity.

I believe, with a perfect faith, that the love of God is the highest duty of His creatures, and that the pure and upright heart is the chosen temple of Jehovah.

I believe, with a perfect faith, that the Creator (blessed be His name!) is the only true Redeemer of all His children, and that He will spread the worship of His name over the whole earth. [110]

This first attempt to found a "Reform" congregation in the United States failed. Most of the founders returned to Beth Elohim, the congregation from which they had seceded, and which had remained formally Orthodox. Nonetheless, when Beth Elohim dedicated a new building in March 1841, the sermon of dedication included the striking sentence, "this country is our Palestine, this city our Jerusalem, this house our Temple."

The new Reform Judaism explained itself not as the break with the past that it seemed to be, but as the necessary, contemporary expression of what Judaism had always been. It had begun with Abraham's proclamation of the One God; it had safeguarded that faith for many centuries by keeping itself apart from paganism, through a national existence of its own, and a Hebrew language. Separatism was no longer necessary in the new, liberal age; it stood in the way of the moral mission of Judaism to make all of mankind better.

> The strength of Judaism lies precisely in the fact that it has grown out of a full national life and that it possesses both a language and a history as a nation. The idea of Judaism was an all-embracing one. Hence, if it was not to be a drifting shadow, it had to find expression in a healthy national individualism which, on the one hand, saw all of mankind epitomized within itself, but on the other hand, sought to embrace all the world of mankind beyond its own confines. Thus it is a strong point of Judaism that it originally revealed itself in a language which was entirely imbued with the idea and which was the noblest of fruit of a full national life. Judaism was not, however, dependent upon language and nationality; indeed, it survived in all its vitality even after being deprived of both. When its vessel was smashed, its survival was not affected thereby. Because it always had to engage in violent struggle, Judaism remained a closed and separate entity; and yet it has succeeded in transmitting its basic ideals to mankind as a universal heritage. And when the artificial barriers fall, it will continue to retain its universality throughout the course of history. Let us, therefore, look back with joy on our former life as a nation, as being an essential transitional era in our history, and on our language, through which the life of that Jewish nation had taken root in spiritual soil![111]

The battle over Hebrew was fought most vehemently in 1845, at a Rabbinic conference of the Reformers in Frankfort, Germany. The majority had decided to phase out Hebrew entirely. The Reform synagogue would pray in German in Germany, in French in France, and in English in England and America. Zacharias Frankel (1801–1875) would not agree. The break with Hebrew as the language of prayer meant, in his view, that Reform

Judaism was cutting loose from the Jewish past—and veneration of that past was the central component of his Jewish faith. The position taken by Frankel has become the foundation of Conservative Judaism in Europe and in America.

The majority of the Rabbinical Conference decided that Hebrew prayer was only *advisable* and that it would be the task of the rabbis to eliminate it gradually altogether.

I disagree with such a decision, not only because I have a different point of view, but also because I disagree with the tendency of the decision. For this spirit leaves unheeded so many important elements and eliminates the historical element which has weight and power in every religion. In my opinion this is not the spirit of preserving but of destroying positive historical Judaism, which I declared distinctly before the Assembly was my point of view. This spirit of the Assembly deprives all its further decisions of any validity in the eyes of those who adhere to the positive historical position. As I explained to the Assembly, not only voting is important, but also motivation. Only those who have already made up their mind and merely want a formal approval for their position can find a superficial satisfaction in general voting procedures.

For these reasons I find myself moved to protest, not only against the above-mentioned decision, but at the same time to declare that my point of view is entirely different from that of the Assembly and that, therefore, I can neither sit nor vote in its midst.[112]

By the 1880s, before the effects of mass migration of Jews from Eastern Europe were felt in the United States, Reform Judaism dominated. Its doctrines were defined at a Rabbinic conference in Pittsburgh in 1885. They flowed naturally from the views of the Temple in Hamburg, the Reform Society in Charleston, and the theology of Abraham Geiger (1810–1874). Here are three middle paragraphs of the declaration in Pittsburgh.

We recognize in the Mosaic legislation a system of training the Jewish people for its mission during its national life in Palestine, and to-day we accept as binding only its moral laws, and maintain only such ceremonies as elevate and sanctify our lives, but reject all such as are not adapted to the views and habits of modern civilization.

We hold that all such Mosaic and rabbinical laws as regulate diet, priestly purity, and dress originated in ages and under the influence of ideas entirely foreign to our present mental and spiritual state. They fail to impress the modern Jew with a spirit of priestly holiness; their observance in our days is apt rather to obstruct than to further modern spiritual elevation.

We recognize, in the modern era of universal culture of heart and intellect, the approaching of the realization of Israel's great Messianic hope for the establishment of the kingdom of truth, justice, and peace among all men. We consider ourselves no longer a nation, but a religious community, and therefore except neither a return to Palestine, nor a sacrificial worship under the sons of Aaron, nor the restoration of any of the laws concerning the Jewish state.[113]

The most eloquent successor of Zacharias Frankel was Solomon Schechter. The shaping force in the Jewish religion, to Schechter, is the people, the community of believers. The people decides what the Bible means. The community of believers keeps fashioning and reinterpreting the Torah.

The historical school has never, to my knowledge, offered to the world a theological programme of its own. . . . On the whole, its attitude towards religion may be defined as an enlightened Scepticism combined with a staunch conservatism, which is not even wholly devoid of a certain mystical touch. As far as we may gather from vague remarks and hints thrown out now and then, its theological position may perhaps be thus defined: It is not the mere revealed Bible that is of first importance to the Jew, but the Bible as it repeats itself in history; in other words, as it is interpreted by Tradition. The Talmud, that wonderful mine of religious ideas from which it would be just as easy to draw up a manual for the most orthodox as to extract a *vade mecum* for the most sceptical, lends some countenance to this view by certain controversial passages—not to be taken seriously—in which the "words of the scribes" are placed almost above the words of the Torah. Since, then, the interpretation of Scripture or the Secondary Meaning is mainly a product of changing historical influences, it follows that the center of authority is actually removed from the Bible, and placed in some "living body," which, by reason of its being in touch with the ideal aspirations and the religious needs of the age, is best able to determine the nature of the Secondary Meaning. This living body, however, is not represented by any section of the nation, or any corporate priesthood, or Rabbihood, but by the collective conscience of catholic Israel, as embodied in the Universal Synagogue. The Synagogue, "with its long continuous cry after God for more than twenty-three centuries," with its unremittent activity in teaching and developing the word of God, with its uninterrupted succession of Prophets, Psalmists, Scribes, Assideans, Rabbis, Patriarchs, Interpreters, Elucidators, Eminences, and Teachers, with its glorious record of saints, martyrs, sages, philosophers, scholars, and mystics; this Synagogue, the only true witness to the past, and forming in all ages the sublimest expression of Israel's religious life, must also retain its authority as the sole true guide for the present and the future.[114]

In the twentieth century, Reform Judaism has been deeply influenced, and transformed, by the Zionist movement and the creation of the State of Israel. It has officially abandoned the anti-nationalism of its origins. In the last half-century, Orthodox Judaism has become stronger. There has been substantial return to ultra-Orthodoxy, which has maintained, since the days of Rabbi Moshe Schreiber, that Jews should have nothing to do with secular culture. The more modern form of Orthodoxy, which began to fashion itself in opposition to Reform Judaism at its very beginnings, has been maintaining that one could be both fully integrated into the general culture, and a believing and observant Orthodox Jew. This view was defined by Samson Raphael Hirsch. He was the first rabbi in Germany who remained Orthodox, even though he had acquired a thorough secular culture culminating in a doctorate. Hirsch affirmed the value of secular education no less than the Reformers, but he insisted that the Divine teaching revealed at Sinai was an absolute, and that it was not subject to change. His major polemical work was cast in the form of letters to a doubting friend.

> Its history we must learn from it, for Judaism is an historical phenomenon, and for its origin, its first entrance into history, and for a long subsequent time, the Torah is the only monument. And if, at the cradle of this people, we were to hear mystic voices, such as no other nation ever heard—voices announcing the purpose of this people's existence—for which it entered into history, should we not hearken to these voices, and try to comprehend them, that we might thus understand it and its history? It is the

only source of its law, written and oral. . . . Our desire is to apprehend Judaism; therefore, we must take up our position in thought within Judaism, and must ask ourselves, "What will human beings be who recognize the contents of this book as a basis and rule of life given to them by God?" In the same way we must strive to know their extent and bearing from the written and oral law. All of this must take place from the standpoint of the object of all this procedure, the finding of the true law of life.[115]

Modern Orthodoxy affirms both the law of the Torah and participation in the ways and culture of the world. The most eloquent contemporary exponent of that position is Rabbi Joseph B. Soloveitchik. In his most famous essay, *Halakhic Man*, he defined obedience to the Law as the source of fearless personal dignity and as the way in which the believer experiences the nearness of God:

Halakhic man does not quiver before any man; he does not seek out compliments, nor does he require public approval. If he sees that there are fewer and fewer men of distinguished spiritual rank about, then he wraps himself in his mantle and hides away to the four cubits of Halakhah. He knows that the truth is a lamp unto his feet and the Halakhah a light unto his path. His whole being loathes idlers, wastrels, and loafers. Piety that is not based upon knowledge of the Torah is of no consequence in his view. There can be no fear of God without knowledge and no service of God without the cognition of halakhic truth. "A crude man fears not sin, nor is a man ignorant of Torah pious" [*Avot* 2:5]. The old saying of Socrates, that virtue is knowledge, is strikingly similar to the stance of halakhic man. . . .

Halakhic man implements the Torah without any compromises or concessions, for precisely such implementation, such actualization is his ultimate desire, his fondest dream. When a person actualizes the ideal Halakhah in the very midst of the real world, he approaches the level of that godly man, the prophet— the creator of worlds. Therefore, the ideals of righteousness, which the Torah first introduced into the world, are implemented, are actualized and concretized, by halakhists in all their purity and resplendent brilliance. Halakhic man cannot be cowed by anyone.[116]

7

PRAYER

GOD HEARS PRAYER

The Lord hears prayer and He always answers it. This does not mean that He always gives the answer that we want, for His ways are not our ways.

The Holy One, praised be He, longs for the prayers of the righteous.[1]

Rabbi Eleazar said: Prayer is greater than the offering of sacrifices. . . .

Rabbi Eleazar said: Since the day on which the Temple was destroyed, the gates of prayer have been locked, as it is said, "Though I call and cry for help, He shuts out my prayer" [Lam. 3:8]. Nevertheless, the gates of tears have not been locked, as it is said: "Hear my prayer, O Lord, and give ear to my cry; keep not silent at my tears" [Ps. 39:13].[2]

". . . to love the Lord your God, and to serve Him with all your heart . . ." [Deut. 11:13]. What is the service of the heart? It is prayer.[3]

Let then the power of the Lord be magnified, as You have declared, saying: "The Lord is patient and full of mercy, forgiving iniquity and transgression. He will not clear the guilty, visiting the iniquity of fathers upon children to the third and fourth generations." Forgive, I pray You, the sins of this people, according to Your great kindness, as You have pardoned this people from

Egypt until now. And the Lord said: "I have forgiven, as You have asked."[4]

Jonah ben Landsofer (1678–1712) was a Bohemian Talmudist. The passage below is from his last will.

The first thing that should be said [in a father's testament to his children] is the great principle that the purpose of the creation of man is the service of God. The essential part of this service is in man's innermost being and the heart watches over it. This is prayer without any outside thought or preoccupation. Not one in a thousand of those who are burdened with human cares reached this level. Though they understand the meaning of the words of prayer, they do not attain the degree of love which should accompany them. Therefore, whenever something happens to you, write for yourselves some new prayer, being careful not to violate the established laws concerning prayer. Let it be composed of verses of the book of Psalms, especially from Psalm 119. Whoever is unable to do this should pray in Yiddish from the depth of his heart.

None of you should omit praying in Yiddish after the morning prayer, especially concerning those petitions whose fulfillment is most regularly needed in your daily life. Pray that God, praised be He, grant you a contrite and an understanding heart, free of jealousy, and cleared of envy. Pray for sustenance, that it may be acquired honestly and without great burdens which could nullify the Torah and the higher things in your life. Let each one pray that he not give birth to an unruly or a sinful child, God forbid. May He protect you against all sin and iniquity. Pray that God plant the love of Him in your heart, and peace in your home. And pray that your prayer itself be undisturbed by carnal and foul thoughts. Pray that you be granted a good memory to aid in the study of Torah. Each of you is free to choose whatever petition he would like to offer.[5]

Here are two Hasidic insights into the meaning of prayer.

In the palace of the king there are many rooms and there is a key for each room. An axe, however, is the passkey of passkeys, for with it one can break through all the doors and all the gates.

Each prayer has its own proper meaning and it is therefore the specific key to a door in the Divine Palace, but a broken heart is an axe which opens all the gates.[6]

Prayer is an act of daring. Otherwise it is impossible to stand in prayer before God. When imagining the greatness of the Creator, how else could one stand in prayer before Him?

Prayer is a mystery, directed in its essence towards changing the order of the world. Every star and sphere is fixed in its order, yet man wants to change the order of nature, he asks for miracles. Hence, at the moment of prayer man must lay aside his capacity for shame. If men had shame, they would, God forbid, lose the faith that prayer is answered.[7]

Searching for God

Traditional teaching has it that prayer is an address to God, and that He hears and responds. For the last two centuries, many Jewish theologians of various persuasions, from Reform to Orthodox, have moved to imagining prayer as a way of transforming the self by turning to God. The child is no longer standing before the Heavenly Father to solicit His favor; the human being in prayer is remaking himself, by letting God into his life. This newer view is already present in one of the earliest Reformers, David Friedlander (1750–1834):

Every morally conscious man feels a need at certain times to lift his soul toward God. He is dependent upon God. He has need for self-examination. Self-examination leads him to a renewed resolve to keep God's commandments, which religion and reason prescribe for his bliss. As in times of joy and sorrow we share our feelings with our friends, so it is even more pleasant, beneficial and comforting to lay them before the All-forgiving Being. God's abundant love and wisdom are so manifest that only a man devoid of feeling could remain unmoved. At the sight of the marvels of creation, man is reminded of his duty and of his destiny, and he rises to worshipful thoughts which bring him close to God. He is purified. He prays. For true prayer, reason and will must work together. Reason will give us a vivid presentation of God. The will steers us away from extraneous matter, and keeps our thoughts on our conversation with God. Such devout and beneficial prayer will be acceptable to the Lord, and will lead us to the divine qualities of the Almighty, will enlarge our comprehension of them, and will enlighten and correct us. We learn wisdom, kindness, consideration, to deal fairly, to forgive our neighbor's short-comings, and to make the best use of our own capabilities. Prayer will teach the rich man to put his advantage to noble use, and will soothe the turmoil in the mind of the unhappy man, and teach him that even his sufferings are means towards the best end. Prayer will make man happy, confident in times of sorrow, gentle and modest in times of happiness.[8]

Quarrels soon erupted, before the middle of the nineteenth century, over the content of Jewish prayer. The Orthodox insisted that not a word could be changed, for the liturgy represents the inherited doctrines of Judaism. The Reformers insisted that they no longer could believe what is said in many of the prayers. The argument of some "conservatives" that the liturgy be kept intact as a form of historic continuity did not convince rationalist critics. Abraham Geiger was a leading figure among those who insisted on contemporaneity.

Many religious concepts have taken on a more spiritual character and, therefore, their expression in prayer must be more spiritual. From now on the hope for an after-life should not be expressed in terms which suggest a future revival, a resurrection of the body; rather, they must stress the immortality of the human soul. We must eliminate the whole physical pictorialization of the divine household, the detailed description of angelic choirs and holy beasts, which is found especially in the morning prayers. We must recognize the force of prayer and the fulfillment of all our obligations toward God more through the blessed effect which they have on our ennoblement, rather than as necessary obeisance to a command imposed from above. We must value our holy days more because of their potential elevation of our sentiment, rather than because of their historic origin, and in this fashion they must be made part of our prayers. The changes which must be made to achieve these purposes will not be very extensive, for in this respect our prayers do possess a treasure of deep thoughts and sentiments, which only need to be cleansed from disfiguring additions. The change of the order of prayers in accordance with these principles will not deprive the service of its sanctity which a long, honorable history has given it—instead, it will significantly strengthen the force of its inwardness.[9]

Despite rationalist criticism, the need to pray remained deep in the soul even of some secular Jews. They had defined themselves in national terms, as belonging not to a community of believers but to the Jewish people. Yet could they be completely divorced from religious feeling? Near the end of his life, A.D Gordon (1856–1922), the moral leader of Socialist Zionism, wrestled with the meaning of prayer:

> I ask myself, and I wonder whether I am alone in this question: What is the Day of Atonement to us, to those who do not observe the forms of religion?
>
> Facing me are a fact and a possibility. It is a fact that for many generations it was a day which the entire people dedicated to repentance, prayer, and the service of the heart. It presented a possibility to spiritually sensitive people to make their inner reckoning on the loftiest plane.
>
> I ask: Is this day for us merely a heritage from the past, a remnant of antiquity? Do we not really need such a day, especially as part of the national culture we are creating? If this day ceases to be what it has been—if it becomes an ordinary day like all others—will this not represent a great national and human loss, a spiritual disaster from which none of us, neither the people as a whole, nor we, its individual children, can ever recover?
>
> As long as we were penned within ghetto walls, ragged, and cut off from the great life of the world, from man and from his broad and abundant life, we accepted what our ancestors had bequeathed to us. We believed in it and we gave our lives for it. When the walls of the ghetto fell, when we saw the world and all that is in it at close range, when we came to know man and his life, when we added cultural values from without to all this— we realized that the traditions of our ancestors were no longer in harmony with what was growing and developing our own spirits. But did we deeply ponder this problem? Did we analyze and examine what had really become antiquated and unsuitable, utterly useless or decayed? In the final analysis, did we ask: What has become obscured or unacceptable in form only? What needs merely a more fitting and noble form, since it is alive and fresh? What is, in essence, sound, awaiting only a higher regeneration?
>
> During all our long exile we existed by the strength of our religion. It sustained us in our grave and prolonged suffering and inspired us to live—often to live heroically. Is it possible, can the mind entertain the possibility, that such a force is a mere figment of the imagination, of the ramblings of an ignorant soul, and that

it possesses no elemental and lasting core? Has the accepted idea been sufficiently examined and analyzed critically—is it sufficiently founded in logic and in the human spirit—that with the loss of the basis for the blind faith the basis for religion has also been destroyed?[10]

The founder of the Reconstructionist movement, Mordecai M. Kaplan, abandoned, without equivocation, the classic belief in a personal God. The God-idea, to use his terminology, is "the power that makes for salvation," the faith that our goodness is linked to the essential goodness of the universe. Prayer is therefore a way of turning us towards the best of ourselves.

Without the actual awareness of His presence, experienced as beatitude and inner illumination, we are likely to be content with the humanistic interpretation of life. But this interpretation is inadequate, because it fails to express and to foster the feeling that man's ethical aspirations are part of a cosmic urge, by obeying which man makes himself at home in the universe. . . . *The dynamic of ethical action is the spirit of worship, the feeling that we are in God and God in us,* the yielding of our persons in voluntary surrender to those larger aims that express for us as much as has been revealed to us of the destiny of the human race. It is only this emotional reaction to life that can make humanity itself mean more to us than a "disease of the agglutinated dust." . . .

. . . To appreciate fully the meaning of the awareness of God as a Presence, one must actually experience the influence of public worship. . . . Participation in public worship makes one feel at home in the world. . . . Realizing that others share our needs, our hopes, our fears, and our ideals, we no longer feel dependent entirely on our own efforts for our salvation. . . . public worship not only enhances our strength by its suggestion of human cooperation but by banishing morbid fear it gives us renewed confidence in nature itself, enabling us to see in it as well as in humanity the immanence of God. Thus public worship makes us feel not only that we have brothers on earth, but that we also have—to use the traditional metaphor—a Father in heaven, a Power in nature that responds to human need, if properly approached. . . .

Public worship aids us by liberating our personality from the confining walls of the individual ego. . . . Instead of living one small and petty life we now share the multitudinous life of our people. . . .

The function of the traditional liturgy is to have the Jewish people experience the awareness of that God Whom Israel began to know only after centuries of groping and stumbling, and Whom it is still in the process of learning to identify. The liturgy therefore speaks in terms of Israel's historic experience; its language, its figures of speech, its symbols and its rites are derived from the cultural heritage of the Jewish people. . . .[11]

Abraham Joshua Heschel was not a rationalist, like Kaplan, but rather a Hasid, a mystical pietist as became the descendant of a distinguished line of Hasidic rebbes. But, in his much more impassioned language, he expressed his own version of the dominant contemporary outlook, that prayer exists not to petition God for favors but to change humanity.

The focus of prayer is not the self. A man may spend hours meditating about himself, or be stirred by the deepest sympathy for his fellow man, and no prayer will come to pass. Prayer comes to pass in a complete turning of the heart toward God, toward His goodness and power. It is the momentary disregard of our personal concerns, the absence of self-centered thoughts, which constitute the art of prayer. Feeling becomes prayer in the moment in which we forget ourselves and become aware of God. When we analyze the consciousness of a supplicant, we discover that it is not concentrated upon his own interests, but on something beyond the self. The thought of personal need is absent, and the thought of divine grace alone is present in his mind. Thus, in beseeching Him for bread, there is *one* instant, at least, in which our mind is directed neither to our hunger nor to food, but to His mercy. This instant is prayer.

We start with a personal concern and live to feel the utmost. For the fate of the individual is a counterpoint to a larger theme. In prayer we come close to hearing the eternal theme and discerning our place in it. It is as if our life were a seamless garment, continuous with the Infinite. Our poverty is His. His property is ours. Overwhelmed with awe of His share in our lives, we extend ourselves to Him, expose our goals to His goodness, exchange our will for His wisdom. For this reason, the analogy between prayer and petitioning another human being is like the analogy between the ocean and a cup of water. For the essence of prayer lies in man's self-transcending, in his surpassing the limits of what is human, in his relating the purely natural to the Divine.

Prayer is an invitation to God to intervene in our lives, to let His will prevail in our affairs; it is the opening of a window to Him in our will, an effort to make Him the Lord of our soul. We submit our interests to His concern, and seek to be allied with what is ultimately right. Our approach to the holy is not an intrusion, but an answer. Between the dawn of childhood and the door of death, man encounters things and events out of which comes a whisper of truth, not much louder than stillness, but exhorting and persistent. Yet man listens to his fears and his whims, rather than to the gentle petitions of God. The Lord of the universe is suing for the favor of man, but man fails to realize his correlation. It is the disentanglement of our heart from cant, bias, and ambition, the staving in of the bulk of stupid conceit, the cracking of hollow self-reliance, that enables us to respond to this request for our service.

The purpose of prayer is not the same as the purpose of speech. The purpose of speech is to inform; the purpose of prayer is to partake.

In speech, the act and the content are not always contemporaneous. What we wish to communicate to others is usually present in our minds prior to the moment of communication. In contrast, the actual content of prayer comes into being in the moment of praying. For the true content of prayer, the true sacrifice we offer, is not the prescribed word which we repeat, but the response to it, the self-examination of the heart, the realization of what is at stake in living as a child of God, as a part of Israel. These elements which constitute the substance of prayer come into being within prayer.

Is it the outburst of eloquence which makes the infinite listen to our feeble voice? Prayer is not a sermon delivered to God. In oratory, as in any other work of art, we endeavor to lend an adequate form to an idea; we apply all our care to adjusting the form to the content. But in prayer it makes little difference whether we stammer or are eloquent. [12]

In a sense, our liturgy is a higher form of silence. It is pervaded by an awed sense of the grandeur of God which resists description and surpasses all expression. The individual is silent. He does not bring forth his own words. His saying the consecrated words is in essence an act of listening to what they convey. *The spirit of Israel speaks, the self is silent.*

Twofold is the meaning of silence. One, the abstinence from speech, the absence of sound. Two, inner silence, the absence of self-concern, stillness. One may articulate words in his voice and yet be inwardly silent. One may abstain from uttering any sound and yet be overbearing.

Both are inadequate: our speech as well as our silence. Yet there is a level that goes beyond both: the level of song. "There are three ways in which a man expresses his deep sorrow: the man on the lowest level cries; the man on the second level is silent; the man on the highest level knows how to turn his sorrow into song." *(Siach Sarfei Kodesh, Vol. 2, p. 92, #318) True prayer is a song.*[13]

Whatever may be the explanation of prayer, it is an institution. In the halakhah, regular prayer is commanded. From the perspective of a contemporary Israeli thinker, Isaiah Leibovitz, the individual need not imagine himself to be answered by God or to be transported beyond himself. That may or may not happen in prayer, but it is the duty of the Jew to utter the prescribed words at set times. Without such obedience the question of prayer dissolves into vagueness.

. . . The greatness and the power of the prayer which we have in the Siddur [prayer book], the obligatory, fixed prayer as determined by Jewish Law—setting aside the independent interests and motivations of man in favor of his position before God and the acknowledgment of his obligation to worship God—is an obligation borne by everyone alike, under all conditions and in all circumstances, independent of his personal history and whatever happens to him and of his own response to events. Therefore, there is only *one* version of the *Shmoneh Esreh* in the Afternoon Service for a groom about to stand beneath the wedding canopy with his heart's desire and for a mourner who has just returned from the cemetery, from the funeral of the wife of his youth. There is only *one* arrangement of song and psalms in the early Morning Service for one who is enjoying the world's splendor and for one whose world has closed about him in darkness. . . .

The great religious obligation of prayer with total devotion can be understood and has real substance only if we understand it as devoted by man to the worship of God, when he prays with the fixed texts of prayer. It is not possible to obligate every man, in all of life's changing situations, to intend the same words of praise and the same petitions, which in certain situations are absolutely inappropriate for what he feels and needs. However, it is precisely the prayer that one prays because he is *obligated* to do so, and not because he is driven to it by his feelings and his needs, which is a religious act of accepting the yoke of the kingdom of heaven and the yoke of the Torah and the commandments.

For all of these reasons there is no place for the claims or the demands, which are heard from time to time, to amend the *text* of prayer in order to match contemporary human needs, whims, or perceptions. Prayer which matches human needs or whims ceases being a religious act, and becomes one of the activities that man pursues for his own pleasure and for the satisfaction of his spiritual needs, like poetry, music, art, and film. Of course, we have always known that the *text* of prayer, the formula fixed by the Sages, is not from Heaven, that it has no sanctity in and of itself. It has been arranged and determined by human beings like ourselves, according to their judgment and their perception, as to what they saw as the most appropriate and suitable expression for fulfilling the commandment of prayer. The entire sanctity of the text of prayer comes only from this legal decision. . . .

If we should meet in the synagogue a *minyan* or several *min-yanim* of Jews who attend the Morning Service daily, there certainly is none among them who believes that he is going to the synagogue out of a need to inform the Blessed One about his needs; and it is doubtful whether there is one among them who thinks that he, flesh-and-blood, has the power to bless, praise and extol the ineffable. Moreover, there generally is not one of them who feels that his fate on that particular day depends upon his going to the synagogue for the Morning Service. Proof of this is the fact that if he or one of his children should take ill, he will go to the doctor's office, exactly like any heretic, even though in the morning he declared honestly [that God is] "healer of the sick of His people Israel"; and in order to earn a living he will go to work like any atheist, even though in the morning he declared honestly, "You open Your hand and satisfy every living thing with favor"; and if he is worried about the welfare and security of the State of Israel, he will be concerned about tanks and rockets, like anyone who does not believe in the God of Israel; and if the

Commander-in-Chief of the Defense Forces should experience a religious revival and put on *tefillin* every morning, his faith in God will not cause him to change his plans of operation by even a hairsbreadth. So why does a Jew come to the synagogue every day? There is only one answer, and it embodies the depth of faith which is in the Judaism of Torah and Law: I come to the synagogue daily in order to fulfill the commandment of communal prayer.

Prayer is not an attempt to have the Creator intervene in the order of His creation. . . .

Understanding prayer as an expression of worshiping God, and not as an attempt to cause the Creator to intervene in the order of His creation, solves the problem which often arises in religious education, especially in education for prayer: "Why does prayer, and at times the prayer of the righteous, upright and innocent, go unanswered?" And the response is: *There is no prayer which goes unanswered!* . . . Since prayer is only the expression of the worshiper's goal to serve God, the very act of prayer is *the attainment of the goal.* In other words, "*answered* prayer" would be a tautology, and "unanswered prayer" is a self-contradictory concept, like a triangle without three sides. What is the frame of reference here? A person who prays with devotion, with the purpose of worshiping God. "The Lord is near to all who call, near to all who call upon Him in truth."[14]

PRAYER AS COMMANDMENT

To worship God is a spiritual necessity for the believer; to speak to his Maker, to beseech Him, to experience His nearness, and to express gratitude and wonder at His beneficence. It is the nature of Judaism not to leave prayer for man's spontaneous enthusiasm alone. Man must pray with true inwardness, with freshness of feeling, but he must pray regularly at stated times and occasions.

You shall revere the Lord your God. You shall serve Him and cleave to Him.[15]

When you have eaten and are satisfied, you shall bless the Lord your God for the good land which He has given you.[16]

In the second century, after the destruction of the Temple, Rabbi Judah the Prince, the leader of Palestine and of world

Jewry, summarized Jewish law and custom in a six-part work called the Mishnah. The text is second in authority only to the Bible itself. The first section of the Mishnah is *Berakhot* ("Blessings"). It is devoted to the laws of prayer, and the passages that follow are taken almost entirely from it, with the addition of a few passages from other Rabbinic literature.

A note on technical terms: *Sh'ma* refers to the passages from Deuteronomy 6:4–9, 11:13–21, and Numbers 15:37–41, which were prescribed in earliest times as the core of the daily morning and evening prayer. *Tefilah* (or *Amidah*) was composed during the Rabbinic period and was prescribed to be said, along with the *Sh'ma*, morning and evening. The full text of the version of this prayer that is to be said every weekday is reproduced later in this section.

One was reading the section containing the *Sh'ma* from the Torah when the time came for reciting the *Sh'ma*. If he read the passage with the full intention of fulfilling his duty to recite the *Sh'ma*, he has fulfilled his obligation; otherwise he has not.[17]

Craftsmen may recite the *Sh'ma* at the top of a tree or on top of a stone wall, but they may not recite the *Tefilah* in this manner.[18]

A bridegroom is exempt from reciting the evening *Sh'ma* on the first night, or until the close of the following Sabbath if he has not yet consummated the marriage.

When Rabban Gamaliel married, he recited the *Sh'ma* on the first night. His disciples asked him, "Master, have you not taught us that a bridegroom is exempt from reciting the *Sh'ma* on the first night?" He said to them: "I will not let your statements influence me to cast off the yoke of the kingdom of heaven even for a moment."[19]

He whose dead lies unburied before him is exempt from reciting the *Sh'ma*, from saying the *Tefilah* and from wearing *Tefillin*. Concerning the pall bearers and all those who relieve them, those who walk in front of the coffin and those who walk behind it: those who are required for bearing the coffin are exempt, but those who are not actually required are not exempt from reciting the *Sh'ma*. All of them are exempt from saying the *Tefilah*.[20]

The morning *Tefilah* may be said any time until noon. Rabbi Judah says: until the fourth hour [i.e. midmorning]. The afternoon *Tefilah* may be said any time until sunset. Rabbi Judah says: until midway through the afternoon. The evening *Tefilah* has no set time. The additional *Tefilah* may be said any time during the day. Rabbi Judah says: until the seventh hour [i.e. one o'clock].[21]

How many times is one obliged to pray each day? Our Rabbis taught that one is not to pray more than the three times daily initiated by the patriarchs. Abraham initiated morning prayer, as it is written "Abraham went early in the morning to the place where he had stood before the Lord" [Gen. 19:27]. Isaac initiated afternoon prayer, as it is written "Isaac went out to meditate in the field toward evening" [Gen. 24:63]. Jacob initiated evening prayer, as it is written "And he [Jacob] came to a certain place [Hebrew word for "place" is also used, in Rabbinic literature, as a synonym for God], and stayed there that night, because the sun had set" [Gen. 28:11]. And concerning Daniel, too, it is written ". . . he [Daniel] got down upon his knees three times a day and prayed and gave thanks before his God . . ." [Daniel 6:11]. However, this verse does not give the times for prayer. David came to explain "Evening and morning and at noon I utter my complaint and moan, and He will hear my voice" [Ps. 55:18]. Therefore, one is not allowed to pray more than three times a day. However, Rabbi Johanan said: If only man *would* pray the entire day. The emperor Antoninus asked Rabbi Judah the Prince: Is one permitted to pray every hour? When he answered: It is forbidden, Antoninus asked him: Why? He answered: Lest one act irreverently with the Almighty. Antoninus did not accept this as a satisfactory answer. What did Rabbi Judah do? He arose early the next morning to visit Antoninus. Upon his arrival he asked: Does it go well with the emperor? One hour later, he entered the royal chamber to say: O Great Caesar! And with the passing of another hour he said: I bring you greetings, emperor. Antoninus asked him: Why must you degrade royalty? Rabbi Judah answered: Let your ears hear what your mouth is saying. You are but a mortal king, and when I greet you every hour you accuse me of degrading you. Is this not truer still for the King of kings? All the more so one should not disturb Him every hour.[22]

If one is riding on an ass, he should dismount to say the *Tefilah*. If he cannot dismount, he should turn his head toward Jerusalem.

And if he cannot turn his head, he should direct his heart toward the Holy of Holies.[23]

If one is travelling on a ship or a raft, he should direct his heart toward the Holy of Holies.[24]

If one sees a place where miracles had been wrought for Israel, he should say: "Praised be He who wrought miracles for our ancestors in this place." If one sees a place from which idolatry had been rooted out, he should say: "Praised is He who rooted out idolatry from our land."[25]

If one sees shooting stars, earthquakes, lightnings, thunders and storms, he should say: "Praised is He whose power and might fill the world." If one sees mountains, hills, seas, rivers or deserts, he should say: "Praised be the Author of Creation." Rabbi Judah says: If one sees the Great Sea [the Mediterranean], he should say: "Praised be He who made the Great Sea," but only if he sees it at intervals of time. Upon seeing rain or receiving good tidings, one should say: "Praised is He, the Good, and the doer of good." Upon receiving bad tidings, one should say: "Praised be the true Judge."[26]

One who has built a new house or purchased new utensils should say: "Praised is He who has given us life." One should say the benediction for misfortune when it occurs, regardless of any consequent good, and for good fortune when it occurs, regardless of any consequent evil. One who cries out to God over what is past utters a prayer in vain. Thus if a man's wife is pregnant and he says: "May it be His will that my wife shall bear a male," his prayer is in vain. If one returning from a journey hears the sound of lamentation in the city and says, "May it be His will that those who mourn not be from my house," that prayer is in vain.[27]

Rav Judah said: Whoever walks out of doors during the month of Nissan and sees trees which are beginning to bud should say: Praised be He whose world lacks nothing, who created in it beautiful creatures and beautiful trees for people to enjoy.

Mar Zutra bar Tuviah said: How do we know that one should recite a blessing upon smelling something good? It is written, "Let every living soul praise the Lord" [Ps. 150:6]. What is it that the soul enjoys which the body does not enjoy? Fragrances.[28]

No one should taste anything without first reciting a blessing, as it is said: "The earth is the Lord's, and its fullness" [Ps. 24:1]. Whoever enjoys the goods of this world without reciting a blessing has transgressed. [29]

How do we know that one must recite blessings after meals? It is written, "When you have eaten and are satisfied you shall bless the Lord your God . . . " [Deut. 8:10]. This teaches that one is required to recite a blessing after a meal. What about before the meal? Rabbi Ishmael used to say that this can be determined by using the method of reasoning called *kal v'homer* ["from the more lenient to the more stringent," a conclusion reached out of logical necessity]. If one is required to recite a blessing after he has eaten and is satisfied, he surely should do so when he is hungry and desires to eat. . . . How do we know that one must recite a blessing before and after the reading of the Torah [at public services]? Rabbi Ishmael used to say that this can be determined by using the *kal v'homer* method of reasoning. A meal, which is merely for the purposes of sustaining this ephemeral life, must be preceded and followed by a blessing. It surely is logical, then, to infer that this is truer still of the reading from the Torah, which is for purposes of sustaining life eternal. [30]

Rabbi Hiyya bar Ashi, citing Rav, said: A person whose mind is not at ease must not pray. [31]

Rabbi Eliezer said: "The prayer of one who makes his prayer a fixed task is not supplication" (Mishnah *Berakhot* 4:4). How do you define prayer which is a "fixed task"? Rabbi Yaakov bar Iddi said in the name of Rabbi Oshaiya: The prayer of one who prays merely to fulfil a ritual obligation. The sages said: The prayer of one who does not use the language of supplication. Rabba and Rav Joseph said: The prayer of one who adheres to the set form, never uttering anything new. Abba bar Avin and Rabbi Hanina bar Avin said: The prayer of anyone who does not pray at dawn and at sunset. [32]

This summary of laws of prayer is excerpted from the authoritative legal code, the *Shulhan Arukh*, "The Prepared Table," compiled in the sixteenth century by Rabbi Joseph Caro in Safed.

One who prays must be conscious of the meaning of the words being uttered, as it is written, "You will strengthen their hearts; You will incline Your ear" [Ps. 10:17]. Many prayer books with explanations in other languages have been published, and everyone can learn the meaning of the words to be uttered in prayer. If one is not conscious of the meaning of the words, one must at least, while praying, reflect upon matters which influence the heart and which direct the heart to our Father in Heaven. Should an alien thought come in the midst of prayer, one must be still and wait until it is no more.

One should place his feet close together, as if they were one, to be likened to the angels, as it is written, "The legs were a single rigid leg" [Ezek. 1:7], that is to say that their feet appeared to be one foot. One should lower the head slightly, and close the eyes to avoid looking at anything. One who prays from a prayer book should not take his eyes off it. One should place the hands over the heart, the right hand over the left, and pray wholeheartedly, in reverence and awe and submission, like a poor beggar standing at a door . . .

One should utter the words consciously and carefully. Every person should pray according to his own tradition, whether it be Ashkenazi or Sephardi or other; they share a sacred basis. . . .

One must be careful to pray in a whisper, so that he alone will hear his words, but one standing near him should not be able to hear his voice, as it is written of Hannah, "Hannah was speaking in her heart; only her lips moved, and her voice was not heard" [I Sam. 1:13].

One should not lean against any object for even the slightest support. One who is even slightly ill may pray while seated or even while lying down, provided that he is able to direct his thoughts cogently. If it is impossible for one to pray aloud with words, he should at least contemplate with his heart. . . .

When one who is outside of the Land rises to pray, he must face in the direction of the Land of Israel, as it is written, ". . . and they pray to You toward their land . . ." [I Kings 8:48], and in his heart he should be directed toward Jerusalem and the Temple site and the Holy of Holies as well. Therefore those who dwell to the West of the Land of Israel must face the East (but not precisely East, for there are idolaters who pray in the direction of sunrise and their intention is to worship the sun), those who dwell to the East should face West and those who dwell to the South should face North (and those who dwell to the Northwest of the Land of Israel should face Southeast, etc.).

One who prays in the Land of Israel should face Jerusalem, as it is written, ". . . they pray to the Lord toward the city which

You have chosen . . ." [I Kings 8:44], and his thoughts should be focused toward the Temple and the Holy of Holies as well. One who prays in Jerusalem should face the Temple site, as it is written, ". . . when they come and pray toward this House . . ." [II Chron. 6:32], and his thoughts should be focused toward the Holy of Holies as well.

Thus the entire people Israel in their prayer will be facing one place, namely, Jerusalem and the Holy of Holies, the Heavenly Gate through which all prayer ascends. . . .

If one is praying in a place where he cannot discern directions, so that he is unable to know if he is facing in the proper direction, he should direct his heart to his Father in heaven, as it is written, ". . . and they pray to the Lord . . ." [I Kings 8:44]. . . .

One must bow four times during the *Amidah*: At the beginning and at the end of the first benediction and at the beginning and at the end of the *Modim* prayer. When one says "Praised," he should bend the knee, and when he says "are You," he should bend over until the joints of his spinal column stand out, and also bow his head. Then, before one pronounces the name of the Lord, he should begin slowly to stand erect, according to the verse, "The Lord lifts up those who are bowed down" [Ps. 146:8]. . . .

It is forbidden to bow at any other place in the *Amidah*.

After the recitation of the *Amidah*, and before the worshipper recites "May He who ordains the order of the universe bring peace to us and to all Israel," he should bow and take three short steps backward, like a servant taking leave of his master.[33]

THE SYNAGOGUE

Even before the destruction of the Temple, perhaps even in early Biblical days, there were already rudimentary synagogues in ancient Israel. It clearly became the central institution for the cultivation of the faith during the Babylonian captivity. The restoration under Nehemiah and Ezra left a large Jewish Diaspora outside the Holy Land, and that Diaspora increased in succeeding ages. Its central institution was the synagogue. Here the Jews gathered to pray together, but that was not its most important function. The commandment to pray is incumbent upon every individual Jew, three times a day—morning, afternoon, and evening—and there is relatively little difference in the prescribed order of prayer between the service as said in public in the synagogue and the version of it that is prescribed for the individual.

The central function of the synagogue was to cultivate a value perhaps more important than prayer to Jewish faith—study of the Torah. On Sabbath and festivals, people gathered in the synagogue to hear a reading of a passage from the Torah and to be led in the understanding of its interpretation. This is enshrined in the central act of public worship in Judaism on every major occasion, to this day. The Scroll of the Torah, which is written in prescribed ancient form by hand on parchment, is taken from the Ark and an appropriate section is read. On the Sabbath, the cycle of readings from the Torah comprises a consecutive reading of the Five Books of Moses in the course of the Sabbaths of the year. At all other times the selection read is a passage from the Five Books of Moses prescribed for the occasion. A complementary section from Prophets, known as the Haphtarah, is also read on the Sabbaths and Festivals.

It should be added that much of Rabbinic literature, including especially the moralistic sections, really represents ancient homilies given in the synagogue to explain and apply the teaching of the Torah reading.

> They told Rabbi Johanan that there were elderly men in Babylonia. He was surprised, and said, "It is written 'that your days and the days of your children may be multiplied *on the land*' [i.e. in Palestine]. But outside of the land this is not so." However, when they told him that these Babylonians came early to the synagogue and stayed late, he said, "That is what helps them." This corresponds to what Rabbi Joshua ben Levi said to his sons: "Rise early and stay up late and go to the synagogue, that you may prolong your life." Rav Acha, son of Rabbi Hanina asked, "What verse [in Scripture] supports this statement?" He answered, " 'Happy is the man who listens to Me, watching daily at My gates, waiting beside My doors' [Prov. 8:34], and in the next verse it is written, 'Whoever finds Me finds life.' "[34]

This account of the synagogue in Safed arround 1600 reflects a community at the apex of spiritual devotion. Here are the classic and lasting values of the synagogue put into practice at highest intensity.

In all the houses of prayer the whole community [of Safed] assembles immediately after the evening and morning prayer, in five or six groups in each house of prayer. Each group studies before leaving the house of prayer: one of them studies Maimonides seriatim, another Ein Jacob [a skillful arrangement of narratives, folklore, and ethical homilies from the Talmud], the third a section of *Berakhot* [the first tractate of the Talmud], a fourth one section of the Mishnah with commentary, a fifth a halakhah [legal statement] with Rashi and *Tosafot* [commentaries to the Talmud] and the others study the *Zohar* or the Bible only. In this way nobody can be found in the community who begins his daily occupation in the morning without having learned something of our teaching. And the same is done by the whole of Israel at night after the evening prayer.

On the Sabbath the whole people goes into the houses of prayer to listen to the sermons of the rabbis. And on each Thursday the whole community gathers in the big house of learning after the morning prayer and prays there for the good of Israel all over the world, for the banished *Shekhinah* and the destroyed Temple. Special blessings are said for those who sent money for the support of the poor in the Land of Israel, that the Lord may prolong their years, that their affairs may be successful, and that they themselves may be saved from every need and affliction. This prayer is recited by the whole community with great weeping and broken hearts. Before they begin to pray, the great and pious Moses Galanti ascends the pulpit and speaks in humble words and awakens Israel to the fear of the Lord, and brings them nearer to the love of their Creator with the sweetness of his language, the greatness of his wisdom and knowledge, and the abundance of his holiness. After him two heads of the Yeshivot [Talmudic academies], great scholars and saints, ascend the pulpit. One of them is Rabbi Massod Sagi Nahor, who is my teacher and master, known in the whole of Israel for his great holiness and the extent of his knowledge; the other is Rabbi Solomon Maarabi, famous among the whole of Israel for his wisdom, exceptional humility and wonderful piety. They begin to pray with anxiety and trembling and great reverence, and their eyes overflow with tears like twenty-two water brooks. Who would be able in the face of these prayers and loud cries uttered by Israel over the dispersion and destruction, and of the confession of sins, not to repent, not to confess his sins, and not to become zealous threefold?[35]

Here are some liturgical passages from the Sabbath morning Torah Service.

Leader and congregation:
None compare to You, O Lord, and nothing compares to Your creation. Your kingship is everlasting. Your dominion endures throughout all generations. The Lord is King, the Lord was King, the Lord will be King throughout all time. May the Lord grant His people strength; may the Lord bless His people with peace.

Merciful Father, favor Zion with Your goodness; build the walls of Jerusalem. For in You alone do we put our trust, King, exalted God, eternal Lord.

The Ark is opened
Whenever the Ark was carried forward, Moses would say: Arise, Lord. May Your enemies be scattered, may Your foes be put to flight. Torah shall come from Zion, the word of the Lord from Jerusalem. Praised is He who in His holiness gave the Torah to His people Israel.

The Torah is taken from the Ark
Leader, then congregation:
Hear, O Israel: The Lord our God, the Lord is One.
One is our God, great our Lord, holiness is His nature.

Leader:
Proclaim the Lord's greatness with me; let us exalt Him together.

The Torah is carried in procession
Leader and congregation:
Yours, O Lord, is the greatness and the power and the splendor. Yours is the triumph and the majesty, for all in heaven and on earth is Yours. Yours, O Lord, is supreme sovereignty.

Exalt the Lord and worship Him, for He is holy. Exalt and worship Him at His holy mountain. The Lord our God is holy. [36]

On the Sabbath, seven adult members of the congregation are called up to the pulpit, each to stand at the reading desk while a portion of the prescribed Torah Reading for the day is chanted from the Torah Scroll. In many non-Orthodox congregations, women as well as men are given this honor. Following are the blessings recited by those who are called up (those who are given an *aliyah*) before and after the chanting of the Torah portion for which they have been called.

Blessing before the Reading:
Praise the Lord, Source of blessing.
Congregation:
Praised is the Lord, eternal Source of all blessing.
Congregant repeats the above response and continues:
Praised are You, Lord our God, King of the universe who has chosen us from among all peoples by giving us His Torah. Praised are You, Lord who gives the Torah.

Blessing after the Reading:
Praised are You, Lord our God, King of the universe who has given us the Torah of truth, planting within us life eternal. Praised are You, Lord who gives the Torah.

After the Reading is completed, the Torah Scroll is raised:
This is the Torah that Moses set before the people Israel; the Torah, given by God, through Moses.[37]

Congregation rises for returning the Torah Scroll to the Ark.
Praise the Lord, for He is supreme, exalted.
His glory encompasses heaven and earth. He exalts and extols His faithful, the people Israel who are close to Him. Halleluyah.

The Torah Scroll is placed in the Ark.
Whenever the Ark was set down, Moses would say: Lord, may You dwell among the myriad families of the people Israel. Return, O Lord, to Your sanctuary, You and Your glorious Ark. Let Your *kohanim* [priests] be clothed in triumph, let Your faithful sing for joy. For the sake of David, Your servant, do not reject Your anointed.
Precious teaching do I give you:
Never forsake My Torah.
It is a tree of life for those who grasp it,
and all who uphold it are blessed.
Its ways are pleasantness, and all its paths are peace.
Help us turn to You, and we shall return.
Renew our lives as in days of old.[38]

mouth and meditations of my heart be acceptable to You, my Rock and my Redeemer. He who brings peace to His universe will bring peace to us and to all the people Israel. Amen.[41]

This is the first passage of the blessing that is recited after every meal at which bread is eaten.

We praise You, Lord our God, King of the universe who graciously sustains the whole world with kindness and compassion. You provide food for every creature, as Your love endures forever. Your great goodness has never failed us; may Your great glory always assure us nourishment. You sustain all life and You are good to all, providing all of Your creatures with food and sustenance. We praise You, Lord who sustains all.[42]

Before eating bread:

Praised are You, Lord our God, King of the universe who brings forth bread from the earth.

Before drinking wine:

Praised are You, Lord our God, King of the universe who creates the fruit of the vine.

Upon seeing natural beauty:

Praised are You, Lord our God, King of the universe who has such beauty in His world.

Upon seeing one distinguished in Torah studies:

Praised are You, Lord our God, King of the universe who has shared of His wisdom with those who revere Him.

Upon seeing a distinguished leader:

Praised are You, Lord our God, King of the universe who has given of His glory to flesh and blood.[43]

PRIVATE PRAYER

Jewish practice insists on the recitation of the prescribed service. It does not, however, rule out—indeed, it encourages—private devotion. Here are a few examples of personal prayer chosen from literally thousands that might be quoted.

The first is by a second-century rabbi, and appears in the

STATUTORY PRAYER

The first passage below is the beginning of the *Sh'ma*. The long section which follows is the *Amidah*, here given in its weekday morning version. This prayer is recited silently while standing.

Hear, O Israel: The Lord our God, the Lord is One.

Love the Lord your God with all your heart, with all your soul, and with all your might. And these words which I command you this day you shall take to heart. You shall diligently teach them to your children. You shall recite them at home and away, morning and night. You shall bind them as a sign upon your hand, they shall be a reminder above your eyes, and you shall inscribe them upon the doorposts of your homes and upon your gates.[39]

Open my mouth, O Lord, and my lips will proclaim Your praise.

Praised are You, Lord our God and God of our ancestors, God of Abraham, of Isaac, and of Jacob, great, mighty, awesome, exalted God who bestows lovingkindness, Creator of all. You remember the pious deeds of our ancestors and will send a redeemer to their children's children because of Your loving nature. You are the King who helps and saves and shields. Praised are You, Lord, Shield of Abraham.

Your might, O Lord, is boundless. You give life to the dead; great is Your saving power. Your lovingkindness sustains the living, Your great mercies give life to the dead. You support the falling, heal the ailing, free the fettered. You keep Your faith with those who sleep in dust. Whose power can compare with Yours? You are the Master of life and death and deliverance. Faithful are You in giving life to the dead. Praised are You, Lord who gives life to the dead.

Holy are You and holy is Your name. Holy are those who praise You daily. Praised are You, Lord, holy God.

You graciously endow mortals with intelligence, teaching wisdom and understanding. Grant us knowledge, discernment, and wisdom. Praised are You, Lord who graciously grants intelligence.

Our Father, bring us back to Your Torah. Our King, draw us near to Your service. Lead us back to You, truly repentant. Praised are You, Lord who welcomes repentance.

Forgive us, our Father, for we have sinned; pardon us, our King, for we have transgressed, for You forgive and pardon. Praised are You, gracious and forgiving Lord.

Behold our affliction and deliver us. Redeem us soon because of Your mercy, for You are the mighty Redeemer. Praised are You, Lord, Redeemer of the people Israel.

Heal us, O Lord, and we shall be healed. Help us and save us, for You are our glory. Grant perfect healing for all our afflictions. For You are the faithful and merciful God of healing. Praised are You, Lord, Healer of His people Israel.

Lord our God, make this a blessed year. May its varied produce bring us happiness. Grant blessing to the earth. Satisfy us with its abundance, and bless our year as the best of years. Praised are You, Lord who blesses the years.

Sound the great shofar to herald our freedom, raise high the banner to gather our exiles. Gather us together from the ends of the earth. Praised are You, Lord who gathers the dispersed of His people Israel.

Restore our judges as in days of old, restore our counsellors as in former times. Remove from us sorrow and anguish. Reign alone over us with lovingkindness; with justice and mercy sustain our cause. Praised are You, King who loves justice.

Frustrate the hopes of those who malign us; let all evil very soon disappear. Let all Your enemies soon be destroyed. May You quickly uproot and crush the arrogant; may You subdue and humble them in our time. Praised are You, Lord who shatters enemies and humbles the arrogant.

Let Your tender mercies be stirred for the righteous, the pious, and the leaders of the House of Israel, devoted scholars and faithful proselytes. Be merciful to us of the House of Israel. Reward all who trust in You, cast our lot with those who are faithful to You. May we never come to despair, for our trust is in You. Praised are You, Lord who sustains the righteous.

Have mercy, Lord, and return to Jerusalem, Your city. May Your Presence dwell there as You have promised. Build it now, in our days and for all time. Reestablish there the majesty of David, Your servant. Praised are You, Lord who builds Jerusalem.

Bring to flower the shoot of Your servant David. Hasten the advent of Messianic redemption. Each and every day we hope for Your deliverance. Praised are You, Lord who assures our deliverance.

Lord our God, hear our voice. Have compassion upon us, pity

us, accept our prayer with loving favor. You listen to entreaty and prayer. Do not turn us away unanswered, our King, for You mercifully heed Your people's supplication. Praised are You, Lord who hears prayer.

Accept the prayers and offerings of Your people Israel as lovingly as they are offered. Restore worship to Your sanctuary. May the worship of Your people Israel always be acceptable to You. May we witness Your merciful return to Zion. Praised are You, Lord who restores His Presence to Zion.

We proclaim that You are the Lord our God and God of our ancestors throughout all time. You are the Rock of our lives, the Shield of our salvation in every generation. We thank You and praise You morning, noon, and night for Your miracles which daily attend us and for Your wondrous kindnesses. Our lives are in Your hand; our souls are in Your charge. You are good, with everlasting mercy; You are compassionate, with enduring lovingkindness. We have always placed our hope in You. For all these blessings we shall ever praise and exalt You. May every living creature thank You and praise You faithfully, our deliverance and our help. Praised are You, beneficent Lord to whom all praise is due.

Grant peace to the world, with happiness and blessing, grace, love, and mercy for us and for all the people Israel. Bless us, our Father, one and all, with Your light; for by that light did You teach us Torah and life, love and tenderness, justice, mercy, and peace. May it please You to bless Your people Israel in every season and at all times with Your gift of peace. Praised are You, Lord who blesses His people Israel with peace.[40]

This personal prayer is, by custom, always said at the end of the *Amidah*. The prescribed *Amidah* itself speaks in the normal plural, the "we" of Jewish prayer (compare the introductory comment to the Confession, from the Yom Kippur liturgy, to be found in Chapter IV).

My God, keep my tongue from evil, my lips from lies. Help me ignore those who slander me. Let me be humble before all. Open my heart to Your Torah, so that I may pursue Your mitzvot [commandments]. Frustrate the designs of those who plot evil against me. Make nothing of their schemes. Do so because of Your compassion, Your holiness, and Your Torah. Answer my prayer for the deliverance of Your people. May the words of my

Talmud. The second is the prayer of a shepherd, from twelfth-century Germany; the third is by Rabbi Elimelekh of Lizhensk, in eighteenth-century Poland; and the last is an undated prayer composed in Yiddish and used as a meditation by women in the synagogue.

Rabbi Nehunya ben Hakaneh used to utter a brief prayer whenever he entered the house of study and whenever he left it. When they asked him, "What is the nature of this prayer?" he told them: "When I enter I pray that I should not be the cause of any offense, and when I leave I give thanks for my lot."[44]

Lord of the universe!
It is apparent and known unto You
that if You had cattle and gave them to me to tend,
though I take wages for tending from all others,
from You I would take nothing,
because I love You.[45]

Guard us
from vicious leanings and from haughty ways,
from anger and from temper,
from melancholy, talebearing,
and from all the other evil qualities.

Nor let envy of any man rise in my heart,
nor envy of us in the heart of others.
On the contrary:
put it in our hearts that we may see our
comrades' virtue,
and not their failing.[46]

God, it is true, before You there is no night, and the light is with You, and You make the whole world shine with Your light.

The mornings tell of Your mercy, and the nights tell of Your truth, and all creatures tell of Your great mercy and of great miracles.

Each day You renew Your help, O God! Who can recount Your miracles? You sit in the sky and count the days of the devout, and set the time for all Your creatures. Your single day is a thousand years, and Your years and days are unbounded.

All that is in the world must live its life to an end, but You are there, You will always be there, and outlive all Your creatures.

You, God, are pure, and pure are Your holy servants who three times every day cry, "Holy," and sanctify You in heaven and on earth.

You, God, are sanctified and praised. The whole world is filled with Your glory for ever and ever.[47]

SOURCES

1. PEOPLE

1. Gen. 17:1–8.
2. Ex. 6:2–8.
3. Ex. 19:5–6.
4. Lev. 20:22–27.
5. Num. 35:34.
6. Deut. 4:32–40.
7. Deut. 5:1–3.
8. Deut. 29:9–14.
9. Hosea 2:21.
10. *Pesahim* 87a–b.
11. *Song of Songs Rabbah* 1:15.
12. From a letter of Maimonides to the Jews of Yemen, in F. Kobler, ed., *A Treasury of Jewish Letters* (Philadelphia: Jewish Publication Society, 1954), Vol. I, pp. 184–86.
13. Deut. 4:5–8.
14. Deut. 7:6–13.
15. Deut. 9:5.
16. Mishnah *Avot* 3:14.
17. *Berakhot* 6a.
18. *Hullin* 89a.
19. *Megillah* 16a.
20. *Shekalim* 2b.
21. *Leviticus Rabbah* 30:12.
22. Judah Halevi, *Kuzari*, Part II.
23. Amos 3:1–2.
24. Amos 9:7–10.
25. *Song of Songs Rabbah* 1.
26. Gen. 9:8–15.
27. *Genesis Rabbah* 34:8.
28. *Seder Eliahu Rabbah*, Chap. 9.
29. *Exodus Rabbah* 19:4.
30. *Sifra, Aharei Mot* 86a (Weiss edition; Vienna, 1862).
31. From a letter of Maimonides to Hasdai Halevi, in F. Kobler, *op. cit.*, Vol. I, pp. 197–98.
32. *Sifre* Num. 71.
33. *Tanhuma* (Buber), *Lekh Lekha*, 6.
34. *Yebamot* 47a–b.
35. *Tanhuma, Lekh Lekha.*
36. From a letter of Maimonides to Obadiah the Proselyte, in F. Kobler, *op. cit.*, Vol. I, pp. 194–95.
37. Cited in W. Gunther Plaut, *The Rise of Reform Judaism* (New York: World Union for Progressive Judaism, Ltd., 1963), p. 70.

38. *Ibid.*, pp. 70–73.

39. *Ibid.*, pp. 221–22.

40. *Ibid.*, p. 223.

41. Cited in David Philipson, *The Reform Movement in Judaism* (New York: The Macmillan Company, 1931), p. 372.

42. *Ibid.*, pp. 275–76.

43. Ben Zion Meir Hai Ouziel, *Piskei Ouziel* (Jerusalem: Mossad Harav Kook, 1977), No. 68.

44. Solomon Freehof, *Recent Reform Responsa* (Cincinnati: Hebrew Union College Press, 1963), pp. 76–78.

45. Arthur Hertzberg, *Encyclopedia Judaica* (Jerusalem: Keter Publishing House, Ltd., 1971), Vol. 10, pp. 64–65.

46. Kaufmann Kohler, *Jewish Theology* (New York: The Macmillan Company, 1928), pp. 326–27.

47. Mordecai M. Kaplan, *The Future of the American Jew* (New York: The Macmillan Company, 1948), pp. 219–20.

48. Martin Buber, *At the Turning* (New York: Farrar, Straus and Young, 1952), pp. 36–37.

49. Edmond Fleg, "Why I Am a Jew," in Arthur Hertzberg, *The Zionist Idea* (Garden City, N.Y.: Doubleday, 1959), pp. 481–85.

50. Samson Raphael Hirsch, *The Nineteen Letters of Ben Uziel* (New York and London: Funk and Wagnalls Company, 1899), Seventh Letter.

51. *Ibid.*, Fifteenth Letter.

52. Abraham Isaac Kook, "The Rebirth of Israel," in Arthur Hertzberg, *The Zionist Idea*, pp. 424–25.

53. Trans. from the *Weekday Prayer Book* (New York: The Rabbinical Assembly, 1961), pp. 45–46.

2. GOD

1. Gen. 1:1.

2. Isa. 40:12–25.

3. Trans. from *Siddur Sim Shalom*, edited, with translations, by Jules Harlow (New York: The Rabbinical Assembly and the United Synagogue of America, 1985), p. 97.

4. Ps. 23; *ibid.*, p. 523.

5. Ps. 113; trans. from the *Weekday Prayer Book*, *op. cit.*, pp. 173–74.

6. Trans. from the *Weekday Prayer Book*, *op. cit.*, p. 181.

7. Jer. 23:23–24.

8. *Numbers Rabbah* 13.

9. *Berakhot* 10a.

10. *Hullin* 60a.

11. *Genesis Rabbah* 19:7.

12. *The Zohar*, Gen. 103a–b; trans. by Sperling and Simon (London: Soncino Press, n.d.).

13. Saadia Gaon, *The Book of Beliefs and Opinions*, trans. by Samuel Rosenblatt (New Haven: Yale University Press, 1948), Treatise II, Chap. 12.

14. Maimonides, *The Guide of the Perplexed*, trans. by M. Friedlander (New York: Hebrew Publishing Co., 1881), Part I, Chaps. 57–58.

15. *Genesis Rabbah* 1:10.

16. *Hagigah* 14b.

17. Hayyim ibn Musa, in N. Glatzer, ed., *In Time and Eternity* (New York: Schocken, 1946), pp. 74–75.

18. *Berakhot* 7a.

19. *Avodah Zarah* 3b.

20. *Exodus Rabbah* 43:6.

21. Israel Baal-Shem, in N. Glatzer, *op. cit.*, p. 87.

22. Deut. 6:4.

23. Ex. 20:2–7.

24. Ps. 115; trans. from *Siddur Sim Shalom*, *op. cit.*, p. 383.

25. *Mekhilta, Pisha* 5.

26. *Shabbat* 55a.

27. Trans. from *Siddur Sim Shalom*, *op. cit.*, p. 197.

28. Ex. 34:6–7.

29. Deut. 8:5.

30. Isa. 1:12–20.

31. *Sifre* Deut. 307.

32. *Megillah* 31a.

33. *Exodus Rabbah* 3:6.

34. *Leviticus Rabbah* 24:2.

35. *Lamentations Rabbah*, Proem XXII.

36. *Genesis Rabbah* 12:15.

37. Franz Rosenzweig and Nahum Glatzer, *Franz Rosenzweig, His Life and Thought* (Philadelphia: Jewish Publication Society, 1953), pp. 304–5.

38. Deut. 6:5.

39. Deut. 10:12–22.

40. Ps. 117; trans. from *Weekday Prayer Book*, *op. cit.*, p. 178.

41. *Berakhot* 61b.

42. From the Testament of Shabtai Hurwitz. See Hebrew text in Israel Abrahams, *Hebrew Ethical Wills* (Philadelphia: Jewish Publication Society, 1948), pp. 255–56.

43. Moses Luzatto, *Mesillat Yesharim*, Chap. 11.

44. *Ibid.*, Chap. 19.

45. *Ibid.*

46. From *The Testament of Israel Baal-Shem*.

3. TORAH: TEACHING AND COMMANDMENT

1. Deut. 6:20–25.

2. Deut. 30: 11–14.

3. *Makkot* 23b.

4. *Makkot* 24a.

5. *Lamentations Rabbah*, Proem II.

6. *Numbers Rabbah* 17:6.

7. Louis Finkelstein, *The Jews: Their History, Culture, and Religion* (New York: Harper and Brothers, 1949), Vol. II, pp. 1739, 1792–93.

8. *Sifre* Deut. 45.

9. *Yoma* 72b.

10. Mishnah *Avot* 6.

11. *Tanhuma* (Buber), *Yitro* 7.

12. *Lamentations Rabbah*, Proem II.

13. *Sifre* Deut. 48.

14. *The Zohar*, Gen. 190a–b.

15. *Genesis Rabbah* 1:1.

16. *Mekhilta, Bahodesh* 1.

17. Trans. from *Siddur Sim Shalom*, *op. cit.*, p. 201.

18. *Sifra* 86b (Weiss edition; Vienna, 1862).

19. *Sanhedrin* 74a.

20. Saadia Gaon, *op. cit.*, Treatise III, Chap. 10.

21. *Ibid.*, Treatise III, Exordium.

22. Samson Raphael Hirsch, *op. cit.*, Fifteenth Letter.

23. Solomon Schechter, *Studies in Judaism* (Philadelphia: Jewish Publication Society, 1896), pp. 248–50.

24. Kaufmann Kohler, *op. cit.*, pp. 352–53.

25. Hayyim Nahman Bialik, "Address at the Inauguration of the Hebrew University in Jerusalem, 1925," in Arthur Hertzberg, *The Zionist Idea*, *op. cit.*, pp. 282–83.

26. Gen. 17:9–14.

27. Mishnah *Shabbat* 19:5.

28. Mishnah *Nedarim* 3:11.

29. *Yalkut Shimoni, Lekh Lekha* 71.

30. *Yalkut Shimoni, Beshalah* 268.

31. Cited in W. Gunther Plaut, *op. cit.*, p. 176.

32. Cited in W. Gunther Plaut, *The Growth of Reform Judaism: American and European Sources Until 1948* (New York: World Union for Progressive Judaism, 1965), pp. 311–312.

33. Cited in W. Gunther Plaut, *The Rise of Reform Judaism, op. cit.*, p. 177.

34. Yehiel Yaakov Weinberg, *Seridei Esh* (Jerusalem: Mossad Harav Kook, 1966), Vol. 3, No. 93.

35. Judith Kaplan Eisenstein, "The First Bat Mitzvah," in *Keeping Posted* (New York: Union of American Hebrew Congregations, 1982), Vol. XXVII, No. 3, p. 6.

36. Gen. 2:18.

37. Gen. 2:24.

38. Deut. 24:5.

39. Prov. 31:10–31.

40. Mishnah *Ketubot* 5:5.

41. Mishnah *Ketubot* 5:6.

42. Mishnah *Yebamot* 6:6.

43. *Yebamot* 63b.

44. *Yebamot* 64a.

45. *Yebamot* 62b–63a.

46. *Yebamot* 63b.

47. *Sotah* 17a.

48. *Tanhuma* (Buber), *Naso* 13.

49. Nahman of Bratslav.

50. *Sh'elot Uteshuvot Mi-maamakim* (New York, 1959), pp. 111–14.

51. *Ibid.*, pp. 151–56.

52. From the Wedding Service.

53. Cited in Lucy Dawidowicz, *The Golden Tradition: Jewish Life and Thought in Eastern Europe* (New York, Chicago, and San Francisco: Holt, Rinehart and Winston, 1967), pp. 207–9.

54. From *The Complete Works of the Hafetz Hayyim* (Hebrew), *Letters and Essays*, edited by Tzvi Hirsch

Zachs (Jerusalem: Hafetz Hayyim Yeshiva, 1990) Part Two, p. 97.

55. Menahem Mendel Schneerson, "A Woman's Place in Torah," *Sichos in English* (New York, 1990).

56. Louis Epstein, "A Solution to the Agunah Problem," *Proceedings of the Rabbinical Assembly 1930–1932* (New York: The Rabbinical Assembly, 1932), 1930 Convention, pp. 86–87.

57. David Aronson, "*Kedat Moshe Veyisrael,*" *Proceedings of the Rabbinical Assembly 1951* (New York: The Rabbinical Assembly, 1951), pp. 120, 135–36.

58. Saul Lieberman, "Ketubah," *Proceedings of the Rabbinical Assembly 1954* (New York: The Rabbinical Assembly, 1954), pp. 67–68.

59. Eliezer Berkovits, *Hagut* (Jerusalem, 1983), pp. 29–32.

60. Blu Greenberg, *On Women and Judaism: A View from Tradition* (Philadelphia: Jewish Publication Society, 1981), pp. 177–78.

61. Susan Weidman Schneider, *Jewish and Female: Choices and Changes in Our Lives Today* (New York: Simon and Schuster, 1984), pp. 21–22.

62. Cited in Walter Jacob, *American Reform Responsa* (New York: Central Conference of American Rabbis, 1983), pp. 25–31, 41–43.

63. Simon Greenberg, Hebrew essay in *The Ordination of Women as Rabbis: Studies and Responsa* (New York: The Jewish Theological Seminary of America, 1988), pp. 207–10.

64. Ann Roiphe, *Generation Without Memory: A Jewish Journey in Christian America* (New York: Linden Press/Simon and Schuster, 1981), p. 203.

65. Solomon Freehof, *Contemporary Reform Responsa* (Cincinnati: Hebrew Union College Press, 1974), pp. 23–26.

66. David M. Feldman, "Homosexu-

ality and Jewish Law," *Judaism*, Vol. 32, No. 4, Fall 1983, pp. 427–29.

67. *Proceedings of the 1990 Convention* (New York: The Rabbinical Assembly, 1991), p. 275.

68. *Report of the Ad Hoc Committee on Homosexuality and the Rabbinate, Yearbook of the Central Conference of American Rabbis* (New York: The Central Conference of American Rabbis, 1990).

69. Ex. 20:12.

70. Deut. 27:16.

71. *Kiddushin* 30b–31a.

72. *Kiddushin* 31a.

73. *Jerusalem Peah* 1:1.

74. *Pesikta* 23.

75. *Kiddushin* 30b.

76. *Yebamot* 5b.

77. Mishnah *Keritot* 6:9.

78. *Kiddushin* 29a.

79. *Shabbat* 10b.

80. *Jerusalem Shabbat* 1:2.

81. *Kiddushin* 30a.

82. *Sifre, Ekev.*

83. Gen. 32:33.

84. Ex. 22:30.

85. Ex. 23:19.

86. Lev. 11:2–8.

87. Lev. 11:9–11.

88. Lev. 17:10–14.

89. Deut. 14:21.

90. Mishnah *Hullin* 3:1.

91. Mishnah *Hullin* 8:1–3.

92. *Tanhuma* (Buber), *Shemini* 12.

93. Maimonides, *The Guide of the Perplexed, op cit.*, Part III, Chap. 48.

94. Joseph Albo, *Sefer Ha-ikkarim*, trans. by Isaac Husik (Philadelphia: Jewish Publication Society, 1946), Book 3, Chap. 15.

95. Shneur Zalman of Liady, *Tanya*, Chap. 7.

96. Abraham Isaac Kook, *Commentary to the Prayer Book*, in *Olat Raaiah* (Jerusalem: Mossad Harav Kook, 1939), Vol. 2, p. 92.

97. Ex. 23:10–11.

98. Lev. 19:9–10.

99. Deut. 14:28–29.

100. Deut. 15:7–11.

101. Job 29:12–16.

102. From letter of the Jews of Alexandria to Ephraim ben Shamarya and the elders of the Palestinian community of Fostat, in F. Kobler, *op. cit.*, Vol. I, p. 240.

103. Maimonides, *Mishneh Torah, Hilkhot Matanot Aniyim*, Chap. 10.

104. *Shulhan Arukh, Yoreh Deah* 252.

105. Maimonides, *Mishneh Torah, Hilkhot Rotzeach*, Chap. 11.

106. Israel Meir Kagan, *Kuntres Zakhor L'miryam*, Chap. 10.

107. Moshe Feinstein, *Hoshen Mishpat*, (Bnei Brak, 1983) Part II, No. 18.

108. Ben Zion Meir Hai Ouziel, *op. cit.*, No. 32.

109. Immanuel Jacobovits, cited in Fred Rosner, *Modern Medicine and Jewish Ethics* (Hoboken: KTAV Publishing House, 1986), pp. 284–85.

110. Isser Yehudah Unterman, *Shevet Miyehudah Shaar Rishon*, (Jerusalem: Mossad HaravKook, 1983), No. 22.

111. Moshe Feinstein, *Igrot Moshe, Hoshen Mishpat*, Part II (Bnei Brak, 1985), No. 69.

112. Solomon Freehof, in *Central Conference of American Rabbis Yearbook*, (New York: Central Conference of American Rabbis, 1958), Vol. LXVIII, pp. 190–93.

113. Moshe Feinstein, *Igrot Moshe, Yoreh Deah*, Part III (Bnei Brak, 1981), No. 132.

114. Eliezer Waldenberg, *Tzitz Eliezer* (Jerusalem, 1978), Vol. 13, No. 89.

115. Seymour Siegel, "Jewish Law Permits Natural Death," *Shema*, Volume 7, number 132, April 15, 1977, pp. 96–97.

116. *Shabbat* 31a.

117. Samuel Laniado, *Kli Hemda*, in N. Glatzer, *op. cit.*, p. 146.

118. Moses Luzatto, *Mesillat Yesharim*, Chap. 19.

119. Israel Baal-Shem Tov.

120. Nahman of Bratslav.

121. Menahem Mendel of Kotzk.

122. Isaac of Worka.

4. THE CYCLE OF THE YEAR

1. Gen. 2:1–3.

2. Ex. 20:8–11.

3. Ex. 31:12–17.

4. Deut. 5:12–15.

5. Isa. 56:1–7.

6. Isa. 58:13–14.

7. Jer. 17:24–25, 27.

8. Neh. 13:15–18.

9. Mishnah *Hagigah* 1:8.

10. Mishnah *Shabbat* 7:2.

11. *Shabbat* 49b.

12. Mishnah *Yoma* 8:6.

13. *Yoma* 84b.

14. *Shabbat* 118b.

15. *Genesis Rabbah* 11.

16. *Shabbat* 119a.

17. *Exodus Rabbah* 25:12.

18. Judah Halevi, *Kuzari*, Part II.

19. *Sefer Hasidim*, ed. Reuben Margoliot (Jerusalem: Mosad Harav Kook, 1959), Nos. 110, 149.

20. A.J. Heschel, *The Sabbath* (New York: Farrar, Straus and Young, 1951), pp. 6–10.

21. Trans. from *Siddur Sim Shalom, op. cit.*, pp. 435, 437.

22. *Ibid.*, p. 319.

23. *Ibid.*, p. 701.

24. Deut. 16:14.

25. Deut. 16:16–17.

26. Mishnah *Hagigah* 1:1.

27. *Pesahim* 68b.

28. *Pesahim* 109a.

29. *Tanhuma, Pinhas* 17.

30. Ex. 12:14–20.

31. Mishnah *Pesahim* 1:1.

32. Mishnah *Pesahim* 1:4.

33. Mishnah *Pesahim* 2:1.

34. Mishnah *Pesahim* 3:7.

35. Mishnah *Pesahim* 4:1.

36. Mishnah *Pesahim* 10:5.

37. *Yalkut Shimoni, Emor* 23.

38. Mishnah *Pesahim* 10:4.

39. From the Passover Haggadah.

40. Deut. 16:9–12.

41. Ex. 20:1–14.

42. Comment of Rashi to Song of Songs 4:5.

43. Lev. 23:34–36.

44. Lev. 23:39–43.

45. Mishnah *Sukkah* 1:1.

46. *Sukkah* 28b.

47. Mishnah *Sukkah* 3:1.

48. *Sukkah* 55b.

49. *Sefer Ha Hinukh.*

50. Jonathan Eibeschütz, *Yaarot Dvash.*

51. From an unpublished sermon of my father, Rabbi Zvi Elimelech Hertzberg.

52. Lev. 23–26.

53. *Sukkah* 55b.

54. Lev. 23.24–25.

55. Neh. 8:9–12.

56. *Rosh Hashanah* 16a.

57. *Rosh Hashanah* 16b.

58. *Midrash Tehillim* 81 (order rearranged).

59. Maimonides, *Mishneh Torah, Hilkhot Teshuvah* 7:4.

60. Cited in S.Y. Agnon, *Yamim Noraim* (New York: Schocken, 1946), p. 177.

61. *Mahzor for Rosh Hashanah and Yom Kippur*, ed. by Jules Harlow (New York: The Rabbinical Assembly, 1972), pp. 241, 243.

62. *Ibid.*, p. 263.

63. *Ibid.*, p. 251.

64. Lev. 23:27–32.

65. Mishnah *Yoma* 1:1.

66. Mishnah *Yoma* 3:8, as translated in *Mahzor for Rosh Hashanah and Yom Kippur, op. cit.*, p. 605.

67. Mishnah *Yoma* 8:1.

68. Mishnah *Yoma* 8:4.

69. Mishnah *Yoma* 8:5.

70. *Midrash Tehillim* 27:4.

71. Mishnah *Yoma* 8:9.

72. Mishnah *Ta'anit* 4:8.

73. Cited in S.Y. Agnon, *op. cit.*, p. 230.

74. M.J. Gutman, *Belz* (Tel Aviv, 1952), p. 75.

75. Cited in S.Y. Agnon, *op. cit.*, p. 243.

76. High Holy Day Prayer Book.

77. *Ibid.*

78. *The Order of Prayers for Independence Day*, Hebrew (Tel Aviv: The Religious Kibbutz Movement [*Hakkibutz Hadati*], 1968), pp. 9–10.

5. LAND

1. Comment of Rashi to Gen. 1:1.

2. Gen. 17:8.

3. Gen. 47:29–30.

4. Deut. 30:1–5.

5. I Kings 8:27–30.

6. *Tanhuma, Kedoshim.*

7. Mishnah *Ketubot* 13:11.

8. *Ketubot* 110b–111a.

9. *Sifre, R'eh.*

10. *Leviticus Rabbah*, 34.

11. *Kiddushin* 49b.

12. Mishnah *Kelim* 1:6.

13. *Baba Batra* 158b.

14. *Jerusalem Nedarim* 6:8.

15. *Baba Kama* 80b.

16. *Genesis Rabbah* 59.

17. *Kiddushin* 49.

18. Isaiah Hurwitz, excerpt from a letter written in Jerusalem to his children in Prague (1621), in F. Kobler, *op. cit.*, Vol. II, pp. 483–84.

19. Quoted in *T'kumat Yisrael* (Tel Aviv: Karni Publishers, 1958), p. 37.

20. Jer. 9:11–16.

21. Ps. 137:1–6.

22. *Tanhuma* (Buber), *Devarim* 7. The text is unhistorical, for the emperor who conquered Jerusalem was Vespasian, and the commanding general was his son Titus.

23. *Mekhilta, Pisha* 14.

24. Judah Halevi, *Poetry of Judah Halevi*, trans. by Nina Salaman (Philadelphia: Jewish Publication Society, 1928), p. 2.

25. From a letter of Hasdai ibn Shaprut to Joseph, King of the Khazars, in F. Kobler, *op. cit.*, Vol. I, pp. 98–106.

26. From a letter of Joseph, King of the Khazars, to Hasdai ibn Shaprut, in F. Kobler, *op. cit.*, Vol. I, p. 113.

27. From a letter written by Obadiah of Bartinoro in Jerusalem to his father, in F. Kobler, *op. cit.*, Vol. I, p. 304. It is a ritual commandment that as a mark of mourning, garments are rent, whether it be for personal or national grief.

28. From a letter of the community of Salonica to the communities on the route to Palestine, in F. Kobler, *op. cit.*, Vol. I, p. 143.

29. From a letter of the Provençal Jews in Salonica to the Jews in Provençe, in F. Kobler, *op. cit.*, Vol. II, pp. 344–47.

30. The Kaddish of Rabbi Levi Yitzhak of Berditshev, in N. Glatzer, *op. cit.*, pp. 94–95.

31. Solomon ibn Verga, *Shevet Yehudah* (Jerusalem: Mosad Bialik, 1947), pp. 163–64.

32. Jacob Emden, *Shaarei Shamayim*.

33. Jonathan Eibeschütz, *Yaarot Dvash*.

34. Jer. 29:4–14.

35. *Ketubot* 11a.

36. *Genesis Rabbah* 96.

37. *Tosafot* to *Ketubot* 110b.

38. Mordecai Kaplan, *op. cit.*; pp. 128–30.

39. Jer. 31:15–16.

40. *Tanhuma, Noah.*

41. Saadia Gaon, *op. cit.*, Treatise VII, Chap. 1.

42. Jacob Emden, from the introduction to his prayer book, in N. Glatzer, *op. cit.*, pp. 216–17.

43. Nahman of Bratslav, cited in N. Glatzer, *op. cit.*, pp. 206–7.

44. Leo Pinsker, *Road to Freedom*, ed. by B. Netanyahu (New York: Scopus, 1944), pp. 105–6.

45. Theodor Herzl, first entry in his diary (1895), in Arthur Hertzberg, *The Zionist Idea, op. cit.*, p. 204.

46. Solomon Schechter, *Seminary Addresses and Other Papers* (New York:

Ark Publishing, 1915), pp. 91–104.

47. Abraham Isaac Kook, "Orot," in Arthur Hertzberg, *The Zionist Idea, op. cit.*, pp. 419–22.

48. Tzvi Yehuda Kook, placard issued in 1967.

49. Tzvi Yehuda Kook, in *Whose Homeland: Eretz Israel Roots of the Jewish Claim* (Jerusalem: World Zionist Organization Department for Torah Education and Culture in the Diaspora, 1978), pp. 183–184.

50. Shlomo Aviner, in *ibid.*, pp. 114–115.

51. Adam Doron, *The State of Israel and the Land of Israel* (Israel: Beit Berl College, 1988), pp. 487–488, 491.

52. Isaiah Leibovitz, *Judaism, the Jews, and the Land of Israel* (Jerusalem: Schocken Publishing House, 1975), pp. 428–429.

53. Cited in Danny Rubinstein, *Gush Emunim* (Tel Aviv: Hakibbutz Haméuchad, 1982), pp. 98–109.

54. Cited in Danny Rubinstein, *Ibid.*

6. DOCTRINE

1. *Sefer Raziel.*

2. Gen. 1:27.

3. Jer. 9:22–23.

4. Ps. 8:4–7.

5. Syriac Baruch 14:17.

6. Mishnah *Sanhedrin* 4:5.

7. Mishnah *Avot* 3:14.

8. *Avot of Rabbi Nathan*, Version b, Chap. 30.

9. *Sanhedrin* 38a.

10. *Ecclesiastes Rabbah* 7:13.

11. *Genesis Rabbah* 8:5.

12. *Ta'anit* 22a.

13. *Tanhuma* (Buber), *B'hukotai* 6.

14. Judah Halevi, *Kuzari, Part III.*

15. Nahman of Bratslav.

16. *Ibid.*

17. Deut. 30:19.

18. Deut. 11:26–28.

19. Prov. 6:16–19.

20. Mishnah *Avot* 4:2.

21. Mishnah *Avot* 3:15.

22. *Megillah* 25a.

23. *Kiddushin* 40b.

24. *Leviticus Rabbah* 4:6.

25. *Erubin* 13b.

26. *Berakhot* 28b.

27. *Avodah Zarah* 4a.

28. *Baba Metzia* 83a.

29. *Sotah* 14a.

30. *Berakhot* 17a.

31. *Pesahim* 113a.

32. *Pesahim* 113b.

33. *Jerusalem Kiddushin* 66d.

34. *Nedarim* 10a.

35. Mishnah *Eduyot* 5:6.

36. Eliezer the Great, *Paths of Life*. See Hebrew text in Israel Abrahams, *op. cit.*, pp. 40–41.

37. From a letter of Judah ibn Tibbon to his son Samuel, in F. Kobler, *op. cit.*, Vol. I, pp. 156–64.

38. From a letter of Nahmanides to his son, in Israel Abrahams, *op. cit.*, pp. 95–98.

39. Rabbenu Asher, in Abrahams, *op. cit.*, pp. 119–25.

40. Moses Luzatto, *Mesillat Yesharim*, Chap. 11.

41. *Ibid.*

42. *Ibid.*, Chap. I.

43. Israel Baal-Shem Tov.

44. *Ibid.*

45. Nahman of Bratslav.

46. *Ibid.*

47. Eccles. 7:20.

48. Ezek. 18:30–32.

49. *Tanhuma* (Buber), *Hukkat* 39.

50. *Yoma* 9b.

51. *Shabbat* 55a–b.

52. *Nedarim* 32b.

53. *Jerusalem Berakhot* 7d.

54. *Song of Songs Rabbah* to 5:2.

55. *Seder Eliahu Zuta*, Chap. 4.

56. *Midrash Tehillim* 90:16.

57. *Pesikta Rabbati*, Chap. 44.

58. *Leviticus Rabbah* 7:2.

59. *Avot of Rabbi Nathan*, Version a, Chap. 39.

60. Moses Luzatto, *Mesillat Yesharim*, Chap. 5.

61. *Berakhot* 5a.

62. *Baba Metzia* 85a.

63. *Menahot* 29b.

64. *Makkot* 24b.

65. Saadia Gaon, *op. cit.*, Treatise V, Chap. 1.

66. Israel Baal-Shem Tov.

67. Nahman of Bratslav.

68. Menahem Mendel of Kotzk.

69. Martin Buber, *At the Turning*, *op. cit.*, pp. 55–56.

70. André Schwarz-Bart, *The Last of the Just* (New York: Atheneum, 1960), pp. 372–74.

71. Yaakov Glatstein, *Shtralndike Yidden, Radiant Jews* (New York: Ferlag Matones, 1946), pp. 12–15.

72. Yoel Teitelbaum, *Sefer Va-yoel Moshe*, trans. by Pinchas Peli (Brooklyn, 1961), second edition with supplements, p. 5.

73. *Ibid.*, p. 8.

74. Yoel Teitelbaum, *Kuntres Al Ha-geulah V'al Ha-temurah, On Redemption and Transformation*, trans.

by Pinchas Peli (Brooklyn, 1967), p. 19.

75. Issachar Solomon Teichthal, *Eim Habanim S'meichah*, trans. by Pinchas Peli (Budapest, 1943) , pp. 16–17.

76. *Ibid.*, p. 22.

77. *Dissenter in Zion: From the Writings of Judah L. Magnes*, ed. by Arthur A. Goren (Cambridge: Harvard University Press, 1982), p. 417.

78. Martin Buber, *Eclipse of God: Studies in the Relation Between Religion and Philosophy* (New York: Harper and Brothers, 1952), p. 34.

79. Zvi Elimelekh Herzberg, *Zaddik Beemunato, The Faith of a Righteous Man* (Jerusalem, 1987).

80. Arthur Hertzberg, "A Lifetime Quarrel with God," *New York Times Book Review*, May 6, 1989.

81. Job 14:7–12.

82. Ps. 6:6.

83. Dan. 12:1–2.

84. Mishnah *Sanhedrin* 10:1.

85. *Sanhedrin* 90b.

86. *Tosefta Sanhedrin* 13:2.

87. *Berakhot* 28b.

88. *Midrash Mishle* 17:1.

89. *Tanhuma* (Buber), *Vayigash* 9.

90. *Berakhot* 17a.

91. *Berakhot* 34b.

92. *Sifra* 85d.

93. Saadia Gaon, *op. cit.*, Treatise VII, Chap. 1.

94. Maimonides, *Mishneh Torah, Hilkhot Teshuvah* 8.

95. Moses Luzatto, *Mesillat Yesharim*, Chap. 4.

96. From the Daily Prayer Book.

97. Trans. from *Siddur Sim Shalom, op. cit.*, p. 525.

98. Isa. 2:2–4.

99. Jer. 23:5–6.

100. Mal. 3:23–24.

101. *Sanhedrin* 98a. Trans. based upon *Mahzor for Rosh Hashanah and Yom Kippur, op. cit.*, p. 698.

102. *Avot of Rabbi Nathan*, Version b, Chap. 31.

103. Saadia Gaon, *op. cit.*, Treatise VIII, Chap. 5.

104. Maimonides, *Mishneh Torah, Hilkhot Melakhim*, in N. Glatzer, *op. cit.*, Chaps. 11–12.

105. Zvi Hirsch Kalischer, *Derishat Tsiyyon*, in Arthur Hertzberg, *The Zionist Idea, op. cit.*, pp. 111–13.

106. From the commentary of Maimonides to Mishnah *Sanhedrin* 10:1.

107. Cited in W. Gunther Plaut, *The Rise of Reform Judaism, op. cit.*, p. 31.

108. Cited in *ibid.*, pp. 33–34.

109. Moshe Schreiber (*Hatam Sofer*, Responsa, Pt. 6, Resp. 84), as cited in Alexander Guttmann, *The Struggle Over Reform in Rabbinic Literature* (Jerusalem and New York: The World Union for Progressive Judaism, 1977), pp. 244–247.

110. Cited in David Philipson, *op. cit.*, p. 332.

111. Abraham Geiger, from *Lectures at the Academy for the Science of Judaism* (Berlin, 1872), cited in Max Weiner, *Abraham Geiger and Liberal Judaism* (Philadelphia: Jewish Publication Society, 1962), p. 151.

112. Zacharias Frankel, letter written on July 18, 1845, submitted to the Rabbinical Conference in Frankfort.

113. From the Platform of the Pittsburgh Conference of 1885.

114. Solomon Schechter, *Studies in Judaism* (Philadelphia: Macmillan, 1896), pp. xvii–xix.

115. Samson Raphael Hirsch, *op. cit.*, pp. 13–14.

116. Joseph B. Soloveitchik, *Halakhic Man*, trans. by Lawrence Kaplan

(Philadelphia: Jewish Publication Society, 1983), pp. 89, 91.

7. PRAYER

1. *Yebamot* 64a.

2. *Berakhot* 32b.

3. *Ta'anit* 2a.

4. Num. 14:17–20.

5. From the Testament of Jonah ben Landsofer.

6. Israel Baal-Shem Tov.

7. Nahman of Bratslav.

8. David Friedlander, writing in 1786, cited in Jakob J. Petuchowski, *Prayerbook Reform in Europe: The Liturgy of Liberal and Reform Judaism* (New York: The World Union for Progressive Judaism, Ltd., 1968), p. 130.

9. Abraham Geiger, cited in W. Gunther Plaut, *The Rise of Reform Judaism, op. cit.*, p. 158.

10. A.D. Gordon (in 1921), cited in Arthur Hertzberg, *The Zionist Idea, op. cit.*, pp. 383–84.

11. Mordecai M. Kaplan, *The Meaning of God in Modern Jewish Religion* (New York: Behrman's Jewish Book House, 1937), pp. 244–49, 251–58, 261–63.

12. Abraham Joshua Heschel, *Man's Quest for God* (New York: Charles Scribner's Sons, 1954), pp. 15–16.

13. *Ibid.*, p. 44.

14. Isaiah Leibovitz, *Conversations About the Ethics of the Fathers and About Maimonides* (Jerusalem and Tel Aviv: Schocken Publishing House, 1979), pp. 56–60.

15. Deut. 10:20.

16. Deut. 8:10.

17. Mishnah *Berakhot* 2:1.

18. Mishnah *Berakhot* 2:4.

19. Mishnah *Berakhot* 2:5.

20. Mishnah *Berakhot* 3:1.

21. Mishnah *Berakhot* 4:1.

22. *Tanhuma* (Buber), *Miketz* 11.

23. Mishnah *Berakhot* 4:5.

24. Mishnah *Berakhot* 4:6.

25. Mishnah *Berkahot* 9:1.

26. Mishnah *Berakhot* 9:2.

27. Mishnah *Berakhot* 9:3.

28. *Berakhot* 43b.

29. *Tosefta Berakhot* 3.

30. *Mekhilta, Pisha* 16.

31. *Erubin* 65a.

32. *Berakhot* 29b.

33. *Kitzur Shulhan Arukh*, Section 18, *Hilkhot T'filat Shmoneh Esreh*.

34. *Berakhot* 8a.

35. From the letter of a Moravian Jew, Shlomoh Shlomiel, son of Hayyim, written from Safed in 1607, in F. Kobler, ed., *op. cit.*, Vol. II, pp. 395–96.

36. Trans. from *Siddur Sim Shalom, op. cit.*, pp. 395, 399.

37. *Ibid.*, pp. 401, 403, 411.

38. *Ibid.*, pp. 423, 427.

39. *Ibid.*, p. 101. Deut. 6:4–9.

40. Adapted from *Siddur Sim Shalom, op. cit.*, pp. 107–121.

41. *Ibid.*, p. 121.

42. *Ibid.*, p. 759.

43. *Ibid.*, pp. 710–711.

44. Mishnah *Berakhot* 4:2.

45. *Sefer Hassidim*, trans. in N. Glatzer, ed., *Language of Faith* (New York: Schocken, 1947), p. 78.

46. *Ibid.*, p. 74.

47. *Ibid.*, p. 14.

Arthur Hertzberg, professor emeritus of religion at Dartmouth College, is visiting professor of the humanities at New York University and visiting scholar at Columbia University's Mideast Institute. The former Rabbi of Temple Emanu-el in Englewood, New Jersey, he has taught at Hebrew University in Jerusalem and at Princeton University. He has served as president of the conference on Jewish Social Studies and as senior editor of the *Encyclopedia Judaica*. He is the author of a number of books, including, *The Zionist Idea, The French Enlightenment and the Jews,* and *The Jews in America,* and has contributed extensively to leading journals, among them *The New York Review of Books* and *The New York Times Book Review.*

Jules Harlow, a native of Iowa, received rabbinic ordination at the Jewish Theological Seminary of America and serves as Director of Publications for The Rabbinical Assembly. He is a liturgical editor and translator whose work includes *Mahzor for Rosh Hashanah and Yom Kippur* and *Siddur Sim Shalom,* a prayerbook for Shabbat, Festivals, and Weekdays. Rabbi Harlow is a translator of modern Hebrew literature, most notably short stories by the Nobel Laureate S.Y. Agnon. His editions of textbooks for children, including *Lessons from Our Living Past,* are widely used in religious schools.